Postmodernism

Postmodernism:

The Key Figures

Edited by

Hans Bertens
and
Joseph Natoli

BLACKWELL
Publishers

Copyright © Blackwell Publishers Ltd 2002

First published 2002

2 4 6 8 10 9 7 5 3 1

Blackwell Publishers Inc.
350 Main Street
Malden, Massachusetts 02148
USA

Blackwell Publishers Ltd
108 Cowley Road
Oxford OX4 1JF
UK

Library of Congress Cataloging-in-Publication Data

Postmodernism : the key figures / edited by Hans Bertens and Joseph Natoli.
    p. cm.
    Includes bibliographical references and index.
ISBN 0–631–21796–7 (alk. paper — ISBN 0–631–21797–5 (pbk. : alk. paper)
    1. Postmodernism. I. Bertens, Johannes Willem. II. Natoli, Joseph P., 1943–

B831.2 P683 2002
149′.97—dc21   2001043233

British Library Cataloguing in Publication Data

A CIP catalogue record for this book is available from the British Library.

Typeset in 10.5 / 12.5 pt Ehrhardt
by Kolam Information Services Private Ltd, Pondicherry, India

This book is printed on acid-free paper.

Contents

Contributors

Eyal Amiran, Michigan State University
Martine Antle, University of North Carolina, Chapel Hill
Peter Atterton, University of San Diego
Philip Auslander, Georgia Institute of Technology
Robert Bernasconi, University of Memphis
Hans Bertens, Utrecht University
Ronald Bogue, University of Georgia
Peter Bondanella, Indiana University
Rocco Capozzi, University of Toronto
Jim Collins, University of Notre Dame
Todd F. Davis, Goshen College, Indiana
Theo D'haen, Leiden University
Ewa Domańska, Adam Mickiewicz University, Poznań
Christopher Douglas, Furman University
Evelyn Fishburn, University of North London
Roy C. Flannagan, Francis Marion University
Jean-François Fourny, Ohio State University
Joanne Gass, California State University, Fullerton
Paula Geyh, Southern Illinois University, Carbondale
Greg Giesekam, University of Glasgow
Philip Goldstein, University of Delaware
Jennifer Harvie, Goldsmiths College, University of London
John G. Hatch, University of Western Ontario
David Herman, North Carolina State University, Raleigh
Sean Homer, University of Sheffield
Thomas B. Hove, University of Illinois at Urbana-Champaign
E. Ann Kaplan, State University of New York at Stony Brook
Douglas Kellner, University of California at Los Angeles
Marcia Landy, University of Pittsburgh

Robert L. McLaughlin, Illinois State University
Steven Monte, University of Chicago
Joseph Natoli, Michigan State University
David G. Nicholls, Bilkent University
Susana Onega, University of Zaragoza
Sheldon Penn, University of Leicester
Nancy Perloff, Getty Research Institute
Dominic Pettman, University of Geneva
Nicoletta Pireddu, Georgetown University, Washington, DC
Arkady Plotnitsky, Purdue University
Karlis Racevskis, Ohio State University
Frans Ruiter, Utrecht University
Hugh J. Silverman, State University of New York at Stony Brook
Madeleine Sorapure, University of California, Santa Barbara
James A. Steintrager, University of California, Irvine
Galin Tihanov, Merton College, Oxford
Wendy Wheeler, University of North London
Richard D. Wolff, University of Massachusetts, Amherst

Introduction

Although we clearly cannot do without them, few of us are straightforwardly happy with the terms postmodern, postmodernism, and postmodernity. While it is obvious that they are here to stay, we still tend to tolerate them as temporary substitutes for the more appropriate or convincing terms that will sooner or later come along. Examples abound of "postmodern" writers, artists, and theorists who have with varying degrees of indignation – and varying arguments – refused the label. Equally telling is the fact that a good many postcolonial critics, who are arguably among postmodernism's many heirs, have assiduously distanced themselves from postmodernism in arguing that their politically inspired work is fundamentally different from the wholly apolitical postmodern criticism that the postcolonial perspective has fortunately transcended.

Perhaps the main problem with postmodernism is that it would appear to have been used for so many different purposes and to have been applied to so many different things that there is always at least one usage of the term – say, postmodernism as a wholly self-reflexive, anti-referential, and apolitical movement in literature and the arts – that a given writer, artist, or theorist who might otherwise identify with the postmodern can, with reason, seriously object to. On closer inspection, however, this supposedly protean character of the term is more manageable than it would seem to be. There is no denying that the term has shifted its base somewhat since it came into circulation thirty years ago and it is equally true that it covers widely different phenomena. However, the question of, for instance, postmodernism's politics – or lack of them – is not only decided by postmodernism itself, but also by the position of the critic who addresses it. What one critic sees as wholly apolitical may for the next one be a provocative, if subtle, statement. Rather ironically, postmodernism, which has substantially contributed to the politicization of contemporary art and theory, has also been among its first victims. But this, of course, is usually the effect of revolutions.

The confusion that surrounds postmodernism is then in some measure due to radical differences in political appreciation. But it also has to do with the problematic fact that the term is used to refer to a wide and rather heterogeneous variety of phenomena. In a book published some years ago, called rather grandly *The Idea of the Postmodern: A History* (Bertens 1995), one of us suggested that it might be possible to distinguish between postmodernism's many guises on the basis of the object or objects a specific use of the term referred to. If we look at "postmodern" and "postmodernism" from this angle, different fields of reference to which the terms are frequently applied emerge. This introduction will briefly review the three major fields of reference – which one could also see as levels of aggregration – and in so doing hopefully enable the reader to position the key figures in the development of postmodernism in its widest sense that this book will cover.

At the most concrete, practical level, postmodernism refers to a new set of literary and artistic practices that emerged in the course of the 1950s, gained momentum in the 1960s, and dominated many artistic disciplines during the 1970s and – at least early – 1980s. In some disciplines – dance, photography, literature – postmodernism initially referred to a new self-reflexivity that radicalizes the self-reflexive tendency in modernism; in others – painting, sculpture, architecture – it signals a return to the representational practices that had been banned by an anti-representational modernism. That return to representation, although almost always political, is also ironic and usually not without self-reflexive elements. To complicate matters, in some of these disciplines, notably dance and literature, postmodernism refers to both an initial self-reflexivity and a later return to – ironic forms of – representation. Later critics have sometimes tried to withdraw the label "postmodern" from the radical self-reflexivity that, in one way or another, informs many artistic disiplines in the postwar period, and have argued that because of its radicalization of originally modernist concerns, "late modern" would be a more appropriate term for this resurgence of self-reflexivity.

On a more abstract level postmodernism denotes a set of philosophical propositions that are centered around the rejection of Realist epistemology and of the Enlightenment project that builds upon that epistemology. These – mostly negative – propositions include the denial of the Cartesian autonomous, and self-identical subject, of the transparency of language, of the accessibility of the real, of the possibility of universal foundation, and so on and so forth. In its quarrel with self-determination, with whatever presents itself as objective, transcendent, and universal, this postmodernism stresses other-determination, desire, contingency, change, difference, and absence (of self and meaning). The major sources of this theoretical postmodernism are to be found in French poststructuralism. In its early stages it borrows liberally from Roland Barthes and Jacques Derrida, while later on it incorporates (elements from) the writings of Jacques Lacan, Jean-François Lyotard, Gilles Deleuze (usually in combination with Félix Guattari), and, especially, Michel Foucault. In its later stage this postmodernism begins to share Foucault's preoccupation with power and knowledge and to accept his contention that they cannot be separated from each other and constitute an inextricable power/knowledge knot. Foucault is also the driving force behind this postmodernism's interest in the institutionalization of power/knowledge and in the marginalization of the "other" in the modern world. In particular in its focus on the "other" postmodern theory is hard to distinguish from postcolonial theory as it began to take shape in the second half of the 1980s. Postcolonial theorists like Homi Bhabha and Gayatri Chakravorty Spivak are as indebted to poststructuralism as postmodern theory, even if their primary focus is the postcolonial subject and the postcolonial condition.

In its most ambitious form, postmodernism – which at this level of aggregation we might as well call postmodernity – seeks to describe a new sociocultural formation and/or economic dispensation that according to a number of theorists has at least in the Western world come to replace modernity. Here we find an impressive array of wide-ranging interpretations of our late twentieth-century and early twenty-first century condition. For Jean-François Lyotard, this "postmodern condition" is the result of the failure and acute discomfiture of the so-called grand narratives that underpinned and legitimized modernity. For Fredric Jameson, postmodernism means the world-wide victory of an aggressive, entrepreneurial capitalism and a concomitant disorientation and "waning of affect" that we all suffer from, and the collapse of the Marxist distinction between base (the mode of production) and superstructure (culture, in its widest sense). For Jean Baudrillard, who gives the old Marxist notion of alienation a different twist, we have lost all sense of authenticity and live in a world-wide simulation that we helplessly take to be reality. By way of contrast, for the social scientist Ronald Inglehart postmodernism implies an important shift – supported by massive empirical data gathered from forty-three (mostly Western) societies – from materialist to so-called "postmaterialist" values. Since this process of postmodernization is driven by intergenerational population replacement, it will, under unchanging conditions of affluence, go on well into the new century, leading to a full-fledged postmodernity that will "emphasize human autonomy and diversity instead of the hierarchy and conformity that are central to modernity" (Inglehart 1997: 27).

With Inglehart we are back in the 1960s, when to its very first theorists postmodernism – amongst other things – implied freedom, a liberation from the stifling conventions and orthodoxies of the 1950s. If the development toward a greater tolerance and an increased acceptance of difference that Inglehart signals does indeed have a solid basis in (recent) historical reality, then we should perhaps combine his analysis of our current sociocultural condition with that of Jameson and see postmodernity as the uneasy and often contradictory coexistence of the outcomes of two related struggles that have their origin in the 1960s: one of them over the economy and the other over culture. Although this way of seeing things is admittedly more pertinent to the situation in Western Europe than to that in the United States, it is by no means irrelevant to recent American history. The mid-and late 1960s seemed for many young Western intellectuals to herald the dawn of a new, politically progressive and emancipatory era. The new left of the 1960s – for which the left of the 1950s was as much of an obstacle on the way toward a brighter future as the right – saw itself as engaged in an epic struggle with the forces of conservatism, a contest for which all over the Western world the Vietnam war provided a perfect focus. For the young leftist intellectuals of the 1960s it seemed only a matter of time before the right would be definitively consigned to history. Whatever our view of recent history, we can agree that the leftist utopia of the 1960s never materialized. We can perhaps also agree that thirty years onwards this struggle between the left – the new left of the 1960s – and the right has resulted in a strange paradox. There can be no doubt whatsoever that the right has won in the economic sphere. In the last twenty years we have witnessed what at this point in time would seem to be the irreversible victory of capitalism over alternative economic arrangements. And Jameson is surely right in telling us that capitalism has by now penetrated every imaginable sector of contemporary society, in the process obliterating the old distinctions between economy and culture and the public and the private.

But the new left of the 1960s has also scored a decisive victory. In spite of a resistance that has by no means disappeared and that should not be underestimated, the left has won the struggle over culture – with culture defined in its widest sense. The leftist cultural agenda, including multiculturalism, pluralist sexual identities, minority rights, identity and single-issue politics, down to unexpected marriages of high and low culture, has shaped our current climate. The cultural stratifications, hierarchies, exclusions, and solemnities of 1950s modernity have been forced into the background, as has the ethical order that underpinned it. Seen from this perspective, postmodernity is indeed characterized by the general absence of larger orders – to paraphrase Lyotard somewhat disingenuously – including that of ethics (witness for instance the legalization of euthanasia in the Netherlands in early 2001). Postmodernity, then, can be said to stand for the acceptance of difference and the celebration of heterogeneity within an overwhelmingly capitalist framework.

At first sight, this humanistically oriented acceptance of difference and the posthumanist insistence on *différance* that we find in postmodern theorizing may well seem to have nothing in common. Together, however, they constitute an intense self-examination on the part of the postwar West. In France this self-examination, in which the historical guilt of the West in its relations with the non-Western world – the colonial Other – occupies a central place, was triggered by the Algerian war. In the US this self-examination, which had already begun under the pressure of the Civil Rights movements, gained crucial momentum with the Vietnam war. Looking back, we can see how in the wake of this moral self-scrutiny the Holocaust, which up till then had been seen as an almost inexplicable historical aberration, began to be interpreted within the framework of the modern West's relations with the non-West and in that light took on even more frightening aspects. As a result, wholly in line with the concurrent development of a new, post-Fordist, capitalism, all that seemed solid once again melted into air. For those who clung to a – usually much-diminished – humanism, the new awareness of the West's historical guilt pointed to an acceptance of difference and social heterogeneity and to relatively untheoretical modes of social engineering. For those who rejected humanism as theoretically indefensible and – worse – as a central factor in the modern West's relations with the Other (both internal and external), *différance* became a central concept in their attempts to deconstruct the assumptions that have historically legitimized the West's extraterritorial interventions.

At this panoramic level of generalization, then, postmodernity is characterized by both an aggressive, entrepreneurial capitalism and an intense and prolonged wave of self-examination taking different but related forms. It should be obvious that no manageable collection of essays – manageable for its editors and publisher, that is – can hope to do justice to what must be seen as a massive sociocultural formation, not even if it focuses on its key figures. And what is "key" in the first place? What strange politics – any postmodern theorist will ask – has led to a packaging of postmodernism/postmodernity from such a prepostmodern perspective? And isn't a selection of key figures inevitably circular? Aren't these the key figures precisely because we have allowed them to define the postmodern for us, and with it their own status as key figures? Wouldn't they lose their key status if we approached postmodernism from an alternative perspective? These are valid questions to which we can only offer pragmatic answers. In good postmodernist fashion, we have opted for an eclectic approach and sought to represent a large variety of postmodern voices – postmodern by their own and others' declaration – and of important but not necessarily well-intentioned commentators on the postmodern. We are very much, and somewhat uncomfortably, aware that other editors might have made other choices. Why the Coen brothers and not Woody Allen? Why one hostile critic of postmodernity – Fredric Jameson – and not another – Jürgen Habermas? Or Terry Eagleton, for that matter? Why not Laurie Anderson, Kathy Acker, Bruno Latour, Guy Debord, Richard Brautigan, David Salle, Slovoj Žižek, Linda Hutcheon, William Gibson, Madonna, David Harvey, Sherrie Levine, Edward Said, Maurice Blanchot, Steve Reich, Philip Glass, Marshall McLuhan, Donald Barthelme, Zygmunt Bauman, Joseph Beuys,

Hélène Cixous, Jeff Koons, Bret Easton Ellis, Richard Powers, Clifford Geertz, and many, many others? But one might also ask: are those who are absent more significant than those who are represented? And can't we approach the postmodern from various but ultimately equivalent angles? Whatever the answer to this last question, the astonishing fertility of the postmodern project does not leave us much of a choice. But selectivity is not necessarily a disadvantage: it may well serve as a shortcut to what is really at stake. We hope and expect that the selection of key figures that we have made is as representative of the postmodern as any other.

Hans Bertens
Joseph Natoli

1

Peter Ackroyd

Susana Onega

In "(Post)Modern Polemics," after commenting on the great variety of points of view held by the critics attempting to characterize the postmodern, Hal Foster (1984: 67–79) suggests that in the field of literature the word "post-modernism" is an umbrella term, used to cover two main, widely divergent modes. One, related to poststructuralism, would be profoundly antihumanistic in its metafictional critique of representation, while the other would be neo-conservative in politics and deeply humanistic in its claim to return to history. In an introductory survey to postmodernism Hans Bertens likewise concludes that, for all the important differences in approach, scope, and theoretical positioning of postmodernist writers, they all respond to two major postmod-ernist modes: "one mode that has given up referentiality and meaning, another one that still seeks to be referential and sometimes even tries to establish local, temporary, and provisional truths" (1993: 65). Foster's and Bertens's conclu-sions echo Patricia Waugh's contention that the basic dilemma confronting contemporary art is the realization "that the world as such cannot be repre-sented. In literary fiction it is, in fact, possible only to 'represent' the *discourses* of that world." Inevitably, "language soon becomes a 'prisonhouse' from which the possibility of escape is remote" (1984: 3–4).

These critics' words bring to mind the basic tension at work in the writings of Samuel Beckett and Jorge Luis Borges, the two late modernists singled out by John Barth (1967: 29–34) as the only writers who had seriously tried to transcend modernism, going beyond the writing innovations of Joyce and Kafka. Beckett responds to the anxiety produced by the impossibility of being original by creating minimalist texts peopled by self-begetting authors-characters who struggle between the compulsion to write themselves into existence and the overriding temptation of silence. Borges's alternative is

This chapter is part of a research project financed by the Spanish Ministry of Education and Culture (PB 97–1022).

to imagine writers and readers trapped in an all-enveloping and self-begetting textual world, a "Library of Babel" made of infinite spiraling shelves and staircases endlessly reflected in numberless mirrors. This absolute world/ library contains "every possible combination of the twenty-odd orthographic symbols, that is, everything that is thinkable" (1989: 467; my translation).

One generation after Beckett and Borges, John Fowles parodied the modernist obsession with originality and closure in his satiric novel, *Mantissa* (1982; see Onega 1989: 123–36). He created a writer, Miles Green, who is in hospital trying to recover from a bout of amnesia. In keeping with Roland Barthes's tenet that writing involves pleasure, a form of *jouissance*, Dr. Delfie treats Green with a curious shock therapy consisting of the induction of an orgasm. The orgasm unexpectedly metamorphoses into the delivery of a child, which, open and read, turns out to be a text beginning with the same words with which Fowles's novel, *Mantissa*, begins. The reader then realizes that the strange pink and gray hospital room really looks like the inside of a skull, Miles Green's skull in fact, and that, like the protagonist of Flann O'Brien's *At Swim-Two-Birds* and of Beckett's *Malone Dies*, *The Unnamable*, and *Endgame*, Green's area of activity is restricted to the inside of his head. The ensuing chapters are just different versions of Miles Green's futile struggle with his doctor/muse for omniscient control and autonomy in writing. Once and again Green fails in his attempts to transform his muse into a dumb geisha, and he has to accept the fact that the text has a life of its own and constitutes the ultimate reality as a source, rather than a product, of linguistic activity and brain functioning. In other words, that the text is the ultimate reality as a source of Green's own self-identity.

In his other novels Fowles seriously tried to find a way out of Beckett's minimalism and Borges's prisonhouse of language by seeking to reconcile the realistic elements he had inherited from the English literary tradition with the experimental and mythical elements of the French literary tradition which he learnt about during his university years at Oxford. In *The French Lieutenant's Woman* (1969) the metafictional and realistic elements are combined with the mythical pattern of the hero's quest, which, as the writer himself acknowledges, underlies all his novels and short stories (see Foulke 1985–6: 370). And it is still present in *A Maggot* (1986), his latest novel to date and his most powerful historiographic metafiction (see Hutcheon 1988:5). *A Maggot* appears bafflingly inconclusive and unstructured at a surface level, making good the Derridean contention of the endless deferral of meaning. However, at a deeper level, the contradiction coheres in a perfectly closed, mythical pattern that follows Jung's scheme of the quaternity (see Onega 1989: ch. 6). Invariably, Fowles develops this basic quest pattern – a young, purblind hero undertaking a physical and spiritual journey for maturation and self-integration – against a historical background.

In the same way that Fowles's absorption of the English and the French literary traditions may account for his tendency to combine realistic and experimental elements in his fiction, Ackroyd's biography shows two salient and divergent traits. The writer himself has noted how at Cambridge – where he obtained a double first in English (1968–71) – he was greatly influenced by "the English school of poetry" (in Onega 1996: 211), represented by J. H. Prynne, Andrew Crozier, Ian Patterson, and Kevin Strutford, who were trying to revitalize English poetry along the cosmopolitan and experimental lines set by John Ashbery and the New York school of poetry. Ackroyd was subsequently granted a Mellon Fellowship to carry out postgraduate research at Yale University (1971–3), where he continued reading and writing "language poetry" (see Onega 1998: ch. 1). The results of his research were published in *Notes for a New Culture*, which shows Ackroyd's familiarity with the basic tenets of post-Saussurean linguistics and post-Barthesian literary theory, in particular with the realization that accepting the Derridean contention that language is perpetually distant from its origin amounts to reducing literature to "*le jeu de la forme*, the free play of linguistic forms without origins" (Ackroyd 1993 [1976]: 144).

In *The Great Fire of London* (1982) Ackroyd tests this definition of language. He writes a sequel to *Little Dorrit* in which various characters compete with each other in order to impose their own version of Dickens's novel without realizing that all these versions are equally subjective and distorting misreadings of the original novel. Thus, *The Great Fire of London* reveals its condition of autonomous and self-begetting linguistic universe, a Borgesian Library of Babel endlessly yielding different versions of itself and constantly begetting and trapping within its textual walls derivative characters and authors alike. By contrast, in *Chatterton* (1987), the poet Charles Wychwood liberates himself from Beckettian solipsism and the anxiety of influence in following Chatterton's ideas about creative plagiarism. At the moment of his death, Wychwood has a vision of himself entering (like Oscar Wilde at the end of *The Last Testament of Oscar Wilde* [1984] and Clement Harcombe at the end of *English Music* [1992]) an atemporal and absolute World of Art, a compound cosmic body-and-voice, made up of the great poets and artists of the past, whom Wychwood joyfully joins with the help of Chatterton and Meredith, adding his voice to a unison that strongly recalls both Borges's supra-individual Spiritual Voice (Worton and Still 1990: 13), and the modernist conception of the underworld as the crypt of the ancestral dead whose poetic voices are given new life by their incorporation into the work of new poets (see Smith 1990: 3–4).

The other salient trait in Ackroyd's biography is the fact that he is a Londoner educated as a Catholic. His Englishness and Catholicism are acknowledged by the writer as the two most influential elements in his early formative years. Catholicism has given Ackroyd a sense of the sacred that survived even his lapse into agnosticism (Onega 1996a: 209), and he refers to London as "the very landscape of my imagination" (1998a: 4). Whenever Ackroyd is asked to define his work he always says that it is "English" and that it shares with writers such as Dickens and Shakespeare a very English sensibility, which "is in part antiquarian, partly visionary" (in Onega 1996a: 217–18). Still, he positions himself at the margin of the English literary tradition – "I'm not really part of the main stream of English fiction. I'm sort of a little bit on the side of it" (in Schütze 1995: 172) – and, although he admits that "working and living in the late part of the twentieth century there must be some psycho-streams which affect one," he refuses to align himself with postmodernism: "But whether you could call it postmodernism I don't know. Certainly I don't read any theoretical work on postmodernism. I have not read the literary or critical texts on that" (in Schütze 1995: 172).

Ackroyd forcefully defended the "Englishness" of his work in a lecture entitled "The Englishness of English Literature" (1995), where he explained that the most salient feature of the true English sensibility is the love of ritual inherited from Catholicism, which survived the Reformation in such popular art forms as the ballad, music hall, pantomime, and vaudeville. His contention is that contemporary English writers such as Iain Sinclair, Michael Moorcock, and the poet Douglas Oliver share with him what he called in another lecture a specific "Cockney visionary sensibility," which he defines as "a living inheritance that has everything to do with the spirit of place and with the nature of the city, and is present in the art of music-hall comedians like Dan Leno and Charles Mathews, novelists and playwrights like Henry Fielding and Charles Dickens, painters like Turner and Hogarth, and poets like William Blake" (1993b). Consequently, Ackroyd's characters are often drawn on the pattern of well-known pantomime or music-hall characters such as Punch and Judy or Miss Havisham who, according to Ackroyd, was created by Dickens after watching Mathews impersonate a lady dressed entirely in white.

Realism-biased critics are prone to resent the unreality of these characters without realizing that their cardboard quality forms an intrinsic part of Ackroyd's overtly fictional and textual world. The pantomimic excesses in novels such as *The Great Fire of London* or *First Light* (1989) share with Dickensian and Shakespearean comedy the same type of "English" creative genius that is brought to perfection by Angela Carter in novels such as *Nights at the Circus* (1984) and *Wise Children* (1991), and is also present in Charles Palliser's *The Quincunx* (1989) and Jeanette Winterson's *Boating for Beginners* (1985) and *Sexing the Cherry* (1989).

Where in Fowles's fiction the end of the hero's quest is symbolized by his transformation from collector into artist/creator, in Ackroyd's novels the hero's quest for maturation often involves his metamorphosis from clown,

Fool, or wandering beggar into music-hall comedian or "monopolylinguist." This is what happens to Tim Harcombe at the end of *English Music*, after having been repeatedly associated with the Fool by his father (1992: 15), and by himself (23). Nicholas Dyer in *Hawksmoor* (1985), Oscar Wilde in *The Last Testament of Oscar Wilde*, and Laetitia Spender in *The Great Fire of London*, are recurrently associated with wandering beggars. Farmer and Boy Mint in *First Light* physically resemble clowns rather than peasants (1989: 19). Damian Fall, the astronomer in *First Light*, is associated with the Fool by another character (95). Ralph Kempis, the Royalist leader of Mary Mount in *Milton in America* (1996), is called fool (230) and also clown (231) by Milton, as is Goosequill, Milton's amanuensis (110). Plato describes himself as a "clown" in *The Plato Papers* (1999: 57), a novel that was published on April Fools' Day. In *Dan Leno and the Limehouse Golem* (1994), Dan Leno puts an end to the serial murders by absorbing them into the healing ritual of the music hall.

As in Jeannette Winterson's *The Passion*, the structure of *English Music* reproduces the double-loop arrangement of the major arcana of the Tarot. The odd-numbered chapters contain episodes of Tim Harcombe's past life told by himself, while in the even-numbered chapters the reader has access to Tim's trances or dream-like visions. This alternation of events and visions echoes the physical and spiritual aspects of the Fool's quest. As in *The Passion*, the reproduction of Tim's quest at the structural level transforms *English Music* into a textual replica of the quester's path that the reader can follow analogic-ally (like the reader of *The Pilgrim's Progress* or *The Divine Comedy*), in order to achieve his or her own self-maturation and cosmic integration.

In *Hawksmoor*, likewise, the alternation of narrative voices and periods and the temporal circularity of the novel recalls the twelve-month structure of a cosmogonic cycle, imitating Nicholas Dyer's attempt to reproduce God's act of the creation of the cosmos. The transcendental ladder to heaven formed by Dyer's churches is thus reproduced structurally, offering the reader the possibility of climbing it analogically, in order to bring about his or her own ascesis (see Onega 1998: ch. 3). But the most accomplished example of book as textual/transcendental labyrinth is *The House of Doctor Dee* (1993a), whose chapter distribution replicates the structure of Dr. John Dee's hieroglyphic monad, his esoteric symbol of the *anthropos*, expressing the complex unity of man and cosmos (see Onega 1998: ch. 3; 1999: ch. 3).

Thus, Ackroyd manages to suggest the possibility of transcendence in "visionary" (or Blakean) terms, without the need to postulate a dualistic metaphysics. As I pointed out elsewhere (Onega 1997), the paradoxical closure thus achieved is the most salient trait of British writers of historio-graphic metafiction. Nicholas Dyer's septilateral ladder to heaven, Dr. Dee's hieroglyphic monad, and the double-loop structure of the Tarot are all arche-typal figurations of mandalic totality expressing the symbolic reconciliation of man and cosmos. To these may be added others such as the quincunx that structures Lawrence Durrell's *Avignon Quintet* (or *Quincunx*) and Charles Palliser's *The Quincunx*, a novel that takes to virtuoso extremes the combination of pattern and randomness, offering the reader an apparently neat though complex plot structure at surface level that, however, hides incompatible and morally disturbing alternatives. The reader's discovery of what may be described as a "hideous narrative of incest" within the "hidden narrative of bastardy" (Onega 2000: 151–63) gives the thematic center of the novel the *regressus in infinitum* structure characteristic of the quincuxial center, simultaneously suggesting the illusion of a center for the whole novel, that is, of unitary meaning, and the absence of a center, that is, of infinite variations of meaning.

In conclusion, where loss of faith in transcendence left Beckett's Molloy, Malone, and "the unnamable," Fowles's Miles Green (*Mantissa*), and Winterson's Henry (*The Passion*) secluded in a solipsistic textual void, for ever condemned to the endless rewriting of their own self-perceptions, and where Spenser Spender and the other author-characters in *The Great Fire of London* were trapped in a Borgesian Library of Babel without the possibility of escape, in his later novels Ackroyd (like Fowles, Winterson, and Palliser in the above examples) manages to suggest the possibility of transcendence by having recourse to myth. Rereading Borges in the light of Chatterton and Blake, he transforms the all-enveloping prisonhouse of language into a transcendental labyrinth of paper and ink, a mystical ladder to heaven that, however, can only be climbed analogically by a willing act of the imagination. Thus, Ackroyd manages to affirm and deny the reconciliation of self and world in the contradictory terms singled out by Foster, Bertens, Waugh, and Hutcheon as the basic characteristic of postmodernist fiction.

2

Louis Althusser

Richard D. Wolff

Louis Althusser (1918–90) produced a large body of writing that enacts the twentieth century's confrontation between postmodernism and Marxism. His life and texts have enabled each movement to work deep, continuing, and contested effects on the other. In criticizing classical Marxism's modernist commitments, he made a postmodern Marxism both necessary and possible. In the 1960s and 1970s, Althusser sought to disconnect Marxism from both the absolutist epistemologies (empiricism and rationalism) and the determinist ontologies (humanism and structuralism). Most of the classical forms of Marxism had shared those epistemologies and ontologies with the bourgeois social theories that Marxists otherwise opposed. By inaugurating the explicit postmodern break within Marxism, Althusser opened the modernist–postmodernist debate about its future that continues inside Marxism (Callari and Ruccio 1996).

At the same time, Althusser's work confronted postmodernists with a parallel problem. With undisguised partisanship, his work provocatively posed the difference between Marxist and non-Marxist kinds and directions of postmodernism. Contrary to those postmodernisms that endorse dissociation from social struggles – on grounds of complexity, uncertainty, undecidability, and so on – Althusser's postmodern Marxism argued for active social struggle. Against postmodernisms that criticize and dismiss Marxism as if it were a totally modernist project, Althusser projected a postmodern Marxism (built around his concept of "overdetermination") that is immune to such criticism. Strategically, his work offers to postmodernism – still largely a movement of thought operating at rarified social levels – one means of connecting to a movement for more broadly social as well as theoretical change. Althusser implicitly suggested that to survive and grow in the twenty-first century, both postmodernism and Marxism would benefit from an effective alliance.

As a philosopher he reached the highest professional rank in France (rector of the École Normale Supérieure in Paris) and fully engaged the intense debates swirling around his contemporaries: especially Sartre, Foucault, Derrida, and Lacan (Kaplan and Sprinker 1993). He likewise participated in the complex rethinkings and extensions of the works of Spinoza, Montesquieu, Machiavelli, Hegel, and Bachelard (Callari and Ruccio 1998; Montag and Stolze 1997). As a Marxist, he joined the French Communist Party in the 1940s and eventually became its best known and most controversial theoretician in relation to such central issues as economic determinism, humanism, Stalinism, and Maoism. While choosing to remain within the Party – "because of its ties to the working class" – he simultaneously became its most profound critic. His intimate personal life was as intensely interrogated an object of his systematic thought as were philosophy and politics. He struggled throughout his life to understand how his French father and mother, emotionally distant and yet dominating figures, shaped his life during and after his youth in Algeria. He returned repeatedly to think through his cathartic experiences in a German prisoner-of-war camp and his complex and conflicted sexuality in their relationships to his philosophy and his politics. His immersion in the relationship with his wife Hélène was both context and catalyst for his life's commingling of philosophy, politics, and personal intimacy. Althusser's connection to postmodernism emerges in his drive to accord all three aspects of his life their own unique dynamics and effectivities on – in his words, their "overdetermination" of – one another. As the autobiographical *The Future Lasts Forever* (1993) shows, he let no one aspect function as the essential determinant of or the master narrative for the totality of his life.

Althusser's relation to postmodernism – a term that never figured significantly in his writings – appears clearly in his anti-essentialist and anti-foundationalist concept of "overdetermination." He borrowed and adapted this concept from Freud's *The Interpretation of Dreams* to formulate his break not only from the economic determinism that characterized classical Marxism but also from *any* determinist social theory. That is, he opposed any logic that presumed, sought, and found an essential cause of – a master narrative to account for – social conditions and changes. Such reasoning – reducing social events to but a few of the infinity of causal influences "overdetermining" them – was complicit, he thought, in many of the mistakes and failures of Marxist movements. Essentialism or determinism inside Marxism represented interpretations of Marx – we may label them "modernist" – that Althusser rejected. In his view, Marx had gone well beyond merely attacking bourgeois theory's denial of the social effectivity of economic processes and interests in general and of class exploitation in particular. Marx had begun a new philosophy and new methodology of social analysis that broke from determinism per se. Althusser's first famous book of essays, *For Marx* (1969), presents basic arguments for understanding Marx as making a systematic break with modernism's embrace of deterministic reasoning.

Althusser undertook a rereading (he called it "symptomatic") of Marx with the goal of discerning and explicating his unique philosophy, the "problematic(s)" that literally informed his writings. By showing how Marx's mature work (above all *Capital*) exhibits but never explicitly renders a new mode of social analysis, Althusser refuted what he saw as his fellow Marxists' uncritical and strategically disastrous absorption of pre-Marxian, bourgeois philosophies and social analysis: their very different problematics. *Reading Capital* (1970) commences many specifications of a postmodern Marxism that contrasts sharply with the modernist mainstreams of *both* the non-Marxian and the Marxian traditions of social theory.

Since Althusser held that all aspects of any society are overdetermined – constituted as the effects of all other aspects – it followed that each aspect exists in/as a complex of pushes and pulls emanating from all the other aspects. Hence, everything exists in/as a complex set of infinitely diverse contradictions, a conceptualization of contradiction more complex than the more dualistic notions usually attributed to Hegel. These interdependent notions of overdetermination and complex contradictions gave to Althusser's Marxist philosophy a distinctive and controversial combination of epistemological and ontological elements with considerable affinities to postmodernism.

Epistemologically, Althusser believed that all analysis is particular, partial, and partisan; it could not be otherwise since no theory can grasp an infinity of overdeterminations. Thus, theory is rhetorical in the classical sense. Here he built on the classical Marxian insight that culture was the scene of a battle between worldviews – bourgeois versus proletarian, materialist versus idealist and so on – but he pointed significantly further. Marxism itself was not exempted from the ranks of ideology. It was no more an absolute truth than were the formulations of its enemies. Since every possible object of thought was complexly overdetermined and contradictory – with an infinity of dimensions corresponding to the infinity of its overdeterminants – no explanation, theory, analysis, or knowledge of that object could claim to be "complete" or "true" or "objective" absolutely. All human thought is partial and limited by the framework through which it helps to construct that object itself and to focus on some of the aspects of that object. All theories, Marxism included, are like flashlights used to navigate the darkness of a space. Each flashlight deployed by each navigator illuminates (constitutes the visible) in its distinctive way, depending on where and how it is used. But each flashlight necessarily also renders other parts of that space invisible; the parts that become lit thereby determine the parts consigned to the shadows. Marxism's problematic – its particular mix of what it illuminates and what it occludes – is significantly different from the problematics of other theories.

This epistemological position shook classical Marxism, and it still does. It swept away notions of historical inevitability, of capturing *the* laws of motion of capitalist society, of guaranteeing particular revolutionary strategies or tactics. Althusser's reception within the French Communist Party and across the left internationally has ever been rocky. Modernism, albeit in different forms, runs deep, no less on the left than the center and right. Against Marxism as the master narrative of truth battling with the corrupt ideologies of capitalist privilege and mystification, Althusser counterposed a Marxism that was one kind of thinking, the elaboration of one problematic struggling among others. Some of those others were enemies, some allies, and some yet to be determined in their position relative to Marxism. Philosophy was the site of an endless battle – a taking of positions, a war of position – among problematics with significantly different impacts on their society. Moreover, the problematics changed one another even as each was itself an overdetermined and contradictory element of the social totality.

Althusser was thus a relativist philosopher, but with this key difference: he never abandoned his commitment to communism and Marxism. His relativism did not entail any undecidability, political neutrality, or political quietism; on the contrary, it informed his intense, lifelong partisanship. All theories, as aspects of society, participate in overdetermining all the other aspects of that society: its politics, culture, and economics. Theories matter; they are material; their proponents and opponents struggle. Which problematic an individual deploys affects everything he or she does. The more individuals deploy a Marxist problematic, the more society will be influenced in directions very different from those fostered by, say, individuals committed to fascist or liberal problematics. What matters are the differences among and hence the different social effects of alternative theoretical problematics. Althusser's intense engagement in philosophical and political struggles – within and beyond Marxism – aimed to advance the social position of one problematic and its desired effects against others. He did not need and rejected notions of absolute truth and claims of having "accounted for reality" as the trappings of bourgeois philosophies and sciences (their modernism) seeking adherents by reactionary appeals to a religiously grounded notion of absolute truth (God).

Ontologically, Althusser's overdetermination entailed what he called an "aleatory materialism." Social structure always has an infinity of dimensions, and social changes always have an infinity of causes and consequences. Marx, Althusser argued, made visible an aspect of society that others had missed, namely class. Marxism was thus a social theory that illuminated the class structures of social life and inspired a movement to transform contemporary class structures – from exploitative/capitalist to communist.

Class is not, for Althusser, the essential determinant of anything. His commitment to overdetermination implies no less. Since Marx and Althusser had read philosophy and social theory widely, both knew that for thousands of years others had spoken about classes in society. What Marx and Marxism offered that was new, then, was a *different* concept of class. Marx's analysis across the three volumes of *Capital* defined and elaborated class as the processes of producing and distributing surplus labor. Before Marx, class had usually meant a group of people distinguished from other groups by the property they owned, the power they wielded, or their self-consciousness. Marx's work made class – as a surplus labor process that impacted social structures and changes – visible, whereas other problematics (including those deploying other concepts of class) had either missed, marginalized, or hidden it. Althusser's work alludes to this point but does not specify Marx's new concept of class. Marxists influenced by Althusser have since begun to do so systematically – showing how individuals participate in multiple, different class processes occurring at such diverse social sites as enterprises, households, and the state (Resnick and Wolff 1987; Fraad, Resnick, and Wolff 1994; Gibson-Graham 1996).

Althusser's Marxism presumes an endless exploration, never finished, of the open-ended way in which the non-class processes of any social totality overdetermine the class processes and vice versa. For Althusser, Marxist activities (discursive and otherwise) are part of the socially overdetermined, evolving self-criticism of capitalist society over the last 150 years. Marxist activities intervene in and thereby change the ceaseless flux of interacting class and non-class processes comprising society. The effects of Marxist interventions, aimed at ending class exploitation and achieving communist society, will depend on all the other discursive interventions and all the non-discursive social processes with which they interact. No underlying causality and no telos govern that interaction. Social history is unalterably open. Althusser's Marxism must struggle within that openness; no modernist closure is available (Resch 1992).

Althusser's commitments to a very particular kind of postmodern Marxism (or Marxist postmodernism) appeared also in his own work's evolution. Indeed, the ongoing work of the French Institut de la Mémoire de l'Édition Contemporaine is collecting Althusser's voluminous unpublished work and producing valuable French and English editions (e.g., Althusser 1996, 1997). An early interest in French structuralism developed into a profound critique of it in his *Essays in Self-criticism* (1976). Analyzing the state as an ideological apparatus of contemporary capitalism led him subsequently to recognize and explore the family, through his autobiographical memoir of his own family, as another such apparatus. In common with so many French Marxists after the failed anti-capitalist uprising there in 1968, he went back to interrogate his Marxism for how it contributed to that failure. Unlike many others, he proceeded to rethink Marxism, not to reject it or to imagine himself a "post-Marxist." That is, he found in critical rereadings of Marx and Marxism the tools with which to develop Marxism in new directions that included self-critical departures from some of his own previous formulations. The new directions included not only some of the most incisive and sophisticated critiques of Stalinism yet produced, but also ever-deeper elaborations of overdetermination as both an epistemological and ontological position. Alongside rereading Marx and Marxism he engaged the "postmodern condition" and its theoretical expressions as important resources – if critically interrogated and transformed – for a Marxism for the next century. Althusser's legacy is a basis for and a provocation to the construction of a postmodern Marxism.

3

John Ashbery

Steven Monte

Period terms do not acquire currency or validity because they provide a comprehensive framework for understanding an era: they suggest trends, point to areas of contention, generate interesting readings, provide perspective on developments. It can therefore be counterproductive to demand more than a working definition of a period term, or to disparage a term because the period in question evidences so wide a range of styles that no one label will suffice. As a conceptual frame, postmodernism is no more or less comprehensive than modernism or romanticism in this respect, and potentially as productive – perhaps more so to judge by the quantity of criticism written in its behalf or against it over the last twenty years. To assess whether postmodernism "succeeds" or "fails" as a conceptual framework thus requires one to explore not so much the nature of the concept as the consequences of employing the term. It is from this perspective that the work of John Ashbery, one of the leading figures of postmodern poetry, if not the paragon of it, paradoxically gains from being considered from outside the framework of postmodernity.

Postmodernity means many and sometimes contradictory things in the world of academic criticism. Ashbery himself has found the postmodern label confusing and applied it to his own work in an idiosyncratic way:

> As for postmodernity, I think I can recognize it in architecture and even in music, but I hardly see what it corresponds to in literature. My idea is to democratize all forms of expression, an idea which comes to me from way back, maybe from Whitman's *Democratic Vistas* – the idea that the most demotic and the most elegant forms of expression equally deserve to be taken into account. It seems to me that postmodernism is a little bit that. (Bleikasten interview, 1993: 7; my translation)

Ashbery grants that his work is postmodern in so far as postmodernism implies a democratization of forms of expression – a weak sense of the term, especially when Ashbery in the same breath mentions that this idea may go back to *Democratic Vistas*. (He might as easily have said Wordsworth's preface to *Lyrical Ballads*, though the context of the interview, conducted in French for a French audience, seems to have urged forward the issue of Americanness that also comes up in Ashbery's interviews in Poland and Britain.) In other interviews, Ashbery has spoken of the democratization of discourses as a specific goal of his when writing *Three Poems* (1972), a book of prose poetry championed by readers as diverse as Harold Bloom and the Language poets for its blurring of genres and mixture of high and low discourses (see Labrie interview, 1984: 31; and Stitt interview, 1983a: 55). From this point of view, Ashbery's poetry, especially his prose poetry, is postmodern according to his own minimal notion, though the poems themselves arguably make his general aims clear without depending on postmodernism as a conceptual framework.

Some critics have been more specific. Margueritte Murphy argues that the prose poem in general fits Lyotard's definition of the postmodern, "the unpresentable in presentation itself," and that *Three Poems* is especially postmodern not only because it comes after the works of Stein and Williams, but also because it subverts generic conventions and discourses in new ways (1992: 170–2). To illustrate her point, she discusses the ambiguity of the pronouns and related features of *Three Poems*, emphasizing the work's submergence of the "lyric I," the polyphonic character of its prose, and, in general, Ashbery's "poetics of inclusion." Stephen Fredman also argues that Ashbery "chose to include"; he supports Robert Creeley's assessment of *Three Poems* as "a possible way out of the postmodern dilemma of the self" and discusses among other things the poem's self-declared problem of selectivity and its ruminations on art's ability to mimic life's way of happening (1990: 117). Marjorie Perloff routinely considers Ashbery postmodern and places his work in a tradition of a "poetics of indeterminacy" (1981, 1990). Like Murphy, Perloff comments on the ambiguous pronouns of *Three Poems* in such a way as to suggest that they disrupt the notion of the self implicit in the romantic "lyric I"; unlike Murphy, her version of postmodernism is Jameson's, not Lyotard's:

> In the consciousness of the postmodern poet, fragments of earlier poetry float to the surface, not to be satirized . . . but as the "blank parody" Fredric Jameson has defined as pastiche, which is to say, the neutral mimicry that takes place when there is no longer a norm to satirize or parodize. When Ashbery's speaker asks, "Have I awakened? Or is this sleep again?" he is not satirizing Keats's "Ode to a Nightingale" . . . (1990: 282)

One dissenting voice among critics is John Shoptaw's, whose analysis of a passage near the beginning of "The New Spirit" ("For we judge not, lest we be judged, yet we are judged all the same") shows that "Jameson's blanket generalization [about parody and pastiche] blurs the textual specifics of post-modern poetry" (1994: 133). Shoptaw also points out that "Not all of *Three Poems* is equally or similarly 'democratic': 'The New Spirit' emphasizes private and romantic discourse; 'The System' foregrounds public discourse; and 'The Recital' features both pragmatic and personal writing" (1994: 133). In a different vein altogether, Andrew Ross discusses Ashbery's work in the context of modernism (1988).

Leaving aside the question of whether Ashbery is postmodern, it is possible to tease out the interpretive effects of considering him as such. Critics who think of Ashbery as postmodern tend to locate and privilege qualities of his writing such as indeterminacy, democratization of discourses, subversion of generic constraints, self-referentiality (especially in so far as the poetry questions its own authority and, in general, deconstructs itself), anti-monumentalism, polyphony, dialogism, and open-endedness. The resulting portrait may be an idealization of certain values and beliefs of our historical moment. At the same time, however, an emphasis on indeterminacy, anti-monumentalism, and the like suggests something important about Ashbery's poetry and prose poetry, if necessarily via some distortion of literary history. As with the idea of a distinctly American prose poem, the idea of a postmodern Ashbery or a postmodern genre informs reading experiences through the attention it brings to bear on a particular set of interpretive issues and its propaganda value. The postmodern framework very likely affects interpretation in other ways as well, if not by a kind of grain-of-truth logic then negatively, through the effort involved in overcoming the expectations which the category "postmodernism" carries with it.

The literary-historical cost of a postmodern Ashbery is a straw-man version of modernism. Bringing the prosaic into poetry, for example, is not only as long-standing a project of modern poetry as Ashbery intimates in his comment about *Democratic Vistas*, but also an idea with which modernists like Eliot were particularly obsessed. Ashbery's poetry is, needless to say, very different from Eliot's poetry, perhaps antithetical to it in some ways, but the differences between the two poets have little to do with reductive oppositions like dialogic versus monologic, open-ended versus closure-oriented, and perhaps even postmodern versus modernist when the former is used in any but its chronological sense. Ashbery's own comments on his poetic aims are illuminating in this regard:

> Everybody knows Mallarmé's dictum about purifying the language of the tribe. In my case I don't feel it needs purifying. I try to encourage it. (Murphy interview, 1985: 20)

> My mind wants to give clichés their chance, unravel them, and so in a way contribute to purifying the language of the tribe. (Jackson interview, 1983b: 72)

The contradiction between Ashbery's statements need not imply a confusion or misrepresentation of aims nor even a change of opinion. Like Eliot, Ashbery is concerned with bringing the prosaic into poetry: the Mallarmé dictum he cites is suggestively closer to Eliot's "purify the dialect of the tribe" from *Four Quartets* than to the original "Donner un sens plus pur aux mots de la tribu." The connotations of the word "purify," however, seem inappropriate for Ashbery's project. In the Murphy interview Ashbery states clearly that he feels the language of the tribe does not need purifying, and in the Jackson interview Ashbery qualifies his assertion with the phrase "in a way contribute to purifying." As Ashbery has suggested in remarks comparing Eliot's and Auden's use of everyday language, Eliot's poetry may simply not go far enough in incorporating the prosaic into poetry. In his interview with Louis A. Osti, for example, Ashbery remarks, "In Eliot, the language of 'The Tribe' always strikes me as a kind of an appendage rather than something that is part of the core of the poetry as in early lyrical Auden" (1974: 93; also see Labrie interview, 1984: 30; Stitt interview, 1983a: 38–9; and Murphy interview, 1985: 23).

Generally speaking, however, postmodernism implies more than a difference in degree between itself and modernism, and it is from this perspective that an interpretation emphasizing Ashbery's postmodernism risks overlooking some of the most meaningful tensions in his work. The problem of selectivity evoked in the opening page of *Three Poems* illustrates this point:

> I thought that if I could put it all down, that would be one way. And next the thought came to me that to leave all out would be another, and truer, way.
> > clean-washed sea
> > > The flowers were.
> These are examples of leaving out. But, forget as we will, something soon comes to stand in their place. Not the truth, perhaps, but – yourself. It is you who made this, therefore you are true. But the truth has passed on
> > to divide all.
> > > > > (*Three Poems*, 1972: 3)

It is important to notice, as most critics have, that the problem of selectivity has aesthetic, autobiographical, and philosophical implications. It is also crucial to observe that omission and inclusion are associated in some way with verse and prose, respectively (Bloom 1985: 74; Murphy 1992: 168–9; Shoptaw 1994: 126). Ashbery's solution to the problem, however, is much more ambiguous than the desire to include everything might indicate, especially if the choice of prose is supposed to imply this poetics of inclusion. As Shoptaw has pointed out, the opening statements of *Three Poems* reverse the expected sequence of inclusion and omission, "putting the way of total prose not after but before the 'truer' way of fragmented lyric" (1994: 126). It is furthermore not clear whether the desire to include in fact wins out over selectivity. A convincing argument can be made that the narrator of *Three Poems* deliberately chooses *not* to include everything, or perhaps has no choice in the matter whatsoever.

It is not as if an aesthetics of inclusion or a postmodern perspective provides an entirely inappropriate framework within which to interpret Ashbery's *Three Poems*. Nor is *Three Poems* an essentially exclusionary and modernist work. The emotional and argumentative movements in Ashbery's poetry are often dialectical. Ashbery's poems may, for example, swerve away from the monumentalism they evoke, but in the process they betray some attraction for the monumental and other things they apparently deny themselves, perhaps even create an atmosphere of desire through rhetorical denial. In either case, as Ashbery suggests in an early poem that questions the monumental, the poet or the reader builds "a mountain of something" merely by "pouring energy into this single monument" of the poem ("These Lacustrine Cities," *Rivers and Mountains*, 1966: 9). Monumentalism, non-democratic discourse, and related qualities may, in other words, be secretly wished-for in the short run, and unavoidable in the long run, in spite or because of the poem's rhetoric. An exclusive emphasis on Ashbery's postmodernism tends to ignore these tensions and in effect short-circuits an important source of the poetry's energy.

But perhaps it is through the poetry's constant turnings and twistings (its sudden shifts between high and low diction; its discontinued arguments and narrations; its skepticism toward authoritative, comprehensive answers) that we can situate Ashbery's work in postmodernism, or at least point to one way in which he has added to our sense of the postmodern. As inventive as postmodern poetry has been, any formal feature associated with it arguably has some precedent in earlier literature – if not Anglo-American modernism, then Futurism or Dadaism. We might however be able to distinguish the dialectical patterns of Ashbery's poems, especially his long poems, from modernist predecessors by the degree and manner in which they turn away from their own plots or lines of inquiry. After all, an impulse toward "negative dialectic" makes itself felt even at a grammatical level in the poems, via the frequent appearance of contrasting logical connectives – *yets*, *buts*, *howevers*, and similar expressions:

> Nothing anybody says can make a difference; *inversely*
> You are a victim of their lack of consequence
> Buffeted by invisible winds, *or yet* a flame yourself
> Without meaning, *yet* drawing satisfaction

From the crevices of that wind, living
In that flame's idealized shape and duration.

Whereas through an act of bunching this black kite
Webs all around you with coal light...
(my emphasis; "Fragment," *The Double Dream of Spring*, 1970: 81)

Even here, however, we need to be careful: contrasting adverbs and conjunctions frequently occur in the long poems of Wallace Stevens, for example, especially when used to mark transitions between stanzas and sections, and a negative dialectics may be a general pattern of thought, or of post-Enlightenment thought. Extremely abrupt rhetorical shifts, such as mid-sentence redirections of thought, may be more unique to Ashbery or postmodern poetry, but, even so, they potentially only confirm the suspicion that postmodernism differs from earlier developments in degree rather than substance. In making us more conscious of such features, Ashbery's poetry has at the very least given postmodernism some definition, direction, and play.

The dialectical movements of Ashbery's poetry not only help explain why his poetry gains something from being considered outside the framework of postmodernity, but also point to a way of understanding postmodernism and situating it among other literary-historical frameworks. If the success of a period term is to be judged by the consequences of employing it, then postmodernism should itself be considered from a dialectical perspective – what it is in relation to what it defines itself against. To put it in another way, postmodernism may have once been a more productive framework in which to situate Ashbery's poetry, may soon prove to be so again, and cannot simply be disregarded now because it does not answer to some important interpretive needs. It has attached itself to Ashbery's work in a way that influences even criticism that would like to believe otherwise and readers who have little investment in the concept. For all of their inadequacy and inconvenience, then, literary-historical frameworks are unavoidable: issuing from a dialogue that demands the kind of perspective they attempt to provide, they necessarily participate in, and therefore become part of, that dialogue.

4

Paul Auster

Madeleine Sorapure

Paul Auster has produced a diverse body of work in the past three decades, including poetry, translations, essays, novels, screenplays, a memoir, and an autobiography. Most important in defining his contribution to our sense of the postmodern are Auster's novels, screenplays, and memoir. These works share certain thematic and formal preoccupations that resonate with other contemporary writers. In describing the particularly postmodern qualities of Auster's writing, I focus on three recurring, interconnected, and familiar themes: identity, chance, and storytelling. In fact, in Auster's work these are not so much themes as they are names for clusters of paradoxes and contradictions within which his characters act.

One prominent feature of postmodernism is that it often rejects either/or dichotomies (either identity or multiplicity, either chance or causality, either fiction or reality) and instead embraces a logic of "both/and." One sees this postmodern logic, for example, in the transgressing or collapsing of boundaries (e.g., between masculine and feminine, public and private, mass and elite culture), or again in Linda Hutcheon's description of parody as a perfect postmodern form because it "paradoxically both incorporates and challenges that which it parodies" (1988: 11). However, this claim with regard to the paradoxical nature of human existence can render action problematic. How does one make decisions and take actions when there is no clear sense of what is true, what is right, what is best? Yet Auster's characters are compelled to act and to take responsibility for their choices, all in the face of radical uncertainty and unresolvable contradiction. Moving from the logic of "both/and," in which one accepts uncertainty and contradiction, to the necessity of "and yet," in which one still must act in these conditions, Auster explores the ethical dimensions of postmodernism. To do so requires a modernist subject, capable of self-reflection, interiority, and some degree of psychological continuity, and by situating this subject in a postmodern world, Auster is able to comment on the postmodern condition. As William Dow (1998) argues,

Auster "feels an obligation to bring back selected values, but in a way that recognizes the ruptures caused by the postmodern" (280).

Let me provide a brief example of Auster's postmodern ethics before turning to a more detailed examination of his work. In his memoir *The Invention of Solitude* (1982), Auster attempts to understand the character of his father, an emotionally evasive man of many surfaces and no apparent center; he describes his father as being "three or four different men, each one distinct, each one a contradiction of all the others" (61). Auster frames his project as a search for the "man hidden inside the man who was not there," and says that "the essence of this project is failure" (20). And yet he undertakes the project anyway, for reasons that are ethical and moral in nature: in order to repay a debt (his father left him an inheritance that enabled him to continue as a writer); in order to "save" or "give birth" to his father (he writes, "my father is gone. If I do not act quickly his entire life will vanish along with him" [6]); and in order to create himself as a writer and as a father of a young son ("There is this responsibility for a young life, and in that he has brought this life into being, he must not despair" [156]). In short, this is a biography/autobiography that explicitly recognizes its own futility, accepting the fragmentary and essentially mysterious nature of its subject, and yet the project must be attempted.

Here and elsewhere in Auster's work, the question of identity is repeatedly the site of a profound struggle for characters whose postmodern sense of themselves and of their place in the world shifts, multiplies, disintegrates, and must be reconstituted, if only provisionally. Charles Baxter (1994) observes that Auster combines "an American obsession with gaining an identity with the European ability to ask how, and under what conditions, identity is stolen or lost" (41). Indeed, many of his characters experience a trauma or rupture that causes them to break down completely; often they place themselves in extreme situations of physical deprivation, hunger, solitude, and exhaustion. They strip away all is that is familiar to them, all that had previously sustained them, pursuing a self-sacrifice that leads (or fails to lead) to redemption – or at least to an ability to return to the world. Pascal Bruckner (1995) describes this aspect of Auster's work as "secular asceticism without transcendence, without God" (28). Whether self-imposed or caused by circumstances outside of their control, these situations have the effect of throwing the characters into an intense, even life-threatening period of introspection.

In *Moon Palace* (1989), for example, Fogg lives in New York's Central Park for a number of months, sleeping outside, scavenging for food, pushing himself to the limits of his physical endurance. He explains his motivation: "I thought that by abandoning myself to the chaos of the world, the world might ultimately reveal some secret harmony to me, some form or pattern that would help me to penetrate myself" (80). The park, he says, "gave me a chance to return to my inner life, to hold on to myself purely in terms of what was happening inside me" (58). In the end, though, he is unable to find a "secret harmony," a "form or pattern" that would permit him to fully know himself; rather, he very nearly starves himself to death before being rescued by friends. But the ordeal causes him to recognize his need for others: "To be loved like that makes all the difference. It does not lessen the terror of the fall, but it gives a new perspective on what that terror means" (50). Throughout Auster's work, isolation can paradoxically heighten one's sense of connectedness, and the importance of relationships is affirmed through the character's solitary inner struggles. Anna of *In the Country of Last Things* (1987) saves an old woman named Isabel, and in caring for Isabel and her husband, Anna saves herself: "for the first time in my life there were people who depended on me, and I did not let them down" (58). If this seems like too easy a lesson, it is in fact complicated later in the novel when Anna works for a charity, the Woburn House, which cares for homeless people. The funds are so low and the need so extreme that guests can stay for only ten days and then must return to the street. Some guests plead pitifully to be allowed to stay longer; some even commit suicide rather than return to a life of homelessness and extreme hardship. Anna comments: "The arithmetic was overpowering, inexorable in the havoc it produced. No matter how hard you worked, there was no chance you were not going to fail. That was the long and the short of it. Unless you were willing to accept the utter futility of the job, there was no point in going on with it" (142). Good works do not necessarily do good and they sometimes do harm, but the alternative of not acting is unacceptable. Responsibility is clearly a virtue in Auster's writing, but his characters continually face the question of how to act responsibly and ethically in a situation that is futile, when choices are ambiguous or misleading, when one knows in advance that the project one undertakes will surely fail.

In their efforts to constitute a sense of identity and purpose in a postmodern universe, Auster's characters often take on identities of other characters, becoming substitutes or stand-ins, in essence living the life of another. For example, in *Moon Palace*, Thomas Effing, wandering in the desert and near death, finds a cave with a dead man inside; he takes over the identity of this man: "He would take on the hermit's life and continue to live it for him, acting as though the soul of this man had now passed into his possession" (167). In *City of Glass* (1985), Quinn becomes "Paul Auster" (the narrator wryly remarks that "The effect of being Paul Auster, he had begun to learn, was not altogether unpleasant" [82]). On the one hand, this identity-switching evokes a postmodern fluidity of subjectivity; if a person can simply become another person, what then is unique, definitive, or stable in one's identity? However, it is often by inhabiting the other, as it were, that characters gain access to themselves; the self is defined through the other, even though both self and other remain ultimately unfathomable. Here too the question of responsibility arises, as characters sometimes take on other identities in order to repair harm that they've caused. In *Leviathan* (1992), for instance, Sachs becomes Reed Dimaggio, a man he had murdered; he moves into Reed's house, supports Reed's wife, becomes father to Reed's daughter, and ultimately takes on Reed's anarchist project. Sachs observes, "As long as I was devoting myself to Dimaggio, I would be keeping him alive. I would give him my life, so to speak, and in exchange he would give my life back to me" (253). Similarly in *The Locked Room* (1986), the narrator takes the place of Fanshawe, falls in love with Fanshawe's wife Sophie, becomes father to Fanshawe's son David: "By belonging to Sophie, I began to feel as though I belonged to everyone else as well. My true place in the world, it turned out, was somewhere beyond myself, and if that place was inside me, it was also unlocatable. This was the tiny hole between self and not-self, and for the first time in my life I saw this nowhere as the exact center of the world" (58–9). While at the end of the novel this narrator is more successful than most of Auster's characters in establishing a satisfactory sense of himself and of his place in the world, it's important to note that the place he names as "the exact center of the world" is "unlocatable," a "tiny hole," "nowhere."

The typically modernist quest to solve the mystery of identity, to create a meaningful and workable sense of self, is paralleled as characters in Auster's works look outward and attempt to understand events and experiences around them. They search for patterns and meanings in the signs they encounter and events they experience, but are frustrated both by the postmodern overload of potentially significant information and by the force of chance, coincidence, the arbitrary, and the implausible. Here the figure of the detective, who Auster describes as "the seeker after truth, the problem-solver" (262), assumes importance, and Auster's rewriting of the detective story, in the New York Trilogy and elsewhere, gives insight into his overall approach. Typically the detective first amasses clues and leads; at this initial stage nothing is insignificant, but eventually false leads reveal themselves as false, random data are brought into order, and the solution becomes apparent. The detective, as Quinn puts it in *City of Glass*, "moves through this morass of objects and events in search of the thought, the idea that will pull all of these things together and make sense of them" (9). But in that novel and elsewhere, the problem is that connections, possibilities, and alternatives multiply out of control, and Auster's detective characters find it impossible to discover a pattern or to arrive at a solution. They confront two contradictory options: either "life is no more than the sum of contingent facts, a chronicle of chance intersections, of flukes, of random events that divulge nothing but their own lack of purpose" (*The Locked Room*, 35); or, as Sachs explains in *Leviathan*, "in one of those unbidden flashes of insight, it occurred to him that nothing was meaningless, that everything in the world was connected to everything else" (231). Either abandon oneself entirely to chance, as Nashe does in *The Music of Chance* (1990) when he lets his fate be determined by a single cut of the cards, or adopt a kind of paranoia, as Quinn does at the end of *City of Glass* when he refuses to give up searching for a solution to the mystery. Neither character comes to a happy end, and in this sense Auster's work examines the consequences of radical indeterminacy, as characters realize that they can no longer impose order and meaning on the contingencies of the world.

Frequently in Auster's work the disruptive force of chance shows up in the form of alternatives that are suggested but that never materialize. For example, in *City of Glass*, Quinn is assigned to follow Peter Stillman. With a photograph of Stillman in hand, he goes to the train station and sees two men get off a train, one stooped and unkempt, the other prosperous and elegant, and both could equally be Stillman: "There was nothing he could do now that would not be a mistake. Whatever choice he made – and he had to make a choice – would be arbitrary, a submission to chance. Uncertainty would haunt him to the end" (91). The possibilities of the first Stillman haunt the narrative, suggesting that all of Quinn's efforts are pointless, and that in fact the story itself is pointless since it focuses on a detective who is bound to be unsuccessful because he is pursuing entirely the wrong person. Similarly in *Ghosts* (1986), Blue sees Black reading *Walden*; he buys the book for himself and tries to read it, but he eventually gives up: "What he does not know is that were he to find the patience to read the book in the spirit in which it asks to be read, his entire life would begin to change, and little by little he would come to a full understanding of his situation. . . . But lost chances are as much a part of life as chances taken, and a story cannot dwell on what might have been" (48–9). Here and elsewhere in Auster's work, "what might have been" haunts the story, calling into question the inevitability of the plot, undermining both the purpose of the characters' actions and the authority of the author.

Unpursued alternatives, chance events, arbitrary connections, the improbable and the impossible – these are essential to Auster's storytelling. In addition to these familiar postmodern devices, Auster employs a reflexive and metafictional stylistics. Robert Creeley (1994) comments that Auster is concerned "not only to tell the story but to tell the story of the story in so doing"; it is "an intellectual preoccupation with the possibilities of telling, of making a de facto 'reality' which can meld with the reality we otherwise know" (37). Auster sprinkles autobiographical references and anecdotes throughout his stories, drawing the author into the world of his own creation and blurring distinctions between fiction and reality. Many of Auster's characters are writers and storytellers, attempting to discover themselves through language, using writing as a means to create a semblance of order and meaning in their lives. But language regularly falls short, and characters find that the world eludes the grasp of words. As Auster states in *The Invention of Solitude*, "the story I am trying to tell is somehow incompatible with language. . . . The degree to which it resists language is an exact measure of how closely I have come to saying something important" (32). The elusiveness and resistance of the signified and the deferral and inadequacy of the signifier mark the context in which Auster and his characters construct narratives. Writers in Auster's novels fail to communicate more often (or at least more notably) than they succeed. In *Timbuktu* (1999), for instance, Willy G. Christmas dies with his seventy-four notebooks of "poems, stories, essays, diary entries, epigrams, autobiographical musings, and an epic-in progress" (9) still hidden away in a bus terminal locker. The great Red Notebook written by Fanshawe in *The Locked Room* is finally incomprehensible; the narrator comments that "All the words were familiar to me, and yet they seemed to have been put together strangely, as though their final purpose was to cancel each other out. . . . Each sentence erased the sentence before it, each paragraph made the next paragraph impossible. . . . I lost my way after the first word" (179).

Auster's characters continue to tell stories while recognizing the inadequacies of language; they continue to act while unsure that their actions will achieve the desired result; they continue to pursue an understanding that they know can only be partial and uncertain. In short, they struggle within and against the postmodern condition. What fuels the struggle is an ethical imperative that might best be described as a kind of hunger. In the first essay of his collection entitled *The Art of Hunger* (1992), Auster describes Knut Hamson's art in terms that might equally be applied to Auster: it is "an art of hunger: an art of need, of necessity, or desire . . . , an art that is the direct expression of the effort to express itself. It is an art that begins with the knowledge that there are no right answers. For that reason, it becomes essential to ask the right questions" (18). While Auster continues to ask questions from the perspective of the modern subject, he transforms these questions by placing them within a postmodern context.

5

Mikhail Bakhtin

Galin Tihanov

The serious appropriation of Mikhail Bakhtin's work in the West commenced in the 1960s precisely with poststructuralist interpretations. From the very beginning, Bakhtin was summoned as a thinker, whose ideas could contribute to the postmodern and poststructuralist concerns with meaning, subjectivity, and canon. Thus the study of Bakhtin was initiated as the study of the potential compatibility of his work with the rising agenda of postmodernism and poststructuralism. It was only later, in the latter half of the 1980s, that an historical approach to Bakhtin began to emerge, which questioned his status as the predecessor of a number of modern trends in literary and cultural theory and frustrated the hope that his work can be seamlessly accommodated under the overarching concepts of poststructuralist theoretical discourse. In what follows I briefly review the principal lines of engagement with Bakhtin's thought in the contexts of poststructuralism and deconstruction. In the first two sections attention is drawn to two thinkers whose texts were formative in the debate over how to "use" Bakhtin. Kristeva and de Man are taken to be the emblems of an affirmative-transformative and a skeptical approach, respectively. In the remaining section, a number of key areas of the postmodernist and poststructuralist appropriation of Bakhtin are explored. The conclusion returns to the issue of the historical meaning versus the contemporary significance of Bakhtin's work.

Kristeva and Bakhtin

Julia Kristeva is undoubtedly not only the person responsible for reclaiming Bakhtin for the Western intellectual scene, but also the author of the most serious texts negotiating the foundations of Bakhtin's theory and their potential capacity to stimulate poststructuralist thought.

Kristeva's first text on Bakhtin, "Word, Dialogue, and Novel" (Kristeva 1980 [1967]), written in 1966 and first published the following year in *Critique*, reshapes his notion of dialogicity into the less personalistic concept of intertextuality. Intertextuality is designed to replace the amorphous and too humanistic idea of intersubjectivity; the text emerges as a mosaic of quotations which reflect the interaction of depersonalized texts and languages rather than of subjects. Kristeva regards the Socratic dialogue, which Bakhtin takes to be an important prototype of the novel, as an anonymous construct that testifies to the negation of personality in the act of dialogue. Not surprisingly, her interest is drawn by Bakhtin's interest in carnival, which she considers an entity that cannot be interpreted with the categories of substance, causality, and identity in mind. Carnival is anti-teleological; instead of being driven by an ultimate goal and seeking to flesh out an inherent essence, it liquidates the subject and reveals the unconscious elemental forces of sex and death. Thus Bakhtin is read by Kristeva as a thinker who, by introducing the principles of dialogism and Menippean ambivalence, embodies the process of abandoning the categories of "identity, substance, causality, and definition" in favor of "analogy, relation, opposition" (Kristeva 1980 [1967]: 86).

Kristeva's later analysis of Bakhtin's *Problems of Dostoevsky's Poetics* (Kristeva 1973 [French edition 1970]) traces possible parallels (and differences) between Bakhtin and Freud, thus emphasizing even further the aspect of depersonalization in Bakhtin's theory of the novel. Polyphony, Kristeva argues here, is not the result of the harmonious blend of different voices, but rather the consequence of the language-user becoming "his own otherness," and thereby "multiple and elusive, polyphonic" (Kristeva 1973: 109). Polyphony, thus divested of its connotations of intersubjectivity, is understood as an open and undecided intertextual space, in which "the 'character' is nothing more than a discursive point of view of the 'I' who writes through another 'I'" (Kristeva 1973: 111).

That Kristeva read Bakhtin in a way that strengthened her own case for the importance of psychoanalysis in the rise of (post) structuralist thought can be gathered from her retrospective comments on the two texts discussed above. In an interview granted in 1995 to *Dialog. Karnaval. Khronotop*, the Vitebsk–Moscow journal of Bakhtin studies, she stated that the distance between Bakhtin and psychoanalysis is, after all, too considerable to be bridged by any impartial interpretation. "From the very beginning," Kristeva writes, "I introduced a deliberate 'working' distortion to my perception of Bakhtin. It seems to me that Bakhtin's 'Other' is after all the 'Other' of Hegelian consciousness, and certainly not the bifurcated 'Other' of psychoanalysis. I, for one, wanted to perceive it not as an 'intersubjective Other,' but rather as a dimension disclosing another reality within the reality of consciousness. In other words, the 'Hegelian' Bakhtin was as if twisted by me and turned into a 'Freudian' Bakhtin" (Kristeva 1995: 7).

Paul de Man and Bakhtin

On reading Kristeva's interpretations of Bakhtin's work, one may well argue that her texts foreshadowed a whole range of postmodern theoretical anxieties to be spelled out in the 1970s and 1980s. Yet Kristeva remained largely uninterested in weighing those aspects of Bakhtin's theories that could be thought to work against aligning him with exponents of postmodern and poststructuralist thought. Writing more than ten years after Kristeva's second article on Bakhtin, Paul de Man, in a text originally published in 1983 in *Poetics Today* (de Man 1989), took a close look at Bakhtin's theory of genre only to establish that his notion of language and discourse can be "monologically aberrant" and undermine his "dialogical ideology."

De Man's questioning of Bakhtin starts with a critique of Bakhtin's rigid opposition between the tropological polysemy of poetry and the dialogism of prose. Bakhtin, de Man argues, thinks the trope as an "intentional structure directed toward an object" (de Man 1989: 112); thus trope is endowed with the status of a pure *episteme* rather than a fact of language. This intentionality and the divorce of tropes from language exclude them from both poetic and prosaic discourse and locate them in the field of epistemology.

Unlike tropes, which are in the grip of an object-directed discourse, dialogism in de Man's interpretation of Bakhtin is seen as social-oriented. Leaning predominantly on the Dostoevsky book, he concedes that "Bakhtin at times conveys the impression that one can accede from dialogism as a metalinguistic (i.e., formal) structure to dialogism as a recognition of exotopy" (de Man 1989: 109) in a social and cultural sense. The Dostoevsky book, in this respect, appears to de Man more seminal than "Discourse in the Novel," whose societal models imply class structures and class relations. Thus dialogism in the Dostoevsky book may be taken to suggest that the binary opposition between fiction and fact fades away and no longer applies.

Whether this transition from the textual embodiment of dialogism to the recognition of the other in a situation of real dialogue does indeed take place in Bakhtin is a question de Man leaves open, although his tone betrays skepticism. What matters is that regardless of whether genuine dialogue is attained, Bakhtin nevertheless presents dialogism as a social-oriented discourse. But if this is true, the opposition between trope and dialogism (poetry and novel) should be taken to stand for the deeper opposition between object and society, which, de Man warns, is redolent of reifying theoretical practices (de Man 1989: 112). Even more disturbingly, de Man believes that on certain occasions in Bakhtin's texts dialogism is reduced to a hermeneutic system of question and answer, in which the will to "understand" the primary meaning cancels all attempts at a genuine acceptance of otherness. The normative discourse of hermeneutic appropriation of meaning (cf. Roberts 1989: 116) is bound to frustrate the discourse of difference grounded in otherness. Thus Bakhtin's project is ambivalent and unable to subscribe fully to the deconstructive strategies of transcending binary oppositions and resisting a reductionist approach to alterity.

Meaning and Canonicity

The two preceding sections have demonstrated two different approaches to Bakhtin: claiming him unreservedly for a postmodern and poststructuralist theoretical agenda through "modifying" his thought to fit in with the patterns of indetermination, alterity, semantic suspension, and decentralization of the self (Kristeva); and subjecting his postulates to a patient scrutiny revealing his strongly limited compatibility with the philosophical tenets underlying post-modernism and deconstruction (de Man). Bakhtin's historical distance from postmodernism comes to the fore in an unmistakable fashion when the question of the meaning of cultural forms is posed. For all his admiration for popular culture and the various forms of "life-ideology" (*zhiznennaia ideologiia*), Bakhtin never abandons his reverence for a presumed canon of great art. He retains his fidelity to those works of literature which stand the test of "great time" and participate in the "great experience" of humankind. Bakhtin's dualism of "great" and "small" time, of "great" and "small" experience, so clearly and passionately stated in his texts of the 1960s and 1970s, has its roots, as has already been argued (cf. Tihanov 2000: ch. 1) in the blend of three philosophical traditions. First, there is the neo-Kantian split between fact and value, along with the trust in the potential open-endedness of being, championed in the articles of Bakhtin's close friend Matvei Kagan (cf. Kagan 1922, 1997); second, there is the Hegelian idea of totality, of culture as a world-historical and depersonalized unity, which provides the ground for each sense (*smysl*) to touch on (and be touched by) other senses, thus entering an unlimited dialogue with them; third, there is the serious domestic tradition of Russian eschatologism, which supports the hopes that every meaning can enjoy a resurrection and that every word is hospitably awaited by a "great time" in a second kingdom, where a new and "great experience" will do justice to that which has been forgotten while "small time" lasted. This powerful Christian utopia is one of the main sources of the ongoing magic and attraction of Bakhtin's texts. On the surface, it suggests that everything can be salvaged in "great time"; in reality, however, Bakhtin never deals with works worthy of admittance to "the homecoming festival" (Bakhtin 1986: 170) of meaning other than those already belonging to a presumed canon of great literature (Dostoevsky, Goethe, Rabelais). The mechanisms of this utopian salvation help us answer the question of why Bakhtin's thought survived the challenges of poststructuralism and proved even – for a great many interpreters – compatible with it.

Meaning, in order to be admitted to the bosom of "great time," has to be, as Bakhtin clearly demands (cf. Bakhtin 1986: 170), unstable and – to a considerable degree – depersonalized. Salvation cannot be hoped for before meaning sheds its stable identity and its status of being borne by an author who exercises control over it. Entering the dialogue of "great time" is an act preceded by the relinquishing of authorial claims and the handing over of meaning – in all its changeability – into the care of Time. It is in this never-ending dialogue that a first or a last meaning can no longer exist. But what emerges along this chain of meanings is an unceasing rejuvenation through change, a salvation through inclusion into new contexts. Bakhtin, then, allows his fans to eat their cake without having to mourn its disappearance: the shaken stability of meaning and the humble withdrawal of the author are in fact only a means for purchasing the eternity and dynamic identity of meaning in "great" time.

Laughter, Body, and Participation

In this final section, I briefly discuss carnival and participatory culture as another focus of postmodernist appropriations of Bakhtin, whose claims face the challenge of substantiated attempts to reassess Bakhtin's ideas of popular culture and carnival from the perspective of Left cultural criticism (cf. Brandist 1996) or through attentive historical comparison (cf. Humphrey 2000).

It has been argued, most brilliantly perhaps by David Carroll in an article drawing potential parallels between Bakhtin and Lyotard (Carroll 1987), that in Bakhtin's *Rabelais* laughter is an "affirmation of unresolved and unresolvable contradictions," that it is the opening up to "difference, heterogeneity, and alterity" (Carroll 1987: 88). Laughter indicates, furthermore, sociability, community, and a "non-determined relation to others" (Carroll 1987: 87). Thus carnival, resting as it does on the support of laughter and the non-classical body, is the "fluctuating form of freedom itself, the acting out or performance of non-restraint, flexibility, multiplicity, otherness" (Carroll 1987: 90). To the (Marxist) objection that carnival is no more than a "safety valve" provided by the ruling class in order for energies jeopardizing the status quo to be diverted away from a more significant (political) action, Carroll responds by asserting the character of carnival as an alternative form of social reality that is unrealizable "except in play." Participatory performance, play, and cultural alterity emerge as inextricably interwoven in an exemplary post-modernist reading of *Rabelais*. Yet this would only be a one-sided reading of Bakhtin, and Carroll himself foregrounds the perils of such a simplistic inter-pretation. The dangers stem from the fact that Bakhtin's vision of carnival affirms a notion of alterity materialized in a collectivist action that in its corporeal intensity appears to be expressive of a pre- or post-linguistic notion of otherness (cf. Carroll 1987: 91). In addition, in Bakhtin's optimistic version of carnival, negativity and death are negated and established as no more than sublatable moments in the immortality of the people; but the refusal to recog-nize pain, negativity, and death as irreducible elements of the human condition amounts to a refusal to truly recognize alterity, of whose engendering they are bound to partake. Bakhtin clearly believes that the people's laughter is a form of growing historical consciousness, gradually purging the fears *vis-à-vis* death and cosmic upheavals; the material foundation of this attitude is seen in the "body of the species" (*rodovoe telo*), a Hegelian construct which is placed above the death-and-life dilemma. Immortal and thus invulnerable to the forces of historic change, all this body knows are the powerful swings of sublation between "*stirb und werde*" (Bakhtin 1984: 250) which underwrite the grand narrative of the people's unfailing and ever-present omnipotence.

Similarly, the participatory nature of carnival in Bakhtin's Rabelais book cannot be unequivocally regarded as an indication of a culture built upon contingency of value and in denial of grand narratives. Carnival does indeed obliterate the boundary between viewers and participants; referring to the wedding feast as a carnivalesque event, Bakhtin asserts: "during that period there are no footlights, no separation of participant and spectators. Everybody participates" (Bakhtin 1984: 265). Undoubtedly, Bakhtin here follows closely Nietzsche's *The Birth of Tragedy* (Section 8), where Nietzsche stresses the absence of differentiation between viewer and actor in Greek tragedy. But in the introduction to *Rabelais*, Bakhtin interprets the participatory nature of carnival in this recognizably Hegelian mode: "Carnival has universal dimen-sions; it is a special condition of the entire world, of the world's revival and renewal, in which all take part" (Bakhtin 1984: 7); and a few passages later: "One can express this also thus: in carnival, life itself plays, enacting – without a stage, without footlights, without actors, without spectators, that is without any specifically artistic and theatrical features – another free form of its materialisation, its regeneration and renewal on *better terms*. The real form of life is here at the same time its revived *ideal form*" (my emphasis). A philoso-phy-of-life glorification of the universal unity of life blends here with a version of the Hegelian equation of the rational and the real. Bakhtin, however, substitutes "ideal" for Hegel's "rational," thus bringing an undeniable strain of often unconcealed utopianism into his text.

It would be fair to say, in conclusion, that appropriating and interpreting Bakhtin has over the last two decades been a business more willing to inscribe him in current debates than to contextualize his thought in its historical ambience. The endeavors to claim Bakhtin for a postmodernist and poststructuralist theoretical agenda, while remaining seminal and stimulating, have evolved on the far side of analyzing his work on its own, historically posited terms. While firmly integrated in the repertoire of postmodernist and poststructuralist thought, Bakhtin's notions of alterity, of participatory culture, and of negotiated (weakened) authorial control over meaning, emerge from an intellectual context which lends them the birthmarks of a confident subscription to ideas that are hardly compatible with a critique of grand narratives or with a mistrust of eternal cultural principles shaping the human condition.

6

John Barth

Theo D'haen

The American author John Simmons Barth, born May 27, 1930 in Cambridge, Maryland, has played a central role in the debate around postmodernism, both with his novels and stories and with two seminal essays, "The Literature of Exhaustion" (1967) and "The Literature of Replenishment" (1979b).

Barth burst on the American literary scene with *The Floating Opera* (1956) and *The End of the Road* (1958). Both novels can best be read against the background of existentialism, prominent at the time in both Europe and the United States. The protagonists, Todd Andrews in *The Floating Opera* and Jacob Horner in *The End of the Road*, do not really see why they are in this world, and they do not know which direction to give to their existence. Andrews reaches the logical conclusion that there is no valid reason to go on living. When about to take his own life, though, it comes to him in a flash that: "There's no final reason for living (or for suicide)"! Horner finds himself in the grip of a catatonic paralysis, simply because he cannot make up his mind as to what he should do next. In order to give some shape to his life, he borrows the attitudes and motives of other people. As a result, he becomes hopelessly entangled in a *ménage à trois* that ends with the death – following an abortion – of his lover, and with his own move to a private clinic run by the same quack that performed the disastrous abortion. Notwithstanding their serious subject matter, *The Floating Opera* and *The End of the Road* bristle with humor and wit. In fact, in these early works Barth, rather than uphold existentialism, subjects it to a subtle but pervasive irony.

The Floating Opera and *The End of the Road* have a contemporary American setting, and their protagonists are credible, if somewhat eccentric, specimens of Barth's contemporary co-citizens. As in the late 1940s and early 1950s the tenor of American fiction was predominantly realistic, Barth's first novels were initially interpreted accordingly, and thus faulted for being a moral and nihilistic. What went virtually unrecognized at the time is precisely what makes these novels into early examples of postmodernism: their pervasive irony and self-reflexivity. *The Sot-Weed Factor* (1960), Barth's next novel, precludes any realistic interpretation. The central character of this novel is Ebenezer Cooke, a fictive reincarnation of the real-life writer of the long satirical poem "The Sot-Weed Factor" of 1708. The language in which the novel is couched and the generic conventions it answers to – primarily those of the picaresque – are those of the period in which the story is set. Yet, Barth pushes these conventions to extremes: unlikely coincidences abound, and so do doubles, as well as instances of cross-dressing and mistaken identities. Barth's extremely self-conscious use of all these devices, then, strongly foregrounds the role of the author in shaping his narrative.

The tension between extreme coincidence, or chaos, and extreme plotting, or control, is characteristic of how the early postmodernists (Hawkes, Gaddis, Pynchon, Coover, Barth himself) look upon the world. That is why so many postmodern novels revolve around a plot or conspiracy of which it is never resolved whether it is more than just a figment of the protagonist's imagination. So also with Ebenezer Cooke in *The Sot-Weed Factor*. Of course, the question as to whether the world is ruled by chaos or order posed itself for earlier writers, too. Barth's eighteenth-century predecessors solved the problem by using the narrative–technical means at their disposal to make sure that in the end everything was set right in accordance with divine providence, and hence with the era's worldview or ideology. For the postmodernists, of course, such a sleight of hand is impossible. On the contrary, Barth foregrounds the dilemma of the postmodernist author, and consequently of postmodern man, by emphasizing the arbitrariness of his authorial interventions. *The Sot-Weed Factor*, then, via parody and pastiche unveils how worldviews or ideologies impose themselves on the world through language, and hence also through literature.

In *Giles Goat-Boy* (1966) Barth again fastens upon specific and well-defined subgenres: science fiction and the campus novel. The "cannibalization" of such "minor" genres is in itself characteristic of postmodernism. On the one hand, it signals a revolt against Modernism's cultivation of "high" literature. On the other hand, the stereotypical plots and characters, and the hackneyed style and vocabulary, of these "formula-genres" illustrate the conventionality of representation that the postmodernists wish to draw attention to. The subtitle of *Giles Goat-Boy* – "or, The Revised New Syllabus" – refers to the New Testament. The story of the redeemer of man and the founding father of a new faith is transposed to the near future, and to the setting of an American university campus. The self-reflexive use *Giles Goat-Boy* makes of prefaces, afterwords, "cover-letters," "post-tapes," and "post-scripts," radically undercuts any claims to referential veracity or truth the reader might be looking for.

Giles Goat-Boy is typical of the 1960s for the way in which it questions norms and values that went unchallenged in the 1950s. As a pastiche of the

Bible, the novel is an outright attack upon the sanctimonious piety of the WASP-majority that in the 1950s set the religious and moral tone of the United States. It also ridicules the Cold War mentality of the Eisenhower era. Moreover, *Giles Goat-Boy* criticizes then dominant ideas of unbridled technical and industrial development. Instead, it advocates the back-to-nature idealism of the flower power movement – though here too undercut by irony. For a short while, *Giles Goat-Boy* enjoyed a cult status. Now, it is one of Barth's least-read books.

The same cannot be said of *Lost in the Funhouse* (1968), Barth's first and still most important collection of stories. In 1967 Barth had published "The Literature of Exhaustion," an essay in which he argued that certain fictional techniques, more particularly those usually associated with realism, could no longer serve contemporary authors. The task in hand was to turn the exhaustion of this kind of literature into a source of inspiration for a new kind of literature. This is what he saw Beckett, Nabokov, and particularly Borges as doing. Small wonder, then, that when *Lost in the Funhouse* appeared, it was looked upon as offering recipes for escape from the impasse Barth saw contemporary American fiction as having reached. Later, when the term "postmodernism" increasingly came to be used to label the kind of fiction that Barth and like-minded authors wrote, "The Literature of Exhaustion" came to be considered as one of the earliest programmatic statements of postmodernism.

What all stories of *Lost in the Funhouse* have in common is that they are intensely metafictional and self-reflexive. In other words, they are not so much preoccupied with *what* they tell as with *how* they do so, and with the possibilities and impossibilities of storytelling. In fact, most of these "Fiction[s] for Print, Tape, Live Voice," really ought to be seen as radical experiments in narrative technique. The first "story," for instance, is only two pages long, one recto and one verso. A narrow vertical banner, reading "ONCE UPON A TIME / THERE WAS A STORY THAT BEGAN," runs the outside length of both pages. The body of the story comes down to a set of instructions as to how to turn the vertical banner into a Moebius-strip, thus causing the text on it to run on endlessly. This first story in the volume bears the appropriate title of "Frame-Tale." The second story, "Night-Sea Journey," is the first-person account of a human spermatozoid en route to the egg it is going to fertilize. At the same time this story presents an allegorical survey of the most important philosophical currents in human history, a condensed history of the world, and a foreshortened version of the life of every man. "Title" and "Life-Story" are reflections on writing itself, and at the same time recount the "story" of such a reflection. Other texts are literally meant for "Tape" or "Live Voice," and only take full effect when performed in the right medium.

The title story of *Lost in the Funhouse* fills us in on an episode in the life of Ambrose Mensch, the protagonist of those few stories that at first sight strike one as "realist." At the same time, this particular story is yet another meditation on writing itself, and on the life of the writer. The "funhouse" of the title is a hall of mirrors that doubles as a maze. It is "really there" in the story, while via *mise-en-abîme* it serves as an allegory for the fiction it features in. When the protagonist, then, gets lost in the funhouse, this has implications on both the level of the story itself and on the metafictional level.

Lost in the Funhouse was written in the midst of the turbulent 1960s, and in his introduction to the reprint of "The Literature of Exhaustion" in *The Friday Book: Essays and Other Nonfiction* (1984), Barth himself admits that both the essay in question and the texts he wrote in that same period were inspired by the social and political unrest then affecting the United States. The State University of New York in Buffalo, where Barth taught at the time, counted an unusually high number of "radicals" among its faculty. The experimentalism of *Lost in the Funhouse*, then, its resistance to traditional forms of narrating and writing, can be seen as the literary equivalent to the more general social and political revolt characteristic of the period and of Barth's more immediate milieu.

Barth did not abandon literary experimentation in his subsequent works, but he did not pursue the radical politics implicit to *Lost in the Funhouse*. The latter collection had closed with "Menelaiad" and "Anonymiad," two stories for which Barth sought inspiration in classical themes, myths, and characters. He steered the same course in *Chimera* (1972), an interlocking series of three novellas prompted by Greek mythology and the *Arabian Nights*. Of course, neither in *Lost in the Funhouse* nor in *Chimera* does Barth limit himself to simple retelling; here again, it is the story *of* the story that takes center-stage.

In 1979 there appeared *LETTERS*, a massive novel, as well as the essay "The Literature of Replenishment," which, like its predecessor "The Literature of Exhaustion," first appeared in the *Atlantic*, and has since been reprinted in *The Friday Book*. Barth's later discursive prose was collected in *Further Fridays: Essays, Lectures, and Other Nonfiction 1984–1994* (1995). In "The Literature of Replenishment" Barth applies the term "postmodernism" to his own work, and specifically to *LETTERS*. In the same breath he praises Borges, Fowles, García Márquez, and Calvino for striking a healthy "mix" between the accomplishments of the traditional novel, the technical achievements of Modernism, and yet more recent narrative experiments, and for at the same time reviving the magic of storytelling.

In the most literal sense, *LETTERS* is a "rewrite" of Barth's own earlier work. Most characters originate from Barth's previous novels and stories. In the later novel they present us with an alternative view of their experiences in those earlier texts in which they featured as protagonists. Barth himself features as "the author," who in the putative "rewrites" of his own earlier texts by their respective protagonists therefore "really" also engages in rewriting his own life and works. In fact, *LETTERS* effectively converts Barth's oeuvre up to 1979 into a self-referential universe. As far as its immediate action is concerned, the novel is set in the politically and socially volatile 1960s, and centers upon a series of conspiracies as determinants of American history. Yet, the book, by mouth of its putative character-author "Barth," refuses to bring any of these plots to a conclusion. "Barth" explains this reluctance as follows: "the real treasure (and our story's resolution) may be the key itself: illumination, not solution, of the Scheme of Things." In other words: it is more important to reveal how the world as we know it is a verbal construction, a "story," than to suggest solutions that, given the verbal nature of "our" world, can never be "true" solutions anyway. *LETTERS*, then, is a clear illustration of how the early generation of American postmodernists, of which Barth is such an eminent representative, is caught in the prisonhouse of language. Implicitly, this comes down to a recognition of the failure of the attempt to link literary experiment and moral and political renewal. *LETTERS* means "the end" of this particular "road" for Barth.

In fact, *LETTERS* in practice also marks the end of "postmodernism" as the dominant strain in American literature. After 1979 Barth's generation of experimental white male authors, though it still continued to command critical respect, effectively ceded the literary center to a younger generation of predominantly female and multicultural authors. The critics hailed *LETTERS* as a masterwork, but the book seems to have gone virtually unread by the wider public. It also barely features in the critical discussion after 1979. This is even truer of Barth's later books. *Sabbatical* (1982), because of its obviously autobiographical elements, at first sight seems more realistic than *LETTERS* but soon turns out to be a rehash of most of Barth's by now well-worn themes. It even seems as if Barth in this book signals his own awareness of having turned some corner when he starts to parody his own earlier work, and to criticize his own earlier experimentalism. *The Tidewater Tales* (1987) involves yet another act of rewriting, this time of *Sabbatical* as well as of Barth's own earlier work and of Western literary history. *The Last Voyage of Somebody the Sailor* (1991) and *Once Upon a Time: A Floating Opera* (1994) continue in the same vein. Both have the *Arabian Nights* as their most immediate matrix. Both, however, also show the autobiographical element growing ever stronger.

The autobiographical tendency culminates in *On with the Story* (1996). This collection of stories takes up the theme of *Lost in the Funhouse* in that it analyzes the power of stories to create an alternative universe. In this particular case, fiction creates a world of laughter to counter the horror of everyday existence for a couple evidently growing older, with one of them staring death in the face. *LETTERS* rounded off a body of work that explored the link of postmodern literature to the public world. *On with the Story* concludes a period in which Barth ever more intensely sought to do the same for the private world. However intrinsically interesting this later work may be, it fails to hold the wider appeal of the earlier work. As to technical experimentation, it adds little if anything to the achievements of the latter. As to themes, it is out of tune with the multicultural dominant of the 1980s and 1990s. The work for which Barth will be remembered, then, is that from *The Floating Opera* in 1956 to *LETTERS* in 1979. This is the work that helped shape the course of American literature in the period in which it appeared, that is to say in the heyday of (American) postmodernism.

7

Roland Barthes

David Herman

Roland Barthes was the son of a Protestant mother and a Catholic father, the latter a lieutenant in the French navy who was killed in action a year after his son's birth in 1915. At 18, Barthes wrote his first text, a pastiche of Plato, and a year later he helped found the DRAF, an anti-fascist political group. From 1935 to 1939, Barthes studied French and the Classics at the Sorbonne. Exempted from military service because of a history of pulmonary tuberculosis, Barthes continued to participate in protests against fascism. During the Nazi Occupation, Barthes was a teacher in Paris, with several relapses of his tuberculosis forcing him to abandon his postgraduate studies and recuperate in sanatoria in France and Switzerland. Unable to find work in Paris after the war, Barthes accepted a job as a librarian and then a teacher at L'Institut français in 1947–9 in Bucharest, Romania, subsequently moving to the University of Alexandria, where he was introduced to structural linguistics by A. J. Greimas and where he contributed articles to prominent left-wing periodicals.

Back in Paris, Barthes worked during the 1950s at the Centre national de la recherche scientifique, first as a lexicographer and later in the sociology section. He published *Writing Degree Zero* in 1953 and *Mythologies* in 1957, and from 1960 to 1962 served as Chairman of Sciences économiques et sociales at the École Pratique des Hautes Études, where until his death in 1980 (from injuries sustained in a traffic accident) Barthes held the position of Directeur d'études in the "sociology of signs, symbols, and representations." In 1976, Barthes was also elected to a Chair in Literary Semiology at the prestigious Collège de France. After publishing such high-structuralist works as "The Structuralist Activity" (1992 [1964]), *Elements of Semiology* (1967 [1964]), "Introduction to the Structural Analysis of Narratives" (1977 [1966]), and *The Fashion System* (1990 [1967]), in 1968 Barthes initiated in his seminar the autocritique of structuralism that would eventuate in the publication of *S/Z* (1974 [1970]). This influential text was the result of a postmodernist turn that unfolded both within Barthes's own oeuvre – as evidenced by writings such as "The Death of the Author" (1977 [1968]), "From Work to Text" (1977 [1971]), *The Pleasure of the Text* (1975 [1973]), *Roland Barthes by Roland Barthes* (1977 [1975]), and *Sollers Writer* (1984 [1979]) – and also in the critico-theoretical discourse to which Barthes's later work gave impetus. The scope and nature of Barthes's postmodernist turn, together with its implications for subsequent developments in literary and cultural theory, will be my specific concerns here. A guiding assumption in what follows is that Barthes's uniquely double identity, his role as one of the world's foremost practitioners first of structuralism and then of post-structuralism, gives his postmodernist turn an especially emblematic status, and makes his mid-career shift as momentous in its own way as Ludwig Wittgenstein's or Henry James's.

Focusing special attention on the transitional period (ca. 1968–71) during which Barthes made his turn, I organize this brief discussion by revisiting – and sketching some historical context for – the seven "principal propositions at the intersection of which [Barthes saw the idea of] the Text as standing" in his 1971 essay "From Work to Text." (I follow Barthes in capitalizing the word *text* when it denotes not a particular text but the notion of "the text" as such – i.e., the *textness* of texts, one might say, though at the risk of reifying what Barthes instead described as a process involving, on the one hand, scriptors who manipulate and recombine previously existing texts and, on the other hand, readers who are not passive consumers but rather active co-creators of the Text [cf. Barthes 1977 [1968]; 1974 [1970]]. In other words, like Barthes I use *Text* as a mass noun, like *water* or *space*, and *text* as a count noun, like *cat* or *pencil*.) I draw on this pivotal, quasi-programmatic essay in part because it conveniently encapsulates ideas that helped define the later Barthes's work, which in turn helped shape the discourses of postmodernism. More than this, though, the essay can be read as a kind of internalized dialogue or debate, with Barthes adopting a persona who now embraces key tenets of Derridean poststructuralism, for example, and who thus takes issue with the author's earlier, staunchly structuralist persona, champion of a classically semiolinguistic approach to literary and cultural analysis.

Of course, given the complex derivations and multiple denotations of the term *postmodernism* (Natoli and Hutcheon 1993), tracing the shift from structuralist to poststructuralist motifs in Barthes's essay (or even in his corpus as a whole) will not be tantamount to mapping his affiliations with postmodernist thought generally. Yet reexploring Barthes's seven themes, and the context in which he propounded them, should throw light on the theorist's turn. The themes can illuminate, too, how Barthes's fellow-travelers and successors built on his work to develop the styles of inquiry that came to be associated with postmodern theory – and, for that matter, with theories of postmodernism.

Barthes's Turn in Context

In stating his seven propositions, Barthes made the caveat that they should be construed less as argumentations than as enunciations or "touches" (Barthes 1977 [1971]: 156). The self-reflexivity, playfulness, and anti-exhaustive spirit of Barthes's proviso can be said to flow directly from the new, postmodernist research paradigm that his essay goes on to outline. As Barthes puts it at the end of the essay, "a Theory of the Text cannot be satisfied by a metalinguistic exposition: the destruction of meta-language . . . is part of the theory itself" (164). Despite or rather in consequence of what can be viewed as a distinctively postmodern relativism – i.e., a refusal to distance his own discourse from the research object to which it stands in some relation other than exposition or explanation – Barthes does nonetheless set out both diachronic and synchronic criteria for distinguishing the (postmodern or postclassical) Text from the (pre-postmodern or classical) work. My next section focuses on the defining attributes of work versus Text. Here I wish to suggest that Barthes's very attempt to draw this distinction helps contextualize his postmodernist turn.

Adopting at first a diachronic perspective, Barthes opens his essay by arguing that the limits of applicability of the idea of the work began to manifest themselves with the advent of that radical interdisciplinarity which is one of the hallmarks of postmodernism, and which enabled the Text to become an object of inquiry in the first place. Barthes's own structuralist investigations, which looked to linguistics as a pilot-science for literary and more broadly semiotic analysis (Dosse 1997; Herman 1997), contributed to the interdisciplinarity that spawned the Text, even though for the Barthes writing in 1971 the Text had ceased to be describable in structuralist terms. Drawing an analogy with developments in the natural sciences, Barthes suggests that, for its part, the work is the correlate of phenomena studied in classical, Newtonian physics. By contrast, the Text is the correlate of phenomena studied in Einsteinian or postclassical physics, a mode of inquiry that "demands that *the relativity of the frames of reference* be included in the object studied." In just the same way, argues Barthes, "the combined action of Marxism, Freudianism, and structuralism demands, in literature, the relativization of the relations of writer, reader and observer (critic)" (156).

Barthes's characterization of the Text as a field of forces encompassing texts *about* the Text marks a distinct break with claims he had earlier promoted under the auspices of structuralism; resonates with other later writings by the theorist; and anticipates the reflexive, relativistic profile of various discourses that emerged as part of the same critique of classical, pre-postmodern theories of theory-making – i.e., theories premised on a division between ways of studying phenomena and the phenomena being studied. The seamless continuity of the Text, its status as a dynamic network of signifiers amid which the analyst is obliged to situate his or her own discourse, contrasts with what the Barthes of 1964 had described as a distinction between the object and the method of structuralist analysis: "The goal of all structuralist activity, whether reflexive or poetic, is to reconstruct an 'object' in such a way as to manifest thereby the rules of functioning (the 'functions') of this object" (1992 [1964]: 1128). Similarly, in his 1966 "Introduction to the Structural Analysis of Narratives," Barthes had characterized stories as one "idiom" among others that could be illuminated by the "linguistics of discourse," which he cast as a metalanguage in which textual or supersentential linguistic units (actants, functions, indices, informants, etc.) could be described and explained. By the time of *S/Z*, in which Barthes reflected on how analyzing a single text could produce insights into the Text, the theorist had erased the boundary between method and object, or rather reconstrued the object as the best source of methods for its own investigation. "The single text," Barthes now argued,

> is not an (inductive) access to a Model, but [an] entrance into a network with a thousand entrances; to take this entrance is to aim, ultimately, not at a legal structure of norms and departures, a narrative or poetic Law, but at a perspective (of fragments, of voices from other texts, other codes), whose vanishing point is nonetheless ceaselessly pushed back, mysteriously opened: each (single) text is the very theory (and not the mere example) of this vanishing. (1974 [1970]: 12)

This relativization of frames of reference, whereby textual analysis becomes less the application of a particular model than the practice of reflecting on the possibilities and limits of models for analyzing the Text, will become the signature of Barthes's later work, whether the specific text under consideration is the novelistic discourse of the Marquis de Sade (Barthes 1976 [1971]); the photographic images, notes, manuscripts, drawings, publications, discussions, and memories that make up the text of Barthes's own life (1977 [1975]); or the "encyclopaedia of affective culture" that can be assembled, bit by bit, through painstaking study of the lover's discourse (Barthes 1978 [1977]). More generally, the discourses of postmodernism have at once theorized and enacted this same shift; their chief goal is no longer explanation as such, but instead a testing of the limits of applicability of competing explanatory models. For instance, Jacques Derrida's concept of "closure" – his insight that any critique of Western metaphysics must borrow from the heritage of concepts it aims to surpass (Derrida 1986 [1966]: 86–8; 1981b [1972]: 17–36) – bears a distinct family resemblance to Barthes's new methodological (or meta-methodological) focus. (Herman under review makes the stronger claim that Barthes's encounter with Derrida's early writings in part *caused* Barthes to abandon his previous, structuralist dissociation of method and object.) Likewise, in the field known as the Social Study of Science, itself an important site for postmodern interdisciplinarity, a whole subdomain of research centers around the "reflexive thesis" (Ashmore 1989). According to this thesis, which is continuous with Barthes's meta-methodological turn, researchers should work to expose the more or less covertly self-referential status of scientific claims. Whatever their overt form, such claims need to be studied "as local, contingent accomplishment[s]" specific to and reflective of "the culture of the laboratory setting" in which they are formulated (Woolgar 1988: 18).

Turning from Work to Text

Focusing in on the seven propositions or themes set out in "From Work to Text," I shift now from the broader contexts of Barthes's reorientation to some of the specifics of the turn itself. Designed to provide a basis for distinguishing between classical ideas of the work and postclassical conceptions of the Text, these themes also afford a thumbnail sketch of the later Barthes's approach to literary and cultural analysis – an approach that can be viewed, in retrospect, as canonically postmodern. To suggest the canonic status of Barthes's themes, I briefly synopsize each proposition and then indicate the generative role it has played in the discourses of postmodernism.

Method; reading

Barthes's first proposition is that "[t]he Text is not to be thought of as an object that can be computed." Barthes writes: "the work can be held in the hand, the text is held in language, only exists in the movement of a discourse," such that "the Text is not the decomposition of the work, it is the work that is the imaginary tail of the Text" (1977 [1971]: 156–7). Hence, Barthes emphasizes, "*the Text is experienced only in an activity of production*" (157). This proposition echoes Barthes's emphasis, in *S/Z*, on readers' use of codes of signification to participate in the active structuration of texts, instead of merely passively appreciating works as pregiven, inert structures (1974 [1970]: 18–21). In short, overlapping with the theme of *reading*, Barthes's theme of method points ahead to reader-response and other contextualist approaches to literary interpretation (Fish 1980; Holland 1975; Iser 1978). To cite a remark from Barthes's discussion of reading: whereas the work is an object of consumption, "[t]he Text (if only by its frequent 'unreadability') decants the work (the work permitting) from its consumption and gathers it up as play, activity, production, practice" (162). Thus "the Text requires that one try to abolish (or at the very least to diminish) the distance between writing and reading, in no way by intensifying the projection of the reader into the work but by joining them in a single signifying practice" (162). Both the theme of method and the theme of reading prefigure, then, what would become a central concern in such subfields of postmodern theory as identity studies and cultural poetics: namely, the (socioculturally structured) interface between particular texts and their contexts of reception.

Genres and filiation

Another proposition put forth in "From Work to Text" is that "the Text does not stop at (good) Literature; it cannot be contained in a hierarchy, even in a simple division of genres. What constitutes the Text is, on the contrary (or precisely), its subversive force in respect of the old classifications" (157). This theme can be traced back to M. M. Bakhtin's (1981 [1934–5]) investigations into the polygeneric origins and dialogic profile of novelistic discourse, but it also flows from and anticipates a broader deconstructive critique of evaluative hierarchies (Derrida 1976 [1967]). The theme of genre foreshadows, too, the rise of popular culture as a target for postmodern theory (Marcus 1989), as well as the questioning of the text/context distinction by New Historicists and practitioners of cultural studies (Greenblatt 1995). Taking their cue from Barthes's distrust of established generic categories, these history- and culture-oriented approaches study the circulation of nonliterary as well as literary texts at particular moments in history, which are assumed to acquire their distinctive character precisely from the modes of textual circulation at issue.

Further, the theme of genre is bound up with what Barthes terms *filiation*. Whereas works are caught up in an institution that bears striking similarities to that of patrilineal descent, originating from an author and standing in a relation of consecution *vis-à-vis* other works, the dominant metaphor of "the Text is that of the network; if the Text extends itself, it is as a result of a combinatory systematic" and it can be "read without the guarantee of its father" (161). Discrete, autonomous works, linked to one another in a causal and chronological sequence, give way to the Text viewed as a network of reversible, nonlinear intertextual relations, only a small subset of which can be captured by classical concepts such as "genre," "allusion," and "citation." Growing out of the work of Bakhtin and V. N. Voloshinov (1973 [1929]) before being rearticulated by Francophone theorists such as Julia Kristeva (1980) and Barthes, *intertextuality* not only became a watchword of postmodern theory (Hebel 1989) but also sounded the death knell of the author (Barthes 1977 [1968]). Barthes's scriptor does not create works *ab novo*, but only multiplies lines of connection between nodes in the intertextual network, into which his or her own identity as scriptor inevitably gets reabsorbed. Hence "the *I* which writes [any particular] text, it too, is never more than a paper-*I*"; i.e., "no longer privileged, paternal, aletheological, [the *I*'s] inscription is ludic" (161). It was while disputing this last claim that Michel Foucault (1984 [1969]) recuperated the idea of the author from a new, differently postmodern perspective. Foucault foregrounded the historically variable but nontrivial role played by authors' *names*, hypothesizing an "author function" that serves to classify discourses and also to anchor them to material circumstances bearing on their production and interpretation.

Signs, plurality, and pleasure

Barthes's essay explores three other themes – that is, three other dimensions along which work and Text can be contrasted. For one thing, whereas the work "closes on a signified," the Text "can be approached, experienced, in reaction to the sign" (158). In so far as modes of signification oriented around the signified involve either evident or hidden meanings, the work is thus the proper province of philology or hermeneutics, as the case may be. By contrast, "[t]he Text . . . practices the infinite deferment of the signified, is dilatory; its field is that of the signifier," whose study unfolds not "according to an organic process of maturation or a hermeneutic course of deepening investigation, but, rather, according to a serial movement of disconnections, overlappings, variations" (158; cf. Deleuze and Guattari 1983 [1972], 1987 [1980]). In consequence, the Text is, like language in the Derridean conception, "structured but off-centred, without closure" (159). Indeed, Barthes's essay here reveals the impress of Derrida's arguments concerning the "transcendental signified" (Derrida 1986 [1966]: 83–6; 1976 [1967]: 44–73). In those arguments Derrida extended and radicalized Saussurean linguistics by construing language as a decentered system – a system in which signification is a function of the limitless play of differences, rather than a result of language's capacity to denote extralinguistic referents. Likewise, many of the artifacts studied by postmodern theorists in the late 1970s and the 1980s were viewed as fields of signification rather than works signifying something definite or even discernible. During this period terms like *undecidability* and *indeterminacy* took their place alongside *intertextuality* as watchwords of postmodernism.

In fact, as Barthes suggests in his essay, one way of talking about the Text's infinite deferment of the signified is to talk about its radical plurality. The Text is plural not because (like the work) it is ambiguous and can be assigned several candidate interpretations, but instead because it involves an explosion, or dissemination, of meanings, a "*stereographic plurality* [born of] its weave of signifiers (etymologically, the text is a tissue, a woven fabric)" (159). Barthes had advanced similar arguments in *S/Z*, drawing there his influential distinction between classical, "readerly" (*lisible*) works, which he characterized as only parsimoniously plural, and postclassical, writerly (*scriptible*) texts, which are limitlessly plural and thus "make the reader no longer a consumer, but a producer of the text" (1974 [1970]: 4; Plotnitsky 1997 explores links between Barthes's readerly/writerly distinction and the ideas of Georges Bataille). What is more, the text's irreducible plurality renders illusory "any inductive-deductive science of texts" (1977 [1971]: 159–60), negating (among other modes of inquiry) Barthes's own earlier attempts to write a "grammar" of a particular class of texts, i.e., narratives (Barthes 1977 [1966]). Plurality also connects back up with the themes of filiation and genre. For in so far as it accords to every particular text the status of "the text-between of another text," the emphasis on textual plurality places a question mark next to the study of the sources and influences of works, "the citations which go to make up a text [being] anonymous, untraceable, and yet *already read*" (160).

Finally, calling for a new, hedonistic aesthetics, Barthes draws one last distinction between work and Text. He closes his essay by suggesting that whereas the pleasure of the work remains a pleasure of consumption, that of the Text entails *jouissance*, i.e., "pleasure without separation" (164; cf. Barthes 1975 [1973]). To be sure, Barthes here introduces ideas of a psychoanalytic (specifically, Lacanian) provenance (Lacan 1977 [1949]). These ideas, interwoven with the poststructuralist, reader-response, and sociocontextualist concepts also outlined or anticipated in Barthes's essay, would emerge as yet another important strand in the Text of postmodern theory. More than this, however, Barthes's distinction between the guilty pleasure of consumption and the *jouissance* of co-production helps account for the continuing vitality of his own work. Arguably, Barthes's postmodernist turn, accomplished with a brilliance and panache impossible to mimic, has had such generative power precisely because it cannot be reproduced. Barthes instead scripted strategies by which the turn might be enacted – co-created – as part of the process of interpreting his own discourse.

8

Georges Bataille

Jean-François Fourny

A contemporary of Breton, Camus, and Sartre, Georges Bataille (1897–1962) is one of the very few members of his generation to have achieved a real posterity and to still be considered relevant to postmodernity. A most paradoxical thinker, bookish librarian by day and patron of brothels and strip shows by night, Bataille cannot be reduced to one school of thought, even if he involved himself in all the major intellectual debates of his time, be they related to surrealism, Marxism, or existentialism. While it had always tended to remain in the shadows of Breton and, later, Sartre, Bataille's thought was brought to the fore in the 1960s by poststructuralism. However, this posthumous lionization of Bataille was achieved through an appropriation of his thought and a selective emphasis on certain of its aspects at the expense of others. In what follows, and as Natoli and Hutcheon (1993) and Jameson (1991) suggest, I will use the terms "poststructuralism" and "postmodernism" as two interchangeable ways to refer to the same historical moment.

From Bataille's early writings to his very last, the sacred (in its opposition to the profane) is the central category of his thought and is treated as an anthropological given, at a time when Marxism dominated the French intellectual scene. However, Bataille's sacred is multifaceted and reversible, so as to include eroticism, obscenity, and most elements that usually generate repulsion in us.

Drawing on Marcel Mauss and other authors related to the French ethnographic tradition, Bataille linked sacrifice, eroticism, the potlach, and luxury as instances of a fundamental human need to waste or destroy surpluses. Repressed or neglected by the "great narratives" of the nineteenth century, such as Hegelianism or Marxism, Bataille reintroduces, into these two systems of thought, irrationality, obscenity, sacrifice, pure negativity, "heterogeneity," *l'impossible* and sovereignty, all different names for the excess (or "accursed share").

The heterogeneous or *l'impossible* are to be understood here as what is beyond language and reason, and cannot be named, and include mystic or erotic ecstasies as well as horror. Bataille saw language as a linear continuum that fragments and distorts the immediacy of violent and overwhelming experiences, such as eroticism or sacrifice, that suspend the usual psychological or social norms, and that provide the individual with an experience of "sovereignty." This last term is to be understood in Nietzschean terms – that is, when all social and moral conventions fade, so that the individual is returned to an immediacy that ignores both the future and utility. Through eroticism death thus becomes the celebration of life.

Using a binary opposition borrowed from Henri Bergson, Bataille defines the individual in terms of discontinuity, as opposed to life, which itself is continuity through the different generations. Orgasm then becomes a foretaste of death, since lovers briefly lose themselves in each other, hence the expression "little death." As for death, it returns the individual's discontinuity to the overall continuity of life. The solemnity and petrified silence of sacrifice also abolish individuality and for a short time merge it into a larger collective entity, that of the community which becomes one and the same. And this is also what Bataille saw at work in Saint Theresa's ecstasy or erotic rapture, as she felt she was dissolving and becoming one with God. In some ways, it could thus be said that what Bataille called the sacred was just another name for violence.

Along with his taste for verbal violence and pranks, a taste shared with the surrealist generation, Bataille remained utterly fascinated with totalitarian regimes and their ritualistic displays of physical force. He interpreted the emergence of fascism as the return of long-repressed archaic elements, leading to a reorganization of the sacred along its two polarities, one being holy, official, and stabilizing, the other malevolent, dark, and destabilizing. During the late 1920s, he quarreled with André Breton because he felt that surrealism was excessively "Icarian," or too tempted by purity and idealism, while Bataille himself craved for materialism and obscenity. In other words, as amply demonstrated in Bataille's novel *Blue of Noon* (1936) and in some of his pornographic novels, holiness and purity were also to be found in debauchery, crime, and infamy. This other road to "sainthood" can be compared to certain branches of Buddhist Tantrism and is reminiscent of Baudelaire's "double application to heaven and hell."

In the 1930s Bataille entertained the idea of founding a new paradoxical science called *heterology*. Its mission would have been to build a knowledge of what is "other" – that is, of what is expelled by scientific knowledge because it resists rationalization, and must be kept at bay by society and its institutions.

It is also in the 1930s that Bataille joined Le Cercle Communiste Démocratique, a dissident communist faction headed by Boris Souvarine that opposed Stalinism. The group was soon torn apart by irreconcilable views of the revolution, some of its members seeing it as a means to an end (such as Simone Weil, cruelly caricatured in *Blue of Noon*), others as an end in itself

– or, for Bataille, as an orgy of violence and destruction. Bataille was later to briefly attempt to organize a secret society, whose members were to have been bound forever by the intense emotional experience generated by an actual human sacrifice.

Such was Bataille's fascination with violence that, in the general framework of eroticism as he defines it, beauty is always desired precisely in order to be degraded and reduced to its animalistic components. In this sense, the sexual act is always a form of rape, because it aims at breaking the bodily integrity of the partner. This is where Bataille's fundamental concept of *transgression* comes into play.

Taboo and transgression cannot be separated, and cannot exist without each other: they are another anthropological given, inherent to humankind. The law exists in order to be broken, and its very existence calls for its violation (a point Michel Foucault will later pick up most productively): in this sense the twinned concepts of prohibition and incest are both complementary and positive. The taboo on murder and violence, which is common to most cultures, calls for sacrifice as a ritualized transgression of this very taboo, as well as for crime. Eroticism would also be probably meaningless, were it not for the strict control imposed on sexual activity by most societies. Humankind is in fact defined by the existence of taboos (and transgressions), since the transition from animality to humankind takes place through the establishment of a set of religious prohibitions (against incest, or contact with corpses, for instance). Hence the fascination generated by criminals such as Gilles de Rais in the Middle Ages (those we would today call "serial killers"), who took transgression to the limit, to a point where language cannot truly account for the horror generated by unspeakable crimes, for erotic and religious ecstasy, for sacrifice, or for anything supremely high or supremely low.

Essentially an anthropologist and a religious historian, deeply influenced by Alexandre Kojève's reading of Hegel and by the works of ethnographers, a different Bataille emerges during the postmodern period.

If we take the *Tel Quel* group as a point of focalization for the emergence of "theory" in the 1960s, we see that Bataille, along with Artaud, Dante, Joyce, Mallarmé, and de Sade, quickly entered a pantheon of writers who were all credited for having experienced the "limits" (in Philippe Sollers's terms), or for having initiated a "revolution" in language (in Julia Kristeva's terms). However, Bataille's instrumental vision of language ("Je fais du langage un usage classique"), and main concern with emotional intensity, disappeared even as his thought was reinscribed within the register of writing (*écriture*).

Poetic excess, violence, madness, all at *the textual level*, were the order of the day, as what thought could not think, and as what discursive language could not represent. The *Tel Quel* group (mainly through Sollers) situated Bataille within a general trend aiming at destroying bourgeois subjectivity. Meanwhile, for Michel Foucault, transgression was to replace contradiction and dialectical thinking, and the "excess" of language was meant to trangress philosophy itself. His *Madness and Civilization* (1961) can also be read as a history of excesses, limits, and "accursed shares" that are silenced and rejected by society. Although Bataille felt ill at ease with the Western philosophical tradition which he found estranged from the body and from emotions, Jacques Derrida (1978 [1968]) linked him with Heidegger in his attempt to deconstruct the "metaphysics of presence." Furthermore, Derrida located Bataille (as well as Antonin Artaud) in the space opened by what he called "the end of representation" (*clôture de la représentation*), that is, when language experiences its own limits, a critical moment for the advent of poststructuralism.

As for psychoanalysis, especially in its Lacanian version, it tended to displace the sacred/profane opposition with that of the conscious/unconscious. It also linked transgression to desire, and, by treating the unconscious in linguistic terms, completed the reinscription of Bataille at a purely textual/linguistic level (Guerlac 1997).

Tailoring Bataille to its needs, postmodernism favors the open and unfinished aspect of his work that somehow called for its appropriation by this very postmodernism. In formal terms, Bataille's "mystic" texts (*La Somme athéologique* [1973]) mirror the very notion of excess they tackle: Bataille multiplies drafts, digressions, fragments, and dots, so as to subvert traditional linear and dialectical reasoning. However, some of his most sober and rigorous texts, which offer an evolutionary frame for understanding the development of humankind since prehistory (*Theory of Religion* [1992/1976], *The Tears of Eros* [1989/1961], and to some degree *The Accursed Share* [1988/1967]) are rarely quoted, if not actually *expelled* from the Bataillean corpus.

Finally, postmodernism is naturally attracted to Bataille's cultivation of parody and pastiche. *Blue of Noon* is a humorous and provocative caricature of Dostoevsky and of the engagé novels of the 1930s, such as those written by André Malraux. *Méthode de méditation* (1953) borrows, in a most ambiguous manner, from Ignacio de Loyola's *Spiritual Exercises*. It could also be said that Bataille never really freed himself from the surrealist aesthetic, and somehow represented a dark and carnivalesque version of André Breton.

The work of such a protean writer leaves many questions unanswered. Identifying with Nietzsche, like many French intellectuals of his generation, Bataille shared with him the experience of losing his faith at an early age: it would thus not be so farfetched to suggest that Bataille's writings constitute a never-ending settling of accounts with Catholicism. From another point of view, Jürgen Habermas (1987 [1983]) links Nietzsche, Heidegger, and Bataille in ascribing to them a common attempt to erase Reason and the principle of individuation, and to go back to archaic times predating Western civilization, so as to rediscover a rather phantasmatic Dionysian element.

9

Jean Baudrillard

Douglas Kellner

French theorist Jean Baudrillard is one of the foremost critics of contemporary society and culture, and is often seen as the guru of French postmodern theory. A professor of sociology at the University of Nanterre from 1966 to 1987, Baudrillard took the postmodern turn in the mid-1970s, developing a new kind of social analysis that went beyond the confines of modern social theory. He is ultimately important as a critic of modern society and theory who claims that the era of modernity and the tradition of classical social theory is obsolete and that we need a novel mode of social analysis adequate to the emerging era of postmodernity. A prolific author who has written over twenty books, Baudrillard has commented on the most salient cultural and social phenomena of the contemporary era and developed one of the most influential modes of postmodern theory.

From Marxism to the End of Modernity

Although in the 1960s Baudrillard participated in the tumultuous events of May 1968 and was associated with the revolutionary Left and Marxism, he broke with Marxism in the early 1970s and remained politically radical, though unaffiliated, for the rest of the decade. Like many on the Left, Baudrillard was disappointed that the French Communist Party did not support the radical 1960s movements and he also distrusted the official Marxism of theorists like Louis Althusser, whom he found dogmatic and reductive. Consequently, Baudrillard began a radical critique of Marxism, one that would be repeated by many of his contemporaries who would also take a postmodern turn (see Best and Kellner 1991, 1997).

Baudrillard argues that Marxism, first, does not adequately illuminate premodern societies which were organized around symbolic exchange and not production. He also argues that Marxism does not critique capitalist societies radically enough and calls for a more extreme break. At this stage, Baudrillard turns to anthropological perspectives on premodern societies for hints of more emancipatory alternatives. Yet it is important to note that this critique of Marxism was taken from the Left, arguing that Marxism did not provide a radical enough critique of, or alternative to, contemporary productivist societies, capitalist and communist. Baudrillard concluded that French communist failure to support the May '68 movements was rooted in part in a conservatism that had its origins in Marxism itself. Hence, Baudrillard and others of his generation began searching for more radical critical positions.

The Mirror of Production (1975 [1973]) and his next book, *Symbolic Exchange and Death* (1993 [1976]), are attempts to provide ultraradical perspectives that overcome the limitations of an economistic Marxist tradition. In the latter book, Baudrillard produces a distinction between the logic of production and utility that organized modern societies and the logic of simulation that he believes is the organizing principle of postmodern societies. He postulates a rupture between modern and postmodern societies as great as the divide between modern and premodern ones that are the foundation of classical social theory. In theorizing the epochal postmodern rupture with modernity, Baudrillard declares the "end of political economy" and of an era in which production was the organizing principle of society. Following Marx, Baudrillard argues that this modern epoch was the era of capitalism and the bourgeoisie, in which workers were exploited by capital and provided a revolutionary force of upheaval. Baudrillard, however, declared the end of political economy and thus the end of the Marxist problematic and of modernity itself:

> The end of labor. The end of production. The end of political economy. The end of the signifier/signified dialectic which facilitates the accumulation of knowledge and of meaning, the linear syntagma of cumulative discourse. And at the same time, the end simultaneously of the exchange value/use value dialectic which is the only thing that makes accumulation and social production possible. The end of linear dimension of discourse. The end of the linear dimension of the commodity. The end of the classical era of the sign. The end of the era of production. (Baudrillard 1993 [1976]: 8)

The discourse of "the end" signifies his announcing a postmodern break or rupture in history. We are now, Baudrillard claims, in a new era of simulation in which social reproduction (information processing, communication, knowledge industries, and so on) replaces production as the organizing principle of society. In this era, labor is no longer a force of production but is itself "one *sign* amongst many" (1993 [1976]: 10). Labor is not primarily productive in this situation, but is a sign of one's social position, way of life, and mode of servitude. Wages too bear no rational relation to one's work and what one produces but to one's place within the system (1993 [1976]: 19ff.). But, crucially, political economy is no longer the foundation, the social determinant, or even a structural "reality" in which other phenomena can be interpreted and explained (31ff.). Instead we live in the "hyperreality" of simulations in which images, spectacles, and the play of signs replace the logic of production and class conflict as key constituents of contemporary societies.

From now on, capital and political economy disappear from Baudrillard's story, or return in radically new forms. Henceforth, signs and codes proliferate and produce other signs and new sign machines in ever-expanding and spiraling cycles. Technology thus replaces capital in this story and semiurgy, the proliferation of images, information, signs, replaces production. His postmodern turn is thus connected to a form of technological determinism and a rejection of political economy as a useful explanatory principle – a move that many of his critics reject (see the studies in Kellner 1994).

Symbolic Exchange and Death and the succeeding studies in *Simulacra and Simulation* (1994 [1981]) articulate the principle of a fundamental rupture between modern and postmodern societies and mark Baudrillard's departure from the problematic of modern social theory. For Baudrillard, modern societies are organized around the production and consumption of commodities, while postmodern societies are organized around simulation and the play of images and signs, denoting a situation in which codes, models, and signs are the organizing principles of a new social order where simulation rules. In the society of simulation, identities are constructed by the appropriation of images, and codes and models determine how individuals perceive themselves and relate to other people. Economics, politics, social life, and culture are all governed by the logic of simulation, whereby codes and models determine how goods are consumed and used, politics unfold, culture is produced and consumed, and everyday life is lived.

Baudrillard's postmodern world is also one of radical *implosion*, in which social classes, genders, political differences, and once-autonomous realms of society and culture collapse into each other, erasing previously defined boundaries and differences. If modern societies, for classical social theory, were characterized by differentiation, for Baudrillard postmodern societies are characterized by dedifferentiation, or implosion. For Baudrillard, in the society of simulation, economics, politics, culture, sexuality, and the social all implode into each other, such that economics is fundamentally shaped by culture, politics, and other spheres, while art, once a sphere of potential difference and opposition, is absorbed into the economic and political, while sexuality is everywhere. In this situation, differences between individuals and groups implode in a rapidly mutating dissolution of the social and the previous boundaries and structures upon which social theory had once focused.

In addition, his postmodern universe is one of *hyperreality* in which entertainment, information, and communication technologies provide experiences more intense and involving than the scenes of banal everyday life, as well as the codes and models that structure everyday life. The realm of the hyperreal (i.e., media simulations of reality, Disneyland and amusement parks, malls and consumer fantasylands, TV sports, and other excursions into ideal worlds) is more real than real, whereby the models, images, and codes of the hyperreal come to control thought and behavior. Yet determination itself is aleatory in a nonlinear world where it is impossible to chart causal mechanisms and logic in a situation in which individuals are confronted with an overwhelming flux of images, codes, and models, any of which may shape an individual's thought or behavior.

In this postmodern world, individuals flee from the "desert of the real" for the ecstasies of hyperreality and the new realm of computer, media, and technological experience. In this universe, subjectivities are fragmented and lost, and a new terrain of experience appears that for Baudrillard renders previous social theories and politics obsolete and irrelevant. Tracing the vicissitudes of the subject in contemporary society, Baudrillard claims that contemporary subjects are no longer afflicted with modern pathologies like hysteria or paranoia, but exist in "a state of terror which is characteristic of the schizophrenic, an over-proximity of all things, a foul promiscuity of all things which beleaguer and penetrate him, meeting with no resistance, and no halo, no aura, not even the aura of his own body protects him. In spite of himself the schizophrenic is open to everything and lives in the most extreme confusion" (1988: 27). For Baudrillard, the "ecstasy of communication" means that the subject is in close proximity to instantaneous images and information, in an overexposed and transparent world. In this situation, the subject "becomes a pure screen, a pure absorption and resorption surface of the influent networks" (1988: 27).

Thus, Baudrillard's categories of simulation, implosion, and hyperreality combine to create a new postmodern condition that requires entirely new modes of social theory and politics to chart and respond to the novelties of the contemporary era. His style and writing strategies are also implosive, combining material from strikingly different fields, studded with examples from the mass media and popular culture in a new mode of postmodern theory that effaces all disciplinary boundaries. His writing attempts to itself simulate the new conditions, capturing its novelties through inventive use of language and theory. Such radical questioning of contemporary theory and the need for new theoretical strategies are thus legitimated for Baudrillard by the radicality of changes in the current era.

Into the 1990s

During the 1990s, Baudrillard published a series of books which continued to comment on contemporary events and to postulate a break within history in the space of a postmodern *coupure*, though he usually distances himself from other versions of postmodern theory. The 1990s texts continue the fragmentary style and use of short essays, aphorisms, stories, and aperçus that Baudrillard began deploying in the 1980s and often repeat some of the same ideas and stories. These writings can be read as a continual commentary on current social conditions, along with a running dialogue with Marxism and poststructuralist theory. Yet after his fierce polemics of the 1970s against competing models of thought, Baudrillard's dialogue with theory now consists mostly of occasional asides and his mode of analysis consists of ruminating on contemporary events and trends.

Baudrillard develops in these works "theory fiction," or what he also calls "simulation theory" and "anticipatory theory," to simulate, grasp, and anticipate historical events which he believes outrun all contemporary theory. The current situation, he claims, is more fantastic than the most fanciful science fiction, or theoretical projections of a futurist society. Thus, theory can only attempt to grasp the present on the run and try to anticipate the future. However, Baudrillard has had a particularly poor record as a social and political analyst and forecaster. As a political analyst, Baudrillard has often been superficial and off the mark. In an essay "Anorexic Ruins" published in 1989, he read the Berlin wall as a sign of a frozen history, of an anorexic history, in which nothing more can happen, marked by a "lack of events" and the end of history, taking the Berlin wall as a sign of a stasis between communism and capitalism. Shortly thereafter, rather significant events destroyed the wall that Baudrillard took as eternal and opened up a new historical era.

In a sense, there is a parodic inversion of historical materialism in Baudrillard. In place of Marx's emphasis on political economy and the primacy of the economic, for Baudrillard it is the model, the superstructure, that generates the real in a situation he denominates the "end of political economy" (1993 [1976]). For Baudrillard, sign values predominate over use values and exchange values; the materiality of needs and commodity use values to serve them disappear in Baudrillard's semiological imaginary, in which signs take precedence over the real and reconstruct human life. Turning the Marxist categories against themselves, masses absorb classes, the subject of praxis is fractured, and objects come to rule human beings. Revolution is absorbed by the object of critique and technological implosion replaces the socialist revolution in producing a rupture in history. For Baudrillard, in contrast to Marx, the catastrophe of modernity and eruption of postmodernity is produced by the unfolding of technological revolution. Consequently, Baudrillard replaces Marx's hard economic and social determinism with its emphasis on the economic dimension, class struggle, and human praxis, with a form of semiological idealism and technological determinism where signs and objects come to dominate the subject.

Baudrillard has never been as influential in France as in the English-speaking world and elsewhere. He is an example of the "global popular," a thinker who has followers and readers throughout the world, though, so far, no Baudrillardian school has emerged. His influence has been largely at the margins of a diverse number of disciplines ranging from social theory to philosophy to art history, thus it is difficult to gauge his impact on the mainstream of social theory, or any specific academic discipline. He is perhaps most important as part of the postmodern turn against modern society and its academic disciplines.

Baudrillard thus emerges in retrospect as a transdisciplinary theorist of the fin-de-millennium who produces signposts to the new era of postmodernity and is an important, albeit hardly trustworthy, guide to the new era. In my view, Baudrillard exaggerates the break between the modern and the postmodern, takes future possibilities as existing realities, and provides a futuristic perspective on the present, much like the tradition of dystopic science fiction, ranging from Huxley to cyberpunk. Indeed, I prefer to read Baudrillard's post-1970s work as science fiction which anticipates the future by exaggerating present tendencies, and thus provides early warnings about what might happen if present trends continue. It is not an accident that Baudrillard is an aficionado of science fiction, who has himself influenced a large number of contemporary science fiction writers.

However, in view of his exaggeration of the alleged break with modernity, discerning whether Baudrillard's most recent work is best read as science fiction or social theory is difficult. Baudrillard obviously wants to have it both ways with social theorists thinking that he provides salient perspectives on contemporary social realities. And yet more cynical anti-sociologists are encouraged to enjoy Baudrillard's fictions, his experimental discourse, his games, and play. Likewise, he sometimes encourages cultural metaphysicians to read his work as serious reflections on the realities of our time, while winking a pataphysical aside at those skeptical of such undertakings. Thus, it is undecidable whether Baudrillard is best read as science fiction and pataphysics, or as social theory and cultural metaphysics, and whether his post-1970s work should be read under the sign of truth or fiction.

10

Jorge Luis Borges

Evelyn Fishburn

The most immediate link that comes to mind between postmodernism and Borges is their "exasperating slipperiness": if few theoretical terms have elicited such controversy over their meanings and cutoff points as postmodernism, few writers can be said to occupy as many and as contradictory literary positions as Borges. Borges's work has been variously defined as quintessentially fictional, dealing totally with irreality and exclusively self-referential, but also as criollista, having meaningful links with an historical context and postcolonial anticipations. On the one hand, Borges has been seen as a classical writer; on the other, a modernist, exemplifying all aspects of the avant-garde, and, of course, as postmodernist, by, among many, Hutcheon, Natoli, McHale, and most emphatically by Fokkema (1984: 38), who wrote: "It can be argued that Postmodernism is the first literary code that originated in America and influenced European literature, with the possibility that the writer who contributed more than anyone else to the invention and acceptance of the new code is Jorge Luis Borges."

Writing mainly in the 1930s and 1940s, Borges did not set out to be a postmodernist, but, like Kafka creating his precursors (Borges 1970: 234), the traces of postmodernism are now detectable throughout his work. Foucault famously opened his groundbreaking questioning of realist epistemology, *The Order of Things*, with a quotation from Borges's "Chinese Encyclopedia," Baudrillard alluded to his teasing piece "On Exactitude in Science" (Borges 1999: 325), in which a map of the Empire is the size of the Empire, ultimately replacing it, as the perfect trope for his idea of the simulacrum, and Genette, in his study of intertextuality in *Palimpsestes* (1982), makes explicit reference to Borges's use of the term (in "Pierre Menard, Author of Don Quixote"). Most discussions on Borges's postmodernism focus on literary aspects, but since his work is increasingly being read with attention to its autobiographical, historical, and political resonances this emphasis may widen.

The qualifiers "Borgesian" and "postmodern" are, of course, not synonymous and both terms would be considerably reduced by any exclusivist comparison, and yet their overlap is considerable. This essay will not offer a definitive discussion of a subject that is by its very nature resistant to clarity and synthesis, but will limit itself to exploring some of the more interesting contact zones, looking at ways in which Borges's fiction can be reread from a postmodernist perspective.

"If I am rich in anything, it is in perplexities, not in certainties" was Borges's upbeat way of expressing what Lyotard would later call the postmodernist loss of faith in grand narratives. An essential skepticism permeates his work, seeking constantly to undermine our belief in all systems of knowledge and global explanations, and indeed questioning the very possibility for such systems to exist. Rather than in their truth, their value would lie, for Borges, in their ability to astonish, that is to say, as "branches of the literature of fantasy" (1999: 74). McHale seems to echo this idea when he talks of postmodernist metanarratives proffered tentatively in the key of "as if," that is to say, "as no more (but no less) than a strategically satisfying fiction" (1992: 24). Borges's fictions are often set in the same tentative key, as metaphors of what the world would be like if certain "truths" or metanarratives were true, so that if metaphysical idealism were a possible reality our planet would be as minutely coherent as Tlön ("Tlön, Uqbar, Orbis Tertius"); if chronological time did not exist, Hladik's secret miracle need not have been "secret" (see "The Secret Miracle"), and in eternal, circular time, we would all, eventually, write the Odyssey (see "The Immortal"). But, as first put forward in "Tlön" and in what is now a preferred mode of postmodernism, these fictionalizations of belief systems (metaphysical idealism, subjective time, eternity) carry within them their own counterargument, playfully undermining the value of their own truth.

Postmodernism is not simply concerned with dismantling the Enlightenment's notion of an ascertainable objective truth, or with distinguishing between truth and falsehood (a distinction imaginatively blurred in "Emma Zunz"), but with proposing the notion of a decentered reality in which a multiplicity of truths collide in unhierarchical existence (Natoli 1997: 135–40). This idea underpins "The Garden of Forking Paths," one of Borges's most radical fictions, written in 1941, during World War II. In this story a novel takes the shape of an ivory labyrinth of symbols and the univocality of traditional fiction is dispersed into several contradictory voices, violating the flow of time and of causality, and the logic of expectation. Mixing a variety of genres (history, espionage, theory of fiction, confession), the story enacts its own proposition, the multiplicity of reality, by juxtaposing different accounts of it. Prefiguring Hutcheon, it questions how we access the past by giving us two versions of it, that of a famous British military historian alongside a highly complex "fictional" explanation given from the point of view of the "enemy." Undermining the totalizing claims of nationalisms, the British side is represented by an anti-British Irishman and the German by an anglophile Chinese spy.

The interconnectedness of the discourses of history and fiction is also suggested in "The Theme of the Traitor and the Hero," which, in Hutcheon's words again, problematizes the making of both genres. In this story, the traitor is given a hero's death in order to advance the cause he had betrayed. Borrowing from previous fictions (the death of Caesar, as recounted by Shakespeare, and the witches' warnings to Macbeth) and prefiguring a historical event (the shooting of Abraham Lincoln in 1865), the 1824 nationalist conspirators fabricate a plot of historical deception. Neither "Garden" nor "Theme" is nostalgic for the past (this is not to deny nostalgia in Borges), but both serve to illustrate the way the past is always ideologically and discursively constructed.

Postmodernity's contention that universal statements are inevitably partial and relative is imaginatively elaborated in "The Aleph," a story much preoccupied with poking fun at the notion of universality by positing a plurality of universes. The title, which refers to a (fictitious) small disc of around one inch diameter in which the whole universe may be glimpsed, is apposite, as the aleph denotes the first letter of the Hebrew alphabet believed, in the Cabbala, to encompass all other letters and numbers (humorously, the story is the *last*, not the *first*, story in the collection of that title which it presumably encompasses). It is also used in mathematics (in Cantor's set theory) as an integer symbolic of all other integers and, by extension, of infinity. Throughout the story there are several mentions of or allusions to "universal" mirrors and "universal" poems all paradoxically reflecting different "universes," thereby relativizing and discrediting the totalizing notion of a single universe. Another way in which all attempts at encompassing totality are ridiculed in Borges is by his witty assault on encyclopedias, both for their globalizing and classifying pretensions. In a passage now made famous by Foucault's discussion of it (see above), Borges's teasing enumeration of disparate entries on categories of animals in "a certain Chinese encyclopaedia . . . (a), belonging to the Emperor; (b), embalmed; (c) tame? Sucking pigs; (d) sirens; etcetera," whilst pretending to inform on a charmingly exotic Oriental mindset, parodies the constructed order of our own post-Enlightenment thought system and exposes the subjective rationale upon which it is erected ("The Analytical Language of John Wilkies," in *Other Inquisitions*). The disintegration of boundaries is a favored means of critiquing their subjective nature and Borges excels in terms of originality, daring, and inventiveness in the way he draws together fundamentally dissimilar concepts, which, in the words of Foucault, "glitter separately in the dimension, without law or geometry" (1973: xvii).

Borges undermines the truth-value of accepted categories by blurring their parameters both at the discursive and at the thematic level: the sacred and the profane in "The Zahir," where the mundane search for sartorial perfection of an aspiring socialite is placed on a par with religious preoccupations of the Talmudists or the metaphysical quests of the followers of Confucius; the cultured and the popular in "Evaristo Carriego," an early text loosely based on a popular poet of the "margins" (it was to be called "*Seneca* in the Margins" [my emphasis]); the trivial and the transcendent in "Pierre Menard, Author of Don Quixote," where the pedantic minor poet has an insight of literally groundbreaking consequence for the reading of literature; the real and the ideal in "Tlön".

A noted characteristic of postmodernist fiction is its self-reflexivity, its self-conscious preoccupation with the problem of language, a deficient tool, unable to reflect a reality which is itself only partially and unreliably accessible. Borges's texts flaunt their fictiveness in titles such as "Artifices," "Fictions," or, as in a well-known English collection of his best-known work, *Labyrinths*. In the imagined world of "Tlön, Uqbar, Orbis Tertius," reality and fiction are said to belong to different ontological levels, the land of Uqbar having two imaginary regions, Mlejnas and Tlön, to which its fiction refers. However, as always in Borges, there are no closed polarizations: it is not the *either/or* of Cartesian thought but the *both/and* of the postmodernist disintegration of essences so that when the fictional Tlön sends its invading *hrönir* (hot, heavy objects made presumably of words or ideas) to infiltrate our reality, this invasion is not suggestive of a triumphalist synthesis but offers an intimation of the extent to which the real is porous to the unreal, objectivity to subjectivity. "Tlön, Uqbar, Orbis Tertius" anticipates postmodernist concerns with language by suggesting the possibilities of a totally differently organized code, one with verbs and adverbs, but no nouns: this noun-free linguistic code is, of course, entirely consistent with the idealist nature of the world of Tlön and would appear to underline the traditional nexus between language and the world, were it not for its eventual invasion and acceptance in a realist, noun-based world such as our own.

Serious postmodernist questions relating to the different ontological levels of our reality are also asked in "Funes, his Memory." By contrasting the mental world of the narrator with the heightened sensitivity (after a fall) of the eponymous character, the story posits two of the many possible levels of accessing reality, talking about it, and remembering it, one which the narrator considers "normal" and the other magnified through the protagonist's exceptionally developed powers of perception. Thus, "With one quick look, you and I perceive three wineglasses on a table; Funes perceived every grape that had been pressed into the wine and all the stalks and tendrils of its vineyard... Funes could continually perceive the quiet advances of corruption, of tooth decay, of weariness" (1999: 135–6).

The arbitrary and conjectural cutoff points of language are clearly suggested by Funes's irritation that the dog seen in profile at 3.14 p.m. should be indicated by the same noun as the dog seen frontally at 3.15 p.m. Funes's ludic proposal, to replace "the unnecessarily cumbersome" numerical system with infinite proper nouns highlights through exaggeration the ultimately contingent quality of all language systems, even our most naturalized.

Like language, memory works on abstraction and "now (that) his perception and memory were perfect" (1999: 135), to remember a day Funes needed a day. The greater his vision of reality, the more he was weighed down by detail, the more incapacitated he became to think, to manipulate ideas, to survive: Funes died an old man, at the age of twenty-one. As in many other stories ("The Writing of the God" and "Three Versions of Judas," "Death and the Compass"), plenitude is presented in a postmodernist spirit as negative, leading to paralysis, madness, or death. In "The Aleph" the revelatory vision mentioned earlier is expressed in one of the most lyrical prose passages in all of Borges, yet the epiphanic experience, far from being uplifting, leads to the vulgar vindictiveness of the jealous narrator.

Beyond the structuralists' declaration of "the Death of the Author," one of the paradoxes of the postmodernist crisis of representation is the reinvestment of importance attached to the authorial voice. For, as convincingly argued by Bertens (1995), if a text is deemed to be dealing in relative rather than absolute truths it becomes ever more important to establish whose "truth" is being put forward. "Pierre Menard, Author of Don Quixote" is a story that humorously announces, in its very title, the problematics of authorship, making the astounding suggestion that Cervantes's masterpiece could have and has been written afresh, by someone else, at another time and place. In what has been declared "the perfect pastiche," "Pierre Menard" proffers two radically different readings of the same declaration. The phrase "truth, the mother of history" is oppositionally interpreted, first, in the discourse of Cervantes, where the connection between truth and history was assumed to be factual and absolute, and then, in the discourse of the fictional Pierre Menard, where, written in the wake of William James, it assumes an exclusively pragmatic connotation. This assertion, which would appear to uphold reception theory, continues to be author-dependent in the teasing suggestion that difference is not only according to when a text is written, but also by whom. Every text can be read anew simply by assuming it to have a different author, as for instance Thomas à Kempis's *Imitatio Christi* as if written by James Joyce, or Céline. Although Borges appears to reemphasize the authority of the authorial voice, it is not the realist authorial voice that is reinstated but an infinity of imaginary authors, whose different enactments of the same texts suggest Derridean *différance*. With this "Pierre Menard" illustrates the idea of every text being a palimpsest, an eternal site of intertextuality. Invoking Deleuze and Guattari's concept of the rhizome, de Toro has pointed out the unhierarchical and antiteleological use of allusion in Borges, arguing the essential separateness between source and text, a point of departure, to be forgotten, "without any semantic implication" (1994: 41). Whilst agreeing that Borges's use of allusion is uncanonical, my own reading has tended toward finding new possibilities of interpretations in the interplay between what has been said in the original and what is being said in the Borges text. Colás (1994: 46–8) places the discussion of allusion in a postcolonial context, arguing that Borges's use of allusion does not result in transculturation because "it is sealed off from other social practices." Balderston (1993), whose work on allusion is by far the most extensive to date, implicitly problematizes this view by refocusing Borges's work and revealing a very real, politico-historical basis for the fiction.

The relationship between postmodernism and postcolonialism cannot be argued here, but in so far as they are both concerned with difference and with dismantling monolithic representations of centrality, Borges's views, and fiction, may be considered relevant. In "The Argentine Writer and Trad-ition," an essay that has become *de rigueur* in most discussions of postcolonial theory, Borges has argued the importance of the margins as a privileged site from which to interpret a culture: "I believe that we Argentines . . . can handle all European themes . . . without superstition, with irreverence . . . which can have, and already does have, fortunate consequences" (1970: 218).

This idea is provocatively dramatized in "Guayaquil." Inverting the usual notion of Europe as center and Latin America as margin, it deals with the rivalry between a "central" criollo historian and his "marginal" opponent, a recent immigrant refugee from Central Europe, over who will be appointed as the national representative entrusted to interpret a newly discovered historical document. Needless to say, the outsider is deemed to be the better qualified candidate. "The Search for Averroës," a story that anticipates Said's ground-breaking work on Orientalism, also deals with cultural difference, exposing the way the center unthinkingly appropriates the "other." The narrator begins by mocking the eponymous Islamic philosopher for his attempt to interpret concepts beyond his cultural reach only to turn the tables on himself for attempting to write a story set in a Middle Eastern culture he knows only through Western mediations.

To summarize: throughout his fiction Borges conveys the postmodern con-dition, "inventing allusions to the conceivable which cannot be presented" (Lyotard 1985: 81; perceiving the aesthetic phenomenon as "the imminence of a revelation which does not occur" [Borges 1970: 223]). But to call Borges a postmodernist writer is to make a postmodernist assertion of a truth only partial and relative, in collision with other truth–claims (as listed at the beginning of this essay). For Borges was not a systematic thinker and did not espouse postmodernism any more than he espoused any other "ism" with which he has been identified, which at least had the result of preventing him from falling into the (postmodernist) trap of systematizing the negation of systems.

11

John Cage

Nancy Perloff

In 1972, as the term "postmodernism" was beginning to gain currency, the American composer John Cage offered the following observations on the new music. His remarks, first made during the recording of a film for television, appeared later in the periodical *Protokolle-Wiener Halbjahresschrift für Literatur, Bildende Kunst und Musik* (1974) and then in the journal *October* (1997):

> The two kinds of music now that interest me are on the one hand a music which is performed by everyone....[M]ore and more in my performances, I try to bring about a situation in which there is no difference between the audience and the performers. And I'm not speaking of audience participation in something designed by the composer, but rather am I speaking of the music which arises through the activity of both performers and so-called audience...The other kind of music that interests me is one which has been traditionally interesting and enjoyable down through the ages, and that's music which one makes oneself without constraining others. If you can do it by yourself you're not in a situation of telling someone else what to do. (Cage and Helms 1997: 82–3)

Cage's writings, his often detailed written instructions for performance, his explanations of compositional procedure, and his musical scores, all produced during a long and prolific career (b. 1912, d. 1992), provide extraordinarily rich and varied evidence of his role as twentieth-century modernist and as source for postmodernist aesthetics. The vast modal differences underlying the writings, scores, and live performances also point to problems inherent in applying a "modernist" or "postmodernist" label to John Cage. In the early 1970s, Cage clearly endorsed collaborative musical performances in which the audience worked together with performers, fusing art with its environment, and in which the composer's will did not constrain participants' activities. This decentered, collaborative, and heterogeneous principle for musical performance seems very postmodern. Yet the decisive presence of Cage's ego

("I like," "I try to bring about"), as well as the value he attached to historical musical practice, steered a modernist course. He designed and determined the performance situation, no matter how many participants were involved, and relied on his invention of chosen traditions from the past.

Did Cage tend more toward "modernism" or "postmodernism"? How is his radical contribution best understood? Cage moves between the seemingly oppositional contexts of postmodernism in the 1970s and 1980s, and European modernism in the early twentieth century, with reference especially to the art of Erik Satie (whom Cage championed), Italian Futurism, and German Dada. Cage's friendship and intellectual exchange with Pierre Boulez during the early 1950s offer a third vantage point. Although the three contexts are quite separate, stylistically and chronologically, each is integral to the evolving Cage oeuvre. Yet none alone accounts for his radicality. Through a discussion of these settings, Cage reveals himself to be an experimentalist and an avant-garde figure who believed in his responsibility to change the world through new music.

Writers on music have used "postmodernism" less frequently than critics in other fields. Even when comprised of quotation and appropriated sounds, music is an abstract language. In the case of Cage, a particularly complex scenario emerges. Here we have a composer who wrote poetic texts and mesostics, transformed the score into a visual object, and created music to be performed with dance and theater. Owing perhaps to the revolutionary changes Cage introduced in the meaning of musical composition, critics have skirted the issue of Cage's postmodernism, identifying him instead as a leader of the late twentieth-century avant-garde. By reviewing the postmodernist debate in relation to Cage, what conclusions might be drawn about the usefulness of "postmodernist" or avant-garde in defining his art?

The few critics who address Cage's links to postmodernism (Henry Sayre, Richard C. Hobbs, David Shapiro, Thomas Hines) identify his collaboration with Robert Rauschenberg and Merce Cunningham, beginning with their Dadaist "Happening" at Black Mountain College in 1952, as a significant impetus for the avant-garde of the 1970s. They define Cage's collaborative work on the "Happening" and on experimental dance in New York City as instances of "theatricality," a term applied by Michael Fried in 1982 to contemporary painting and sculpture which "depends for its effects of 'presence' on the staging, the conspicuous manipulation, of its relation to an audience" (Sayre 1989: 9) In the years following Fried's introduction of the term, "theatricality" came to coincide with "postmodernism" and shifted from single media art to a performative art revealed through the collaboration of performers and audience, and of high and vernacular media, sounds, and images. The modernist frame disappeared in postmodernism, replaced by contingency and fragmentation.

The experimental performance or "Happening" which Cage created and staged in the dining hall at Black Mountain College placed the performers in the aisles among the audience and presented a range of simultaneous but unrelated events: John Cage on a ladder reciting either his Meister Eckhart lecture, lines from Meister Eckhart, a lecture on Zen Buddhism, the Bill of Rights, or the Declaration of Independence; Merce Cunningham dancing around the chairs; Rauschenberg standing in front of his paintings or playing scratchy Edith Piaf recordings at double speed; David Tudor playing a prepared piano and a small radio; and M. C. Richards and Charles Olson perched on a different ladder and reading from their poetry. No narrative unfolded. But the events witnessed by the audience were staged and could be enhanced and refined by the performers, in the course of performance (Harris 1987: 226; 228). In both respects, Cage's "Happening" was a new form of theater.

This theatricality and the close link between performance and composition prompted Sayre to identify Cage, Rauschenberg and Cunningham as the originators of postmodernism. Sayre supported his argument with a discussion of important documents such as the "Interview with Roger Reynolds," published in 1962 in the Henmar Press catalogue of Cage's compositions, the essay "Composition as Process," and individual compositions. In the Roger Reynolds interview, Cage redefined the nature of composition. Composition was not a finished, static object performed before an audience of passive listeners, but, rather, a changing acoustical experience subject to each individual (performer and auditor) in the performance space. Since the performance action might have no beginning, middle, or end, and no discernible ordering of events, the composition as process opened the possibility for many different receptions and critiques by the audience. The French philosopher Roland Barthes concurred with the argument that Cage introduced a new music. Barthes's analysis of this break linked the new role of performance with the idea of multiple signifiers in Cage's music and the ceaseless production of new signifiers during the act of listening. Here Barthes implicitly concurred with Sayre's view that the performative requirements of Cage's music defined its novelty and hence its postmodernism.

Both the dancer Yvonne Rainer and the critic and philosopher Theodor Adorno discussed Cagian ideas associated with postmodernism, and attacked them as apolitical and uncritical. In talking about Cage's impact on her dance, Rainer praised the precedents he established for a new nonhierarchical, indeterminate organization, but argued that this nonhierarchy still failed to enable us to, as Cage would have it, "wake up to the excellent life we are living." On the contrary, she asserted, the critical insights gained from new methods of indeterminate composition and performance lead us to *question* whether the life we lead is so excellent, so just, so right, and how and why we have been led to believe this (Sayre 1989: 8). Adorno attacked Cage for the practice of indeterminacy, the freedom to let sounds be sounds, the aesthetic of a composition's interpenetration with its surroundings. The philosopher endorsed, instead, relative autonomy of the work of art from its social conditions, believing both in the composer's independence and his exertion of some control, so that the work assumed a critical function in relation to society (Joseph 1997: 90; 95).

In *The Imaginary Museum of Musical Works*, Lydia Goehr took a different tack on the radical nature of the ego in Cage. She argued that Cage did not succeed in abdicating control of, and hence distance from, the musical performance and attributed this "failure" to a split between his theory (his ideas and aspirations) and his actual musical practice. Goehr posited that a chance-inspired musical work like the celebrated 4'33", premiered by David Tudor in 1952, still operated within the protocols of the concert hall. The concert setting conveyed a message to the audience about when to applaud and how to behave during the performance. The fixed duration told the audience to follow this behavior during an allotted time period. Cage intended to relinquish control over the performance, so that the sounds of audience and space would produce the contents of the piece. In Goehr's view, however, theory and practice went their separate ways, since specific performance instructions circumscribed the range of random sounds and events (Goehr 1992: 261–4). Whereas Rainer and Adorno believed that a stronger ego would present a critique of social conditions, Goehr asserted that Cage's performances were the result of a powerful ego, which imposed choices that inadvertently *strengthened*, rather than undermined, the work-concept.

In seizing upon Cage's theatricality as a source for postmodernism of the 1970s, critics overlooked the emergence of collaborative and mixed-media performance in Europe as early as the 1910s (Sayre 1989: 9). Satie's "lyric comedy in one act... with dance music by the same gentleman," *Le Piège de Méduse* (Medusa's Trap) (1913), was revived as part of a Satie Festival organized by Cage at Black Mountain College in 1948. While fully notated and scripted (far from a chance piece), *Piège de Méduse* experimented with absurdist word-play, outrageous disjunctions between dialogue and stage action, and mixed media (dance, theater, music) (Whiting 1999: 449–60). It surely influenced Cage's Black Mountain "Happening" staged four years later with Cunningham. *Méduse* coincided with the Italian Futurists' organization of concerts of new sounds and with the Dadaists' creation of a new form of poetic recitation. Luigi Russolo, the pioneer of Futurist music, broke the "limited circle of pure sounds" by composing scores for *intonorumori* (noise-intoners). He designed these instruments to simulate the sounds of the street and of vernacular life. For German Dadaists such as Kurt Schwitters and Raoul Hausmann, new performance expressed itself in an abstract poetry, in which the formal visual patterns of words and letters served also as scores for poetic recitation.

The modernist theater of Satie, Russolo, and Schwitters offers but three examples of performance genres which preceded and inspired Cage. He studied the aesthetics of the past and borrowed from musical and philosophical traditions that intrigued him, in order to invent his own voice (Pasler 1994: 125; 133). It is important to recognize this practice as we define Cage's position *vis-à-vis* postmodernism. Whereas postmodernist artists referred to historical practices through techniques of quotation and *bricolage*, Cage used history as an intensive research process involving reinterpretations of tradition from his contemporary vantage and leading to the discovery of a personal style.

Cage's serious study of the past began early in his career, during lessons in counterpoint and analysis with Arnold Schoenberg in Los Angeles (March, 1935–Summer, 1937) and during a six-month stay in Europe in 1949. Cage spent the bulk of his time in Paris, where he went regularly to the Bibliothèque Nationale to study the life and work of Satie – one year after he had arranged the celebrated Satie performance at Black Mountain. During his visit, Cage also pursued Virgil Thomson's suggestion to contact Boulez, the most prominent French composer of the postwar avant-garde. The two developed a close friendship, which continued through correspondence when Cage returned to New York in November, 1949 (Nattiez 1993: 4–7). Cage was thirty-six, and Boulez twenty-four.

When he first met Boulez, Cage was searching for matrices with which to organize his works, particularly their rhythmic structure. A letter he received from Boulez in August, 1951 suggests the nature of their Paris conversations. Using technical terms, Boulez described how the notion of the twelve-tone series could be generalized to apply not only to frequency but to intensities (volume), attacks, rhythm, and even timbre. (Nattiez 1993: 99ff.). Boulez spoke of the "serial structure" of each musical parameter and introduced corresponding tables which mapped out the serial organization. This letter so impressed Cage that he translated much of it and published it in 1952 in the journal *Transformations*, with commentaries by Morton Feldman, Christian Wolff, and Cage. By bringing together the French serialist Boulez with American composers of chance and indeterminacy, Cage made a statement about the new music. He affirmed the common goal of composers of new music to isolate and compose for individual musical parameters, so that the parameters could then be integrated in different combinations.

Boulez's admiration for Cage hinged on their common interest in doing away with Western European harmony and defining sound instead as an aggregate of timbre, frequency, attack, and duration. In a lecture Boulez delivered on Cage on June 17, 1949 (while Cage was in Paris), Boulez praised his colleague for "making use of sound complexes," instead of "pure sounds." In the published version of this lecture (entitled "Possibly"), which appeared in 1952 in *La Revue Musicale*, Boulez expanded this point:

> We also owe to John Cage the idea of sound complexes; for he has written works in which, instead of using pure sounds, he employs chords which have no harmonic function, being essentially a sort of amalgam of sounds linked to timbres, durations, and intensities. (Nattiez 1993: 9)

Boulez was most likely thinking of the sounds of Cage's prepared piano, a magical transformation of the piano into a percussion instrument capable of producing different timbres when materials (such as string, rubber band, metal coils) were inserted between the strings. During the 1940s, Cage had composed many pieces for prepared piano with which Boulez was clearly familiar.

The basis for friendship between the two young composers was solid: an interest in structural relations between musical parameters, in mathematical tables which charted out the different parameters, in sonic aggregates, in the idea of the series. They parted ways, however, as Cage became increasingly interested in chance and in a new performance situation. Boulez had always been critical of Morton Feldman's "imprecision" and "simplicity," but in a letter of December, 1951 Boulez lashed out at Cage's use of chance in *Music of Changes* (1951):

> The only thing, forgive me, which I am not happy with, is the method of absolute chance *(by tossing the coins)*. On the contrary, I believe that chance must be extremely controlled: by using tables in general, or series of tables, I believe that it would be possible to direct the phenomenon of the automatism of chance, whether written down or not ... there is already quite enough of the unknown. (Nattiez 1993: 17)

In *Music of Changes*, Cage used the *I Ching*, or Chinese *Book of Changes*, to create charts corresponding to three musical parameters: sound, duration, dynamics. To compose his piece, he tossed the dice (Boulez's coins), obtained numbers referring to different cells in his charts, devised a sound aggregate with the resultant frequency, duration, and dynamics cells, then threw the dice to construct the next sound. In Boulez's view, Cage left too much to chance.

In his rejection of Western harmony and his application of the idea of the tone row of Schoenberg and Webern to all aspects of musical structure, Boulez stood as a leading avant-garde figure. He was not, however, a postmodernist, for reasons that are clear from his response to *Music of Changes*. Neither Boulez's theory nor his practice represented an intent to remove the ego, make the auditor central, and fuse art with life. Seen in relation to Boulez, Cage was the American experimentalist who used the discipline practiced by Boulez to redefine both musical composition and performance, and to introduce randomness. Unlike those of Boulez, Cage's experiments involved collaboration with artists in other media (Cunningham in dance, Rauschenberg and Johns in painting and set design, filmmakers, video artists). Recasting the modernism of Satie, Italian Futurism, Dada, and other early modernist movements, Cage infused the vernacular into his composition by giving audiences the freedom to move and participate and, during the 1960s, by conceiving of the work as a disciplined *action* by the performer with or without sounds (Pritchett 1993: 146).

Yet to place Boulez with the avant-garde and Cage with postmodernism is far too simple. The two composers had much in common. Both believed in building upon tradition, in this case the serialism of Arnold Schoenberg and Anton Webern. Both believed that in applying serial structure to all musical components, they were extending and reinterpreting the work initiated by the Second Viennese School to replace functional harmony with a disciplined counterpoint in which one sound did not imply the next. Neither Boulez nor Cage engaged in social and political satire or attack. They tended not to appropriate and combine fragments of social and cultural history, philosophy, or composition to create multiple voices and *simulacra*. Cage, in particular, sought to discover a "suitable past" from which to invent a tradition of which he was the logical heir, the next voice (Pasler 1994: 125; 133). He was concerned to carve his place in history. Absorbed by the past, Cage joined the "mainstream of musical modernism" and set himself apart from the "fading sense of history" and the life in a "perpetual present" of postmodernist culture (Pasler 1994: 140; Connor 1989: 91).

In assessing whether the postmodernist label aptly defines Cagian composition and aesthetics, I have argued that Cage's interest in theater and mixed media may have prefigured postmodernism; I have situated his art in the context of European modernism of the 1910s and 1920s; and I have discussed his work in relation to that of Boulez. The missing link is the contribution of Cage to our understanding of the present world, independently of movements he may have anticipated, echoed, or refuted. With every decade, Cage's work changed dramatically. In the 1950s, he explored procedures of chance and indeterminacy, devising unique graphic notations which performers could realize in myriad ways and raising perplexing questions about critical evaluation based on the written score or on the performance (which always changed). Cage sought to create a world of interpenetrating sounds and to eliminate hierarchy among these sounds (Pritchett 1993: 139; 146). In the 1960s, Cage's aesthetic changed. Rather than treating the composition as a concrete object made up of sounds, he approached it as an action, a process in which the composer set up electronic components, and the performer realized a score that offered broad outlines, but no specifics. For instance, the score for Cage's *0'00 (4'33" no. 2)* of 1962 contained the following sentence: "In a situation provided with maximum amplification (no feedback), perform a disciplined action." By the 1970s, according to James Pritchett, Cage's aesthetic had changed again, preoccupied more with an eclectic mixture of styles than with a single music of the future (Pritchett 1993: 146; 158; 173).

Cage's production was diverse, yet motivated throughout by goals which cannot be contained within the postmodernist rubric. The utopian vision of modernism and American experimentalism led Cage to transform the traditional roles of composer, performer, and audience, and to introduce a vision of "freedom given to disciplined people" to change society and to show the "practicality of anarchy" (Cage and Helms 1997: 81). Cage used chance procedures in order to shift the authorial voice from the composer to the performer and to the individual members of the audience. His move away from self-expression resonates with the multiple voices of postmodernism, although indeterminacy operated within his chosen parameters. In addition, the "postmodernist" rubric does not adequately explain Cage's challenge to musical composition, the revolution he sparked in the 1950s by establishing *difference* between writing (the musical score) and sound (the performance). Cage paved the way for the production of works that were not fully notated or fixed. In the 1960s and 1970s, Fluxus musicians went on to explore this idea of the "open work," which anticipated conceptual art (Pepper 1997: 37–8). The Cagian tension between the written score and the variable performance, the resulting paradox that the score is autonomous, without fixed referent, the treatment of composition as process, the expansion of the possibility for multiple signifiers and critical receptions – such ideas propelled the avant-garde to new terrain. Explored in their own right, they distinguish Cage as a startlingly provocative voice whose originality made room for a new freedom for the contemporary audience.

12

Italo Calvino

Rocco Capozzi

To entertain is a serious job.

(I. Calvino)

Italo Calvino (1923–85) is one of the most read, studied, quoted, and respected contemporary Italian writers at home and abroad. He is also one of the most complex, cerebral, innovative, interdisciplinary, and playfully imaginative metafictional fabulators of the twentieth century. The author's popularity in the English-speaking world came in the 1960s after the publication of *Cosmicomics*, *Invisible Cities*, and *The Castle of Crossed Destinies*. Calvino's fame increased as a result of John Barth's well-known essays, "The Literature of Exhaustion" (1967) and "The Literature of Replenishment" (1979b), in which he considers the fiction of Jorge Luis Borges and Italo Calvino as perfect models of postmodernism. Barth's second article presents Calvino as a writer who "began as an Italian neo-realist (in *The Path to the Spiders' Nest* [1998/1947]) and matured into an exemplary postmodernist (with *Cosmicomics* [1976/1965], and *The Castle of Crossed Destinies* [1973]) who on occasion rises, sinks, or merely shifts to modernism (*Invisible Cities* [1974/1972])" (Barth 1979b: 66).

In "Multiplicity," in *Six Memos for the Next Millennium* (1988b), Calvino admires writers like Flaubert and Borges whose fiction illustrates the notion of the "contemporary novel as an encyclopedia, as a method of knowledge, and above all as a network of connections" (1988: 105). *Invisible Cities*, *The Castle*, and *Mr. Palomar* (1983) are all excellent examples of taking an object or image/concept – be it a city, a story, a myth, a wave, an animal, a picture, a display of cheeses in a store, or a novel – and by continually constructing and deconstructing it in the process of trying to analyze the parts and the whole to arrive at a better understanding of what is under examination. However, we often also notice how a narrator (especially Palomar) is frustrated by the fact that words may be inadequate not only in capturing reality but also in clarifying his own intentions in describing what he thinks or perceives.

At times critics have made too much of Calvino's close reading of Borges or other writers and critics. Given the long history of Calvino's eclectic interests, his vast encyclopedic competence, his overall poetics of *docere et delectare* ("instructing and entertaining"), and his love of fusing interdisciplinary and multimedia elements, he can legitimately be seen as a pioneer of European postmodernism. Calvino's work combines classic and academic culture with popular culture, literary with theoretical and philosophical texts, science and the humanities, past and recent history, and written and visual images. Movie and comic-strip techniques abound in, for instance, *Cosmicomics* and *Tzero* (1967), where cinematic effects combine with techniques of science fiction, romance, and Westerns in a most clever and intertextual fashion. Furthermore, the opening page of *If on a Winter's Night a Traveler* (1979) is also playfully cinematic and intertextual as it recalls scenes from old black-and-white detective movies (like the closing scene in *Casablanca*).

A number of studies of Calvino, such as Howard Carter's *Metamorphoses of Fantasy* (1987), offer an overall picture of the author's so-called evolution from neorealism to postmodernism. These remind us that Italian critics for a substantial period were more interested in the engagé and "realist" Calvino and were not particularly happy with his alleged quick assimilation of the French experimentalism associated with the *Tel Quel* group and with the new fiction advocated by Robbe-Grillet and other promoters of the *nouveau roman*. However, Calvino was hardly an imitator; he was instead interested in finding new possibilities for literature – pretty much as Queneau and the members of the "Oulipo" (*Ouvroir de littérature potentielle* – "Workshop of Potential Literature"; Calvino became a member in 1974) were combining math, science, and literature in order to inject literature with a new life and at the same time increase its artistic potential. As illustrated throughout Calvino's work, under an apparent freedom and playfulness hide constraints and clear logic. This is particularly evident in the carefully constructed frames (in the tradition of Boccaccio's *cornice*) of *Invisible Cities*, *The Castle*, and *Mr. Palomar*.

The notion of literature as a "machine" that generates other literature in using a limited number of units (or elements) to produce an infinite number of texts, is examined in his essay "Cybernetics and Ghosts." This important article on "literature as a combinatorial game" is in part historical, as it takes us from Raymond Lully's *ars combinatoria* to Saussure's concept of the pieces and moves on a "chess board," to Propp's discussion of functions in his *Phenomenology of Fables*, to Greimas's *actants*, and to the type of combinations and permutations suggested by the "Oulipo." It also examines narratological issues linked to semiotics and structuralism and it reveals the author's own ideas on writers and literature as "writing machines." Moreover, it provides a key for the reading of *Invisible Cities* and *The Castle of Crossed Destinies*, the latter of which makes use of the images of tarot and popular cards and is narratologically speaking an excellent demonstration of how "narrative machines" are set in motion and kept going, possibly *ad infinitum*, through a network of associations, combinations, and interpretation of emblems, myths, texts, stories, gestures, and even silence.

Calvino's close attention to the literary climate of his times is amply illustrated in *If on a Winter's Night a Traveler*, – a detective fiction which is both a parody on and a clever illustration of "reader reception theories" (Eco, Iser, Bloom, Derrida). Calvino, like Eco, was uneasy with the shift from the authorial and textual *auctoritas* – especially by poststructuralist and radical deconstructionists – to the reader's freedom to interpret. There is no question that from the first to the last page we feel the authorial presence controlling the actual reader and the readers in the text. Throughout the novel, which is made up of ten opening chapters, Calvino has great fun playing cat and mouse with different types of readers (such as Ludmilla, Lotaria, and Irnerio) who chase after various texts dealing with different fictional genres (such as romance, mystery, and erotic fiction). The author has also plenty to say about critics, professors, translators, and editors. This remarkable demonstration of *mise-en-abîme*, of embedding, rewriting, infinite intertextuality, and other narratological strategies (dating back to Sheherazade and Boccaccio) confirmed Calvino's exceptional skills in creating not just intricate stories but also in dealing with complex philosophical ideas and literary theories.

With the trilogy "Our Ancestors" (1951–9) Calvino had distanced himself from the sociopolitical commitments that Marxist critics were demanding from intellectuals, when many writers and artists were still involved with the engagé, neorealist techniques of the postwar years. In 1956, when the Soviet Union invaded Hungary, Calvino became disillusioned with the silence of the Italian Communist Party and in 1957 he resigned as a member. This came as no surprise to readers who in the trilogy and also in his short stories – especially those of *Difficult Loves* – had noticed Calvino's growing love affair with fantasy and metafictional elements. In *Difficult Loves* we find stories like "The Adventure of a Reader," which is like a miniature of the fully postmodern *If on a Winter's Night a Traveler*. *Difficult Loves* offers us a gamut of existential and psychological meditations on the part of a narrator on his relationship with nature, with others, with time, and with his own mind.

Still, until the late 1960s critics were examining Calvino's work mainly in light of his realism and his long collaboration with Elio Vittorini. This was largely justified with regard to his first novel, *The Path to the Spiders' Nest*, dealing with the anti-fascist Resistance and narrated by a young boy, Pin, who learns from the world of adults about sex and violence; his wartime short stories collected in *Ultimo viene il corvo* (1949; "Last Came the Crow"); *Gli amori difficili* (1970; *Difficult Loves*, written in the late 1940s and early 1950s); and the short narratives *The Argentine Ant* (*La formica argentina*, 1952), *Smog*

(*La nuvola di smog*, 1958), and *A Plunge into Real Estate* (*La speculazione edilizia*, 1963), written as Italy was undergoing major changes in developing from an agricultural into an industrial economy. In these last two stories we see Calvino lament the fate of nature which has almost disappeared in an industrial and consumeristic society. And, of course, we must include his political short novel *The Watcher* (written in the late 1950s and published in 1963). With hindsight we can see that conservative readers had ignored the author's experiments with language, style, and narrative strategies in texts in which fantasy, narratological elements, and the author's attention to literary theories were perfectly fused with existential and sociological themes. Most critics overlooked the fact that Calvino was already deeply involved in a new literature in which ideas, open structures, problems of perception, and the relationships between words, images, ideas, and reality preoccupied him much more than political ideology. This changed in the 1970s as we can see in the criticism published from 1973 onwards (e.g., Calligaris 1973; Bernardini Napolitano 1977; Milanini 1990; and in particular the outstanding essays of Belpoliti and Ricci).

Calvino's experimentation with metafiction may have to some degree increased after his frequent Parisian sojourns in the 1960s (from his contacts with the *Tel Quel* group – and more specifically with writers and critics such as Barthes, Greimas, Robbe-Grillet, Queneau, Perec, and Serres). Moreover, he may have been inspired by his reading of Borges, Stevenson, Nabokov, Barth, and Pynchon. These and other possible influences (Valéry, Ponge, Montale, or Gadda) are undeniable but it should be remembered that Calvino was also becoming skeptical and even critical toward the new theories of the 1960s and 1970s.

The best indication of Calvino's reluctance to embrace any particular new theory on representation or on solving social problems is evident in some of his most quoted essays (see especially "Il mare dell'oggettività" [The Sea of Objectivity], "La sfida al labirinto" [The Challenge to the Labyrinth], "Cibernetica e fantasmi" ["Cybernetics and Ghosts"], and "I livelli della realtà" ["The Levels of Reality"] – the last two have appeared in English in *The Uses of Literature* [1987]). Here we can see his unwillingness to embrace either the *nouveau roman* or the new faith in science and technology that the Italian literary trend "Literature and Industry" seemed to encourage, or the position that literature was essentially all language (Derrida and poststructuralism). In "Il mare dell'oggettività" Calvino warned writers against the level of objectivity advocated by "l'école du regard" and against moving from the sea of subjectivity to a drowning sea of objects and objectivity. In "La sfida al labirinto" he maintained that the role of literature is to "challenge the labyrinth" (a familiar Borgesian metaphor for an imprisoning chaotic reality). He was to illustrate this notion in different ways in his fiction through familiar images of libraries, labyrinths, prison–like or kaleidoscopic and rhizomic structures, networks, and webs. The images of the "inferno" at the conclusion of *Invisible Cities* and of the maze/prison in the final story of *Tzero*, "The Count of Monte Cristo," present clear examples. In both cases man may not escape but he will at least have identified the source and cause of his anguish.

Calvino's skills as an ingenious postmodern fabulator are perfectly exemplified by the galactic picaresque adventures of Qfwfq in *Cosmicomics* and *Tzero*. Drawing in part on some of his favorite writers like Galileo (for the art of combining science and literature), Ariosto, and Borges (as masters of fantasy), Calvino combines science, embedded frames, fables, myths, detective fiction, history, humor, and solving logic problems (see especially the closing stories in *Tzero*), in stories that convey criticism on a variety of social issues. The stories also deal with popular literary theories of semiotics and structuralism (see especially "A Sign in Space" and "The Origin of Birds"). The arbitrariness of verbal signs and the overall issue of signs that can be interpreted in different ways depending on context and culture are familiar themes in Calvino's work (above all in *Cities*, *Castle*, and *Cosmicomics*). Moreover, Calvino includes Lacanian psychoanalysis in the portrayals of innumerable I – Other relationships and of the continual state/conflict of desire. Qfwfq – not just a palindrome, but a perfectly mirrored self-reflection, as the name can be folded on itself: qfv-vfq – is an enigmatic and protean character who forever changes state and form, in time and space, from the time of the Big Bang, through the days of dinosaurs, right up to the present day in New York (shopping at Tiffany's), and who is an acute eyewitness and a humorous commentator. It is both educational and entertaining to share Qfwfq's omniscience. His adventures in space, water, time, and history deal with all sorts of cognitive processes and Qfwfq handles all of them with the ease of someone who has today's knowledge. Moreover, his decentered self, his existential anguish, his solitude, his contemplative nature, and his self-irony are all fictional reflections of a Calvino at a difficult stage of his career who has chosen to "keep in tune with the times" (Capozzi 1989) but at the same time maintains a safe critical and aesthetic distance from what could be passing fashionable literary trends.

Calvino's interdisciplinary approach to literature and his overall ironic/parodic postmodernist use of intertextual echoes and popular culture can be traced back to his trilogy. Here we have the first clear evidence of his art of mixing media (especially cinematic techniques) with history, literature, fables, allegory, irony, and satire as he unleashes some of his most acute criticism of hypocrisy, hedonism, bureaucracy, and the perils of capitalism and modern science.

Critics have identified in the contemplative and phenomenological eyewitness narrator of *Mr. Palomar* many autobiographical characteristics. We also see Calvino mirrored in some of his other alter egos such as Amerigo in *The Watcher*, the complementing team of Polo and Khan in *Cities*, Qfwfq in *Cosmicomics*, or Silas Flannery in *If on a Winter's Night*. And we must also include the narrator in "I Also Try to Tell My Tale," in *The Castle*, who compares his role as a writer to that of "a juggler, or conjurer, who arranges on a stand at a fair a certain number of objects and, shifting them, connecting them, interchanging them, achieves a certain number of effects" (105). In *Mr. Palomar*, we at times get the impression that the focus seems to be inward as the narrator's mind and descriptions become a mirror of the outside world. Palomar observes, catalogues, describes, interprets words as well as silences, meditates on a sunbeam, all in order to reflect the world while he yet never feels in harmony with it. And even though he is frustrated with being able to capture only the surface of things, he keeps on observing and writing.

Calvino's posthumous *Six Memos* are a final testimonial to the author's love for literature. The lectures on "Lightness," "Speed," and "Multiplicity," which deal extensively with writing and narrating, reveal a great deal of Calvino the writer, such as his preferences for short narratives, for encyclo- pedic authors, and his interest in cognitive processes. Throughout *Six Memos* we again encounter the names of writers like Ovid, Valéry, Borges, Gadda, and Perec, testifying to Calvino's love for a literature that is essentially a world constructed by the intellect and a way of creating mental order out of chaos.

Still, Calvino's worlds of fiction, even when they appear to be pure, complex, cerebral, and playful language constructions (*Cities*, *Castle*, or *Mr. Palomar*), or when they seem to derive from the world of literature and intertextuality (*Cosmicomics*, *Castle*, *If on a Winter's Night*), always send us back to the world in which we live. Furthermore, the skepticism shown by several of Calvino's narrators, who feel impotent in the face of chaos or labyrinthine structures, should not be interpreted as pessimism. Marco Polo's words to Khan summarize very well Calvino's philosophy:

The inferno of the living is not something that will be; if there is one, it is what is already here, the inferno where we live every day, that we form by being together. There are two ways to escape suffering it. The first is easy for many: accept the inferno and become such a part of it that you can no longer see it. The second is risky and demands constant vigilance and apprehension: seek and learn to recognize who and what, in the midst of the inferno, are not inferno, then make them endure, give them space. (*Cities*, 165).

13

Angela Carter

Joanne Gass

" 'Is she fact or is she fiction?' " (1984: 7). This question (or is it a challenge?), which bedevils Jack Walser as he tries to uncover the truth about Fevvers, the winged aerialist/heroine in *Nights at the Circus* (1984), also bedevils critics who try to categorize its author, Angela Carter. Like Fevvers, her finest creation, Carter wrote novels, short stories, and essays which defy categorization. Even a cursory review of criticism of Carter's works will reveal that they invite as many interpretations as there are "schools" of criticism in the late twentieth century. She is identified as Foucauldian when she questions discourses of power. She is Bakhtinian when she integrates the carnivalesque and the grotesque in order to disrupt those discourses of power. When she brings capitalism and class privilege, especially British capitalism and class privilege, onto the stage, she reveals her Marxist influences. She deconstructs essentialism and the myth of subjectivity and replaces them with performativity and play. And, as a feminist, she challenges patriarchal structures of all types. Lindsey Tucker says of her work that it "is both grand and vulgar; its deployment of intertextuality is daunting, but it revels in the smells of carnival and the many representations of physicality" (Tucker 1998: 2). She is all of these things, and yet she is not one of them exclusively. Just as Fevvers is a master of the confidence trick, a common angel who exploits all of the myths of womanhood and banks the profits, so Angela Carter exploited and mastered the discursive practices embedded in her culture. Like Fevvers, she refused to be catalogued or categorized, for to be identified meant to be fixed and therefore subject to control, like the Somnambulist and the prisoners of the panopticon prison in *Nights at the Circus* and the puppets in *The Magic Toyshop* (1967). Her characters are often the victims of essentializing discourses who refuse their victimization and set out to dismantle them. And Carter, like her strongest characters, refuses essentializing of any type.

Angela Carter spent her entire creative life exposing the material conditions which determined women's and men's lives. For Carter, having taken Simone de Beauvoir's injunction to women "to know the economic and social structure" of the world in order to become themselves (Beauvoir 1952: 52), set out to probe, with intellect and wit, the real conditions of her and our existences. By "real," Carter meant the quotidian, mundane, unique, and individual facts of our lives. In *The Sadeian Woman* (1979b) she critiques pornography because it universalizes the sexual experiences of individual human beings and ignores the linguistic, social, political, and cultural differences which particularize our existences:

> But no bed, however unexpected, no matter how apparently gratuitous, is free from the de-universalising facts of real life. We do not go to bed in simple pairs; even if we choose not to refer to them, we still drag there with us the cultural impedimenta of our social class, our parents' lives, our bank balances, our sexual and emotional expectations, our whole biographies – all the bits and pieces of our unique existences. (1979b: 9)

Not that she imagined for a moment that we are each independent entities in complete control of our lives; she, like Beauvoir, understood that we are the products of the material conditions which produce us. Pornography like any other discourse which predicates "a universality of human experience is a confidence trick and the notion of a universality of female experience is a clever confidence trick" (1979b: 12).

One of her most frequent universalizing targets was myth and its claim to metaphysical truth and power. In Carter's estimation, myth's power lies not in its metaphysical, universal potency but in its material potency which finds its expression in economic, political, and social discourse and patriarchal oppression. "Myth deals in false universals, to dull the pain of particular circumstances," she says in one of her most often cited remarks about myth in the "Polemical Preface" to *The Sadeian Woman*. She goes on to say:

> All the mythic versions of women, from the myth of the redeeming purity of the virgin to that of the healing, reconciling mother, are consolatory nonsense; and consolatory nonsense seems to me a fair definition of myth, anyway. Mother goddesses are just as silly a notion as father gods. If a revival of the myths of these cults gives women emotional satisfaction, it does so at the price of obscuring the real conditions of life. This is why they were invented in the first place. (1979b: 5)

Angela Carter set out to undermine and eventually to overthrow the rhetorical power of myth, and the instrument she used to effect such a revolution was parody. Nearly all of her novels and short stories parody an accepted literary form and accepted cultural myths to a very serious political purpose. Carter's brand of parody parallels Linda Hutcheon's sense that it is "an apt mode of

criticism for postmodernism, itself paradoxical in its conservative installing
and then radical contesting of conventions" (Hutcheon 1988: 129). Parody of
this type, according to Hutcheon,

> use[s] parody not only to restore history and memory in the face of the distor-
> tions of the "history of forgetting"... but also, at the same time, to put into
> question the authority of any act of writing by locating the discourses of both
> history and fiction within an ever-expanding intertextual network that mocks
> any notion of either single origin or simple causality. (Hutcheon 1988: 129)

Thus parody, in Hutcheon's scheme, serves a double political purpose; it
focuses upon history or genre, then calls its univocal authority into question.
In "Notes from the Frontline," Carter remarks, "language is power, life and
the instrument of culture, the instrument of domination and liberation"
(reprinted in Tucker 1998: 30). From *The Bloody Chamber* (1979a), to *The
Sadeian Woman*, to *Nights at the Circus* and *Wise Children* (1991), she probes
the discourses we use to define and identify human beings, particularly
women, in order to expose the rhetoric of myth and its claim to metaphysical
truth and power.

At the risk of oversimplification, Angela Carter might best be described as a
"Foucauldian postmodern[ist]" after Hans Bertens's designation of the period
of the 1980s in which Foucault dominated postmodern theory and practice
(Bertens 1995: 8). Carter, whose first novel, *Shadow Dance*, was published in
1966 and her last, *Wise Children*, in 1991, apparently found, in her reading of
Foucault, a kindred spirit, for she frequently alludes to him, even beginning
her "Polemical Preface" to *The Sadeian Woman* with a quotation from *Madness and Civilization* (1979b: 3). But Angela Carter was no pale imitator of the
great mind, nor does she perpetrate yet another patriarchal mythology in her
writings. Perhaps she is most like Foucault not so much in the theoretical
discourse but in the laughter which disrupts the order of things. Foucault tells
us that the idea for *The Order of Things*

> arose out of a passage in Borges, out of the laughter that shattered... all the
> familiar landmarks of my thought... breaking up all the ordered surfaces and all
> the planes with which we are accustomed to tame the wild profusion of existing
> things, and... threaten with collapse our age-old distinction between the Same
> and the Other. (Foucault 1973 [1961]: xv)

This laughter undermines the foundations of patriarchal discourse and focuses
our attention on the confidence trick that has kept us fixed in identities which
make victims of us all. Carter's lusty, robust, irreverent, confrontational prose
challenged the accepted "truths" of her time and undermined virtually all of
the cultural myths which keep those subjected to them chained to their

"eternal verities." Among the myths she set out with the determination of a guerrilla warrior to explode are the Freudian myth (especially as perpetuated by Bruno Bettelheim), the myth of male authorship, the myth of fixed subjectivity and identity, the myth of primordial guilt as promoted by Judeo-Christian orthodoxy, and the death-centered myth called by some the "tragic vision" and by a number of feminists, the politics of Thanatos. That she does not replace these myths with another need not disturb us; her fiction provides the material with the use of which her readers can break chains, not manufacture new ones. Lest we think that Carter's guerrilla carnivalesque ignored unpleasant facts, Kate Webb reminds us that Carter was only too aware that

> There are "limits to the power of laughter" – the carnival can't rewrite history, undo the effects of war or alter what is happening on the "news." And there is no transcendence possible in life, Carter tells us, from the materiality of the moment, from the facts of oppression and war. But carnival does offer us the tantalizing promise of how things might be in a future moment, if we altered the conditions which tie us down. It is only the carnival which can give us such imagined possibilities, which is why the creative things that make it up in life are so precious: laughter, sex, and art. (Sage 1994: 307)

Neither Carter nor Foucault meant to replace "the facts" with a jolly, chaotic carnival; they understood the necessity for order and for the discourses which support order-making systems. What they wanted to question was claims made by such discursive practices to universality, transcendence, and Truth, and to point out that all such practices derive their sources and potency from cultural practices.

If, as Foucault suggests, laughter threatens to break up the ordered surface of things, then Carter's approach to the rhetoric of Freudian myths like the Oedipus conflict, penis envy, and castration complex can best be summed up in her comment about D. H. Lawrence in "Lorenzo the Closet-Queen," written in 1975: "those who preach phallic superiority usually have an enormous dildo tucked away somewhere in their psychic impedimenta" (1997: 499). Her attack on the myth of the Oedipus conflict took place on several fronts – in her nonfiction essays, in her short stories, especially in the fairy tales, and in her novels. In her essays, she reminds her readers that "*Oedipus the King* [is] a cultural product with the specific conditions of the time and place of its composition mediating its universality" (1997: 74), and that the "whole theory of Oedipus' conflict is based on the cultural fact of patriarchy rather than on the biological accident of paternity" (1997: 366). Carter likewise objected to that "psychic fiction" of female castration: "Female castration is an imaginary fact that pervades the whole of men's attitude towards women and our attitude to ourselves, that transforms women from human beings into wounded creatures who were born to bleed" (1979b: 23).

Carter's interest in the fairy tale stems, among other things, from her observation that women were the tellers and often the heroines. When Freud and Bettelheim speak about them, they usurp the woman's voice and insert their own "naturalizing" and patriarchal authority over the stories and the women. In her retelling of Grimm's fairy tales, Carter appropriates the narrative voice, returning power to the female voice. For example, in "The Tiger's Bride" in *The Bloody Chamber*, the heroine tells her own story, unlike the Grimm Brothers' version, which we know as "Beauty and the Beast." Sylvia Bryant says of this crucial change in narrative voice:

> By appropriating the personal voice, the girl . . . not only takes charge of telling the narrative of her life, and consequently of the narrative traditions of the fairy tale, but she also makes clear from the start that what blame there is to be assigned lies not with her but with the dominant systems to which she is only a bargaining chip. . . . And in carving out her own life-story, in resisting the story which literary and cultural traditions have patterned for her, her narrative becomes an alternative model for the female subject's desire. (Bryant 1998: 90–1)

Carter uses the female narrator in a number of her novels as well, most notably, *The Magic Toyshop, Heroes and Villains* (1969), *Nights at the Circus*, and *Wise Children*. Each novel has an unorthodox heroine who takes control of her narrative, challenges the "accepted fictions of femininity" (Sage 1992: 170), and, with varying degrees of success, sets out to bring down the edifice of patriarchal control.

Carter does not, however, offer unsullied heroines in return. Her female narrators may be heroic, but they are by no means perfect. Nor does she shrink from the obvious fact that many female characters in fairy tales (and in her novels, as well) are cruel, wicked, weak, and manipulative. She presents them to us unvarnished, warts and all "in a valedictory spirit, as a reminder of how wise, clever, perceptive, occasionally lyrical, eccentric, sometimes downright crazy our great-grandmothers were" (1990: xxii). Carter's heroines, like the women in the fairy tales she collected, are only too aware of life's cruelties, but they speak for themselves; they are not spoken for.

And when they speak for themselves, they challenge the accepted mythologies of the "nature" of women and even of life itself. Fevvers and Dora Chance confront accepted ideas of identity, authorship, and essentialism. Marianne, in *Heroes and Villains*, reminds us that Judeo-Christian guilt is tattooed into our psyches, just as the myth of the Fall is tattooed onto Jewel's back (J. Gass 1995).

In the end, Carter herself challenged the tragic vision, the politics of Thanatos, which is transcendental, metaphysical, and patriarchal and which anguishes over time and death. She offers, instead, a comic vision which focuses upon social constructs and opens them up to subversion, transformation, and change.

Angela Carter's oeuvre encompasses, as it anticipated, many facets of postmodern thought. Hayden White tells us that in

> postmodernist times, it is understandable why people of goodwill, wanting to do justice to the particularities of existence, should turn against totalizing systems of thought which privilege the whole and ignore the parts of life which are to be sacrificed to it. (White 1999: viii)

Angela Carter was a writer of supreme goodwill.

14

Ping Chong

Philip Auslander

Although the word "postmodern" and its cognates seldom appear in critical discussions of Ping Chong's performance work, there are compelling reasons to see him as a preeminent postmodernist. His performances exhibit the distinguishing features of postmodern art, summarized by Craig Owens as "appropriation, site-specificity, impermanence [arguably a basic characteristic of live performance], accumulation, discursivity, hybridization" (1984a: 209). Further, the themes of his performances reflect postmodern ideas of identity and subjecthood.

Owens's list, intended to describe postmodernist strategies in the visual arts, is an appropriate point of reference for Chong, who came to performance from a background in the visual arts and film. Born in Toronto in 1946, Chong grew up in New York's Chinatown and studied graphic art at Pratt Institute and filmmaking at the School of Visual Arts. An interest in dance led Chong to a workshop with postmodern choreographer and performance artist Meredith Monk, whose company he joined and with whom he collaborated on several performances. He founded his own performance group – the Fiji Company, now called Ping Chong and Company – in 1975. He and his collaborators have developed over forty performance pieces, beginning with *Lazarus* (1972), and including *Humboldt's Current* (1977), *AM/AM-The Articulated Man* (1982), *Angels of Swedenborg* (1985), *Elephant Memories* (1990), and *Chinoiserie* (1994).

Chong was attracted to the performance scene of the late 1960s in part because he saw experimental theater as partaking more of the "pageantry, ritual and color" of the Chinese Opera, in which his parents performed, than traditional Western theater (Hong 1995: 55). His performance work reflects the visual opulence of Chinese opera, sometimes relying on images rather than words for expression, and always containing striking visual tableaux. In the prologue to *Nosferatu* (1985), for instance, two angels clad in gray, with gray plastic masks and white shocks of hair (a cross between Pre-Raphaelite grave stones and Kabuki warriors), frolicked, caressed, and wrestled with one another until one tore from the other's breast not his heart but a dry black thing that is like a heart of darkness. (Banes 1998: 277)

Like most of Chong's images, this one is visually very specific, but open-ended in meaning. The visual elegance and polish of Chong's performances, his emphasis on design and production values, seem to constitute a postmodernist gesture related to the slick surfaces of much postmodernist visual art. This visual refinement can also be seen as postmodernist if one construes postmodernist performance to be in reaction against the emphasis on the raw, unadorned physical presence of the performer in much of the "ecstatic" experimental theater of the 1960s (Auslander 1992: 35–55).

Chong is a multimedia artist – his performances typically incorporate acting; written texts; choreography; projected film and slide sequences; puppets; visually rich set, costume, prop, and lighting designs; music; and sound. His productions are hybrids that are difficult to classify – they are sometimes said to be dance, sometimes theater, sometimes performance art. Chong originally called his performances "bricolage theater pieces," referring to anthropologist Claude Lévi-Strauss's concept of bricolage, defined by Chong as "new worlds created out of any and all materials at hand." He uses appropriated material in all dimensions of his productions, frequently borrowing from film. *Nosferatu* (1985) incorporates clips from F. W. Murnau's 1922 silent film and slides recreating the title cards from that film. The figure of the vampire, who in Chong's performance becomes an allegorical figure for the unacknowledged darknesses beneath the smooth surface of Reaganite America, is a live recreation of Murnau's filmic image. The plot of *Fear and Loathing in Gotham* (1975) derives from Fritz Lang's *M* (1931), while the action and visual style are related to film noir. But even as Chong invokes familiar films and styles, he undermines the expectations created by his allusions. The child murderer in *Fear and Loathing*, for instance, is not a psychopath but an Asian immigrant whose murderous rage arises out of frustration at his failure to assimilate to a new culture. Chong alludes to a familiar representation of madness to suggest that the pathology he addresses is social, rather than individual, in origin.

Like any good postmodernist, Chong leaps back and forth across boundaries – including those separating national cultures and that between high and low culture – in his appropriations. In *Nuit Blanche: A Select View of Earthlings* (1981), a performance whose scenes range across the globe and through historical time, Chong prefaces a staging of a Cambodian ritual he found described in a newspaper article with a video recording of the Apollo moon landing. Chong juxtaposes opera and Schubert with Jelly Roll Morton and

1950s pop ballads in *Kind Ness* (1986), a performance concerned with how a group of friends understand differences of ethnicity, class, and taste. Chong's dialogue generally contains familiar clichés, lines from popular songs, and references to television programs. Sometimes, this verbal appropriation is more extensive: the main characters of *Nosferatu*, a group of yuppies, speak largely in words Chong found in magazine articles about wealthy Manhattanites.

Chong not only combines media in hybrid performances, but hybridizes the media themselves. *Nuit Blanche* contains a slide sequence of a man walking down a road that uses a succession of still images to convey movement. Photography is thus hybridized with film, but also with theater, for the sequence probably represents the departure of a character's husband and is thus part of the unfolding live action. In *Kwaidan* (1998), a collaboration with designer Mitsuru Ishii and puppeteer Jon Ludwig based on Lafcadio Hearn's redactions of Japanese ghost stories, Chong recreates the visual syntax of film using theatrical means. In the opening scene of one story, a priest's trek through a mountainous region is played against a pen-and-ink landscape. As the priest nears his destination, larger puppets representing him are substituted for the smaller ones used initially, creating the effect of a cut from long-shot to medium-shot. The climactic scene, in which a demon devours a body over which the priest maintains a vigil, is presented as if shot from above. Chong thus hybridizes media in ways that suggest, contra modernist purism, that no one form has a monopoly on a particular visual language or set of conventions.

Chong's use of texts and narration in his performances renders them discursive in a way that conventional theater is not. He often uses projected texts to define the setting of a scene or to provide information not otherwise represented on stage. Sometimes, these texts are deliberately opaque, yet imply potential meanings. The opening of *Nuit Blanche* includes the projection of a slide bearing

> a name: Abigail Smith – a name that does not recur at any time during the play. Below the name a birth date dissolves into place, followed by the death date, and, finally the cause of death: Small pox. (Chong 1990: 7)

The audience is left to decide just who Abigail Smith may have been and what she has to do with the rest of the performance. *Snow* (Chong 1989b) provides an interesting example of another kind of discursivity. At one point, the stage directions describing a scene that has already occurred on stage are spoken aloud. The performance thus offers the same scene rendered in two different forms of discourse – the theatrical and the verbal. This device foregrounds the role of discursivity and textuality in the performance.

Chong's pieces also frequently incorporate that most discursive of perform-ance modes, the lecture. *Kind Ness* opens with a disembodied voice leading the audience through pairs of slides said to illustrate "What is similar and what is dissimilar" (Chong 1988: 39). *Deshima* (1990), described by Chong as "a poetic documentary" on the subject of Japanese history, has a narrator who provides historical information to the audience. Whereas the lecturing voice in *Kind Ness* argues for absurd similarities and differences between things and is clearly presented satirically, the displayed texts and narration in Chong's work more frequently bring an element of documentary presentation into his performances, making them hybrids of fact and fiction in which it is not always clear which elements are fictional and which factual, and what the relations between fact and fiction are.

Although most of Chong's performances are scripted and incorporate plot and dialogue, they bear little resemblance to conventional drama. The connections between scenes are usually associative rather than causal. *Snow*, for example, "cuts" back and forth among nine different locations in time and geography. The scenes in these locales have no specific relation-ship to one another except the presence of the titular weather phenomenon. The ultimate effect of Chong's storytelling style is that meaning arises more from the accumulation of characters, actions, images, information, and cul-tural allusions than from a causally structured plot.

Perhaps the central theme of Chong's work is the question of identity, also a major issue in philosophical explications of postmodernism. In statements and interviews, Chong always emphasizes that he sees his own identity as a Chinese-American in complex terms. From *Fear and Loathing in Gotham* through *Deshima* and beyond, he has built performances around explicitly Asian subject matter, focusing on the immigrant experience and the history of East–West political relations. Even as he points to the elements of "Asian aesthetics" that appear in his work, however, he resists classification as an Asian-American artist (Chong 1991: 91). He identifies himself, rather, as "a real American artist," underlining "the complexity of the cultural issue of being American." As an artist, Chong sees himself "using what the unmelting pot has to offer" (Chong 1989a: 65–6). For Chong, the term "American" stands for a rich complex of identity formations – including Eastern and Western cultural influences – that cannot be reduced to the unambiguous cultural identities embraced in some versions of identity politics.

Chong's views on identity resonate with postmodern perspectives. Philoso-pher Richard Schacht envisions the postmodern world as one in which "dominant cultures, peoples, social substances" will have been replaced by "a profusion of social and cultural formations, participation in any of which is optional and normatively neutral" (1996: 10). This would be a world "in which there no longer is anything in particular with which any particular person ought to identify, but rather only a decentered and deprivileged multiplicity of available alternative reference points" (Schacht 1996: 7). In his performances, Chong has thematized both the modern world of normative identities and the pain suffered by those who cannot conform to those norms, as in *Fear and Loathing in Gotham*, and the postmodern world in which the normative is losing its hold. A small but telling moment in *Kind Ness*, when one character quizzes his peers, illustrates the deteriorated state of the normative under postmodernism:

> Let's say you're walking through the forest and you sense a large black man carrying a pole. He is (a) a fisherman (*ALVIN raises his hand*) (b) a mugger – (*DOT raises her hand*) (c) God – (*DAPHNE raises her hand*) (d) a poacher. (*BUZZ raises his hand*) Very good. (Chong 1988: 78)

The speaker's approving response indicates that there is no "right" answer here, no normative, socially approved perception, not even a normative prejudice. Each character's reaction, derived from each one's experience and commitments, is valid.

Nuit Blanche can be seen as a representation of the historical transition to the postmodern world Schacht describes. An early scene, set in the 1800s on Estancia la Mariposa, a South American estate, clearly depicts an environment of rigid social norms and patterns of domination. At the end of the next scene, projected titles inform us that the world we have been looking at has fallen apart: the estate "is lost at the gaming tables." "Slavery is abolished," and the servant Berenice is free to make her way to the United States (Chong 1990: 12). The orderly world of clear social relations is gone.

The remainder of *Nuit Blanche* depicts aspects of a world in which social norms like those that governed life at Estancia la Mariposa no longer hold. The scenes in the United States involve a mulatto woman, also named Berenice, who has her own laundry business. Although seemingly locked into a hardscrabble rural life, this Berenice realizes that she has "always wanted to travel" (Chong 1990: 17). On that note, she walks away from her environment. When next we see her, she is rubbing shoulders with the jet set at an unnamed airport. This plotline depicts a postmodern world in which identity is self-defined and subject to change at a moment's notice. A similar freedom to choose one's own identity is enacted by Dot in *Kind Ness*. Dot, who is Jewish and blind, declares that she wants to go to Memphis "to be with my people." Her people turn out to be Blind Lemon Jefferson, Blind Willie McTell, Blind Boy Fuller, Big Mama Thornton, Bessie Smith, Ma Rainey, and John Lee Hooker (Chong 1988: 87). No explanation for Dot's identification with black blues artists is offered. Through the sequencing of blues artists in the list, Chong first encourages the assumption that blindness is the basis of

Dot's identification, then playfully undermines that assumption since only the first three figures named were blind. There is no traceable, traditionally identity-based reason for Dot's decision. She has simply chosen the cultural formation in which she wishes to participate.

Suzanne R. Westfall has pointed out that the absence of norms in the worlds Chong creates on stage leaves the audience as unmoored as his characters often seem to be. Discussing the vampire in Chong's *Nosferatu*, she suggests that we cannot evaluate this figure conventionally as a figure of horror:

> here, Nosferatu is designed to be striking in movement and costume, placed in a designer apartment with beautiful people. . . . In addition, the onstage audience, the characters, are utterly oblivious to the creatures. . . . Consequently, we in the theater have no cues, or rather contradictory cues, for the construction of our response. (1992: 367)

Since 1992, Chong has been engaged in a performance project that takes the issues of identity his work has long addressed as its only subject matter. Entitled *Undesirable Elements*, these "community-specific" performances are based on workshops Chong conducts for residents of various cities, including New York, Chicago, Minneapolis, Tokyo, and Rotterdam. In performance, the workshop participants, generally not professional performers, tell their own stories, sometimes in languages other than English; these stories are interwoven with information about their historical contexts. The participants' identities are revealed to be complex, multilayered, and not assimilable to simply defined categories. To cite but a single example, one participant is a white, female, French double-bass player who had been married to an African-American jazz musician, raised a biracial daughter, and moved to Chicago to play the blues. This musician, and all the participants in the various iterations of *Undesirable Elements* around the world, are postmodern subjects whose identities can be addressed fruitfully only in terms of a multiplicity of reference points (Schacht), not by reference to a cultural norm. By using "real" people drawn from the communities in which the piece is performed, Chong suggests that complex, bricolaged identities are not confined to theory or fiction. They are the rule, not the exception, in the postmodern world.

15

Ethan and Joel Coen

Joseph Natoli

Blood Simple (1983), the first major Coen Brothers release, is inevitably a film one goes back to look at as a "launch" to their careers after they have reached the point of having a "career." It means now in terms of, or in relation to, *Raising Arizona* (1987), *Barton Fink* (1991), *Fargo* (1995), *The Big Lebowski* (1998), and *O Brother, Where Art Thou?* (2000). And because there are qualities in those films now linked to the postmodern, we search *Blood Simple* for its postmodern qualities. We are also predisposed to thinking of those qualities as rudimentary and perhaps barely visible amid classic realist and twentieth-century modernist tones. It seems to be a retelling of Tay Garnett's *The Postman Always Rings Twice* (1946), a *film noir* with a Depression-era edge to it. There is the ugly – in every way – husband of Greek descent, the wife fed up with him, and her lover, an employee of the husband, the murder of the husband, and then the drama of fatal miscommunication between the lovers. The angst of twentieth-century modernism appears in the crack of *film noir*; a tragic vision is reconfigured within the classic realist design of Hollywood film while being duly loaded with the tensions and anxieties already expressed in twentieth-century literature, painting, and music. A postmodern slant to *film noir* samples both naive/classic realist and late modernist *film noir*. "Fear and trembling, sickness unto death" is at once in touch with a sly, witty parodying of the mood, a gleeful immersing in dark *film noir* waters, a rush onto all paths and possibilities without fear of getting back, within an ontological need of finally winding up *someplace* where there is a bit of light, a place to rest. It is a ride for the hell of it – a ride that we have to take, that we may think we are not taking but we are taking nonetheless. It is an unraveling, deconstructive journey – a nomadic wandering that has no clear beginning or end. Who is better than whom, what is better than what, is all in motion. We land someplace, we team up with someone, we pursue a thread of sense. At the same time, we are set in motion again or waiting to take off again.

Blood Simple does *Postman* all over again – self-consciously, so that *Postman* becomes a reality frame for *Blood Simple* whereas a dark reality that cannot be calibrated, theorized, or illuminated is the outside framing of *Postman*. The ontological *mise en scène* of the modernist *noir* is this: darkness swells up out of our own natures and that opaqueness peers out at a world saturated with either its own darkness or ours or both. Of the postmodernist *noir* it is this: darkness swells up out of the *film noir* concoction of reality and we play into it, into its ins and outs, twists and turns, ups and downs, angles and curves, replacing late modernist dread with postmodern storytelling of dread, replacing a direct exposure to an ever-darkening reality with a variety of send-ups of both how we hook up with reality and what that reality may be. Our dread is not absolutist, our confrontation not universalist; instead dread is relative to the story this character is in, and this character's reality-making, while riddled by cultural stories, has no universalist pretensions. It has no claim on us; we are going along for the ride; what is at stake is not our ability to grasp what is real and true for all of reality has turned *noir*. Or the *noir* is at the center. Reality is narrated as *noir*.

We go from the darkness of a postmodern *noir* in *Blood Simple* to the snowy whiteness of *Fargo*. The ludic quality of *Raising Arizona* is in *Fargo* shifted into a postmodern frame, and the Coen Brothers will reproduce this ludic postmodernism in *The Big Lebowski*. The intermediary film that works into the ways in which we frame or narrate reality, and see within the limitations of that framing and narrating, is *Barton Fink*. And because this film is focused on narrating the theory of multiple realities it is most frequently cited as an example of the postmodern aspect of the Coen brothers' work. Interestingly and perhaps ironically, *Barton Fink* has the same sort of postured, abstract quality that typifies the avant-garde, and that we find in a film like David Lynch's *Eraserhead* (1976). There is a kind of comic carnivalesque in both films, a farcical wit and playfulness that is heavily lidded by the concentrated style that is adopted. Both films therefore have an arty, experimental quality, seem filled with arcane symbolism in a late modernist manner. But while Lynch's jump from the studied contrivances of *Eraserhead* to a clash of contrivances in *Blue Velvet* (1986), from avant-garde modernism to postmodernism, is unprecedented, the Coen brothers' jump from *Barton Fink* to *Fargo* and *The Big Lebowski* comes out of a postmodern filmic world Lynch had already screened.

We journey into two radically different life-worlds in *Fargo*. If we consider them first on the level of personal life-worlds, we have Marge and Norm Gunderson, sheriff and bird painter respectively, and then Karl and Gar, kidnappers and murderers. But Marge and Norm also share a social-cultural life-world in the town of Brainerd, Minnesota, home of Paul Bunyan and Babe the Blue Ox. There is a regional quality here, revealed in vestiges of a slow, melodic Scandinavian speech rhythm; we are in a cultural enclave within America, one of the many differing cultural life-worlds that yet are part of the American social order. We are in *The Brainerd Show*, into a special box of ice and cold. From the perspective of the "mainstream," "normative" America that TV has shown us for the past fifty years, the Brainerd world is different, loaded with funny provincial mannerisms, slow-paced, a Mayberry-ish un-hipness, out of step with the times, not in the 1990s, not thinking globally but only reacting locally, marking time not digitally but by the *Farmer's Almanac*. "Gotta eat breakfast," Norm tells Marge. "I'll fix you some eggs." And he does so and later on Marge tells her deputy that Norm fixed her some eggs. The old protocols, the old traditions of life-faring apply here; there are no fads and fashions around to challenge them. It is as if here in these cold northern regions of the Midwest, no one has heard that reality has been replaced by simulacra, that the hyperreal has buried the real.

Where we are going in *Fargo* plotwise pales in interest compared to *how* we are going and how others go in *Fargo*. And we go in accord with our own reality maps, our own timescapes, our own culturally and socially saturated life-worlds. On a path to solving a crime, to finding murderers and kidnappers, we nonetheless live in a world in which people are on other paths and taking different journeys. At 11:30 at night, Mike Nagageeta, a voice from Marge's past, calls her up and wants to get together. Ironically, of course, Marge and Mike only appear to get together; in actuality, they fly past each other. He remains a mystery to her; she solves the murder mystery, but Mike remains a mystery. She is unable to go from the Brainerd reality to the Nagageeta reality. She has no problem connecting with husband Norm, whose daily reality-constructing makes sense to Marge, and neither one of them has any problem in this regard with any of their Brainerd neighbors. They all hook up on the same mental mapping; but Mike throws Marge for a loop. She is surprised that nothing Mike told her turns out to be true. Surprise is no clash; she does not take a step into Mike's world. She stays in Brainerd. In the same fashion, Mike's inexplicability throws the viewer for a loop: the scene makes no sense in the murder plot; it is mystifying; it is a surprise. If you put the surprise behind you as something senseless, as a lapse in the filmmakers' art, and you pick up on the murder plot that you have a map for, then you do not go very far into the postmodern world of *Fargo*.

The ludic quality of a Coen brothers' film comes out of their fascination with the sheer variety of ways in which their characters know, identify, and produce reality and the expected and unexpected ways these characters run into each other. Anticipating clashes of reality frames is part of our audience enjoyment. But the ludic quality reaches toward us, toward our own perceptions, the priorities of our own seeing, the formulae by which we convert seeing into knowing, the inescapableness of producing for ourselves a reality that confirms and actualizes our way of knowing. Every character's way of being in the world is a send-up; but ours is not. These characters live in stories of reality that come right off TV and cereal boxes; but ours does not. We are in touch with reality directly. And we prove our exclusive grasp of "things as they really are" by mastering the lives and worlds the Coen brothers put on display for us. Failure to dominate these worlds and the "meaning" of these films throws us precipitously into the realities we presume our reality surpasses. Thus, the ludic quality of a Coen brothers' film leads us to a defensiveness as we distance our lives from those on the screen, and an offensiveness as we muster up a critique of a filmic reality that lacks coherence, continuity, and closure.

The Big Lebowski pushes us to wondering whether we are unable to command its subject because we are right and there is no subject, there is no rug that ties the whole room together, or that the fact that we are unable to command its subject and are wondering why is precisely what the film's subject has led us to. We discover a "sense of vacancy" in this film and wonder where the "grownup reality" is. Yet, this sense of vacancy is a presence in this film. The film first registers from our "grownup reality" as unplotted, less than purposeful, fractured, disconnected, ludic, maze-like, discordant, surrealistic, incoherent, a jumble, a farrago.

What does it appear like to the Coen brothers? We know from the film *Fargo* that they have a real grip on grownup reality as presently being manufactured in the Midwest. And they cannot see the whole of it without seeing the ludic, farrago dimensions of that reality. For them it appears that grownup reality is always already filled to the brim with unstoppable mania, is always tending to bring its own sobriety and control onto the snowy drifts of the cockamamie where the hard, cold edges of grownup reality finally melt away in the sun. In *The Big Lebowski* all of the grownup reality the Dude becomes entangled in gives way to a musical number *à la* Busby Berkeley. And when the Dude is hit over the head and things grow dark as they do for Dick Powell in Edward Dmytryk's *Farewell, My Lovely* (1944), the Dude does not fall into a deep, dark pool and wind up running through a dark corridor of endless doors pursued by who knows what. Instead, he flies like Superman with arms spread wide over Los Angeles at night with all its lights fluttering below. He has a great, happy smile on his face; he surely dreams he can fly away. And then he is embracing a bowling ball, a look of surprise on his face, as he plummets downward, his flight canceled. He is weighted down and it is the weight of real-world gravity.

As in *Fargo*, all real-world gravity passes through human mediation, which gives it this role or that, assigning it wherever our "sense of realism" sees fit. The Coen brothers greet grownup reality with a "sense of vacancy" and rather than put on *gravitas* they try to take a look at things as if they themselves were not obliged to obey the laws of grownup reality. The roll of the bowling ball, like the Dude's flight over LA, is a metaphor of travel Coen brothers' style, a style of travel it is profitless to object to. Unless you are thoroughly convinced that grownups can and should travel only one way across a reality that allows for only that perspective of travel. Once you settle in for the ride on the Coen brothers' terms you can see that every character in the film, not just the Dude and his bowling buddies, are coming at reality from separate lanes. If reality is only ahead in our lane and if we are the only ones with the proper bowling form, we are the only ones bowling like grownups, then the plot and perspective on lane 50 should mean nothing to us. On the other hand, if you take a postmodern view of things – and the Coen brothers do – then you are going to bowl laterally. Maybe your game will improve and your "sense of realism" expand; maybe your empty frame will get filled in and your "sense of vacancy" shifted back out to empty space. But the ludic postmodernism of the Coen brothers generates the opposite also: your "sense of realism" will contract as you experience a "sense of vacancy" you once could fill but no longer can.

16

Robert Coover

Robert L. McLaughlin

Robert Coover's contribution to our current conception of postmodernism has been his career-long exploration of narrative, especially its power to determine our knowledge and experience of the world. In his fiction Coover recognizes the human need to create coherent, meaning-supplying narratives out of the disparate phenomena of the world, demonstrates the dangerous power these narratives can acquire, and plays with the potentially liberating subversion of these narratives.

In his early works Coover focuses on the paranoiac tendency to find patterns and significance in a chaotic world. His characters' will to interpret results in narratives that support and manifest epistemological belief systems, systems that accrue power far out of proportion to the trivial or mundane phenomena that inspire them. *The Origin of the Brunists* (1966), which follows a millenarian cult from its beginnings in the wake of a mine disaster to its institutionalization as a world religion, illustrates and critiques this process. The cult arises from the need of the West Condon townspeople to find meaning in the explosion that kills dozens of miners and puts many more out of work when the mine is permanently closed; the lighting of a cigarette seems too insignificant to justify such catastrophic results. The hermeneutic enterprises focus variously on the reflections off walls of the miners' headlamps, a dying miner's unfinished and ambiguous note, a charred hand from a miner's body, and the pronouncements of a miraculously rescued but mentally disturbed miner, Giovanni Bruno.

In stressing their insignificance, the novel suggests that the signs are chosen based on how well they can be accommodated to existing belief systems, some widely recognized, some eccentric. The local fundamentalist Christians, Eleanor Norton with her logbooks of automatic writing, Ralph Himebaugh with his chartings of worldwide disasters, the various historic revelatory texts Justin Miller prints in the *Chronicle*, are all discursive systems that can accommodate and make apocalyptic sense of the post-mine-disaster signs.

Moreover, the signs provide the means for these separate systems to become mutually supporting (Norton and Himebaugh "both had staked their lives on some unspecified but cataclysmic event to which they believed their own destinies linked – each lent credence, that is to the other's central hope" [260]), synthesizing into a new belief system with enhanced power.

As this suggests, this meaning-making process becomes stabilized and legitimized as it becomes narratized. Unofficial narratives, gossip and rumors about the Brunists, help to define the group as a group to its members. Then, when the *Chronicle* exposes the Brunists and the national media pick up the story, an official narrative of the cult is created with two results. First, the narrative, in completing the process of finding patterns among signs and significance in the patterns, stabilizes the Brunists' epistemological system by supplying a beginning and middle (incidents now linked narratively into causally related events) to an anticipated end: the end of the world. Up to this point, the Brunists have articulated their end – the apocalypse – and now their various, mutually supporting discursive systems are brought together into a coherent narrative. The second result is a legitimization of the Brunists' epistemological system. Response to the story reaffirms the significance of the hermeneutic pattern: as one Brunist says, "it certainly is another sign we're on the right track.... [It] just has *got* to *mean* something!" (398). This leads to a Weberian rationalization of the group, where their *raison d'être*, the apoca-lypse, becomes secondary to organizing a hierarchy of authority and articulat-ing doctrine.

Coover's novel critiques this entire process in its form and content. Espe-cially in its multiple narrative focalizations, it offers alternative versions of the signs, patterns, and significances to those that the Brunists embrace. These alternatives, by their very presence, undercut the Brunist narrative and the epistemology it supports. This critique is mirrored by the parodic stories of the Last Judgment that Miller receives in the mail from his lover. These stories mock the end that the Brunist narrative anticipates. Implied here is a recognition of the power of narratives and also a cautious suggestion that knowledge can be liberated from would-be totalizing narratives, perhaps through play.

More recently, Coover's focus has moved to an examination of the wide-ranging cultural narratives that worm their way into our consciousnesses and continually regulate our experience of the world. As one character in *Gerald's Party* (1986) puts it, "we learned our lines about love... from fairy tales, then went out in the world and acted them out, not even knowing why it was we had to do it" (74). Coover's method is to undermine the epistemological power of cultural narratives by rewriting them: parodying their conventions and revealing their areas of slippage. His subjects are sometimes specific works – the Cat in the Hat in *A Political Fable* (1980), *Casablanca* in "*You Must*

Remember This" (1987b), *Pinocchio* in *Pinocchio in Venice* (1991), Sleeping Beauty in *Briar Rose* (1996a) – and sometimes entire genres – Westerns in *Ghost Town* (1998) and mysteries in *Gerald's Party*.

In parodying mysteries, *Gerald's Party* explores three issues fundamental to the genre and to our knowledge of ourselves and our world: attention, by which we perceive the phenomena around us, used to notice and understand clues; memory, by which we understand the past, used to elicit testimony and recover clues; representation, by which past events are turned into a coherent story, used to present the solution to the mystery. The novel problematizes all of these, subverting the genre and our reliance on them to make sense of a chaotic world.

The novel is narrated entirely from Gerald's point of view and, excepting a few brief gaps, follows a continuous action, from the discovery of the body at a crowded party to Gerald going to sleep after everyone has finally gone home. Thus the limitations of Gerald's attention are constantly foregrounded: we see how much in the absurdly wild party Gerald misses or notices but misunderstands; there is far too much information for Gerald to sort out and understand. Readers share his confusion as we try to keep track of the seemingly infinite number of partygoers and clues. When, at the end, Gerald says to his wife, instead of "I love you," "You focus . . . my attention . . . " (315, Coover's ellipses), we realize how rarely we have a moment in which our consciousness is focused on its surroundings rather than distracted.

Memory is similarly problematized. It is unreliable, as we see when the various partygoers remember the spot where the first body was found differently. It is also uncontrollably selective, as Gerald realizes: "I found myself running over the night's events in my mind as though hunting for dangerous gaps in the story (but it was the gaps I seemed to remember, the events having faded)" (20). More troubling, because our experiences are always mediated by the many cultural narratives that permeate our consciousness, memories are not necessarily even tied to a past event. As Gerald reflects, "Memories, I realized . . . always come before the experiences we attach them to" (13).

Representation in a mystery comes when the detective presents a narrative representing the story of the murder. This narratizing is an ordering process, bringing coherence and meaning to seemingly disparate and insignificant events. However, in this mystery several attempts to represent the events fail. Nothing the Inspector and his policemen do to recreate the events leading up to the murder, from confiscating all the witnesses' watches to tearing apart a stuffed rabbit to torturing witnesses, makes any sense – much less makes sense of the murder. Moreover, the police add to the chaos, killing at least two more people. When the Inspector announces that the murder has been solved and the police haul someone off to jail, there is no narrative explanation of how this solution was arrived at. Similarly, a play about the murder, performed by the victim's theater friends in the living room and using her body as a character, reveals the participants' eccentricities but provides no meaning for the event. Another attempt to represent the evening's events is in the many videocassettes Gerald and his wife find. This taping of the evening not only fails to provide coherence (the variously labeled cassettes fragment the evening into episodes), but it records an evening that has in many ways eluded Gerald. His wife remonstrates, "You were at a different party" (312). Gerald's experience suggests that in representing life, art offers us multiple versions of the present: which is the *real* one is anybody's guess.

Coover, then, uses the conventions of the mystery novel in order to confuse them and the meaning-making process they enable. He blurs the boundaries between attention, memory, and representation, as representation (in the form of cultural narratives) shapes memory and memory precedes perception. Coover's parody critiques the forms narratives provide to order life; it reveals the arbitrary and contingent nature of the truth these narratives make possible.

Coover's most complex critique of the epistemological power of narratives unfolds in his masterpiece, *The Public Burning* (1977). This highly stylized retelling of the events leading up to the execution of Julius and Ethel Rosenberg captures the web of discourses that we find in the defining American narratives and offers an unlikely candidate to uncover the void they mask – Vice-President Richard Nixon. The novel's structure – chapters focusing on Uncle Sam, personification of American ideology, alternate with chapters narrated by Nixon, while in the intermezzos and elsewhere, historic discourses are presented in experimental forms – reveals, explores, and critiques the workings of power behind the stories of America.

Uncle Sam's discourse is a jumbled parody of American phrases and ideas: "It is our manifest dust-in-yer-eye to overspread the continent allotted by Providence for the free development of our yearly multiplyin' millions, so damn the torpedoes and full steam ahead" (8). His speech both scatters symbolic cues – words that recall longer narratives from American history – and indiscriminately links them, as if to suggest that the individual historicity of each is irrelevant since each is an instance of a larger master narrative: America's divinely granted authority and duty to have dominion over the world. The Rosenbergs' execution must go on, despite questions about their guilt, because it fits in so well with this master narrative, both in the largest sense – US Manifest Destiny struggling to fulfill itself while in conflict with the eternal adversary, the Phantom – and in the most immediate – Soviet aggression in Korea and East Berlin made possible by possession of the A-bomb and thus by the Rosenbergs' betrayal. The story is too good to let facts interfere.

In his chapters Nixon alternates between self-mythologizing, creating his own Franklinesque life story, and reconstructing the case against the Rosenbergs, discovering its many flaws. Oddly, the more he investigates, the more his story and the Rosenbergs' merge; the less secure he feels in his own identity, the more he wonders how small incidents might have made him a different person (an idea Coover later explores in *Whatever Happened to Gloomy Gus of the Chicago Bears?* [1987a]). This leads him to a startling revelation about the power of narrative:

> all men contain all views ... and only an artificial – call it political – commitment to consistency makes them hold steadfast to singular positions. Yet why be consistent if the universe wasn't? In a lawless universe, there was a certain power in consistency, of course – *but there was also power in disruption!* ... I'd understood at last the real meaning of the struggle against the Phantom: *it was a war against the lie of purpose!* (363)

Nixon sees this revelation as a political opportunity: he can use the Rosenberg case as a way of revealing the void at the center of American ideology, and then offer himself as something to believe in. But when Ethel Rosenberg refuses to cooperate, Nixon quickly reclaims his position of most faithful acolyte to Uncle Sam.

Exposing the factitiousness of the American ideology is also the point of the novel's heteroglossia – the many historic texts Coover inserts into his narration: *Time*, the *New York Times*, the Rosenbergs' letters to each other and their sons, trial transcripts, speeches by the President, a play, *The Valiant*, in which Ethel Rosenberg had acted. This heteroglossia works in two ways. First, the very number of texts and the stylized way in which they are presented (as poetry, in an opera) defamiliarize them; their textuality is stressed, their authority is subverted, and their associated ideologies are made suspect. Second, the resulting Bakhtinian dialogue decenters the totalizing impulse of the official American narratives and their implied ideology. This is best seen in the second intermezzo where Ethel Rosenberg's clemency appeal is put into dialogue with President Eisenhower's response. Eisenhower's desire to make his decision and the executions fit coherently with the larger American narratives about law, justice, and democracy is undercut by Ethel's claiming those ideals as the basis for her logic. The final impression is that the Rosenbergs, rather than having betrayed America, have been betrayed by their own naive belief in the truth of the stories America tells about itself.

The result here, as in much of Coover's work, reveals the factitious way in which epistemological narratives are constructed, the dangerous power these narratives can attain, and the necessity of challenging their power through parodic alternative narratives. These ideas, central to Coover's oeuvre, are also central to our understanding of postmodernism.

17

Gilles Deleuze and Félix Guattari

Ronald Bogue

Gilles Deleuze (1925–95) published over twenty works of philosophy, including studies of Hume, Nietzsche, Bergson, Kant, Proust, Sacher-Masoch, Spinoza, Foucault, and Leibniz, as well as *Difference and Repetition* (1969), *The Logic of Sense* (1969), *Cinema 1* (1983), *Cinema 2* (1985), and *Essays Critical and Clinical* (1993). Félix Guattari (1930–92), a psychoanalyst and political activist, wrote several wide-ranging works, including *Psychoanalysis and Transversality* (1972), *The Molecular Revolution* (1977), *The Three Ecologies* (1989), *Schizoanalytic Cartographies* (1989), and *Chaosmosis* (1992). The two are perhaps best known, however, for their jointly authored works: *Anti-Oedipus* (1972), *Kafka: Towards a Minor Literature* (1975), *A Thousand Plateaus* (1980), and *What Is Philosophy?* (1991).

There is good reason not to label Deleuze and Guattari "postmodern." Deleuze hardly mentions the term, and in "The Postmodern Impasse" (1996 [1986]) Guattari formulates a brief but blistering critique of postmodernism, describing it as "nothing but the last gasp of modernism; nothing, that is, but a reaction to and, in a certain way, a mirror of the formalist abuses and reductions of modernism from which, in the end, it is no different" (109). Some commentators on Deleuze and Guattari have followed this line of argument, Goodchild, for example, seeking to wrest their thought from "the unproductive black hole of 'postmodernism'" (Goodchild 1996: 139), and Murphy suggesting that they be viewed as proponents of "amodernism," a tendency that "does not succeed postmodernism, but contests it throughout the postwar period" (Murphy 1997: 23). Nonetheless, Deleuze and Guattari are frequently cited as important forces in postmodern thought. Indeed, in their *Postmodern Theory* (1991), Best and Kellner treat Deleuze and Guattari, along with Foucault, Baudrillard, Lyotard, and Jameson, as primary exponents of postmodern theory, and Niall Lucy devotes a full chapter to their writings in his *Postmodern Literary Theory* (1997). The problem, of course, is that "postmodern" has been used in many different and often incompatible ways, such that even those who accept the label must also distance themselves from others who bear the same designation. Though no single definition of the postmodern fits Deleuze and Guattari neatly, several features deemed postmodern in diverse definitions do characterize their thought. Perhaps we should treat Deleuze and Guattari as inventors of a unique mode of postmodern thought, one that offers creative options within the "postmodern condition" and pathways beyond the "postmodern impasse."

For Deleuze and Guattari, as for many theorists of the postmodern condition, the mechanisms and operations of advanced capitalism are central for understanding the contemporary world. Their take on capitalism, however, does not lead to a passive acceptance of the play of simulacra, *à la* Baudrillard, nor to the abandonment of collective political action save at the local level (a stance Guattari attributes to Lyotard [Guattari 1996/1986: 110–11]). In *Anti-Oedipus* (1983 [1972]), Deleuze and Guattari develop a theory of universal "desiring-production," an incessant and ubiquitous creation of flows and fluxes of affective intensity that connect the heterogeneous components of the material world in multiple and dispersed circuits of activity. They identify two poles in desiring-production, a schizophrenic movement of deterritorialization, whereby fixed codes and regular power relations are uncoded and disrupted, and a paranoiac movement of reterritorialization, whereby codes and power relations are reestablished in organized and restricted circuits of interaction (Deleuze and Guattari 1983 [1972]: 366). The history of capitalism is that of a continual deterritorialization of stable social relations – kinship systems, religious practices, class hierarchies, taboos, etc. – through the conversion of coded and incommensurable elements of the world into commodities capable of being substituted for one another in an indifferent and undetermined system of exchange. But capitalism also continually reterritorializes social relations to ensure its own regular operation, reactivating dead codes and institutions in a cynical pastiche of past practices. The features of contemporary Western culture often deemed postmodern – universal commodification, the reign of simulacra and surface images, the full integration of consumption within production, the waning of affect – are simply the inevitable effects of capitalism's simultaneous processes of deterritorialization and reterritorialization.

Yet Deleuze and Guattari insist that the proliferation of simulacra in a commodity culture of consumption need not induce helpless acquiescence. Primary in desiring-production is deterritorialization, and throughout the social sphere there are points of disequilibrium, zones of instability that may be exacerbated and thereby converted into areas of creative transformation. Inherent in capitalism's tendency to decode and unfix power relations is a revolutionary potential that may be activated through an intensification of destabilizing forces that traverse the social field. And that activation of destabilizing forces may proceed through collective groups of various sizes. Deleuze and Guattari contrast molar and molecular desire throughout *Anti-Oedipus*, and much of their analysis of power anticipates the micropolitics of Foucault's *Discipline and Punish* (1977 [1975]). But the distinction is qualitative rather than quantitative, molar and molecular designating not relative size but modes of relation, the one hierarchical and totalizing, the other nonhierarchical and decentered. Crucial for Deleuze and Guattari is the difference between *subjected groups*, whose identities are prescribed by existing power formations, and *subject groups*, which produce new social relations through unpredictable metamorphoses of power configurations (Deleuze and Guattari 1983 [1972]: 348). The mode of relation of subject groups is molecular, but they may function in diverse quantitative dimensions. Hence, revolutionary political action may involve local struggles and micro-relations, but it may extend as well to broad collectivities and alliances.

Such an analysis of capitalism might imply a foundational ontology, but in this regard Deleuze and Guattari are simply following a strategy common to many postmodern thinkers (Hutcheon 1993) – that of simultaneously asserting and undermining "master narratives," critiquing old accounts and inventing new, with an ironic recognition of the constructed nature of their own models. Deleuze and Guattari's thought is resolutely antifoundational, for in their view "philosophy is always a matter of inventing concepts" (Deleuze 1995: 136), not a matter of representing truth. "There's no truth that doesn't 'falsify' established ideas. To say that 'truth is created' implies that the production of truth involves a series of operations that amount to working on a material – strictly speaking, a series of falsifications" (Deleuze 1995: 126). Yet their philosophy is neither textualist nor constructivist, for it presumes no priority of language or the subject in the production of thought. Language is a mode of action for Deleuze and Guattari. It functions through heterogeneous patterns of power relations that combine practices, institutions, and material entities in separate discursive and nondiscursive "assemblages" (Deleuze and Guattari 1987 [1980]: 88). Words intervene in things, but things take form, interact, and in turn shape practices through processes of differentiation that are distinct from those that produce language. (In this regard, Deleuze sees Foucault's thought as similar to his own [Deleuze 1988: 47–69].) In no sense, then, is Deleuze and Guattari's antifoundationalism a function of a universal play of free-floating signifiers. Nor is it a function of a subject freely constructing a perspective view of the world. Thought proceeds via problems, but problems are not chosen; they impinge on thought, inducing involuntary movements of disequilibrium. Both thought and the thinker emerge in a field of unfolding, self-differentiating differences, the problem that instigates thought being one with a specific configuration of multiple discursive and nondiscursive circuits of activity. The thinker as biological entity growing and interacting in the material world, for example, is inseparable from the problem that impinges on and informs thought. Hence, though philosophy's invention of concepts is contingent, it is not arbitrary, for it follows the lines traced by the problem that unfolds within and as part of the unfolding of a particular world. In short, the thinker does not select the thought so much as the problem-world selects the thinker and the thought.

In their approach to the arts, Deleuze and Guattari do not adopt a typically postmodern stance. They do move freely between works of popular and high culture with indifference to that distinction, especially in *A Thousand Plateaus*, and in this regard they exhibit what Huyssen has identified as a basic postmodern sensibility, but like many other French poststructuralists, they concentrate much of their attention on canonical works of high modernism. (It is this tendency that leads Huyssen to describe poststructuralism as "a theory of modernism" [Huyssen 1993: 136] rather than postmodernism.) Yet their handling of such writers as Proust, Kafka, Woolf, Fitzgerald, Artaud, and Beckett challenges standard modernist readings of these figures. In *Kafka: Towards a Minor Literature*, for example, they reject the received images of Kafka as Oedipal cripple, reclusive "writer's writer," ascetic mystic, or melancholic chronicler of modern alienation and *angst*, arguing instead that he is the creator of an apersonal literary machine that is immediately social and political and imbued with joy and humor. Far from retreating from the world, Kafka detects the "diabolical powers of the future" (Deleuze and Guattari 1986 [1975]: 83) of fascist, Soviet, and capitalist bureaucracies immanent within the Austro-Hungarian Empire. He experiments on the representations of institutions and social relations that circulate in his world, tracing networks of power that pass through the most intimate and the most public spheres alike. He also experiments on the German spoken by Prague Jews, discovering points of variation and disequilibrium that allow him to fashion a foreign language within his own tongue, to induce a stuttering strangeness in his German that is immanent within the language and its social usage. Finally, his letters, diaries, short stories, and novels function as parts of a literary machine plugged into familial, social, and political circuits, a machine defined solely by its movements – its blockages and flows, fits and starts – decentered, non-unified, anindividual.

Deleuze and Guattari find similar literary machines in writers ranging from Kleist, Melville, Lawrence, and Miller to such contemporary figures as Gherasim Luca and Carmelo Bene, thereby suggesting a selective line of filiation that extends from Romanticism through Modernism to the present. The twin principles of aesthetic experimentation and political engagement that inform this antitradition are those of the historical avant-garde (Dada, Surrealism, etc.); the features of dispersion, multiplicity, and asubjectivity are common to many works that revive the historical avant-garde project in what Hal Foster has labeled "a postmodernism of resistance" (Foster 1983: xii). But what is most postmodern about Deleuze and Guattari's approach to the arts is the way they relate the themes of difference, otherness, multiplicity, and becoming to issues of gender, sexuality, race, and class (see Huyssen 1993: 148–9). The artists Deleuze and Guattari admire engage in "minor" practices that contest majority norms and standards. Whatever their actual numbers, white Western male adults constitute the majority, by which various minorities – nonwhites, non-Westerners, women, and children – are measured, categorized, and regulated. Dominant social codes construct and instill majority values, the conventional structures of language, images, practices, and institutions reinforcing and reiterating relations of power and control. For Deleuze and Guattari, resistance must proceed through a becoming-other, a passage between the preestablished categories of male/female, white/non-white, adult/ child, human/nonhuman, that passage constituting a "becoming-woman," "becoming-black," "becoming-child," "becoming-animal" that undoes the binary oppositions of social codes and makes possible the invention of new forms of thought and interaction. The experimentations of writers, painters, and musicians whom Deleuze and Guattari admire are not mere formal innovations in words, images, and sounds, but modes of action that engage immanent relations of power, destabilize them, and open up possibilities for their transformation. The various "becomings" these artists create thereby reinforce the processes of becoming-woman, becoming-black, and becoming-non-Western that play a vital role in the political struggles of gender, racial, and class minorities.

Perhaps it is in their own practice as writers of philosophy, however, that Deleuze and Guattari are most postmodern, for their works both articulate and enact a thought of becoming, difference, multiplicity, and heterogeneity. This is particularly the case with *A Thousand Plateaus*, a collection of fifteen "plateaus" that may be read in any sequence (save the conclusion, which should be read at the end). Each plateau forms a "plane of consistency," a kind of surface of heterogeneous elements that cohere through the trajectories of the becomings, variations, and metamorphoses that fill the surface. If there is a unity to each plateau, it is that of an added part, an extra component produced by the elements that occupy the plateau, yet a part paradoxically presupposed by those elements. The relation between elements of a plateau is that of a "disjunctive synthesis," a paralogical combining through differentiation, the components forming a qualitative rather than a quantitative multiplicity, that is, a multiplicity whose qualities change with any change in the number or nature of its constituents. Within each plateau, various concepts are formulated, extended, and transformed as they are traced through various fields, disciplines, and discourses. In Plateau 14, the concepts of smooth and striated space are elaborated in studies of textiles, music, maritime strategies, mathematics, physics, and art history. Plateau 11 unfolds the concept of the refrain in the domains of music and animal ethology. Plateau 10 treats becomings in horror films, novels, shamanism, warrior cults, music, art, and philosophy.

The various plateaus intersect, coincide, and diverge with one another, suggesting multiple interconnections and zones of resonance. And together they delineate a composite plane of consistency, which comprises the disjunctively synthesized multiplicity called *A Thousand Plateaus*.

Most important, however, is Deleuze and Guattari's compositional *modus operandi*. In *A Thousand Plateaus*, they remark that "it is not enough to say 'Long live the multiple,' difficult as it is to raise that cry. No typographical, lexical, or even syntactical cleverness is enough to make it heard. The multiple *must be made* [Le multiple, *il faut le faire*]" (Deleuze and Guattari 1987 [1980]: 6). Deleuze and Guattari's means of making and doing the multiple is to write together in a manner unprecedented in philosophy. In creating *A Thousand Plateaus*, they report taking turns composing now a sentence, now a paragraph or page in different plateaus, revising as they proceeded, but leaving everywhere traces of the text's genesis. The result is a work whose content and form are genuinely multiple, the creation of no single subject. The concepts, organizational schema, vocabulary, rhythms, and tone are at once distinct and composite, a recognizable plural voice and thought irreducible to either writer's individual style or to a mere juxtaposition of the two. What one reads is an open-ended, dispersional novel of a thought thinking itself into diverging series in compound terminologies and registers, the production not of Deleuze, Guattari, or Deleuze and Guattari, but of the hybrid, multiple – even monstrous – Deleuze–Guattari.

Deleuze and Guattari's is a postmodernism of resistance. They acknowledge late capitalism's play of simulacra, yet they find ample possibilities for creative transformations of social relations through political action in varying spheres of engagement. They reject all forms of foundationalism, but they steer clear as well from the traps of the textualist prisonhouse of language and the implicit voluntarism of constructivist relativism. Their thought is contingent yet necessary, emergent within an unfolding field of discursive and nondiscursive differences that elicits a creative thought-action across a pragmatic domain of forces and concepts. Their aesthetic ignores distinctions of high and low culture and embraces the avant-garde project of fusing formal experimentation and political intervention. The genuine work of art they see as decentered, nonunified, and asubjective, immediately social, and engaged with the struggles of minorities in its diverse minor becomings – becoming-woman, becoming-black, becoming-child, becoming-animal. And in their own writing they adhere to the principles of difference, multiplicity, heterogeneity, and becoming, generating conceptual planes of consistency in a plural voice. In sum, if the postmodern is an irresoluble condition or inescapable impasse, then indeed Deleuze and Guattari are not postmodern theorists, but if it is a specific social, historical, philosophical, and aesthetic situation capable of instigating transformative responses, then they are key figures of the postmodern era.

18

Don DeLillo

Christopher Douglas

"Is DeLillo a postmodern writer or is he a pathologist of postmodernism?" one anxious critic has recently inquired (Cantor 1991: 58). The answer to this too simply formulated question is not a modern either/or, but, fittingly, a postmodern both/and. Born in 1936, Don DeLillo is a difficult novelist of ideas whose work obsessively analyzes the contemporary moment. His provocative subject matters – from advertising, rock music, and sports, to mathematics, language, cults, crowds, disasters, and the assassination of President Kennedy – are made more complicated by some mild formal innovation, and his work has, until recently, been better received by academics and the reviewing press than the reading public. DeLillo's status as a "postmodern" writer may surprise, considering the fact that his work can only marginally be considered in terms of a *formal*, literary postmodernism. Although several critics consider his first three novels metafictional, the novels' quality of self-referentiality is slight in comparison to contemporaries like John Barth and Robert Coover. On the other hand, many consider his 1988 novel *Libra* to be an example of what Linda Hutcheon (1988) has termed historiographic metafiction, with its historiographic ruminations developed by a narrator-character who, charged with the task of writing the secret history of President Kennedy's assassination for the CIA, complains that historical information is being hidden even from him. DeLillo can better be considered postmodern in the *thematic* sense: he is an author whose work, since the early 1970s, has registered certain currents within what Raymond Williams would call the "structure of feeling" known as postmodernism.

Among these currents four stand out in DeLillo's work as narrative fixations to which he repeatedly returns. First is his fascination with popular culture and its incorporation into his fiction in such a way that characterizes postmodernism against the aesthetic of high modernism, as Andreas Huyssen (1986) and Fredric Jameson (1991) make clear. Second is a loss of a sense of originals, which appears in DeLillo's work to be a fictional working out of the theoretical discourse associated with Jean Baudrillard. Third is a mood of simultaneous historylessness and desire for historical context; we see in DeLillo's work "an attempt to think the present historically in an age that has forgotten how to think historically in the first place" (Jameson 1991: ix), but also, maybe, the symptoms of our very inability to think about our present. Finally, DeLillo's postmodernism shares a trait with another American post-modernist, Thomas Pynchon: a mood of paranoia and a suspicion of design.

These four currents have preoccupied DeLillo's critics as well. DeLillo is celebrated as a commentator on contemporary media and popular culture and their daily effects. DeLillo's engagement with popular culture appeared when his fiction first came to light, with advertising in *Americana* (1971), with sports in *End Zone* (1972), and with rock music in *Great Jones Street* (1973). What continues to dominate the critical reactions to his work is the question of DeLillo's attitude toward the culture(s) he portrays – as cultural critic or as enthusiast of such contemporary manifestations. The answer has tended to depend on where a critic located "DeLillo" among his texts' ironic layers, a hermeneutic process that was precisely at stake, for example, in reactions to DeLillo's 1985 novel, *White Noise*. The problem here, as Frank Lentricchia notes, is that though DeLillo writes Swift-like satire, DeLillo does not – or cannot – depend, as Swift could, on his readers sharing his "norms of reasonable behavior" (Lentricchia 1991: 13). In fact, when Lentricchia waded in to this interpretive fray, he had to reiterate the obvious, that *White Noise* was a first-person narrative, with all the epistemological uncertainty that attends that form (Lentricchia 1991: 87–113). One of DeLillo's most clear-eyed interpreters, Lentricchia sees the narrator's mix of high-art and low-brow references as one more layer of irony. Other reactions underscore DeLillo's interesting solution to the problem of the lack of shared norms of reasonable behavior – there isn't one. He merely cuts us adrift to let us fend for ourselves; we have to supply such norms in order to navigate the postmodern world DeLillo's fiction portrays.

Contributing to this interpretive problem of locating DeLillo's attitude to popular and consumer culture is that most of DeLillo's characters seem to exist through a praxis of quotation: many seem like simulations of characters – that is, simulations of simulations of people. In DeLillo's novels, characters watch themselves act and imagine themselves acting. Self-reflection and image supersede innocent intent, unconscious action, or motivation. His characters have been saturated by many media; they already-know the gestures, looks, fashions, and phrases with which they must make do. Characters so composed – sometimes self-consciously so – are part of the absence of authenticity in the postmodern, and on these grounds DeLillo's texts are often read as resonating with Baudrillard's perspective on the precession of simulacra. But what confuses his critics is that DeLillo does not appear nostalgic for the authentic, or for a presimulative social world. His reviewers' accusations that DeLillo fails to create real, "flesh-and-blood" characters stem from this practice wherein his subjects seem to act by a citational ontology: their words, thoughts, gestures come to them (as they come to us, DeLillo's oeuvre implies) from the outside, from the social world that offers the content for speech, emotion, and action. His critics' complaint is thus DeLillo's point, not an imaginative flaw in his fiction. How this practice of quotation develops is well exemplified in the final pages of *White Noise*, where the cuckolded Jack Gladney has to learn a response to his wife's unfaithfulness, and can do so only by accepting the clichéd image of male rage offered to him through his wife and his friend Murry Siskind. Gladney's citation of this image leads him to murder (much as male rage does in the novel of which *White Noise* is a kind of parodic citation, Norman Mailer's *An American Dream*, whose murderous hero is also an academic dealing in dread). But Gladney's shooting of his wife's lover ends farcically, with both wounded but recovering. Here volition and action are simulated as Gladney tries to act the part; what is missing is the passion that might originate such violence. With this representation of a world governed by simulation and quotation DeLillo comes closest to a formal postmodernism. Many of his texts exhibit games with language; here DeLillo mirrors a poststructuralist sensibility that language does not reflect reality, or at least a postmodern sense that language is not necessarily in the service of rationality and logic. Such games include characters' repetition of outside phrases and images as if DeLillo were quoting a novel, or an imagined scene. But they also erupt in the form of the conversational "metonymic skids" (Barthes 1974 [1970]: 92) in *White Noise*, for example, and the intrusive voice of television and its advertising into the narrative flow ("Leaded, Unleaded, Superunleaded"). Furthering the reader's sense of the randomness of language and its unconnectedness to the real world is the DeLillan non-sequitur – "Down in the field boxes they want Gleason to say, 'You're a dan-dan-dandy crowd'" (*Underworld* [26]) – which can be read as DeLillo's trying to register the simultaneity and unconnectedness of experience (and maybe trying to stitch these things together).

DeLillo's work also reflects Fredric Jameson's argument about postmodernism: that we have forgotten our history, and that it is increasingly difficult to form a sense of the present as something within a historical context. In this light, DeLillo's work could be considered a symptom of our historylessness and an attempt to compensate for it. His work takes up the signs of our contemporaneity, things which seem to distinguish our time as different from time past: high technology, advertising, terrorism, suspicion of democratic governments and multinational corporations, religious cults, sports crowds, religious crowds, political crowds, tourist crowds, television, natural and human-made catastrophes, nuclear war. But his work gives us no overall explanation of the present, a strategy that is at once postmodern in that it offers no totalizing picture of the contemporary, and postmodern in a symptomatic sense that Jameson puts forward, that such a comprehensive understanding is no longer possible. Our age thus appears, in DeLillo's novels, as TV collage: we experience the present through media report, the incident or the amazing event, the not-so-amazing CNN "factoid," the fleeting disaster, and the catastrophe. We experience our unrelatedness to the past (we exist after the end of history, Fukuyama thinks) much as do the characters in *White Noise* who cannot accept their own catastrophe until it is represented back to them. What should be palpable and personal awaits simulation so that we might grasp it. For DeLillo, this postmodern condition began with the assassination of President Kennedy:

> As the years have flowed away from that point, I think we've all come to feel that what's been missing over these past twenty-five years is a sense of a manageable reality.... We seem much more aware of elements like randomness and ambiguity and chaos since then. (Cited in DeCurtis 1991: 136)

DeLillo's work is an attempt at thinking the present historically and at trying to manage postmodern reality, but a compensatory attempt ultimately unsuccessful in so far as the work is symptomatic of the problems it registers.

In his fictional history of Lee Harvey Oswald in *Libra*, for example, DeLillo rejects the lone gunman theory and opts instead for a complicated conspiracy that goes awry. This is the plot the Warren Commission never uncovers, and as another DeLillan character notes, all plots tend toward death. DeLillo's fictional history places him within the postmodern mood of paranoia and suspicion of conspiracy in the US; he shares the sense with *The X-Files* that human networks of malicious intent are at work in the seams of the social order. The Commission appears as the tool of modern rationality: evidence, papers, tape recordings, interviews, documents, dental records, scientific studies of bullet trajectories and flesh-and-bone impact studies, multiple agencies, all contributing to explain the event. The Commission's conclusion – that the assassination was the work of a sole, wishy-washy, twice-defected ex-Marine who could not spell – confounds the gravity of the assassination, a disjuncture which gives rise to the postmodern mood of suspicion and dread. *Libra* plugs in to a postwar public's willingness to suspect its own government, a willingness triggered in part by the roles of the CIA and the FBI in spying on and discrediting its own citizens, in their participation in illegal actions abroad (assassinations and in training anticommunist groups with techniques in torture), and at an extreme, the possibility of a coverup at Roswell (a topic ripe for DeLillo's address: all the clichés await him). DeLillo's flirtation with conspiracy, in novels such as *Libra* and *The Names*, although one might name any of his novels in this context, has led columnist George Will to condemn DeLillo as a "bad citizen" for advancing conspiracy against the lone gunman theory in *Libra* (cited in Lentricchia 1991: 3).

This last aspect of DeLillo's postmodernism – what I wish to call his gnosticism – is the largest contribution of DeLillo's work towards unraveling our sense of the present. DeLillo's peculiar place in American – or, better, world – literature is his status as one of several who register a shift in Western thought, from modernity's rationalization to postmodernity's attention to the irrational. DeLillo's work recognizes postmodernism as the new gnosis: against modernity's transparent power of rational thought there is postmodernity's secret knowledge – again. In the nineteenth century, Dostoevsky registered modernity's denial of secret knowledge with the agnostic uncertainty that "God may not exist." DeLillo turns this agnosticism on its head, not by suggesting in response that "God may exist" (such is Cormac McCarthy's dread), but by suggesting that the natural world and the human world exhibit signs of unsettling designs, of secrets, of mysterious groups, of obscure but powerful systems that seem to mimic intent, if not intelligence. In *Libra*, this takes the form of multiple conspiracies against the President by groups ideologically various but structurally identical in that they are governed by secrecy. In *The Names* this attention takes the form of the language cult and, the novel implies, a kind of gnosis that lies within language itself – a fact suggested by the text's interest in glossolalia. In *Ratner's Star*, mathematics itself – another language – is a subject of gnosis as well: as one of its characters puts it, "pure mathematics is a kind of secret knowledge." The terrorist groups punctuating DeLillo's work, from *Players* through *The Names* to *Mao II*, also function in terms of self-propelling secrecy, in which hidden design erupts in violence. *White Noise* manifests several gnostic groups, from the Gladney-led body of Hitler specialists gossiping about the final days in the *Führerbunker* (the subject of DeLillo's *Running Dog* as well) to more technological- and technician-led systems of medical information and disaster-response programs. Tom LeClair (1987) offers Ludwig von Bertalaneffy's systems theory as a hermeneutic paradigm that best explains DeLillo's postmodern attention to the curious designs found in human and in natural organization; Paul Civello (1994) postulates the "field concept" of the new physics as a suitable gloss. DeLillo's metaphysical impulse is channeled in a specifically human and worldly direction. DeLillo's characters' awareness that they are objects of systems of knowledge hidden from them is, in one sense, what Fredric Jameson in a review of *The Names* calls the consolation of paranoia:

> The point is that a paranoid world is the *opposite* of an "absurd" or meaningless one... the world is if anything too meaningful, and there is undoubtedly a

deeper consolation here which translates itself into formal pleasures. (Jameson 1984b: 118)

This formal pleasure of DeLillo's fiction, by which the gnostic qualities of our contemporary era are teased out, results not from the suggestion of meanings below the surface of our everyday life (such is the modernist depth model of metaphysical meaning), but meaning within the whorls of the surface pattern. Zooming in or zooming out, the inexplicable order of fractal systems suggests design: within this surface space is that which Don DeLillo has repeatedly called the postmodern "mystery."

19

Jacques Derrida

Hugh J. Silverman

What would postmodernism be without deconstruction? And what would deconstruction be without Jacques Derrida? Postmodernism – or at least postmodern thought – operates in tandem with deconstruction as its operative theoretical strategy. To think postmodernism without deconstruction is to think heterotopias, multicultural sites, juxtapositions, marginalities, and the very relation of the modern to the postmodern with the risk of the misguided claim that in the postmodern "anything goes." The postmodern (which is not necessarily the same as postmodernism) is carefully motivated. The postmodern places the modern in question by asking how the modern marks its own limits and margins. If this relation between the modern and the postmodern were to be inverted, the new dominance of the postmodern would take place by unfolding the differences between the postmodern and the modern. Such a strategy would be not only deconstructive, but explicitly Derridean. Derridean, then, is already an adjective, an adjective describing that form of deconstruction which is most fully elaborated in the writings and activities of Jacques Derrida.

When Jacques Derrida (b. 1930) published three major books in 1967, he was only thirty-seven years old. Except for his translation and introduction to Edmund Husserl's *Origin of Geometry* in 1962, he was hardly known on the French scene. The almost simultaneous publication of *Speech and Phenomena*, *Writing and Difference*, and *Of Grammatology* was a tremendous feat – launching the career of one of the most important philosophical figures of the late twentieth century. There is no doubt that with respect to the development of postmodernism and its relation to deconstruction, the role of Jacques Derrida has been of massive significance. Indeed, Derrida's theoretical writings – always articulated through the reading of philosophical, literary, critical, political, or intellectual texts – have given a unique character to the last third of the twentieth century, and particularly with respect to the development of postmodern thought. With Derrida, philosophers, critics, and theorists have learned a whole new set of strategies for reading texts, for thinking the role and significance of texts, and for establishing how texts constitute the textures of the contemporary critical and theoretical scene. And since the text for Derrida is not just what is written but more broadly what is inscribed within culture, his concerns for and writings about philosophy, literature, art, politics, and many other areas make evident his attention as much to what is outside the text as to what is inside the text, even if what is outside the text is elaborated, formulated, and iterated textually.

Derrida's writings have not appeared in a vacuum. They clearly arise out of at least three different intellectual traditions as they developed throughout the first half of the twentieth century. These are phenomenology, structuralism, and psychoanalysis.

Phenomenology – as formulated by Edmund Husserl at the beginning of the twentieth century – offers a philosophy of description, accounting for human experience and the objects of that experience. Based on the premise that we can achieve a pure, transcendental, immanent description of our experience of things, offered in a rigorous and presuppositionless fashion, Husserl claims that the transcendental subject can reflect upon the contents of an experiential consciousness and achieve both necessary and apodictic knowledge of the meaning of what is experienced. While this phenomenology was crucial for the existentialism and hermeneutics that followed in both Germany and France, it was the backdrop for the Algerian-born Derrida's formative years as a student in Paris. Indeed, Derrida produced three books in which he takes up Husserl's philosophy: his master's thesis on *The Problem of Genesis in Husserl's Philosophy* (1953–4), his *Introduction to Husserl's Origin of Geometry* (1962), and *Speech and Phenomena* (1967).

Genesis, as he points out in the thesis, could be either a question of origins or a question of becoming. The locus of this question is at the heart of Husserlian phenomenology. Husserl's notion of the transcendental ego or subject is formulated as an origin, the source or condition from which all intentional acts are derived. But the notion of genesis also has to do with the temporal experience of consciousness as it transpires over time at a multiplicity of moments. Consciousness is active, ongoing, and at the same time memorial. Inscribed between these two notions of genesis is a split (between origin and the multiple sites or nodes of specificity) that has come to play an important role in postmodern discourse.

The question of genesis is even further elaborated in the *Introduction to Husserl's Origin of Geometry*, where Derrida raises the further concern about historicity, namely, the relationship between the beginning moments in the history of a particular science (e.g., geometry) and its origins, namely the relation between that science as marked in history and the eternal objects (e.g., right triangles) which are the subject matter of its inquiries. Here again, an indecidability is inscribed at the heart of the science and in the juncture between "beginning" and "origin." And, as we have come to understand, the dissemination of beginnings and origins is one of the principal formulations of the postmodern.

In *Speech and Phenomena*, Derrida focuses on the question of meaning and the sign in Husserlian phenomenology. Meaning – what something means and how meaning is essential to phenomenological description – can be a matter of expression or a matter of content. The sign could be either expression or content, either noetic or noematic (to use Husserl's terms). The sign can be meaningful if it says something or if it expresses something. These are not the same. And the indecidability inscribed within this split is what makes Derrida's question all the more compelling. This split in the notion of meaning or sense (*Sinn*) is crucial to the postmodern, for ultimately postmodern meaning is neither core content nor adventitious expression. The only way meaning can be located in multiple sites is for its expressions to proliferate and therefore its contents as well.

Structuralism is rooted in the semiology of the Swiss linguist Ferdinand de Saussure, a contemporary of Husserl. Saussurean semiology, the general science of signs, was reinvented some thirty years later in the 1940s by the structural anthropologist Claude Lévi-Strauss (in conversation with Roman Jakobson). Where Lévi-Strauss sought to build connections between anthropology and linguistics, he also wanted to show that elementary structures of kinship, of myth, of totems and taboos are not matters for primitives alone, but rather that they are fully distributed throughout different societies and cultures – by virtue of some specifiable transformations, they constitute different versions of the same structure, but, as Derrida shows in "Structure, Sign and Play in the Human Sciences" (his presentation at the groundbreaking Johns Hopkins *The Structuralist Controversy* conference in 1966), there is no centered self or subject located within or behind any of these versions of human structures. Structures repeat, recur in multiple contexts, but they have no centered transcendental subject (as Husserl would insist). This notion of self-decentering became a fundamental tenet of Derridean deconstruction.

Similarly, the very idea of the sign, which is basic to semiology, carries its dual nature (of signifier and signified) into Derrida's notion of the end of the book and the beginning of writing (viz. *Of Grammatology*). The signifier is effaced in the voice or speaking (*phoné*) and writing (*graphé*) is effaced in the *logos* (the reign of meaning, the signified, and the history of metaphysics). The book is the product of an author as transcendental signified. The idea of the book as a work, produced and signified by an external author, is placed in question. The text or the beginning of writing takes its place. As with Michel Foucault's notion of the "absent subject" at the end of *The Order of Things* (1966) and Roland Barthes's "Death of the Author" (1968), this account of the book as work is also linked to the question of the centered epistemological subject in Husserlian phenomenology, which Derrida offers to decenter and deconstruct.

Writing, for Derrida, arises out of the opposition between speaking and writing. Derrida is not seeking to claim that there is anything wrong with speech, but he has been concerned that speaking was given primacy in the Western traditions, and that writing was disfavored. According to the deconstructive strategy, the privileging of speaking over writing can be inverted, but this is not the whole story. What is of interest is what happens between speaking and writing (once inverted). Derrida claims that a new notion of writing arises – what he calls "originary writing" (*archi-écriture*), writing which is neither speaking nor the writing that is opposed to it. This originary writing can also be said to constitute the space of the postmodern, a liminal space that takes shape only out of the juxtapositions of modern objects and modern subjects.

In *Of Grammatology*, Derrida links the work of Saussure to that of Martin Heidegger. As with Heidegger, the hermeneutic successor to Husserlian phenomenology, the notion of ontico-ontological difference (that difference which arises out of the relation of beings to Being) establishes a differential space, similar to the notion of difference in semiology. In semiology, any sign is a sign only by virtue of its differences from other signs. This horizontal difference is matched up with the vertical difference marked by Heidegger's ontico-ontological difference. The crossing of these two differences opens up the space which Derrida calls "originary writing" or just "écriture." The famous essay "Differance" (1966) makes this evident. Derrida invents a new word "differance" as opposed to "difference." When spoken (in a certain way) one cannot hear the difference between difference and differance. But the difference is clear in writing. This example shows that there is a new difference – that between difference and differance – which marks what Derrida is calling "writing" (not the writing which is opposed to speaking, but rather the originary writing that arises out of the difference between the two). Hence, the title *Writing and Difference* (in French: *L'écriture et la différance*), but in French one can also hear "writing is differance" (*l'écriture est la différance*). And this is the key point: originary writing, for Derrida, is difference, this deconstructive difference, which marks the space of the text (as opposed to the work). The text makes no necessary appeal to an author, to a transcendental signifier, to a centered subject, to a constitutive agent that has authority over the text. Although such notions were not at the time in any way linked to postmodernism – as it was coming to be defined in architecture, for instance – by the 1990s, it was feasible to think Derrida's notion of writing as difference in the context of certain postmodern strategies, in particular ones that understand the proliferation of the decentered position of the subject throughout writing, text, space.

Psychoanalysis, spawned in the early twentieth century by another contemporary of Husserl and Saussure, namely Sigmund Freud, raises the question of the subject in terms of the psychic realm of id, ego, and superego. Here the centered subject is split – always split by the ever-present reality of repression and the inaccessibility of the unconscious to conscious life. This split marks a gap, a break, a screen, a mystic writing pad, which both separates and brings together the conscious and the unconscious. Memory traces are inscribed on this screen, traces of experiences which are in principle inaccessible to the conscious life. This place of difference between the conscious and the unconscious is where the period of erasure leaves its marks or traces constituting the locus of the Freudian analysis, a kind of performance of the "scene of writing" (see "Freud and the Scene of Writing" [1966] in *Writing and Difference*).

Derrida's principal interest in Freud has been through his reading of his followers, most notably, Jacques Lacan. Lacan's famous statement that "the unconscious is structured like a language" has allowed him to develop the idea that whatever can be called the unconscious is proliferated and disseminated through the chains of signifiers, words as they narrate a patient's dreams or fears or interpersonal relations. Lacan reads Poe's "Purloined Letter" in which a revealing and embarrassing letter addressed to the Queen is stolen by the Minister. Auguste Dupin is charged with recovering the letter after the police have been unable to find it. Dupin notices the (conspicuously placed) crumpled-up piece of paper on the Minister's desk in the library and returns the next day to replace the famous letter with a substitute. The Queen is thereby restored with what was taken away from her. Lacan's reading of this story emphasizes the role of the letter as a signifier (not as a signified). For Lacan, the letter is both a veiling and unveiling of truth. For Derrida in "The Purveyor of Truth" (1975), republished in *The Post Card* (1980), the letter functions as a signifier for female sexuality – the Queen has the letter between her legs. She must conceal and disclose at the same time. The theft of the letter is potentially quite damaging and so she must recover it without her husband suspecting that it has been stolen. The truth of the letter is also the truth of the narrator, of writing, of the literal, which is never just what it says. Similarly the postmodern has come to be understood as occupying this interstitial zone between the said and the not said, the literal and the metaphorical, the evident and the hidden, the modern and the postmodern.

There is an important link between Derrida's work of the late 1960s and that of the 1970s. This becomes evident not only in "The Purveyor of Truth" ("Le facteur de la verité") – the postal carrier of truth or the truth factor – but also in the essay called "Spurs: Nietzsche's Styles" (1979 [1976]). The question of truth, the question of woman, the question of style are all interrelated here in a reading of Nietzsche's famous statement that "truth is a woman." Here again (as he does often) Derrida turns to Heidegger. Heidegger's account of truth as *aletheia* is that this Greek word (a-LETHE-ia, where Lethe was the mythical river of forgetfulness) means not-hiddenness, non-concealedness, disclosure. Derrida reads this notion of truth as a metaphor for woman's genitalia, disclosing and hiding or concealing. He contrasts the vaginal with the penal (the long oblong object, like a pen, writing instrument, stylus). The stylus is associated with style, with writing, while the vaginal is associated with truth, with openness, with dis-closure. The word "truth" in German (*die Wahrheit*), French (*la verité*), Italian (*la verità*), Spanish (*la verdad*), etc., is feminine. Truth is female. Style is male. Writing the truth happens with style and with the question of truth. It could be claimed that if the postmodern is just style, then it carries no truth. But if it is disclosure and coming out of concealedness, then it has precisely to do with truth. But truth without style (e.g., postmodern style) also cannot be style without disclosure if only in its multiple sites.

In 1972 (as in 1967), Derrida again published three books: *Margins of Philosophy*, *Dissemination*, and *Positions*. Appointed to teach the history of philosophy as *maître de conférences* at the École Normale Supérieure, a post which he maintained for many years, *Margins* reflects this deep engagement with the history of philosophy. Readings of Aristotle, Kant, Hegel, Heidegger, Sartre, Foucault abound. Yet here the thinking of marginalities, borders, edges, and limits becomes crucial. All of these concepts mark the difference between the inside and the outside, between the included and the excluded, between the privileged and the underprivileged. "The Ends of Man" (1968) shows how the question of end can be understood as having dignity (end versus means), goal (telos), and termination. For Kant, one must treat another person as an *end* rather than a means; for Sartre, existing humans determine for themselves a fundamental project or *end*; and for Foucault, the end of man means the *end* of the age in which the concept of the empirico-transcendental subject has dominance. In the latter case, the modern centered anthropological subject evacuates itself from the center of the scene and the postmodern subject as decentered, dispersed, multiple takes precedence.

Similarly, in "Ousia and Gramme" (1968), time in Heidegger is contrasted with time as a now point (Aristotle), as the comprehending of and memory of all that is (Hegel), as the constitution of the now within a web of protentional and retentional consciousness. For Heidegger, temporality is the inscription of difference as an ontico-ontological difference, as the presence [*Anwesenheit*] of that which is present [*Anwesendheit*]. This differential moment is neither that of presence nor of absence, but that of a writing that exceeds the whole history of metaphysics in which these various notions of time are inscribed. Once again a question of writing the difference between this history and what would stand outside it – a standing outside which reinscribes the difference between the inside and outside – reaffirming the margins.

The essays from *Margins of Philosophy* mark both the role of writing and difference as in-between. The tympanum, drum (as in eardrum), membrane, hymen, text mark the place of difference but which can only be articulated by virtue of the opposition of inside and outside, here and there, and so on. This is why the important preface to *Dissemination* also occupies this kind of indecidable status. Does the Preface to a work belong inside it or outside it? Is it part of the book or is it preliminary to it? The Preface is like the membrane, the eardrum which links the inside to the outside. It is writing as difference. "Hors-Livre" is translated variously (by Barbara Johnson) as Outwork, Hors d'oeuvres (what comes outside the meal, the appetizers). The dissemination of writing is situated at these places of difference in between the outside and the inside, between the author and the work, between what belongs and what does not – writing as supplement.

Derrida's interviews in *Positions* reiterate the deconstructive strategy. Find the opposition, go to the less privileged side, reaffirm the less privileged side and name the difference with the less privileged side in order to mark the place of difference, margin, trace, tympanum, membrane, hymen, text. Hence, the much-debated *"Il n'y a pas de hors texte"* (from *Dissemination*) does not mean that the text is all there is, creating an impossible textualism. Rather, it means that what is outside the text is marked by what is inside the text, and what is outside the text is inscribed by its exclusion in the text. The text would have no status without the question of the border, margin, edge of the text, which has no status without the opposition between the inside and outside. So much so that in the essay "Living On: Borderlines" (1979), it becomes evident that in the very question of survival, of living on (as in the case of Shelley, who drowned before completing his last poem "The Triumph of Life"), living on (*sur-vivre*) is not only living on in writing but the living happens in the moment of difference between life and death, at the place of the text, on the border between what is included in the poem and what lives on beyond it.

Derrida's readings of literary texts, not only Shelley, but also Genet, Blanchot, Artaud, Bataille, Ponge, Kafka, Joyce, Celan, et al., is iterated in many different frames. What is postmodern about these readings, as well as being deconstructive, is that they are typically juxtaposed with other texts, other writings from different contexts, in such a way that they mark the places of difference between, where it is the marks of their alternative formulations that are specified and designated. *Glas* (1974), in which Genet is placed alongside Hegel, is a majestic enterprise of two improbable bedfellows. Blanchot's *Death Sentence* (*Arrêt de mort* – Stopping Death/Execution Sentence) alongside Shelley ("Triumph of Life" – Triumph over life, i.e., death/Life triumphant, i.e., living) shows how the juxtapositional strategy comes into play.

And then there is Derrida's turn to discourse about painting. *The Truth in Painting* (1978) situates Derrida within the postmodern frame. Four essays, four voices, four corners of a frame. The preface *"Passe-partout"* makes the point: the *"passe-partout"* goes around the picture, the painting. It also constitutes the matte or cardboard that separates the frame from the picture. And yet, a *"passe-partout"* is also a "skeleton key," or a "universal key," one that opens all the doors. So the *"passe-partout"* now in the place of the "preface" opens all the doors, enframes the issue of painting, and links the frame to the picture. *The Truth in Painting* is squared off by four essays – the reading of parergonality in Kant (as a question of framing), the framework in Meyer Schapiro's critical reading of Heidegger's account of Van Gogh's "shoes," the need for air in Adami's drawings about Derrida's *Glas*, and the very question of the coffin, like a sealed box in which there can no longer be any air. These four corners, metaphors upon metaphors, mark the edges not only of the painting, but also of the modern itself. The question of what can be outside the frame is the postmodern question, or the postmodern condition (as Derrida's friend Jean-François Lyotard called it).

From Derrida's interest in painting, architecture was not far behind. Development of architectural plans for the Parc de la Villette in Paris with Bernard Tschumi and collaboration with the American architect Peter Eisenman on the project (see "Point de folie – maintenant l'architecture" [1987] and "Why Peter Eisenman Writes Such Good Books" [1987]) brings deconstruction full circle into the very domain where postmodernism "began" – in the work of Philip Johnson as reiterated even up to the end of the twentieth century with Frank Gehry's Bilbao Guggenheim Museum. He had already offered a study of photography in his reading of *Droit de regards* (*Right of Inspection*) (1985), a photo-novel by Marie-Françoise Plissart, which raises the question of what the viewer has the right to see, where photographs of nude women engage the relation of seeing to sexuality. And the right to see was then pursued in *Memoirs of the Blind* (1990) as a museum catalogue of paintings depicting blindness. Derrida even participated earlier in films such as *Ghostdance*, in which he played Jacques Derrida.

The topic of ghosts, which recurs often in Derrida's writings, became particularly thematized in *Specters of Marx* (1993). With the fall of communism in Eastern Europe, the ghost of Marx is nevertheless still around. Marx himself had spoken of communism as a specter arising over Europe. Derrida reads Marx in tandem with Hamlet's father's ghost. Hamlet's father's ghost is very much present through traces in the world created by his brother (and murderer and new husband of his murdered brother), traces which mark Claudius's world. The return of Hamlet's father's ghost to avenge the murder can be read as a parallel account of Marx coming back to avenge the Europe which had been laid bare by subsequent forms of communism. Shall we not call them "postmodern ghosts"? The ever-increasing need to address political and ethical issues explicitly, as in "The Force of Law" (1992), his reading of the New Europe in *The Other Heading* (1991), *The Politics of Friendship* (1994), and more recently the topics of hospitality, forgiveness, and perjury have come to preoccupy his work of the 1990s and into the twenty-first century. These important writings show how the postmodern has come to be inscribed in the pressing political issues of our day.

As Derrida came into his own sixties, he began to do more than hold interviews – as he had done for *Positions* and as collected together in *Points ... Interviews, 1974–1994* (1995). He has begun to write his own life, and the autobiographical *Circumfession* (1991) which he prepared in collaboration with Geoffrey Bennington marks the line between biography and autobiography – a theme Derrida had explored earlier in *The Ear of the Other* (1982) in connection with Nietzsche's account of his life in *Ecce Homo*. And as might be expected, his teachers, friends, and contemporaries have begun to depart. Hence along with his account of his own life and past and how he has "lived on," "survived," there are those memorials and requiems of others who have mattered to him. They have become numerous now: Paul de Man, Roland Barthes, Michel Foucault, Emmanuel Levinas, Jean-François Lyotard, and all too many others. These memorial essays will be collected together by Michael Naas and Pascale-Anne Brault in a single volume on mourning (2001). By thematizing the question of death in relation to studies of the gift – *The Gift of Death* (1992) and the recurring theme of religion (1999) and its apocalyptic tones (1979) – Derrida once again returns to the matter of limits, margins, ends but now in terms of giving and returning. Indeed, Nietzsche's eternal return of the same is the metaphor of the will to live one's life exactly as one is living it. Can one imagine any more exquisite gift than what Derrida has returned in his lifelong career of writing and reading our histories, philosophies, literatures, cultures, ethics, religions, politics? With Derrida, the postmodern is inscribed in the modern age that we (we?) cannot not overcome.

20

Marguerite Duras

Martine Antle

Marguerite Duras (1914–96) was born at Gia Dinh in Indochina. She has bequeathed a significant corpus of texts in prose, several volumes of plays, interviews, film scenarios, and films. Her works span the second half of the twentieth century, yet it was not until the scandals provoked by the publication of *The Lover* in 1984 that Duras finally caught the attention of the French public. Duras's work, in which one can identify certain characteristics of *new fiction* or of *new wave cinema*, has evolved independently from all other literary or artistic currents. How, then, can she be situated? Should her works be classified among the writings of the confession era of the 1980s–1990s, a decade that witnessed a massive return to autobiography in France? How does one read the work of Duras in light of postmodern criticism? As we shall see, even if Duras's work does not fully make use of the processes of pastiche and irony typical of the postmodern text, it participates nevertheless in the ending of grand narratives and announces a profound crisis of subjectivity. In particular, Duras deconstructs the mechanisms of power – colonial power, fascism, or masculinity – through a radical requestioning of the social relations of domination.

One of the greatest difficulties in analyzing Duras derives from the fact that, as Michel Foucault has already noted, her works challenge all totalizing interpretation. This may be partly due to her use of what has been called *continuous writing*, a technique most frequently manifested through a rewriting of the same text from one genre to another, or through the mixing of genres within the same work. To give an example, although *La Pute de la côte normande* (1986) is written in prose, it is perfectly situated between the boundaries of theater and film writing. In a similar manner, *Blue Eyes, Black Hair* (1988 [1986]) can be easily read both as a text in prose and as a didascalic text. Punctuated at intervals with commentary addressed to the actors or the readers of the text, the novel insists upon the performative properties of writing. Direct references by Duras to the reading, or the vocalization, of the text emphasize the fact that this writing is in the oral mode. According to Duras, to write is "to take the highway, the general route of speech" (1990 [1987]: 16). This interest in the staging of language, or the "spatialization of voices," is found throughout Duras's works; moreover, she affirms, "I speak like I write." These attempts at inscribing the oral in the written parallel the imprinting of oral language into the written by the authors of postcolonial francophone literature or the authors of *new fiction* in France in the 1980s and 1990s.

Duras's work, then, is distinguished by its radical questioning of the notion of genre. The boundaries of genres become increasingly blurred until they no longer appear to exist in a differentiated state. For Duras, regulated and organized narratives are not "free," and her work is thus by definition open. In this manner, Duras privileges the place of the reader, who must henceforth play a fundamental role in the elaboration of the artistic work.

The fact that Duras's work functions on the levels of both structural and thematic repetition renders the role of the reader all the more complex. The leitmotifs that pervade her entire corpus constitute yet another essential characteristic, and they all stem from some fundamental themes present from her first novels of the 1950s. Duras's narratives defy all chronology, and ceaselessly repeat the same stories, returning over and over to the same point until they form practically identical frameworks that echo from one novel to the next. This is how Duras summarizes all her books: "*The book*, it is the story of two people who love . . . without forewarning. This occurs outside the novel . . . This love exists in the impossibility of being written" (1990 [1987]: 97). Duras's continuous flux affirms the crisis of representation and prepares the path for such techniques as "recycling," characteristic of the French *new fiction* of the 1980s and 1990s. Among the many recurrent motifs in her work, one must note in particular her locations and characters. These characters are drifters, dedicated to wandering, condemned to errancy, representing only the frequently indefinable, multiple facets of a subjectivity that escapes the constraints of representation. Duras's characters evolve in locations and spaces whose geographical references are frequently falsified. The landmarks, whether falsified or imaginary, remain blurred and indeterminate in Duras's geography, which extends from Indochina to India to Japan. Moreover, everything in Duras's writings revolves around a disappearance, a longing, a lack, an impossibility: the impossibility of speaking; the impossibility of telling a story of pain such as that of a childhood in Indochina; the impossibility of overcoming the longing. In *The Ravishing of Lol Stein* (1966 [1964]), Lol is unable to access the realm of language. It is through the devices of cries and laughter that Duras's women access language. The scream of Lol Stein finds its echo in the scream of the woman killed by her lover in *Moderato Cantabile* (1966 [1958]) and in the scream of the beggar in the film *India Song*

(1976 [1973]). In direct opposition to the succession of female characters who do not have access to speech, who are plunged into the depths of silence, unable to narrate their own existences, there is Claire in *L'Amante Anglaise* (1968 [1967]). Claire speaks continuously, and yet she speaks only under certain specific conditions: under the constrictive mechanisms of cross-examination and audio recording. Furthermore, the more Claire speaks, the more truth is removed from her story, from knowing where her cousin's head was hidden at the time of the crime. This ironic gesture by Duras puts us on guard against the traps and pitfalls of language and causes us to reflect upon the ideological conditions of enunciation. For it is not Claire's truth that matters here. For Duras, "to write is not to tell stories. In fact, it is the opposite of telling stories. It is to tell everything all at once. It is to tell one story as well as to tell the absence of this story."

In her filmmaking, Duras also remains silent; she does not tell stories through the image, but rather experiments with movement and sound. She deconstructs the filmic image through the camera's immobility and the representation of static shots. In the film *Agatha* (1981) for example, it is through the spatialization of voices that the spectator attempts to reconstruct the incest. In *La Femme du Gange* (1973), the voices utter "look, see, forget, and remember."

Duras's theater accomplishes another form of rewriting through the exploration of a new conception of language. For example, in the play *Le Shaga* (1968), the female character invents a new language that reaches the limits of the intelligible. All of Duras's characters frequently travel through the memories of their past, passionately yet unsuccessfully attempting to recapture a lost love, a history, a past. This is how the different levels of the representations of desire are endlessly repeated in a work so haunted by the dimensions of memory. From *The Sailor from Gibraltar* (1966 [1952]), the quest for desire is ever present; desire is rendered equally problematic in *Hiroshima, mon amour* (1966 [1960]) by the impossibility of relating, or seeing, the nuclear catastrophe. In Duras's writings, all erotic desire implies a transgression of the forbidden, as in Bataille: incestuous eroticism with the brother, or the narrator's lesbian desire in *The Lover*. Desire and love remain forever in the act of seeing in *Blue Eyes, Black Hair*. A man and a woman, bound to one another by "a contract," submit to the contingencies of a corporeal choreography that is akin to a veritable ritual of simulation, an unending ritual that the characters are powerless to interrupt. Mutual masturbation as a substitute for a sexual relationship is itself doomed to failure. Through its repetitions, the text marks the successive advances and retreats of two bodies toward the other and away from the other. This dynamic of desire implies a process of blinding: to see implies here the closure of the gaze or what Duras herself calls the "blind-gaze."

This process of blinding is already in place in *The Sea-Wall* (1967 [1950]) with the colonial bureaucracy and its control of the Indochina territory. Power and its hierarchical microstructures in this text remain diffused and dispersed. This power is generated from the blindness of the mother, who either does not realize or refuses to see that her land is not cultivable. It is precisely this ignorance and this blindness that push her to impose upon the Vietnamese the injustice she suffers at the hands of the authorities.

From the explosion of Hiroshima, to the "colonial vampirism" in *The Sea-Wall*, to the drama of the Occupation in *La Douleur* (1986 [1984]), to the "general catastrophe" of *Yes, peut-être* (1968), and to the decentering of cultural identities in the modern-day Parisian suburbs (*Summer Rain*, 1992 [1990]), Duras's work perseveres in revealing the mechanisms of power.

The methods Duras employs to explore the enforcement of power over the body lead once again to further requestioning, this time to a reconsideration of the construct of subjectivity. For Duras, the crisis of subjectivity includes a destabilization of the conventional methods of masculine domination. To better denounce the foundations of masculine domination, she goes as far as to declare, "all men are homosexuals." Duras places sadistic men in opposition to inactive, impotent ones. A number of these characters attempt to write a book, but it is a goal they never attain. Among these weak men, it is important to mention the beardless Chinese man from *The Lover* (1985 [1984]) who is dominated and feminized ("He moans, he cries"), as well as the ambivalent figure of the homosexual in *Blue Eyes, Black Hair*, a text that disrupts all notions of genre and gender.

If Duras's work offers other possible readings of the hierarchical construction of power and its implementation on the body, her writing and her interviews cast only a partial light on her political commitments. After the Liberation, Duras became a member of the French Communist Party and was strongly militant until 1950. Throughout her life, she continued to affirm her loyalty and commitment to social and political causes. At times she is inspired by various elements of popular culture or by crimes given high-profile media coverage, such as the murder of a child in the Vosges mountains. The public accusations that she made about the child's mother, Christine Vuillemin, scandalized public opinion in France and jeopardized, for some, the validity of Duras's own political and social beliefs.

Prior to the 1980s Duras was hardly noticed as a writer, but from then on she instantaneously entered the media arena. At a time when numerous French writers were revealing their personal lives to the media in order to advertise and sell their books, Duras instead engaged with the media to establish a position against world injustice, and in particular to denounce the economic consequences of colonization in multicultural France in the 1980s and 1990s. In a series of interviews with her old friend from the Resistance,

François Mitterrand, she denounced the neoliberalism of the end of the twentieth century. Still in the 1980s, Duras collaborated with Amnesty International for the liberation of international political prisoners. Although Duras's political statements cannot all be taken at face value, her interviews and speeches amply testify to her considerable knowledge of and profound sensitivity to the world's cultural diversity. In this sense, and once again, Duras participates in the postmodern debate of the end of the twentieth century, placing great importance on the Other and questioning cultural identity and otherness during this contradictory era of globalization and multiculturalism. She additionally contributes to the postmodern debate by attacking the media and the virtuality of the televised image: "France has half an hour ... daily during which the French population is informed of the day's events ... There is no true news on television." Thus Duras, like her contemporaries, puts the media on trial in the era of globalization, in which they have become, as Serge Halimi (1997) put it, "the new guardians" of our economic system.

21

Umberto Eco

Peter Bondanella

Born in Alessandria (Piedmont) in 1932, Eco began what seemed to be a traditional academic career with a dissertation on St. Thomas Aquinas and aesthetics at the University of Turin. Supervised by Luigi Pareyson and published as *Il problema estetico in San Tommaso* (1956; *The Aesthetics of Thomas Aquinas* [1988]), the book nevertheless plays a crucial role in Eco's later literary career as a postmodern novelist. Among other original arguments in his first book, Eco demonstrated that the workings of scholastic philosophy had a great deal in common with structuralist thought, an approach to critical theory that was extremely popular at the time in Europe.

After working for the Italian state television service and the Bompiani publishing house in Milan, Eco received a Chair of Visual Communications at the Faculty of Architecture in Florence and subsequently moved to the University of Bologna in 1971, where he remains to this day as one of that institution's most famous professors. Eco's first major work – *Opera aperta: forma e indeterminazione nelle poetiche contemporanee* (1962; *The Open Work* [1989]) earned him national renown in 1962 (as well as famously negative reviews from Nobel Laureate Eugenio Montale and Claude Lévi-Strauss) for aesthetic theories that distinguished between what he termed traditionally "closed" works of art, to which he juxtaposed what he believed were the truly avant-garde "open" works, such as Joyce's *Finnegans Wake*, Alexander Calder's mobiles, and the music of Luciano Berio. Eco was primarily responsible for increased critical notice of Joyce's works in Italy, and the section of *Opera aperta* dedicated to the Irish modernist has appeared as a separate book in English (*The Aesthetics of Chaosmos: The Middle Ages of James Joyce* [1989]). More than any other Italian critic or novelist, Umberto Eco knew very well what the boundaries of literary modernism were when he would eventually decide to become a postmodern author himself.

Ever sensitive to the shifts of popular culture and eager to embrace critical theories that were capable of dealing with both high and low culture (a desire not shared by traditional Italian intellectuals), Eco gained a huge audience with a bestseller entitled *Diario minimo* (1963; *Misreadings* [1993]), a witty collection of parodies of various schools of thought (the Frankfurt School, psychoanalysis, Roland Barthes, Antonioni's cinema, cultural anthropology) that were contemporaneously enriching his own writings. While often in agreement with leftist thinkers in support of what he would probably term "progressive" social and political programs, Eco's independent mind prevented him from ever becoming a Marxist, particularly the kind of dogmatic Marxist that characterized so much of Italian intellectual life in the two decades following the end of World War II.

Even before he had achieved international fame as a novelist and semiotician, Eco's career to this point had been marked by a precocious and voracious capacity to assimilate practically every kind of cultural innovation in a wide variety of cultures and eras. This cosmopolitan interest in everything from comic books to linguistic theory produced a number of seminal books in what Eco calls his "pre-semiotic" period. In 1964, *Apocalittici e integrati: comunicazioni di massa e teorie della cultura di massa* (partially translated as *Apocalypse Postponed* [1994]), provided a brilliant discussion of the different approaches taken by intellectuals to popular culture: according to Eco, "apocalyptic" intellectuals, the more traditional brand of European intellectual, often attacked the very notion of "popular culture," while "integrated" intellectuals, more often than not from the Anglo-Saxon tradition, embraced popular culture. He also provided often-reprinted classic discussions of American comic strips, such as Charles Schulz's *Peanuts, Superman,* and *Terry and the Pirates.* A subsequent and equally original collection of essays continued Eco's exploration of popular culture – *Il superuomo di massa: retorica e ideologia nel romanzo popolare* (1976; partially translated as *The Role of the Reader* [1979]) – and this book contained Eco's single most famous essay: "Narrative Structures in Fleming." His analysis of Ian Fleming's first novel (*Casino Royale*) and his superspy hero, James Bond, would lead Eco toward the methodology of semiotics, which he hoped would become a master discipline encompassing all forms of human culture – from graffiti to philosophy, from cartoons to cinema – without the need to divide culture into higher and lower forms.

Eco's fame as a semiotician came at a crucial moment in the discipline's history when the influence of the American philosopher Charles S. Peirce (1839–1914) and his use of the term "semiotics" was beginning to challenge the "semiology" of Ferdinand de Saussure and Roland Barthes. With the publication of *Trattato di semiotica* (1975; *A Theory of Semiotics* [1976]), Eco became an academic superstar, traveling all over the world to deliver lectures in many languages and charming his audiences with his erudition and wit.

Semiotic theory appealed to Eco because it pointed toward a cultural theory that was neither purely literary nor devoted solely to the analysis of high-culture classics. Eco was influenced most especially by Roland Barthes, whose *Mythologies* and *Elements of Semiology* departed from Saussure's purely linguistic model to study French popular culture (soap, wrestling, toys, tourism). Moreover, Eco wanted to counter the Marxist tendency of the times to attack all forms of popular culture, dismissing it as part of the capitalist consumer society Marxists professed to despise and vowed to destroy. Eco rightly believed that such a negative attitude was as blind as the traditional conservative but non-Marxist intellectuals' distrust of anything popular.

A Theory of Semiotics embraces a particular concept of Peirce's, that of unlimited semiosis, which claimed to demonstrate how signification operated by a circularity of references from one sign to another – and not to objective referents in reality, subjective mental states, or Platonic universals. Eco believed this key theory of semiotics would guarantee that social and historical realities would not be ignored by its findings, as he felt they were in the structuralist methodology he had recently embraced and then abandoned. Furthermore, Peirce's theory of unlimited semiosis had the additional attraction of providing a firm philosophical foundation for his own theory of "open" works. In large measure because of Eco's reliance upon Peirce's particular brand of semiotics, the American philosopher's works became more and more popular in Europe.

Eco's ecumenical attentions turned to literature almost at the same time as he was consolidating his position as Italy's most widely cited intellectual with his semiotic theory and his essays on popular culture. As a popularizer of new ideas, often imported from abroad into Italy, Eco wrote essays for Italy's most widely read newspaper, *Il Corriere della sera*, as well as a weekly column for *L'Espresso*, the second of which activities he continues to the present day. On a theoretical level, Eco's most important work during the decade before he turned to writing novels was *Lector in fabula: la cooperazione interpretativa nei testi narrativi* (1979; only partially translated as *The Role of the Reader: Explorations in the Semiotics of Texts* [1979]). *Lector in fabula* discusses the reader's presence in the story and sets out to define the Model Reader, something every author must construct. The Author is defined by Eco as not so much a concrete person as a textual strategy establishing semantic correlations and activating the Model Reader. Much of the book is taken up with fascinating discussions of the interaction between the Model Reader, Text, and Author and how such notions have implications for the study of literature. What is important about Eco's theories of the role of the reader is that, like so many other postmodern writers, he assumes that a text has many levels of meaning and that few of them are exhausted by the "intentions" of the Author.

With the 1980 publication of his first novel, *Il nome della rosa (The Name of the Rose)*, Eco seemed to combine all his previous intellectual interests:

popular culture, medievalism, the detective novel, semiotics, literary theory. The book earned him numerous literary prizes and sold tens of millions of copies all around the globe. No other Italian work of this or any other century has enjoyed such commercial or critical success, and it may be said without exaggeration that the appearance of the book firmly established the presence of the postmodern novel in Italy. Eco's own assessment of his work in *Postille al "Nome della rosa"* (1983; *Postscript to "The Name of the Rose"* [1994]) makes it perfectly clear that the novel has been conceived as a purely postmodernist performance and even provides one of the most convincing and useful definitions of the term "postmodern." In the postscript, Eco underlines the concepts of pastiche, parody, and revisiting the literary past as the essential elements of postmodernism: books always speak of other books. The postmodern attitude is humorously compared to a lover who must find an original way to express his love for a woman. Since he knows he cannot simply say "I love you," because the sophisticated woman has already heard that before, he finds a postmodern solution in the declaration: "As Barbara Cartland would put it, I love you madly." Eco thus sums up the postmodern mentality as "irony, metalinguistic play, enunciation squared." His novel provides ample demonstration of his mastery of a postmodern fictional style that had few Italian practitioners at that moment in time. It seemed to contain something for everyone. For the mass-market reader, Eco offered a "whodunit" indebted to Conan Doyle's Sherlock Holmes, a medieval monk-detective figure who attempts to solve a series of ghastly murders in a forbidding monastery. For the academic critic or the intellectual, Eco's novel was filled with arcane historical references, medieval philosophy, and anachronistic references to modern critical theory (Peirce), science, and literature (Borges).

Eco's two subsequent works of fiction were less popular but no less postmodernist in their reliance upon pastiche, combining the most erudite forms of literary theory and arcane information about the past with traits of the mass-market thriller, adventure or mystery story. And like his first venture into postmodern fiction, each book also embodied some of Eco's cultural and literary theory. In *Il pendolo di Foucault* (1988; *Foucault's Pendulum*), Eco recounts the adventures of a group of friends working for publishers in Milan who stumble upon a plot to take over the world that stretches back to the Templars, the Rosicrucians, and other modern apocalyptic fanatics. Besides being an immensely erudite work that traces the history of centuries of groups convinced they have a lock on absolute truth, *Foucault's Pendulum* also satirizes the literary theory of deconstructionism. As a novel about overinterpretation and even paranoid interpretation where fanatics relate anything to everything else without regard for the standards of logic, it should be read together with two theoretical works on the subject of interpretation: *I limiti dell'interpretazione* (1989; *The Limits of Interpretation*); and the Tanner lectures Eco presented at Cambridge University, subsequently published as *Interpretation and Over-interpretation* (1992).

While Eco's early fame as a literary theorist of the "open" work had stressed the reader's response playing an active, even a dominant, role in literary interpretation, his experience as a practicing novelist convinced him that the rights of interpreters had been overstressed, and in these two important works, Eco argues that while a text can have many senses, it is not theoretically possible for a text to embody *every* sense. In the process of discussing postmodern theories of interpretation (especially deconstruction), Eco uses his erudition to show that most so-called "postmodern" theories are really pre-antique. In particular, they have an affinity with the kind of second-century hermeticism that rejected the categories of formal classical logic and argued, as do the paranoid characters in Eco's second novel, that many things may be true at the same time even when they stand in open contradiction. *Tout se tient* ("everything is connected") becomes the leitmotif of Eco's novel and for many contemporary theories of interpretation that display what he calls "hermetic drift" or the "uncontrolled ability to shift from meaning to meaning, from similarity to similarity, from a connection to another." In *Foucault's Pendulum*, a secret document supposedly proving a diabolical plot to take over the world actually turns out to be an ancient laundry list.

Eco's third novel, *L'isola del giorno prima* (1994; *The Island of the Day Before*) is best read against the backdrop of the prestigious Norton lectures Eco delivered at Harvard University in 1992–3 and subsequently published as *Sei passeggiate nei boschi narrativi* (1994; *Six Walks in the Fictional Woods*). In his third novel, Eco presents a pastiche of the historical romances of Alexandre Dumas, *Robinson Crusoe*, and *Treasure Island* in a fascinating account of Baroque culture of the seventeenth century with particular emphasis upon that century's attempts to measure longitude. Since the measurement of longitude concerns the question of time, it is of interest to the novelist as well as to the scientist. Much of the charm of this book lies in its hilarious presentation of the many bizarre ideas typical of seventeenth-century science that seem ridiculous until the clever reader understands that many such ideas are extremely close to exemplary notions of postmodern thought. Obviously influenced by the theoretical work of Omar Calabrese, one of his university colleagues at the University of Bologna, whose book *L'eta neobarocca* (1987; *Neo-Baroque: A Sign of the Times* [1992]) traces similarities between the Baroque period and the postmodern experience, Eco's novel juxtaposes the often foolish scientific mistakes (as well as the startling discoveries) made during the Baroque period by a number of scientists and literary theorists, such as Kepler, Galileo, Tesauro, Donne, or Marino; these notions are implicitly related in the complex text to postmodern ideas espoused by such diverse contemporary critical thinkers as Barth, Harold Bloom, Foucault, Peirce, and Derrida, to mention only a few of the authors relevant to the novel.

If a single image could be created to express Eco's postmodern fiction, it would certainly be that of the palimpsest - usually a vellum or parchment document which has been written upon several times with remnants of earlier and not completely erased writings still visible. Eco's literary creations are postmodern palimpsests, pastiches of other literary works or critical theories that are revisited with irony or even parodied by a master craftsman of contemporary fiction. *Six Walks*, in some respects, revises some of Eco's early negative views of popular writers (such as Ian Fleming) in the light of Eco's own experience as a novelist. Moreover, as the title suggests, his discussion of the nature of literature owes much to an earlier series of Norton lectures delivered by Italo Calvino (*Six Memos for the Next Millennium*). Calvino ranks with Eco as Italy's most famous postmodernist fiction writers, and it is not surprising that if Eco's books speak of other books, one of his best works should also speak of Calvino.

Eco's literary and philosophical production has always been prodigious. His latest book, *Kant e l'ornitorinco* (1997; *Kant and the Platypus: Essays on Language and Cognition* [2000]), represents an attempt to rewrite *A Theory of Semiotics*. In particular, it presents an intriguing discussion of how the human mind deals with previously unknown objects. Departing from Marco Polo's difficulty in describing a rhinoceros (he could only relate it problematically to the unicorn, something he had obviously never actually seen), Eco relates this thorny problem of classification to the theories of Kant and Peirce. Pride of place is reserved for the humble platypus, an animal that human experience finds difficult to categorize because of its puzzling shape.

Umberto Eco's taste for parody, pastiche, and ironic revisitations of other literary or philosophical texts constitutes an integral part of his complex personality. Since his personality and the demands of postmodern literary theory or practice have so many points of convergence, it is not surprising that his works have been more widely read and translated than those of any other Italian writer of the late twentieth century.

22

Frantz Fanon

Robert Bernasconi

Frantz Fanon (1925–61) is still perhaps best known in the United States as the philosopher of violence and decolonization who, beginning in the late 1960s, posthumously inspired the Black Power movement. However, from the perspective of postmodernism, Fanon can be appreciated as a thinker who both interrogated subject-formation and promoted radical difference in the face of the universalizing tendencies of phenomenology and psychoanalysis. Because his works are a natural starting-point for any exploration of the relation between postmodernism and what, depending on one's point of view, might be called postcolonialism or colonial discourse analysis, Fanon has become a site of contestation in the continuing debate over the political stakes of postmodernism. But, however amenable he might be to a postmodern reading, the existential component of his works is irreducible.

Frantz Fanon was born in Martinique. Among his *lycée* or high-school teachers was Aimé Césaire, who in the 1930s had been one of the founders of the negritude movement. Although Fanon would throughout his short life issue strong criticisms of the concept of negritude, particularly the less political, more literary version of it espoused by Leopold Senghor, Césaire's impact on Fanon was lasting. Above all, Fanon learned from Césaire that even the best representatives of European civilization were responsible for colonial racism, thereby leading him to approach the received wisdom of the West with a healthy skepticism. Fanon joined the Free French army and served in Morocco and Algeria, as well as France. He was wounded in action and so he returned to Martinique. In 1947 he returned to France, this time to study. In 1951 he was awarded a medical degree from the University of Lyon. While in Lyon, Fanon attended the lectures of Merleau-Ponty and read Sartre closely. In addition to his familiarity with the most recent developments in existential phenomenology, Fanon also developed an extensive knowledge of psychoanalysis, including the early publications of Jacques Lacan. All of this was brought together in his 1952 study of anti-black racism, *Black Skin, White Masks*.

Fanon's *Black Skin, White Masks* is presented as an attempt to address the inferiority complex that at the time was widely ascribed to the colonized. Fanon initially referred this diagnosis to Aimé Césaire, who proposed it in *Discourse on Colonialism*, but Fanon devoted a chapter to a discussion of the use made of it by Octave Mannoni, an ethnologist and follower of Lacan. In *Prospero and Caliban: The Psychology of Colonization* (1950), Mannoni had argued that the Malagasy suffered from a dependency complex that made them ripe for colonization. According to Mannoni, it is when specifically the educated Malagasy "forgets his or her place" that he or she pays for it with an inferiority complex. By contrast, Fanon set out to show that what he called the psychoexistential complexes of blacks were the product of the colonial situation. Fanon's argument was that this feeling of inferiority must be seen as arising from the internalization of economic oppression. As a result, psychoanalysis was incapable of solving the problem on its own. What is needed is a restructuring of the world. But whereas a unilateral solution at either the individual or societal level is ruled out, there is also no automatic interdependence between them: "such a systematic tendency is contrary to the facts" (1952: 11).

Throughout *Black Skin, White Masks* Fanon criticized the homogenizing tendency of the dominant schools of thought of his day. Although clearly inspired by Sartre and Merleau-Ponty, Fanon was at the same time highly critical of both of them for ignoring the specificity of black existence. The central chapter of *Black Skin, White Masks*, chapter 5, is an existential phenomenological description under the title "the lived experience of the black," a phrase that deliberately evoked Merleau-Ponty. In that chapter Fanon attacked Sartre for offering a phenomenology of the body that was blind to the fact that blacks experience their body quite differently from whites (1952: 138). Similarly, in chapter 6, he argued that the theories of Freud and Adler do not apply to blacks (1952: 141). While recognizing, following Canguilhelm, that the concept of normality is problematic, Fanon claimed that whites enjoy a correlation between the life of the family and the life of the nation that is denied to blacks: a "normal" black child becomes abnormal on contact with the white world (1952: 143). By showing how white psychoanalysis has ignored, or at best misconstrued, the structures of racism as they affect blacks, Fanon went on to show that it was likely that classic psychoanalysis had also failed to understand a certain masochism that arises from the way whites, particularly in the United States, identify with blacks, at the same time that they persist in their racism (1952: 176–8).

Fanon did not set out to proclaim universal truths. He repeatedly warned that his conclusions were valid only for the Antilles, even if broader categories, like that of the Negro, had to be introduced because the white gaze imposed on blacks the uniformity of a single type. If Fanon went to great lengths to show that the black soul is a white man's artifact (1952: 11), thereby recalling Sartre's dictum that the anti-Semite makes the Jew, it was not only to show the impact of white racism. Fanon sought to acknowledge that anti-black racism had forged the black identity and that that identity needed to be utilized as a political force to combat racism and its instruments. But that did not stop him from proclaiming that the notions of a black identity and a white identity are both ultimately unacceptable (1952: 197). His position was therefore not as different in this respect as is sometimes thought from that proposed by Sartre in "Black Orpheus," where negritude was located as the second term in the dialectic, between white supremacy and a future universalism. It is telling, therefore, that when Fanon opposed Sartre, it was on the grounds not that Sartre was wrong, but that such ideas were destructive of black zeal (1952: 135). At the same time, Fanon was clear that he was not positing a universal human type that could be studied in terms of its deviations (1952: 197). His approach was opposed to abstract liberal humanism. In its place he advocated a concrete and so ever-new understanding of man (1952: 22).

After completing *Black Skin, White Masks*, Fanon toyed with the idea of writing a study of Richard Wright, but his frenetic activity in Algeria, where he had gone to work in a psychiatric hospital, led instead to a collection of essays, *Year Five of the Algerian Revolution*, known in English as *A Dying Colonialism*, which was published in 1959. It is a valuable antidote to decontextualized readings of Fanon, even though that same tendency toward decontextualization has perhaps encouraged some feminist readers to deal harshly with his essay on the veil. However, a plausible defense has been developed by Sharpley-Whiting (1998).

Fanon completed *The Wretched of the Earth* (1991 [1961]) in the knowledge that he was dying of leukemia. The book is best known for its theory of violence. Some extreme statements can be found there. For example, Fanon wrote: "For the colonized, life can arise only from the decomposing cadaver of the colonizer" (1991 [1961]: 93; my trans.). However, Fanon was not nearly as indiscriminate in his advocacy of violence against the colonizers as Sartre was in his preface. In *The Wretched of the Earth* Fanon was continuing, albeit in another, more political register, to explore some of the issues that had already preoccupied him in *Black Skin, White Masks*. So, for example, he wrote: "At the level of individuals, violence is a disintoxifying force. It frees the colonized from his inferiority complex and from his despair and action, it makes him fearless and restores his self-respect" (1991 [1961]: 94; trans. modified). Fanon claimed that violence organized by the leaders helps the masses understand social truths (1991 [1961]: 147). Violence illuminates the consciousness of the people and directs them against any pacification. It unifies. In this way, a certain violence not only frees the colonized from their inferiority complex, but is supposed to justify the rhetoric of a new humanity that pervades *The Wretched of the Earth*. It is a rhetoric that had already been introduced in *A Dying Colonialism* to describe the experience of revolutionary action in Algeria, but that in *The Wretched of the Earth* was generalized and postponed to an indeterminate future.

The extraordinary closing lines of the book read: "For Europe, for ourselves, and for humanity, comrades, we must cast the slough, work out new concepts, and try to set afoot a new man" (1991 [1961]: 316; trans. modified). The claim is that just as the colonizer made the colonized, so decolonization is the creation of new human beings (1991 [1961]: 36). Decolonization means more than depriving the colonizers of their power. Fanon insisted that the Third World ought not to be content to define itself in terms of the values that preceded it, but should find its own values, method, and style (1991 [1961]: 99). But even though the general tenor of *The Wretched of the Earth* was that of antagonism, it should not be assumed that Fanon had altogether left behind his earlier more conciliatory approach. Only a couple of years earlier Fanon had called for a humanism built to the dimensions of the universe which would unite the oppressed with those who are already sovereign (Fanon 1988: 114). Although Fanon's corpus is relatively small, it seems that on many crucial issues it is always possible to juxtapose one text with another markedly different one. This has opened the way to a variety of different readings, including some by significant theorists of postmodernism.

The postmodern appropriation of Fanon is best exemplified by Homi Bhabha. In his foreword to the English edition of *Black Skin, White Masks* (1986; reprinted in Gibson 1999), Bhabha constructs a Fanon who refused "the ambition of any 'total' theory of colonial oppression" (Fanon 1986: x). Bhabha's Fanon is indeed, in Benita Parry's phrase, "a premature poststructuralist" (Parry 1987: 31). However, having conceded that Fanon was not all he wants him to have been, Bhabha proceeds to rewrite *Black Skin, White Masks* quite openly. By examining those points where Bhabha finds himself under most pressure to revise Fanon's texts to bring them into conformity with postmodernism, one readily identifies the points of tension between Fanon's texts and (a certain version of) postmodernism.

Even though he initially recognizes the role of Fanon's existentialist evocation of the "I" in restoring the presence of the marginalized, Bhabha seems willing to sacrifice it to present a reading of Fanon that emphasizes his Lacanian aspects, even if it means ignoring what Fanon himself has to say against Lacan (Fanon 1986: 161 n. 25). According to Bhabha, Fanon is too quick to name the Other and too ready to treat the Other as the fixed phenomenological point of a culturally alien consciousness. According to Bhabha, "The Other must be seen as the necessary negation of a primordial identity – cultural or psychic – that introduces the system of differentiation which enables the 'cultural' to be signified as a linguistic, symbolic, historic reality" (Bhabha, in Fanon 1986: xviii). So far as Bhabha is concerned, Fanon's insight into the ambivalences of identification is compromised by his tendency to have recourse to antagonistic identities.

Bhabha may be right to claim that Fanon can be at times criticized for oversimplifying the opposition between colonizer and colonized, but Fanon's strategy can be seen in a slightly different light when it is juxtaposed with that of deconstruction. Deconstruction, according to Derrida, takes the binary oppositions that dominate Western metaphysics, reverses the hierarchies implicit within them, and then displaces the oppositions. If the hierarchy between colonizer and colonized is assimilated to this model, as a certain postmodernism tries to do, it can seem, particularly on the basis of *The Wretched of the Earth*, that Fanon simply reversed the terms of the hierarchy but perpetuated the division. Nevertheless, as I have already noted, there are passages in Fanon that argue explicitly for a humanism that seeks to unite the oppressed and the oppressors. This raises the possibility that it is not so much that Fanon vacillates between strategies, as that he recognizes, in good deconstructive fashion, the necessity of both stages. That is to say, he keeps in mind the construction of a new humanity without supposing that one can move there by edict. The battles still must be fought and the victims remembered.

Those postmodern critics of Fanon who complain that he too often leaves the terms of the opposition intact, proceed in a manner not unlike that for which Fanon himself criticized Sartre: they are liable to destroy black zeal. In that case, the problem would not be that Fanon was too quick to name the Other, but that Bhabha was too quick to renounce those names. In effect, this is part of the argument made by Cedric Robinson (1993) and, on slightly different grounds, by Lewis Gordon (1995) against postmodern readings of Fanon.

Henry Louis Gates, Jr. offers a different route to a postmodernist Fanon when in "Critical Fanonism" (1991) he describes how critics like Edward Said and Homi Bhabha, by presenting Fanon as an opponent of fixed identity, have also reduced him to a global theorist *in vacuo*. Gates claims that in their effort to construct a version of Fanon that can participate in debates inspired by postmodernism about the decline of grand narratives and identity theory, they have paradoxically deprived him of his context. This leads Gates to argue not only for a rehistoricization of Fanon, but one that encourages us to develop an understanding of our own theoretical reflections as equally provisional, reactive, and local. However, this is an argument that follows more readily from a reading of *Black Skin, White Masks* than from *The Wretched of the Earth*.

Black Skin, White Masks is not an easy book to read, for either whites or blacks. Fanon held up a mirror to his readers, particularly his black readers, but at the same time he did so within the framework of a progressive infrastructure that was supposed to allow blacks to chart their way on the path to disalienation (1952: 184). This complex strategy, which has helped to solicit a wide variety of readings of the book, is amenable to a postmodern reading, but it ultimately remains impenetrable if one omits its existential component. So long as one keeps Fanon's politics and especially his opposition to racism and colonialism firmly in the foreground, his works are much less porous or polyvocal than is sometimes thought.

23

Michel Foucault

Karlis Racevskis

When asked about his thoughts on postmodernism, Michel Foucault usually responded by indicating that he knew very little about a concept that did not really interest him. It is obvious today, of course, that Foucault's thought has played a major role in the constitution and elaboration of what could be called a postmodern critical awareness. What Foucault contributed to set in place, then, is a critical approach seeking to disclose the special character of a mindset called "modernity." From a genealogical standpoint, it was not so much a question of defining a period or announcing its ending as of examining the discontinuity in thinking our history – a discontinuity that had become a marking characteristic of our age. As Foucault saw it, "rather than seeking to distinguish the 'modern era' from the 'premodern' or 'postmodern,' I think it would be more useful to try to find out how the attitude of modernity, ever since its formation, has found itself struggling with attitudes of 'counter-modernity'" (1984b: 39).

It was a struggle he found reflected in the work of Kant, one of modernity's most prominent figures. While Kant's influence on Western thought was clearly fundamental, it was also highly problematic, Foucault found, since it had produced two divergent paths in philosophy:

> It seems to me that Kant founded two great critical traditions according to which modern philosophy has divided itself. Let's say that in his great critical opus, Kant posed and founded the philosophical tradition that asks the question of the conditions under which true knowledge is possible and, from there, we can say that a whole segment of modern philosophy has presented itself and developed since the 19th century as an analytic of truth. (1984a; *Dits et écrits* 4: 687)

Now the attempt to found knowledge in truth had mainly induced an anthropological sleep in philosophers and was therefore inherently deluded to Foucault's way of thinking. On the other hand, he credited Kant for having founded a critical tradition he considered a most inspiring and fertile source of philosophical investigation. It was in a minor essay entitled "Was ist Aufklärung?" that Foucault located one of the German philosopher's most insightful contributions. Foucault recognized that, with the publication of this article, "the question of the 'present moment' becomes, for philosophy, an interrogation from which it can no longer be separated" (1985; *Dits et écrits* 4: 766). The effect of Kant's reflections, accordingly, had been to suggest that philosophy could be considered a part of a general historical process, as well as a system of interpretation that provided the means for deciphering history, for uncovering the historical conditions giving rise to philosophy itself.

Foucault thus identified Kant's meditation on the Enlightenment as the source of a second important critical tradition. In Germany, the thinking outlined in the essay had inspired an historical and political reflection on society that could be traced "from the post-Hegelians to the Frankfurt School and Lukács, by way of Feuerbach, Marx, Nietzsche, and Max Weber." In France, it was above all through the history of sciences that a philosophical approach to the question of the Enlightenment had developed and Foucault singled out the writings of Koyré, Bachelard, Cavaillés, and Canguilhem as works that "functioned as important centers of philosophical elaboration, to the extent that they displayed under different angles this question of the Enlightenment, so essential to contemporary philosophy" (1985; *Dits et écrits* 4: 767).

The critique of the *Aufklärung* inevitably brought into question the very concept of the Enlightenment. It was an interrogation in which the history of sciences, especially in the particular form that Georges Canguilhem gave it, had had a central importance in intellectual debates in France, Foucault thought. What gave Canguilhem's contribution its importance was the elaboration of an approach that stood opposed to Kant's analytic of truth. The originality of Canguilhem's thought, for Foucault, resided in the paradoxical evidence that "this historian of rationalities, himself so 'rational,' is a philosopher of error." Underlying Canguilhem's philosophy was the recognition that "error is at the root of what constitutes human thought and its history." The life and history of humans revolve around and in response to a condition that is marked fundamentally by chance, unpredictability, and error. As a consequence, conceptual schemes and rationalizations can be seen as ways of coping with error, as strategies meant to compensate for the reality of chance at the heart of human affairs:

> The opposition of true and false, the values we attribute to both, the effects of power that different societies and different institutions link to this division – all this is perhaps only the latest response to this possibility of error, which is intrinsic to life. If the history of science is discontinuous, that is, if it can be

analyzed only as a series of "corrections," as a new distribution of true and false which never finally, once and for all liberates the final moment of truth, it is because there too, "error" constitutes not the forgetting or the delaying of the promised accomplishment, but the dimension proper to the life of humans and indispensable to the time of the species. (1985; *Dits et écrits* 4: 775)

The awareness of this aspect of human existence brings about two important consequences. If we recognize, first, that knowledge is more likely to be "rooted in the 'errors' of life" than to provide an opening to "the truth of the world," then we become aware of the need to completely reformulate the whole theory of the subject. Second, this recognition also produces a different understanding of the relationship between error and truth: "Error is not eliminated by the muffled force of a truth that would emerge, bit by bit, from the shadows, but by the formation of a new way of 'speaking true' [*dire vrai*]." What passes for scientific truth at any given moment, for example, is the mark of a provisional state of affairs. And the recognition of the provisional status of the conceptual systems accounting for the real informs, in turn, the self-reflexivity whose importance was first recognized by Kant.

Paradoxically, the notion of error is thus given a positive role to play: the recognition of the tenuous nature of truth is what opens up the possibility of thinking the subject's freedom. Thus, once we become aware that what we are and what we think are aspects of our being that are not dependent on a preordained order of things, once we realize that events, actions, and thoughts are subject to contingency and chance and not to law – either divine or human-made – then we also become aware of the freedom and possibilities inherent in the present moment. It is in this sense that Kant's famous *sapere aude* becomes an ethical injunction to assert one's freedom through the exercise of one's critical faculties. It is to this extent also, Foucault thought, that we are indebted to the Enlightenment because it still serves to valorize "the principle of a critique and a permanent creation of ourselves in our autonomy: that is, a principle that is at the heart of the historical consciousness that the Enlightenment has of itself" (1984b: 44). The application of this principle, Foucault tells us, is also what will free us from what he calls "the blackmail of the Enlightenment," which he perceives as an unwritten moral obligation to be either for or against the Enlightenment, a compulsion that is created by a constant "historical and moral confusionism that mixes the theme of humanism with the question of the Enlightenment." As it frees itself from the fallacious notion that lets us perceive a discursive formation as the expression of a human essence, critique becomes archaeological in its method,

> in the sense that it will not seek to identify the universal structures of all knowledge or of all possible moral action, but will seek to treat the instances

of discourse that articulate what we think, say, and do as so many historical events. And this critique will be genealogical in the sense that it will not deduce from the form of what we are what it is impossible for us to do and to know; but it will separate out, from the contingency that has made us what we are, the possibility of no longer being, doing, or thinking what we are, do, or think. (1984b: 46)

The important lesson of the Enlightenment for Foucault is, then, an awareness that freedom is possible, that it is a potential always present in what we do and think, a chance to be sought out and taken whenever it presents itself. There is no causality inherent either in our existence or in history, no plan or foreordained truth to guide it. This does not mean that anything goes, however, or that humans can do or think anything they like. The elaboration of a critical perspective requires vigilance and discipline – if we are to effectively free ourselves from a number of illusions and delusions due, precisely, to the inability to see that a certain legacy of the Enlightenment has made us prone to error. Thus, for example, the two themes of progress and freedom have proven to be contradictory. The growth of technological capability has resulted in an increased capacity for control and domination in such areas as economic production, social regulation, and communication. The pressing question for our time has therefore become, "how can the growth of capabilities be disconnected from the intensification of power relations?" (1984b: 48).

The investigation of the present-day constitution of power relations involves cognitive, ethical, as well as political considerations, because it aims to disclose the effect discourses and practices have on the formation of our consciousness of ourselves. Consequently, the question to be raised is threefold, suggests Foucault: "How are we constituted as subjects of our own knowledge? How are we constituted as subjects who exercise or submit to power relations? How are we constituted as moral subjects of our own actions?" (1984b: 49). Whatever serves to validate our knowledge, our politics, and our ethics is to be viewed in terms of limitations inherent in our ways of thinking. These are limits to be disclosed, defined, and, eventually, overcome and reconfigured.

At the same time, such striving is always to be seen as tentative, experimental, and itself prone to erring. As Kant himself was aware, any critical standpoint is to be taken as a position within a cultural, epistemological, and political context informing it. The critic's task will therefore consist "in showing how and in what way the one speaking as a thinker, as a scientist, as a philosopher is himself a part of this process and (even more) how he has a certain role to play in this process, in which he will therefore figure as both an element and an actor" (1984a; *Dits et écrits* 4: 680). What appears to Foucault as the most important part of the Enlightenment's legacy is thus an attitude that translates into a will to resist the forces of subjectification. Kant interprets the Enlightenment as a striving to emerge from a state of minority. Foucault, in turn, relates Kant's definition of minority to a lack of courage in the face of an excessive authority: consequently, "we must *dare* to refuse to be led, to refuse to let ourselves be completely governed by others" (Fimiani 1998: 63).

The decision to assume the responsibility to think for oneself also entails the acceptance of a "morality of uncomfortableness," as the title of one of Foucault's book reviews suggests. In his discussion of *L'ère des ruptures* by Jean Daniel, who was the founding editor of *Le Nouvel Observateur*, Foucault finds that what motivates Daniel is precisely the attitude Kant identifies in his essay on the Enlightenment: it is "the desire to find out what is hidden under this precise, floating, mysterious, absolutely simple word: 'Today'" (1979 [1966]; *Dits et écrits* 3: 783). Indeed, Foucault notes that the very foundation of the journal was already an expression of such an attitude, of a desire to clarify the prevalent consciousness of the day. And, as it "narrates how the work and the struggle to clarify an indistinct consciousness ended up by unraveling the evidence that had given it birth," Daniel's book succeeds in disclosing the coming to awareness that marked its time. First to unravel, as a result, were the grand historical referents – capitalism, the bourgeoisie, imperialism, socialism, the proletariat – as well as any attempts at maintaining the "heroism of political identity." The evidence of what once was certain dissipated in the light of experience – the arbitrariness of set convictions appearing only long after their certainty had evaporated. On the other hand, what had been invisible became suddenly visible, as all the truths that had been taken to be self-evident were shown to rely on supports belying their self-evidence. What became clear, as a result, was that "each certitude can only remain secure by virtue of a supporting ground that remains unexplored" (1979 [1966]; *Dits et écrits* 3: 787).

In the wake of Foucault's archaeological and genealogical analysis of modernity, what present-day critiques of our cultural imaginary provide most notably is an awareness of the irreducible complexity of our world; they also bring out the reasons why the process of making sense of the world and of creating norms by which to live is more demanding than modernity imagined. A postmodern critical perspective makes us understand that this sense and these norms are not available to us preformed, that they have not been inscribed from the beginning of time in a book of eternal and universal verities. On the other hand, once they are brought down to earth, the values and meanings that inform our lives become our responsibility once more: we now know that, if they are to be, these norms and this sense need to be reaffirmed, reformulated, or created anew through a never-ending process of debate and negotiations.

24

John Fowles

Susana Onega

John Fowles's literary career began in 1963 with the publication of *The Collector*, a short novel written during a break from work on *The Magus* (1966). The following year he told an interviewer that contemporary British writing was "not too healthy," that it was "too insular, too privately embroiled" and that the "provincial" school to which "some of our best younger writers belong" was too self-enclosed (in Newquist 1964: 220). Fowles was separating himself here from what Blake Morrison (1980) later termed "The Movement," the kind of anti-experimental and anti-cosmopolitan trend associated with novelists and poets such as Kingsley Amis, John Braine, Alan Sillitoe, John Wain, David Storey, Philip Larkin, D. J. Enright, Robert Conquest, John Holloway, Elizabeth Jennings, and Thom Gunn, considered to be the mainstream postwar English trend by such influential critics in of the 1960s as Frederick R. Karl, James Gindin, and Rubin Rabinowitz. In the field of drama, The Movement was paralleled by "The Angry Young Men," a phrase coined by J. Russell Taylor in his book *Anger and After* (1962), who may have taken it from John Osborne's *Look Back in Anger* (1956). Together with Osborne, the most important playwrights belonging to this trend include Shelagh Delaney, John Arden, and Brendan Behan. The phrase was soon employed both for playwrights and novelists belonging to The Movement, such as Kingsley Amis and John Wain, as well as Collin Henry Wilson, John Gerard Braine, David Storey, and Alan Sillitoe.

A few years later, in an interview with Lorna Sage (1974: 33), Fowles was to admit his interest in French literature, especially in the medieval romance and the *nouveau roman*. However, Fowles's relationship with this cosmopolitan, extremely experimental trend was never unproblematic. In an essay entitled "Notes on Writing a Novel" (1968: 88–97), where he comments on some of

This chapter is part of a research project financed by the Spanish Ministry of Education and Culture (PB 97–1022).

the memoranda he had written while he was writing *The French Lieutenant's Woman* (1969), he says that "Alain Robbe-Grillet's polemical essay *Pour un nouveau roman* (1963) is indispensable reading for the profession even where it produces no more than total disagreement" (Fowles 1968: 89). As he explains, one of Robbe-Grillet's answers to his "key question: *Why bother to write in a form whose great masters cannot be surpassed?*" (89–90), is a fallacy in that "it reduces the purpose of the novel to the discovery of new forms: whereas its other purposes – to entertain, to satirize, to describe new sensibilities, to record life, to improve life, and so on – are clearly just as viable and import-ant" (91).

As early as 1968, then, Fowles was already advocating the renewal of the novel form while preserving its intelligibility and the old humanist values of classic realism, that is, he was expressing the desire to reconcile the modernist "consolation of form" with the "longing for the return to the traditional relish in story-telling," the very reconciliation that Linda Hutcheon considers to be the defining characteristic of postmodernist fiction. According to Hutcheon, the type of novel that best fulfills this contradictory poetics is "historiographic metafiction," by which she means "those well-known and popular novels which are both intensely self-reflexive and yet paradoxically also lay claim to historical events and personages," a type of novel in which "the theoretical self-awareness of history and fiction as human constructs (historio*graphic* *meta*fiction) is made the ground for its rethinking and reworking of the forms and contents of the past [and which] always works *within* conventions in order to subvert them" (Hutcheon 1988: 5).

The attempt to renew the novel from within, subverting its own conven-tions, provides the key for an understanding of Fowles's work as a whole. In *The French Lieutenant's Woman* – arguably the first British historiographic metafiction (Onega 1993a: 47–61) – Fowles seemingly attempts to imitate the conventions of Victorian realism until chapter 13, where imitation unexpect-edly gives way to parody, as the omniscient narrator mischievously admits that he does not know who Sarah is and that the story he is telling "is all imagination" (1969: 97), thus shaking to its foundations the willing suspension of disbelief of the reader. Elizabeth Rankin (1973: 193–207) has pointed out that, thematically, *The French Lieutenant's Woman* fictionalizes the Darwinian metamorphosis of the last Victorian aristocrat into the first existentialist. From this perspective, the unmasking of the unreliability and contingency of the narrator may be said to echo at the structural level Charles's metamorphosis. At the end of the novel, protagonist and reader are left in a strikingly similar position: turning from a Victorian into an existentialist, Charles loses his reassuring belief in a well-ordered, unitary cosmos, immediately accessible to the subject, and experiences the agonizing vision of the void, as he contem-plates the abysmal gap separating himself from the world. Likewise, with his/

her trust in the reliability and omniscience of the narrator irreparably shattered at the end of the novel, the reader finds himself/herself sharing Charles's bafflement and alienation, as the fictional world fragments and appears unattainable by unmediated perception.

Charles's and the reader's anagnorisis echoes that of David Williams, the purblind abstract painter in *The Ebony Tower* (Fowles 1974: 9–113), when, confronted with *The Moon-Hunt*, one of Henry Breasley's masterpieces, he realizes that, in this as in most of the old master's work, the picture grew out of the absorption and parodic rejection of a centuries-old tradition, in this case of "Uccello's *Night Hunt* and its spawn down through the centuries; [giving it] an essential tension, in fact: behind the mysteriousness and the ambiguity (no hounds, no horses, no prey ... nocturnal figures among trees, but the title was needed), stood both an homage and a kind of thumbed nose to a very old tradition" (23).

David's discovery that contemporary art can only achieve genuine originality and creativity by standing in a parodic relation to the formidable Western tradition it stems from echoes John Barth's well-known contention in "The Literature of Exhaustion" that "if Beethoven's Sixth were composed today, it would be an embarrassment; but clearly it wouldn't be, necessarily, if done with ironic intent by a composer quite aware of where we've been and where we are" (1967: 31). For Barth, the truly creative writer is one capable of giving birth to a new literary form out of the ironic absorption and rejection of the "exhausted" form preceding it. In a later essay (1979b), Barth describes postmodernist literature as characterized by a double, contradictory impulse to absorb and transcend not just one "exhausted" form but two: classic realism and modernism, the very combination Fowles experiments with once and again in his own fiction. It does not come as a surprise, then, when Barth offers a long list of postmodernist writers, most of them American and continental European – Barthelme, Bellow, Coover, Elkin, Pynchon, Vonnegut, Mailer, Barth himself, Nabokov, Butor, Robbe-Grillet, Cortázar, and Calvino – adding to them just one British writer, John Fowles.

In *The Collector*, the novelistic form Fowles sets out to parody is that of Movement fiction. The collector, Frederick Clegg, is not just a rebellious son of the welfare state who refuses to abide by the social rules imposed on him, but rather a dangerous psychopath, the product of a deeply troubled, unstructured working-class family and the victim of a heavily repressive nonconformist background. As Robert Huffaker (1980: 75) has pointed out, the timid butterfly collector turned woman collector and murderer, like the gang of psychopaths in Anthony Burgess's *A Clockwork Orange* (1962), constitutes an extreme and blood-curdling parodic version of the postwar "angry young man." At the same time, however, *The Collector* fictionalizes an archetypal situation: the Bluebeard-like man who punishes the woman's curiosity and disobedience (Newquist 1964: 219; Grace 1984: 245–62). From an archetypal perspective, Miranda's death and Clegg's incapacity to abandon his collecting and voyeuristic activities and to learn the language of art Miranda has been trying to teach him during her confinement may be read as the double failure of kidnapper and kidnapped to round off their respective maturation processes – in Clegg's case, his evolution from collector to creator and, in Miranda's case, from young creator-to-be to mature creator/magus (Mellors 1975: 65–72).

In *The Magus*, Nicholas Urfe, a collector of "girlfriends" and a would-be poet, suffering from existentialist bad faith, undergoes a series of trials set for him by "the magus," Maurice Conchis, with the help of two mysterious twin sisters. As in the mythical hero's quest, the trials are both physical and psychological. Nick suffers an agonizing phase of deterministic despair, as he is made to confront the existentialist void. But after he masters his angst and accepts the void, he is seized by the *delirium vivens*, the passion to exist that comes together with the realization that he is free to shape his life as he likes. This realization of personal freedom brings about his maturation, or transformation from collector into artist/magus.

In every novel by John Fowles, collecting and creating are the metaphors for expressing what he considers to be two basic ways of relating self and world. Already in *The Aristos* (1980 [1964]) – Fowles's "Self Portrait in Ideas" – the writer draws an implicit opposition between self and world when he refers to the I's constant awareness of "the otherness of things" (Fowles 1980: 84). Nearly thirty years later, he continues to speak in similar terms in *The Nature of Nature* (1995), when he warns the reader that the "world is not just stranger than we think; it may be stranger than we can think" (Fowles 1995: 95). Making his own Virginia Woolf's belief that "there is a lethal enmity between words and nature" (91), he contends that classifying and naming a thing distort its "beingness," what D. H. Lawrence called "the existingness in things" (26–7), since: "Even the simplest knowledge of the names and habits of flowers or trees . . . removes us a step from total reality towards anthropocentrism . . . it destroys or curtails certain possibilities of seeing, apprehending and experiencing" (26–7).

Fowles's words show his awareness of the position of writers like Joyce, Beckett, and Robbe-Grillet and of critics like Roland Barthes and Jacques Derrida, for whom language is not a transparent and utilitarian medium, but rather a self-sufficient and autonomous sign-system without meaning or referent. The realization that language can only signify itself led the modernists to the logical conclusion that the only accessible reality is the inner reality of self-perception. Thus, Samuel Beckett's work grows out of the tension between his obsessive compulsion to record the inescapability of self-perception, confronted with his conviction that language cannot communicate meaning. Characteristically, the great Irish writer expresses this tension by creating authors-characters, like Molloy, Malone, or "the unnamable," who struggle between the need to write themselves into existence and the temptation to yield to silence/death.

The modernist and poststructuralist definitions of language open a gap between self and world that Fowles will once and again try to bridge by attempting to recuperate the creative power of language. In *The Tree* (1979), he explains that human beings have always tried to come to terms with the world in two basic ways: by using language logically in order to name and classify things and to impose rational order over the natural chaos of the external world; or by using language intuitively in order to express their own individual feelings about the world and about themselves. The first is the collective language of scientists, the second, the poetic language advocated by William Wordsworth for the individual artist. With Wordsworth, Fowles believes that, for all the radical otherness of nature, poetic language can aspire to capture its essence by following the promptings of the natural laws inscribed in the human heart. Consequently, the maturation processes of his heroes necessarily involve the abandonment of the "scientific" attitude to nature of the collector and the adoption of the intuitive and symbolic language of art, the only type of language capable of expressing the complexity and otherness of nature and of reconciling self and world (Onega 2000).

In *Daniel Martin* (1977), Fowles attempts to find a way out of Beckettian solipsism and the "prisonhouse of language" (Waugh 1984: 34). The novel begins at the moment when Daniel Martin decides to put an end to his successful career as a cinema-script writer in order to write an autobiographical novel, or, in Beckettian terms, in order to write himself into existence. At the end of the novel, Dan – like Nicholas Urfe at the end of *The Magus* – has overcome his predatory tendency to collect women, has learnt the value of true love, and – like David Williams in *The Ebony Tower* – has discovered the capacity of art to pin down reality: "To hell with cultural fashion; to hell with élitist guilt; to hell with existentialist nausea and above all, to hell with the imagined that does not say, not only in, but behind the images, the real" (Fowles 1977: 454).

This "happy" ending is disturbed, however, in the last paragraph of the novel, when the reader is surprised to discover that Daniel Martin has not written his autobiographical novel yet. Also disturbing is the reader's realization that Dan's pseudonym, "Simon Wolfe," can be rearranged to form the name FOWLES (Simon WOLFE) (Wolfe 1979: 182; Conradi 1982: 95), and that Dan's unwritten last sentence, "Whole sight, or all the rest is desolation," is in fact the first sentence in John Fowles's novel, *Daniel Martin* (7). As Fowles metafictionally undermines the protagonist's illusion of freedom, the boundaries between the real and the imaginary, the written and the unwritten collapse. The novel becomes a Borgesian Library of Babel, trapping within itself character, narrator, and flesh-and-blood author, who are thus revealed as the fragmented facets of a unique subject, a kind of Borgesian supra-individual composite subject, standing astride the boundaries of fiction and reality (Onega 1995: 93–105; 1996b: 29–56).

In an interview with Jan Relf, Fowles explained that he had removed from the original draft of *The French Lieutenant's Woman* a whole final passage, in which "the author figure . . . was in fact an escaped lunatic. It was quite funny, but it was out of the tone of the book" (in Vipond 1999: 127). This image of an author figure in a lunatic asylum is the image out of which *Mantissa* (1982) grows, a satiric novel written in homage to yet another great Irish modernist, Flann O'Brien. In *At Swim-Two-Birds* (1939), O'Brien imagines a writer, Dermot Trellis, obsessed with the idea of creating a human being by means of a process of "aestho-autogamy." Trellis eventually succeeds in begetting a character, John Furriskey, not, however, *ex nihilo*, since he acknowledges the influence of a late writer of romances, William Tracy, as his dominant predecessor. Trellis is a ludicrous example of the naive author who happily relies on his authorial ability to create his own subjective textual universe, even though, in fact, his created characters usually refuse to obey him and even drug him in order to lead secret lives while he is fast asleep. In *Mantissa*, an amnesiac writer, Miles Green, wakes up in a cell in a lunatic asylum, which (like the cells in *Malone Dies*, *The Unnamable*, or *Endgame*) neatly resembles the inside of a skull. Following Roland Barthes's theory that reading produces pleasure (*jouissance*), Dr. Delfie, Green's doctor/muse, helps him overcome amnesia by means of the artificial induction of an orgasm which unexpectedly metamorphoses into the delivery of a text made up of a series of ludicrous and repetitive versions of Green's struggle to silence his muse and to achieve control over his creation/himself. Needless to say, Green's newly born text is not original but – like Daniel Martin's – identical to Fowles's text entitled *Mantissa* (Onega 1989: 123–36; Pifer 1986: 162–76).

Fowles returns to historiographic metafiction in *A Maggot* (1986), a wonderfully rich novel situated in Augustan England, which Fowles himself has related to "South American magic realism" (in Vipond 1999: 142). The protagonist, Mr. Bartholomew (or Mr. B.), an occultist magus, undertakes a journey from London to Dolling Cave in Devon in the company of his deaf-mute servant, Dick Thurlow, a maid addressed as Louise, but really called Rebecca Lee, and two other men, Francis Lacy and Sergeant Timothy Farthing, also traveling under assumed names. At the end of the journey Mr. B. disappears in the cave without a trace and Dick Thurlow is found dead, hanging from a tree with a posy of violets growing out of his mouth. Henry Ayscough, the Tory barrister who tries to solve the mystery by applying rational methods, is – like the realism-biased reader – incapable of unraveling the truth, since each witness offers a puzzlingly different account: for Francis Lacy the events at the cave were infernal, for Rebecca, celestial – just as in Peter Ackroyd's *The House of Doctor Dee* (1993a), where London is both a hell and a heaven, depending on Doctor Dee's way of imagining it.

Only by renouncing the Aristotelian either/or logic in favor of the dualistic logic of myth can the contradictory versions gathered by Ayscough acquire an unassailable logic and the multiplicity of names and characters' roles gain overall significance. From a Jungian perspective, the journey becomes an archetypal hero's quest for individuation and cosmic integration, with Mr. B., the Christ figure at war with the Father, standing for the conscious or ego; his deaf-mute manservant and suspected twin brother for the unconscious; and Rebecca Lee for the anima. From an archetypal perspective, Mr. B.'s disappearance and Dick's death – like the disappearance of another eighteenth-century occultist, Nicholas Dyer, at the end of Peter Ackroyd's *Hawksmoor* (1985) – can only be interpreted as evidence that, after sacrificing his unconscious and reconciling himself with his anima, Mr. B. has managed to bring about his transformation from man to *anthropos* and his cosmic integration by means of ascesis (Onega 1989: 137–63).

Mr. B., who is an endless storyteller, had hired the other travelers to perform a series of roles while keeping them in the dark about the real aim of the journey. In this sense, we might say that he, like Daniel Martin and Miles Green, consciously tried to control his life, to write the script of his own existence for the *comoedia vitae* (Fowles 1986: 22). However, as the Richardsonian echoes of his name suggest, Mr. B. is only a fictional character, trapped in a novel entitled *A Maggot*. From this perspective Mr. B.'s final disappearance can only be interpreted as evidence that he – unlike Daniel Martin and Miles Green, but like the Tory MP John Marcus Fielding in "The Enigma" (Fowles 1974: 185–239), and also like Nicholas Dyer in Ackroyd's novel – has managed to step out of Fowles's text, thus liberating himself from "the prisonhouse of language" and becoming, like Fielding, "the *Deus absconditus*, the God who went missing" (235).

Thus, in *A Maggot*, Fowles offers his most nuanced answer to the questions about self, world, and text he had been tackling in his earlier fiction. He uses parody, pastiche, and the metafictional undermining of realism-enhancing mechanisms in order to convey the fragmentation and isolation of the self, while simultaneously managing to transcend this isolation and fragmentation in mythical terms, thus suggesting that, although the world cannot be represented with the fidelity of a mirror, it can be symbolically evoked, as archaic civilizations did through myth and as visionary writers like Blake or Wordsworth also tried to do, using the power of their creative imaginations to transform the flux of experience into meaningful patterns.

Looking at the situation of the British novel in the 1980s and 1990s and at the emergence of new writers of historiographic metafiction such as Peter Ackroyd, Charles Palliser, Jeanette Winterson, Salman Rushdie, or A. S. Byatt, who are trying to renew the novel form in Britain along the lines of Fowles's work, that is, by the combination of metafiction and myth with the rewriting of history, one cannot help but realize the importance of the writer who originated what we can now describe as the most promising and truly creative postmodernist trend that has appeared in Britain in the last thirty years.

25

Carlos Fuentes

Sheldon Penn

As one of the leading authors of the Latin American literary "Boom" that reached its peak in the 1960s and 1970s, the Mexican writer Carlos Fuentes has achieved international recognition as a novelist. He has held positions as a visiting lecturer both in the United States and in England, continues to be a familiar figure at both academic conferences and public readings, and has made numerous contributions to newspapers in Europe and the Americas. Coupled with his oft-mentioned desire to be recognized as a contributor to a universal body of literature, it should come as little surprise that Fuentes has gained a high profile outside of Latin America. This status is also reflective of a cross-cultural impulse that is fundamental to much of Fuentes's writing. Central to many of his novels and short fictions is the investigation of the relationship between cultures and between the Old and New Worlds. This exploration finds its roots in the author's own multinational and trilingual upbringing (as the son of a diplomat Fuentes was born in Panama, soon moved to the United States, and spent time in Geneva). During the early years of his career Fuentes maintained a strongly Marxist position. He continued to support the Cuban Revolution, a galvanizing political force for "Boom" writers, when others had rejected it. Finally, Fuentes himself gave up hope for this cause when, in his own words, "the Cubans developed their tropical socialist realism and began to excommunicate people" (Fuentes 1981: 171). Since this time Fuentes has remained left of center, but has gradually come to favor a social democratic stance.

Fuentes has received a great deal of attention from anglophone theorists of the literary postmodern. Two texts from the 1980s that provided influential definitions of literary postmodernism, Brian McHale's *Postmodernist Fiction* (1987) and Linda Hutcheon's *A Poetics of Postmodernism* (1988), both cite examples of Fuentes's fiction as illustrative paradigms. Indeed, with reference to *Terra Nostra* (Fuentes 1976), McHale goes as far as to state that "this novel is, along with Pynchon's *Gravity's Rainbow* (1973), one of the paradigmatic texts of postmodernist writing, literally an anthology of postmodernist themes and devices" (1987: 16). Both McHale's and Hutcheon's theses are probably guilty of oversimplification as a result of their zeal for a systematized position. Most importantly, they both fail to consider sufficiently the various cultural, socioeconomic, and political contexts particular to the production of their chosen postmodern texts. I shall discuss this problem in due course, but Hutcheon's theory of postmodernism in particular is worth pursuing nevertheless for the considerable insight that it provides for a reading of Fuentes's work.

Hutcheon's postmodernism is defined in opposition to that of Marxist thinkers such as Fredric Jameson who have identified the phenomenon as a negative condition pertaining to late capitalism. She argues that postmodernism is "contradictory, resolutely historical and inescapably political" (Hutcheon 1988: 4), challenging Jameson's and others' positions that it is homogenizing, ahistorical, and politically disinterested. Conceding that postmodernism might be a result of mass consumer culture, Hutcheon asserts that it seeks to challenge and critique its socioeconomic context rather than to celebrate it. Her analysis of the postmodernist position is focused largely through a type of novel that she labels "historiographic metafiction."

The postmodernism of this fiction is defined by Hutcheon as a shift within modernism rather than as an outright contradiction to it, the prefix "post" being indicative of the liminal complexities of the mode that is subversive rather than destructive (1988: 5). Postmodernism, therefore, looks to advertise its own problematics, hence Hutcheon's indication of its contradictory nature. It is the metafictivity of these novels that simultaneously attracts censure from anti-postmodernists and approval from Hutcheon. Her "historiographical metafiction" strives to make clear that the production of historical discourse is dependent upon narratival representation. It demonstrates this contention by continuously reflecting its own narrative back onto itself. For Hutcheon it can only be this self-reflexivity that troubles the anti-postmodernists, because paradoxically, the postmodern novel is in a general sense more historically focused than most modernist literature. Hutcheon sees the postmodern novel as a return to history, but stresses that this new investigation emphasizes its own inherent difficulties. History is no longer approachable as a raw unrepresented truth; it only acquires meaning through each new representation. This brand of "metafiction" also critiques the "liberal humanism" of modernism. With reference to Jean-François Lyotard, Hutcheon argues that postmodernism challenges the "master narratives" of the modernist novel with multiple micronarratives that provide competing and contrasting viewpoints. This shift reorientates discursive control toward the text and away from the centralizing (and elite) figure of the author. The postmodern novel does not dispense with master narratives altogether, but by including them it highlights and explores their historical construction. This process is typical of the "denaturalization" of narrative that Hutcheon recognizes in "historiographical metafiction."

In many respects Carlos Fuentes's *Terra Nostra* is an excellent example of such a text. The novel represents the author's single most ambitious engagement with the historical foundations of Latin America. Its endlessly entwined narrative jumps from the Paris of 1999, to Hapsburg Spain, Tenochtitlan at the time of the conquest, Tiberius's Rome, and to a Mexico of the future. *Terra Nostra*'s aims and strategies reflect very closely those laid down in Linda Hutcheon's argument. Referring to the novel in an interview, Fuentes describes it as "an excursion into Mediterranean culture, into all the worlds we come from, and into the creation of power in our society" (Fuentes 1981: 162). The novel is an attempt to bring together the foundational narratives of Spanish American culture in order to "de-naturalize" them and expose their ideological agendas. It does this by flagging up the constructedness of its own narrative. Following Hutcheon's "historiographical metafiction," *Terra Nostra* does not recount a history but foregrounds the production of history by the way in which it openly juxtaposes and interconnects the conflicting narratives that comprise Spanish American culture. Most importantly this reengagement with history is shown to be a function of the novel itself, and the image of the "Terra Nostra" revealed is self-consciously fictional. The cultural narratives are rewritten in the eternal present of the text. Each rereading is a reenactment of the past and therefore the potential conception of a new and different future. The "Terra Nostra" exists simultaneously on two different but interconnected levels, being both the external reality of the Latinate world and the text itself. History and narrative are inseparable.

Above all *Terra Nostra* is a novel of contradiction. It is all but impossible to decide upon a coherent reading because the narrative has neither temporal center nor primary narrator. Characterization is fluid, and, in adherence to Hutcheon's formula, fact and fiction are deliberately merged. The King Philip of the novel would appear to be Philip II, but he is married to Queen Elizabeth of England and his life spans the depictions of real events of Spanish history separated by over a hundred years. As well as historical figures, Fuentes includes characters from various literary sources. The central female character bears the name of Fernando de Rojas's anti-heroine Celestina, and there are appearances by Ezra Pound's Pollo Phoibee and Jorge Luis Borges's Pierre Ménard among others. As Hutcheon points out with reference to the real-life but fictionalized character Ambrose Bierce from Fuentes's *The Old Gringo* (1986 [1985]) (Hutcheon 1988: 155), the blurring of the ontological condition of novelistic characters serves to problematize our relationship with history. In this instance, the reader is aware of the real existence in the past of Philip II, but the novel's depiction makes clear that our understanding of that figure is dependent upon a narrative process that has no direct access to a pure or unreflected reality. *Terra Nostra* asserts that such a realization can have an empowering effect. Paradoxically, the postmodern hermeticism of *Terra Nostra*, a novel that folds in upon itself at every twist of the narrative, also provides a critical distance.

This is evident as we reach the final scene of the novel, which would appear to be the depiction of a redemptive sexual fusion between the characters Pollo Phoibee and Celestina. On the face of it, we are presented with an enactment of the apotheosis of the master narrative, a moment of mythical and philosophical closure. Several disparaging critics have duly criticized Fuentes with such a reading, but this is to ignore the novel's final postmodern irony. The sexual fusion serves to ironize closure rather than to celebrate it. The scene demonstrates how "historiographical metafiction" subverts the metanarratives of modernist literature from within. Any notion of the sublime is undercut by the text's radically self-reflexive and intertextual style. The sexual encounter is written as pornography and the final description is a rewriting of the Bible: "for dust thou art, and unto dust thou shalt return – without sin, and with pleasure" (Fuentes 1976: 890). This not only indicates the novel's final textualization of its own story, but shows a deliberate juxtaposition of registers that is commonplace in postmodern fiction. *Terra Nostra*'s return to origins is in fact a reiteration that emphasizes the impossibility of an unmediated disclosure of either beginnings or ends, the eschatological conclusion to the novel being an ironic comment on the desire for historical closure. By revealing the act of its own narration, *Terra Nostra* shows that history is made in the present. This performative strategy is a deliberate critique of two ideologies of history that plague contemporary Spanish America: a Catholicism that views the world as a place in which to kill time before death, and industrial capitalism's false teleological march into a future in the name of progress.

Hutcheon's outline of "historiographical metafiction" is clearly appropriate to *Terra Nostra* in many respects, but risks ignoring a particular set of problematics that exist within Fuentes's specifically Latin American context. Both McHale's and Hutcheon's readings of postmodernism see it chiefly in terms of a reaction to the modernist aesthetic but tend to take the wider, cultural, political, and socioeconomic as a given. The interdisciplinary debate around postmodernism in Latin America which gathered momentum some years after that of the United States and Europe is concerned with defining postmodernisms specific to societies that have experienced a very uneven modernity in comparison with those of the countries of the center. Many novelists, including Fuentes, have often made the point that Latin America is a subcontinent still searching for its own modernity. A popular early criticism of postmodernity in Latin America was that it was a wholly inappropriate mode for a society that had not experienced modernity apart from an alien imported form, whether that be economic, political, or aesthetic. Most have now come to see this view as oversimplistic, preferring to analyze these structures as forms of a hybrid culture (see, for example, Néstor García Canclini's *Hybrid Cultures: Strategies for Entering and Leaving Modernity*).

In Latin America the tension between modernism and postmodernism has a character particular to itself. In Fuentes's writing, and especially his novels up until the 1980s, this tension is revealed by a far greater modernist presence than McHale's and Hutcheon's analyses allow for. *Terra Nostra*, for example, betrays certain totalizing impulses that cannot be described as ironically postmodern. In this novel Fuentes undeniably shows a European canonical orientation, and a utopian impulse particular to Latin American thought that Anglo-American postmodernism fails to recognize. Contradictions surface in Fuentes's novels and essays that cannot be merely attributed to the inherent contradictory nature of Hutcheon's postmodernism. Despite Hutcheon's insistence that the "post" prefix does not signify a completely new chronologically orientated aesthetic, the notion of some form of cultural rupture cannot be denied. This cultural break is completely at odds with Fuentes's own position on the role of Hispanic culture that he has maintained from *La nueva novela hispanoamericana* [The New Spanish American Novel] (1969) through to his latest collection of criticism, *La geografia de la novela* [The Geography of the Novel] (1993a).

For Fuentes, Spanish American culture has always been a positive and potentially liberating force in the face of a discontinuous and iniquitous society. This cultural vision also tends to spread beyond Hispanic literature to incorporate world literature into a universal project of liberation via the power of creative imagination. This vision has the historical commitment of Hutcheon's postmodernism but also more than an echo of the utopianist belief in the power of the artist and the importance of tradition, attitudes that tend to be associated with modernism. It is perhaps not unsurprising that when asked to define his position on postmodernism in an interview on his novel *Christopher Unborn* (1989 [1987]), Fuentes likened his own approach to an amalgamation of Mikhail Bakhtin and Jürgen Habermas (Ferman 1997: 99–100). The many voices of his novels are thus reflected in Bakhtin's heteroglossia with this difference always seen within the context of Habermas's community of consensus.

Fuentes has continued to write novels informed by the postmodern debate, although in recent years his work has altered somewhat from the (nearly) classic "historiographical metafiction" of *Terra Nostra*. Common to his novels from the late 1980s till the present is the particular Latin American postmodern awareness of speaking from the periphery. Added to this is the increasing awareness of the global political and economic context that has seen a shift from a bipolar to a more multipolar share of power. Fuentes's novels and essays have both recognized the contradictory implications of this new order for Latin America. In *La geografía de la novela*, Fuentes seems optimistic about the future of a global situation that offers the potential for new power centers following economic and technological change. However, in a speech he made in 1992, he warns against the global adoption of the North American ideology of *laissez-faire* free-market capitalism now that there seems to be no alternative metanarrative (Fuentes 1993a: 76–7). Mexico is, of course, a country for which this problem is particularly acute. In *The Crystal Frontier: A Novel in Nine Short Stories* (1997), Fuentes explores the paradoxical relationship between two countries with such radically different cultural identities and disproportionate economic situations. The novel examines the real and metaphorical border between these two peoples that is at once increasingly porous and yet unbridgeable. The stories show that the rapid blurring of this border, created by economic necessity, produces on the one hand tragic circumstances born of misrecognition, and on the other, epiphanic moments of interconnection. The micronarratives of this text perhaps seem closer than *Terra Nostra* to the spirit of postmodern antifoundationalism. There is a far greater mix of high and popular cultural references and less of a sense of artistic resolution. The hope for the growth of understanding, economic equality, and social justice is provided by the act of telling the stories themselves. Fuentes's historical conviction has not altered; the past and the future are still made in the present.

26

William H. Gass

Thomas B. Hove

For his stylistic pyrotechnics and his experiments with narrative form, William H. Gass is often grouped with a cadre of American postmodern fiction writers that includes John Barth, Donald Barthelme, Don DeLillo, Stanley Elkin, William Gaddis, Joseph Heller, Joseph McElroy, Richard Powers, and Thomas Pynchon, to name a few. Gass's fiction takes place primarily in the American Midwest and the inner reaches of consciousness. But his role as director of the International Writers' Center at Washington University, the breadth of his erudition, and the range of his sociopolitical concerns make him a truly international figure. Although he distrusts the term "postmodernism," his affinities with literary postmodernism can be seen in his experiments with fictional form and his ambivalent treatments of the modernist ideal of the artistic genius who stands above and apart from reality.

For Gass, as for the pragmatist philosopher William James and the many recent continental and postcolonial enemies of metaphysics, truth lies not in finished products and unanswerable arguments but rather in continually unfolding processes of skeptical inquiry and exploratory troping. In his non-fiction, Gass strives not for a mimetic or logical truth but rather for an "essayistic" one: "the essay interests itself in the narration of ideas – in their unfolding – and the conflict between philosophies or other points of view becomes a drama in its hands; systems are seen as plots and concepts as characters" ("Emerson" 23). These features that define Gass's essays can also be found in his fictions. In both forms, the most important feature of Gass's style is its abundant variety of metaphors. Rather than imitate reality, Gass believes fiction's purpose is to add to it, to create new forms of consciousness that will alter the ways we view the world. In attempting to broaden the possibilities of consciousness with the tools of skeptical inquiry, free-flowing essayistic forms, and metaphoric clusters, Gass joins a long tradition of writers whose influence he repeatedly avows, among whom are Plato, Thomas Browne, Emerson, Nietzsche, Valéry, the James brothers,

Wittgenstein, Rilke, and Stein. As his most complex fictional voice says of his own private explorations of consciousness, "my subject's far too serious for scholarship, for history, and I must find another form before I let what's captive in me out. Imagine: history not serious enough, causality too comical, chronology insufficiently precise" (W. Gass 1995: 107). This comment only begins to suggest Gass's quarrels with the realist tradition.

As expressed in his essays, his fictions, and his notorious series of debates with John Gardner, what Gass distrusts most about the realist tradition is its lack of self-consciousness about its own conventionality. In addition, Gass believes that the conventions of realist verisimilitude cannot adequately portray certain modes of consciousness that are in no way less "real" than those offered up by the realist mode. The realist demand for a straightforward portrayal of probable events, situations, and linguistic forms jeopardizes the heightened linguistic styles and varied emotional effects that Gass would like to investigate. His narratives and essays offer a fluid mixture in which a variety of modes – the expository and the fictive, the mimetic and the experimental, the active and the passive, the hierarchical and the associative – exist side by side, and Gass never suggests that one side of these polarities has a more direct purchase on reality or consciousness than the other. As several of Gass's critics have noted, his stories always rely heavily on the conventions and techniques of realism, particularly his gripping novella "The Pedersen Kid," which could not achieve its suspenseful effects without adhering to conventional realist techniques of pacing, scene-setting, and characterization. But in spite of his polemical attacks on Gardner and realist conventions, Gass considers literary realism to be a mode equally as valid as any other mode. Gass objects only when people begin to insist that realism, or any other mode, is the only "true" mode, or the "best" one.

In keeping with the modernist tradition, Gass's characters always attempt to create imaginary worlds elsewhere, away from the chaos and disappointments of everyday life. But in Gass's postmodern take on this tradition, his narratives show how these imaginary refuges fall victim to invasion, contamination, dissipation, or disintegration. At other times, Gass shows how, in spite of their self-referentiality, imaginary constructions can intervene in the real world, for better or, more often, for worse. Gass's protagonists are not the confident, superhuman figures of high modernism who transcend the circumstances that blight their everyday existence. Rather, they are all-too-human beings equally as baffled and confused about life as everyone else is. Accordingly, their imaginative constructions can be redemptive and ruinous at the same time.

In his fictions, Gass typically focuses on a solitary consciousness beset by disrupting and troubling forces from outside. This beset consciousness will try to escape from those forces into an imaginary realm of its own construction.

But in doing so, it will inevitably change the world – sometimes intentionally, but usually inadvertently. Gass's most extensive and profound treatment of this theme is the historian William Kohler's exploration of "the fascism of the heart" in *The Tunnel* (1995). According to Kohler, Nazi history and anti-Semitism grew out of not only Enlightenment master narratives but also the universal private impulses felt by anyone who has known disappointment and needs to relieve that disappointment with fantasies of domination, scapegoating, and revenge. Throughout all of Gass's fiction, similar potentially predatory and destructive imaginative constructions intrude upon an otherwise neutral reality in a variety of ways, but usually through the mediation of language.

As with many of Gass's postmodernist contemporaries, language often takes center stage in his work, and linguistic style is the primary medium in which imaginative constructions are built and through which they transmit their energies. Yet Gass is more ambivalent than modernist writers about the nature of these energies. While style can serve a redemptive, liberating function, Gass also shows how it can very easily be enlisted in enterprises of domination and colonization. In one of Gass's most alarming treatments of this theme, William Kohler's mentor, the German historian Magus Tabor, draws explicit comparisons between linguistic representation and domination. According to one of Tabor's theories, since language occupies most of our consciousness, historians can be equivalent to conquerors and occupying armies, for historians can make a whole nation, society, or "race" into their own construction and subordinate those real entities to their own imaginary scheme of ordering. Moving one step beyond this assumption, Tabor justifies German nationalism's specific enterprise of domination with exhortations such as the following: "Don't you see that when a man writes the history of your country in another mother-language, he is bent on conquest? ... His history will be yours. **Per-force!** I say make others – why be made?"

Following in his Hobbesian tracks, Tabor's disciple William Kohler writes a historical study of Nazism, anti-Semitism, and fascism titled "Guilt and Innocence in Hitler's Germany." Kohler's historical research leads him to wonder whether anyone can be blamed for the impulse to "make others" in order to survive in the war of all against all, and whether the act of writing history could ever be anything but "a superficially plausible apologia for tomorrow's acts of robbery or cowardice, revenge, rape, or other criminalities already under way." The 652 pages of *The Tunnel* – Kohler's inverted monument to his own subjectivity – function as his application of these Hobbesian impulses to humanity in general, whose universal history he attempts to create through his ruthless self-explorations, his testimonies for the Party of Disappointed People (PdP), and his speculations about the "fascism of the heart." Tabor's and Kohler's historiographic ambitions thus reflect the modernist impulse to master the imperfect, undefined, chaotic world. But Gass's postmodern ambivalence toward this impulse highlights its sinister associations with the imperialist and genocidal horrors of recent history. Blake illustrated this theme two centuries ago in the figure of Urizen, but this theme pervades so much recent fiction that it has become a commonplace reflecting a postmodern self-consciousness about the legacies of nationalism, imperialism, ethnocentrism, and the monotheistic assumptions of these social forces.

In Gass's fiction, as in the criticism of George Steiner, the Holocaust is one possible outgrowth (albeit not a necessary one) of the attempt to shape the world according to a coherent, self-referential linguistic construction or master narrative. Such outgrowths can be much less cataclysmic than the Holocaust, as in Jethro Furber's effect on Brackett Omensetter's life in *Omensetter's Luck* (1997 [1966]), or Luther Penner's obsessive eye-for-an-eye approach to life in "The Master of Secret Revenges." But the impulse underlying these disparate enterprises is potentially the same. His speculations on a universal impulse toward domination underlying language indicates Gass's dissatisfaction with reductive social constructionist views of language and motivation, but it would be misguided and simplistic to lump Gass with his creation Kohler and label him a dogmatic naturalist. His warnings against the misuse of language, however, reflect only a part of his complex attitude toward language. In linguistic style, Gass locates not only identity's predatory impulses and its reactive power against perceived enemies but also a more positive, productive, and potentially redemptive form of power. As he has often said, the protagonists of his books are the characters with the richest language, or the names attached to the best sentences.

But a rich language and a complex consciousness are mixed blessings. For Gass, as for Emerson, a linguistically mediated self-consciousness constitutes a secular version of the Fall. Such linguistic self-consciousness separates us from the angst-free animal world and dooms us to unhappiness. This theme is treated briefly in some of Gass's shorter works, and in the character Lou in *The Tunnel*. But it is most extensively developed in *Omensetter's Luck*. Like Melville's Billy Budd, Gass's Brackett Omensetter dwells in a prelinguistic state of existence that preserves him from the gnawing miseries of self-doubt and self-consciousness. Accordingly, Omensetter's neighbors Henry Pimber and Jethro Furber envy his freedom from self-consciousness and yearn for a similar prelinguistic state of existence in which they, too, could be oblivious to their insecurities, limitations, and disappointments. But Gass's narratives always reveal the impossibility of sustaining a mode of being like Omensetter's prelinguistic lack of self-consciousness. Ultimately, language and the self-consciousness it brings are what Gass believes make us fully human. Occupying the linguistic realm of self-consciousness is something that must simply be endured with forbearance – or not, as in the case of Henry Pimber, Gass's milder version of John Claggart, who commits suicide because he realizes he can never attain the state of being he attributes to Omensetter.

What Gass sees as "human," though, is certainly not the coherent self of the Enlightenment and of literary realism. Nor is it the autonomous, "expressive" self of romanticism and modernism. Rather, it is a fragmented, decentered self that must struggle to define its own identity and match up the demands of self-definition with the ever-changing pressures of the social and material worlds. Accordingly, the self is not only decentered but extremely fluid and porous. These aspects of the self are reflected in Gass's constant oscillation between self-reflexivity and referentiality. Consciousness for Gass is not a stream but rather an agglomeration and a march and a collage of signs (1997 [1995]: 212). The voice that constitutes the self, moreover, requires at least a speaker, a hearer, and an overhearer ("On Talking"). To be a self at all, one must always already consist of these three disparate persons and a wide variety of symbols.

Accordingly, many of Gass's tales portray the risks and dangers of an interiority mapped out in linguistic style. His characters' escapes into the inner reaches of consciousness almost always result in a beleaguered, injurious, or sometimes self-destructive solipsism, as with Henry Pimber and Jethro Furber in *Omensetter's Luck*, Jorge Segren in "The Pedersen Kid," the narrator of "Mrs. Mean," Fender in "Icicles," the poet-narrator of *In the Heart of the Heart of the Country* (1968), and all the main characters of the novellas collected in *Cartesian Sonata* (1998). *The Tunnel*, purportedly an unfinished preface to the study of "Guilt and Innocence in Hitler's Germany" that William Kohler cannot bring himself to finish and pass on to the public, serves as Gass's largest and most elaborate document of obsessive interiority. Kohler obsesses over his preface and cannot finish his book mainly because he believes his study fails to capture the private workings of what he calls "the fascism of the heart." But while Kohler obsessively tunnels into his heart, the concerns of the public world catch up with him: his colleagues get ahead of him, his wife correctly senses the vengeful impulses behind his writing, and his writing itself comes to resemble the self-destructive alcoholism of his mother.

But time and again, Gass's work demonstrates the unavoidable compulsion to explore interiority in order to learn what it can tell us about such matters as motivation and action. For example, in the *"Kristallnacht"* section of *The Tunnel*, Gass's meditations on the lures and risks of interiority make up one of the most thrilling studies of motivation and agency in recent fiction. Within American fiction, some of the high points of this tradition are Melville's *Billy Budd* (1924), Faulkner's *Absalom, Absalom!* (1936), and Philip Roth's *American Pastoral* (1997). Reflecting on Herschel Grynzspan's assassination of the Nazi officer Ernst Eduard vom Rath, on his own participation in the anti-Semitic violence of the *Kristallnacht*, and on the confused motives and unintended consequences of both events (probably by way of Arendt's discussion of them in *Eichmann in Jerusalem* [1963]), Kohler develops a theory of history according to which "inadvertence rules our roost" (324). By exploring the variety of discrepancies between motivations and consequences in a world full of so many competing allegiances and interests, Kohler's *Kristallnacht* meditation explores several important postmodern concerns. First, it reflects the inescapable complexities of modern social existence, and the unintended consequences these complexities often produce. Second, it challenges the modernist hope, somewhat more pronounced in Faulkner and Mann, that if we can come up with a complex enough account of how the unconscious works, we can ultimately attribute certain motivations to certain actions. Third, it challenges the pieties and system-building impulses of moral, religious, political, and psychoanalytic master narratives. As always, Gass challenges such system-building impulses and master narratives through his complex figures of speech and his insistence on skeptical, essayistic form. Like many of his academic and literary contemporaries, Gass worries about the tenuous influence that knowledge can have on reality, or thought on action. When Kohler notes that "there were at least three correct conclusions to be drawn" about the sociopolitical ramifications of Grynzspan's assassination of vom Rath, he is also careful to point out the most disturbing conclusion of all, expressed with a troubled hesitation that betrays compassionate impulses that Kohler usually denies in himself: "To the Jews it didn't matter how many. Might be drawn. Or colored in. Correct conclusions" (333).

As the faint but nevertheless audible notes of compassion in Kohler's remarks suggest, the pitfalls and failures produced by the escape into an imaginary interior realm are not the whole story in Gass. Even though he is too skeptical to accept without reservations the high modernist creed that imaginative constructions transcend reality and therefore ought to shape it in their image, his fiction works against the reductive tendencies in recent postmodern fiction and criticism that reject art's potential to offer transcendence or redemption. On the one hand, Gass shows that the transcendence and redemption both art and verbal style might offer are no match for the predatory Hobbesian impulses so deeply entrenched in our behavior, or for what Fredric Jameson calls the "alienating necessities of history." But on the other hand, Gass shows that transcendence and redemption can remain possibilities, and he resists the tendency of much politically charged criticism to absorb art wholly into its own sphere of polemical, regional ad-hoccery. Admittedly, art, like alcoholism, drug abuse, or any other form of escapism, can amount to a self-destructive evasion of urgent social responsibilities and political or moral commitments that cry out for our attention. But it can also be the only form of commitment that a self-confessed "parasite" like Gass is best suited to pursue in a world full of many different possible forms of commitment. This theme is most movingly brought out in Kohler's portrait of his mother, from whose alcoholism he makes "a wholly romantic connection between her time-eating activities and . . . this scribbling I do at night" (631).

But for Gass the novelist, and the admirer of an essayist like Emerson or a poet like Rilke, not only domination and escape but redemption can lie in the beauty and complexity of linguistic style. That such redemption can only be tentative and provisional in no way cancels out its psychological reality and its potential to serve as a positive historical force. As Gass has said of Emerson, encountering an invigorating style can send one's audience "away with their hearts a little higher in their chests, in a Dionysian mood, intoxicated by their own powers and possibilities, not by bottled artificialities, drugs, the false-hoods of gambling and war, or still further fraudulent rites." Even though, after such a moment of elevation, "the freshly inflated soul begins immediately to leak" ("Emerson" 37), and even though the despicable traits of characters like Jethro Furber and William Kohler seem so heavily to outweigh the redemptive potential of their linguistic style, Gass shares the hopeful note struck somewhat more strongly in Emerson and William James: "To fly in the face of a fact . . . is not to strike a solid wall, but to feel the fact yield, if only a bit" ("Emerson" 36).

27

Antonio Gramsci

Marcia Landy

The *Prison Notebooks* published in 1948 were a great influence on the thinking of many Italian intellectuals of the Left and particularly of postwar European filmmakers. They constituted an important intervention for Left politics in those years as a means of rethinking the politics and culture of Italian fascism. Gramsci's writings were a critical reservoir for the Left to develop strategies in the interests of forging counterhegemony in the years of transition from the fascist regime to "democracy" in the immediate postwar era. This was a time when many dissident individuals and groups were struggling to create a new vision of Italian society in the aftermath of the war and the struggles of the Resistance.

Even with the disillusioning victories of the Christian Democrats in the late 1940s and early 1950s, Gramsci's writings were a source for identifying the tendencies of capitalism to rejuvenate itself through innovation and restructuring of class relations. His work was to become more widely disseminated throughout Europe and in the United Kingdom in the 1960s and 1970s, giving rise to new forms of cultural analysis that were also directed to rethinking prevailing forms of Marxist analysis and traditional Left forms of political organization. This discussion selects three areas of Gramscian thought which I believe are also at the heart of poststructuralist and postmodernist theorizing about history, the role of intellectuals, and relations between culture and politics.

The particularly iconoclastic dimensions of Gramsci's thought that were to have important repercussions from the 1960s onward involved his unrelenting struggle against what he termed "economism." Economism signified for Gramsci the reduction of individuals and groups and events to "mechanical causes," that is, to the inexorability of economic determinism associated with forms of scientific Marxism. At the same time that Gramsci inveighed against the interpretation of social change in purely quantitative terms, he also sought to avoid the reductive character of "ideologism," which he defined as a valorization of individual volition, uniqueness, and freedom from cultural and political restraints. In examining questions of causality, he wrote: "a common error consists... in an inability to find the correct relation between what is organic and what is conjunctural" (Gramsci 1978: 178).

Gramsci's methods of cultural and political analysis were geared to overcoming the problematic of configuring causality beyond economism and ideologism. In order to challenge these two extremes, he was drawn to a rethinking of Italian history, examining the role of intellectuals in relation to the state and civil society, and to developing an understanding of the inter-relations of the state and of civil society. His thinking led him (and subsequent students of his work, e.g., Louis Althusser) to examine their interpenetrating roles in the exercise of coercion and of modes for creating the illusion of consensus and independence from the state. In particular, his analysis bears a connection to more contemporary notions of overdetermination. He sought to identify multiple lines of determination.

Hence, Gramsci's writing was deeply implicated in historical and philosophical analysis, and his examination of Italian history becomes an exercise in locating certain concepts that are transposable to other parts of the world and also to more recent political analysis. His analysis of the Risorgimento as a "passive revolution," or what he also termed "revolution/restoration," is a major contribution to forms of historicizing, addressing the problems of identifying difference and repetition. Or, in the language of Gilles Deleuze,

> We are right to speak of repetition when we find ourselves confronted by identical elements with exactly the same concept. However, we must distinguish between these discrete elements, these repeated objects... In every case repetition is difference without the concept. (Deleuze 1994a: 223)

In investigating the Risorgimento, Gramsci is not only addressing a moment in time that has been superseded, but one that bears signs of repetition. He is identifying a process whereby "sectors of the working–class movement are transformed into politically harmless elements not threatening the fundamental social relations by absorption into more traditional political organisation" (Sassoon 1987: 207). Of "passive revolution" he wrote:

> [T]he course of events in the Risorgimento revealed the tremendous importance of the demagogic mass movement, with its leaders thrown up by chance, improvised, etc., nevertheless in actual fact taken over by the traditional organic forces – in other words, by the parties of long standing. (1978: 112)

Gramsci's particular use of the word "revolution," usually identified with radical social and political transformation in behalf of subaltern classes, suggests irony (in the spirit of Marx's *Eighteenth Brumaire of Louis Napoleon*), since Gramsci is describing a restoration of the old order under a new rubric and with a new rhetoric through state reformism. However, it is clear that Gramsci does not restrict his analysis to this retrospective glance at Italy. More generally, he has nineteenth-century Europe in mind. Most importantly, he has in mind the notion that Italian fascism, like the Risorgimento, bore the characteristics of what he termed a passive revolution. Fascism was able through the "legislative intervention of the State, and by means of the corporative organization" (1978: 120) to produce economic reforms in the interest of traditional ruling classes (with the incorporation of friends and allies through economic concessions) and at the expense of the populace at large. Gramsci's analysis of the realignment of ruling and traditional social and economic forces seems particularly cogent for the present.

A striking but not surprising characteristic of the last decades of the twentieth century is the restructuring of capitalism and the redistribution of economic wealth at the top in the abandonment of the welfare state. (See, for example, Stuart Hall's analysis of Thatcherism as an instance of passive revolution. Hall's discussion does not apply merely to the UK but also to the United States and to other areas of the globe.) The purely economistic and bureaucratic tendencies of the revolution from above can be seen to reign triumphantly. Much current critical analysis has chosen to move in other directions, preferring to see the present as the inauguration of new, utopian or dystopian, possibilities, as a break from, if not the end of, past history. The current focus on historicizing would profit from a careful reading of Gramsci's notes on historical process. Rather than leading in the direction of linear and totalizing forms of thinking, his analysis of past history in his "Notes on Italian History" and in "The Modern Prince" is implicated in questions of repetition and difference, essential for a proper examination of the persistence of the past and of teleological thought. His relevance to postmodernity resides in his recognition of the interdependence between philosophy and historical analysis so as to enable a proper recognition of multiple causal determinants, and of the tendency, in the words of Giuseppe di Lampedusa, for "everything to change so that everything can remain the same." Thus, the ability to recognize difference in sameness is still very much at stake in the assessment of historical determinations.

Since assessments of history are not divinely ordained but constructed, and since these constructions are themselves historical, the role of intellectuals is integral to Gramsci's thought. The Gramscian enthusiasm of the 1960s and 1970s paid particular attention to redefining education and the role of intellectuals, in particular, distinctions between traditional and organic intellectuals. In the *Prison Notebooks*, Gramsci makes the following distinctions concerning intellectuals. He writes that:

When one distinguishes between intellectuals and non-intellectuals, one is referring in reality only to the immediate function of the professional category of the intellectuals; that is, one has in mind the direction in which their specific professional activity is weighted.... This means that, although one can speak of intellectuals, one cannot speak of non-intellectuals, because non-intellectuals do not exist... There is no human activity from which every form of intellectual participation can be excluded. (1978: 9)

These statements may sound particularly out of place in our current era, in which *homo economicus* is in the ascendant and in which we are told we live in an era where meaning has been eclipsed and certainly where rationality has vanished. And there are the recent debates about the bankruptcy of "public intellectuals" who have become as commodified as other cultural artifacts – cinema, television, news reportage and commentary, academic scholarship, and so on. How, then, do Gramsci's notes on the role of traditional and organic intellectuals have any analytic cogency? The distinction he made between traditional and organic intellectuals is by no means simple: the distinction is not as it has been romanticized and diluted, a mere binary distinction between state and dissident intellectuals.

Rather than providing a blueprint of the role of intellectuals in society, Gramsci's investigations of intellectual work are as overdetermined as his analysis of history. First of all, his comments are set in the impossible but necessary context of trying to explore the possibility of creating "a new stratum of intellectuals," one that "becomes the foundation of a new and integral conception of the world" (1978: 9), but Gramsci is no more a utopian thinker than are Michel Foucault or Gilles Deleuze. He is aware of the deleterious and long-standing effects of state power and of the difficulty, if not impossibility, of altering events. Moreover, he does not prescribe a specific image of the new intellectual. His work is directed toward an exploration of the changes wrought historically in the role of intellectuals from the Renaissance in Italy to the 1930s under Mussolini's regime. As such, his observations are tentative rather than definitive, investigative rather than programmatic, and historical rather than ahistorical.

He regards the role of the intellectual as inseparable from the prevailing modes of production, and, furthermore, given the constant changes mandated by capitalist production, the position of the intellectual is neither constant nor isolated from the social relations of production. Thus, he can write that: "In the modern world the category of intellectuals has undergone an unprecedented expansion" (1978: 13). Here he has in mind not only professional academics but administrators, bureaucratic functionaries, military personnel, and technology experts. Thus rather than making a simplistic distinction between well-meaning radical social critics and "traditional intellectuals" who occupy educational, research, or administrative positions, Gramsci has complicated for his own purposes of analysis these roles. Instead of slinging mud at the reigning powers as intellectual traitors, he has issued a challenge to rethink "a whole series of problems and possible questions for historical research" (1978: 115). Most importantly, Gramsci's analysis of intellectuals is closely tied to an historical examination of institutions (e.g., the Catholic Church) that have been responsible for the creation not only of "traditional" but also of "organic" intellectuals. He offers a complex analysis of the contradictory social and political elements involved in the formation of intellectuals: not all traditional intellectuals are class traitors and not all organic intellectuals are from the working class.

Consonant with his commitment to explore avenues for creating different forms of social life is the role of the "party" as he conceived it. In other words, Gramsci's challenge to rethink intellectual work is not only central to an understanding of late capitalism but a prerequisite for contemplating the possibility or impossibility of social transformation. As ever, the misrecognition of the nature of intellectuals is the greatest obstacle for envisioning change.

Aligned, then, to the role of the intellectuals in society is yet another area where Gramsci's thought converges with the problematic of understanding postmodernity. Much has been written on the role of culture, particularly of mass culture under capitalism. Following his lead from the 1960s to the end of the century, scholarship has focused on the role of media, seeking to uncover the "common sense and folklore" of cultural production. In his concern with the creation of a "popular culture," one expressive of the needs of the people, he is aware that in Italy there was in fact no popular culture but a dependency on foreign literary models, particularly those from France.

The creation of a popular culture was important in so far as Gramsci understood the importance of culture in creating the conditions for transforming subaltern classes into the dominant class. While his allusions to cinema are sparser than his comments on literature, he seems to acknowledge implicitly the dominance of narrative forms that extend into the cinema. However, his comments on the operatic suggest that, for example, Verdian opera is "responsible for a whole range of 'artificial' poses in the life of the people, for ways of thinking, for a 'style'" (1985: 373). Under the rubric of the operatic, Gramsci subsumes the uses of language, oratory, lectures, the theatricality of the law courts, and even "sound films." Gramsci is not setting himself up as an arbiter of correct cultural artifacts and promoting a taste for tendency literature on behalf of proletarian concerns. Instead his writings on cultural production are investigative. He is concerned to examine how cultural artifacts are residual sources of cultural values and attitudes and, even more, are deeply imbued with "the process of intellectual civilizing" (1985: 382).

Thus his investigation is not merely descriptive nor one of cataloguing abuses but of acknowledging the importance of connecting cultural work to the maintenance of political priorities. However, he does not suggest a simple correlation between culture and politics. The problem is far more complex, revealing again his commitment to an understanding of the multiple determinants and changes in culture. For example, he writes in relation to researching the art of printing that "implicit in this research [is] that of the quantitative as well as qualitative modifications (mass extension) brought about in ways of thinking by the technical and mechanical development of cultural organization." And, in relation to "spoken communication," he writes that it

> is a means of ideological diffusion which has a rapidity, a field of action, and an emotional simultaneity far greater than written communication (theatre, cinema and radio, with its loudspeakers in public squares, beat all forms of written communication, including books, magazines, newspapers and newspapers posted on walls) – but superficially and not in depth. (1985: 382–3)

Critics who have followed Gramsci have sought to identify the changing character of mass cultural production and to locate in it vestiges of earlier cultures, its "common sense." His comments on common sense as a residual aspect of these earlier cultures in conjunction with new forms of communication have contributed to reevaluations of the role of mass culture as more than mere "entertainment" devoid of meaning. Critics have also sought to locate in these works signs of resistance, and an overt or implicit critical reaction to prevailing social and political conditions.

If current critical literature on the culture of postmodernity has focused on readings of cultural texts that reveal their complicity with the dominant culture or explore their resistance to it, they have not yet found ways to bring that analysis to bear on the political implications of their insights. The mainly descriptive, even diagnostic, character of cultural studies has lost track of the necessary work of exploring ways of connecting culture to political action. Gramsci's writings on cultural texts are not merely an attempt to describe the victimage of the subaltern condition, to diagnose its psychic castration, and its imbrication in unrealizable desire; they are attempts to forge modes of thinking in the interests of different forms of action. His writings are still very relevant to the dilemmas of postmodernity.

28

John Hawkes

Roy C. Flannagan

Gauging the postmodern status of a given writer is sometimes complicated by the shifting nature of both the critical term and the career trajectory of the writer in question. As John Hawkes's career progressed, his fiction employed different facets of postmodernist and modernist technique. In "The Literature of Replenishment," his good friend John Barth pronounced Hawkes's novels "examples of fine late modernism" (1979b: 66). In a *Contemporary Literature* essay on the topic, John Unsworth (1991) described Hawkes's work as "postmodern," with the hyphen perhaps denoting its close affinity to modernist writing. Meanwhile, Donald Greiner described him as "a master of American postmodernism" (1991: 211). The truth of any of these claims depends upon where one focuses along the arc of Hawkes's career and how one defines one's terms. There is no doubt that his work in the 1940s and 1950s helped inspire the heyday of postmodern literature in the 1960s. Hawkes's stubborn refusal to give his readers any epistemological certainty, his parody of popular genres, his emphasis upon image instead of plot, and his continual experimentation with narrative form establish him as an early American postmodern innovator.

Hawkes began his career imitating Hemingway by driving ambulances in World War II. He found he could translate his World War II experiences into evocative prose under the mentoring of Albert Guerard at Harvard. In these early attempts, Hawkes developed the free-floating details, the macabre humor, and the narrative incoherencies of his writing style and created an avant-garde aesthetic that repudiated the conventional expectations of realist fiction. In an early interview, he proclaimed that "plot, character, setting, and theme" were "the true enemies of the novel." In their stead, he chose to emphasize "structure," the "[r]elated or corresponding event, recurring image and recurring action" (Enck 1991: 65–6) as the most important elements of his fiction. He strove to substitute the ambiguity of the image and the motif for the usual narrative concerns of who, what, where, when, and why. The result can be confusing; the reader can try to decipher what is going on or can just give in to the experience of disconnected but often violent and evocative details that build up to landscapes of postwar squalor. Hawkes was interested in creating mystery and beauty and not in letting it make sense for the reader.

In terms of content, Hawkes's work is not especially postmodern. Most comfortable imaginatively recreating European locales such as France, England, Renaissance Italy, and Germany, Hawkes does not revel in American popular culture. He avoids high-tech or scientific subjects and eschews conspiracy theories. Except in the case of *Adventures in the Alaskan Skin Trade* (1985), he mostly disdains autobiographical fiction. He does not dwell ironically on the simulacra created by the media. In fact, he scarcely refers to television or movies (*Whistlejacket* [1998], however, is devoted to a photographer). He obsessively returns to favorite motifs and themes such as horses, landscapes, erotic images, the effects of war, morbid humor, and grotesque ways to die. Many of his earlier works share much with Eliot's *The Waste Land* in their attempt to convey a fractured state of mind through a devastated landscape, and in this respect he seems more modernist in orientation.

While his choice of subjects can seem haphazard, his method of drawing upon semi-subconscious images for his fiction does provide continuity through his writings. As he said in an interview, "I write out of a series of pictures that literally and actually do come to mind, but I've never seen them before. It's perfectly true that I don't know what they mean, but I feel and know that they have meaning" (Graham 1966: 452). Hawkes may begin with a series of mental images that he threads into a narrative, but the narrators in the novels after *The Lime Twig* (1961) have recognizable similarities. As Paul Emmet points out, "each successive narrator moves further into the unconscious; each successive narrator is, in one sense, the *same* person with progressively more self-knowledge" (1991: 191). Hawkes may vary his technique and use of point of view, but his impulse to plumb the unconscious remains.

In his first fully realized novel, *The Cannibal* (1949), Hawkes juxtaposes two stories concerning the small German town of Spitzen-on-the Dein in 1914 and in 1945 respectively, showing how the nationalistic delusions of the Germans led directly to postwar disillusionment and despair. As Albert Guerard points out in his introduction to the first edition, *The Cannibal* reads like Kafka's *Amerika* in reverse (1950: xi). In both cases, the writers create dreamscape-like representations of other countries without much concern for verisimilitude. While there is some naturalized characterization of the town's functionaries and a loose plot, the novel is most effective in creating a wasteland panorama reminiscent of the drawings of George Grosz, a cultural portrait in diametric opposition to the American baby-boom consumerist culture of the same period.

Whatever Hawkes leaves behind in his neglect of narrative coherence in these earlier novels, he gains in hallucinatory intensity. He forces the reader to think analogically, to apprehend imagery without any clear sense of context or explanation, and in this way he foreshadows one particular postmodern trend. In *Practicing Postmodernism, Reading Modernism* (1992), Patricia Waugh, following Nietzsche, notes how postmodernist writers tend to favor the "luminous detail" over the "concept." She writes that "Concepts are not reflections of essences in reality, but disguised or 'dead' metaphors used to organize the chaos of sensations which is experience" (1992: 35). Postmodernists desire to "experience the world as a continuous flux of radically contingent detail" (1992: 34), and this typifies Hawkes's earliest novels, written long before the major postmodern experimentation of the 1960s.

The Cannibal had its impact: critics were either outraged or entranced, but writers including Robert Coover, John Barth, Saul Bellow, and Flannery O'Connor began to follow Hawkes's career with interest. As Tony Tanner points out, Hawkes's entropic landscapes of waste and postwar stasis foreshadow those of Burroughs and Pynchon (1971: 203). In his next novel, *The Beetle Leg* (1951), Hawkes locates that entropy in the American West and parodies the Western just as *The Cannibal* explodes the conventions of the war novel. *The Beetle Leg* has as its main motif a man buried in a large earth dam and a grotesque scene where a man fishes a dead baby out of the river, but as a whole the novel shows up some of the risks of Hawkes's method. Because there is so little characterization, its characters become indistinguishable from the snakes in the desert or the drift of the dam. Moreover, motorcycle outlaws occasionally pop up in the course of the narrative, but the reason for their presence is never given. They operate as random forces of evil much like the dogs of war in *The Cannibal*. Everything quickly seems emblematic and insufficiently developed.

While many of the early postmodernists (John Barth, Donald Barthelme, Kurt Vonnegut, Thomas Pynchon) were writing their major experimental fiction in the 1960s, Hawkes wrote his in the 1940s and 1950s and produced comparatively little in the 1960s, during which time he moved toward more realist conventions with his use of first-person narration. In 1961, Hawkes finished one of his best novels, *The Lime Twig*. This novel takes the grimy British world of Graham Greene's *Brighton Rock* (1938), a noirish thug-filled landscape, and shows how dreams can entrap people just as a limed twig can entrap birds. Hawkes begins with the Beckett-like voice of a man named Hencher living with his mother at various cheap flats around London during the blitzkrieg. Once again, there is little sense of causation, and a muckraking reporter Sidney Slyter and some detectives mock the reader's attempts to make narrative coherence out of the dreamlike and often violent scenes. Compared to the static Western tableau of *The Beetle Leg*, the pulp-fiction conventions here greatly energize Hawkes's prose as if he needed some gangsters to kick some fun into his static Gothic effects. Once Hencher dies, kicked to death by a horse, his two middle-class friends, Michael Banks and his wife Margaret, get ensnared in a gang's attempt to enter a horse named Rock Castle in a race. Banks imagines himself as the studly romancer of multiple girls, but he is just being lulled along as a front for the gang as they beat and eventually kill his wife. He is blinded by his desire to live an adventure. So the entire novel becomes a meditation on the dangers of dreams, although one told in a dreamlike, violent way. Hawkes goes beyond parody into a kind of metafiction deeply critical of the novel's illusionist power. Contextualizing experience can not only prove dangerously misleading, it can get one killed.

In subsequent novels, the tension in Hawkes's fiction moves from dystopic vision to a surprisingly pastoral appreciation of sensual love. *Second Skin* (1964) remains of interest because it exemplifies his shift in emphasis from dystopic nightmare to a more lyrical celebration of life. It is told solely from the perspective of Skipper, the perpetually embarrassed and deluded narrator, as he tries to control the forces of lust and suicide surrounding his daughter. Hawkes frames the narrative within the island paradise of Skipper's later years, but one remembers the flashbacks where he continually loses control over himself in his barely suppressed attraction for his daughter. While the images remain self-reflexive (a green tattoo metamorphoses into an iguana clamped onto a character's chest), and the landscapes veer wildly from western deserts to tropical islands, the basic storyline charts Skipper's gradual mastery over the forces of death and destruction around him. From here on through the "trilogy" of the next three novels, *The Blood Oranges* (1971), *Death, Sleep, and the Traveler* (1974), and *Travesty* (1976), Hawkes moves deeper into the psychology of his central characters and farther away from the postmodern disruptions of his earlier work.

Travesty deserves consideration for both the extreme absurdity of its narrative framework and for its more postmodern use of technology, in this instance a car, to propel its narrative. Like J. G. Ballard's *Crash*, *Travesty* eroticizes a car wreck, in this case one that the unnamed narrator decides to participate in one evening with his unwilling daughter and her fiancé in the car. The narrative, which alludes to both Camus's *The Fall* and Camus's death in a car crash, sticks completely to the voice of the deranged man who decides to turn his death, and those of the others in the car, into a kind of art work. Since he is driving too fast for the others to stop him, he has the whole short novel to chat about whatever he likes, including sexual fantasies, the French countryside, and his passengers' whining about their imminent death. Since Hawkes never allows anyone any reprieve, the novel is delightfully perverse, a kind of study in the excitement of annihilation. Through the narrator's rambling sickly-aestheticized voice, Hawkes even parodies his own recent shift to the celebration of the lyrical and the sexual.

After *Travesty*, Hawkes went on to write many more novels in the 1970s, 1980s, and 1990s, many of which used postmodern techniques, but he never broke ground in narrative form in quite the way he did in the 1940s and 1950s. Whereas before he created fictions out of his subconscious, later he seemed far too self-conscious, pandering to Freudian analysis in *The Passion Artist* (1979), self-parodying his equine obsessions by having a horse narrate *Sweet William: A Memoir of Old Horse* (1993), and placing a live frog in his narrator's stomach as the central interest in *The Frog* (1996). Where once his style was laconic but dense with imagery, now it became perfumed, smooth, and decadent. His decision to parody French pornography in *Virginie: Her Two Lives* (1981), led to passages of mawkish excess. For example, take this bathhouse scene:

> But never had there been such soap! Mere soap it was, but what a forbidden glossy egg on Sylvie's palm! How could she so ingenuously offer him the soap, knowing as she must that once he trusted his awkward fingers to close on the slippery cake, which might well slip away once more in his agitation, he would enter in a bargain with Sylvie defined not by what the soap actually was but by what it meant? So much was undeniable. The two of them might have been in a bath together! (1981: 125)

Hawkes here tries to narrate two parallel bawdy stories from the perspective of an innocent eight-year-old girl. He might have figured this was a brave experiment with an incongruous subject matter, but the result is maudlin and coy, with exclamation marks to denote joyful surprise. The problems with *Virginie: Her Two Lives* characterize much of his later work. He continued to experiment, but the Gothic tension was gone.

Looked at as a whole, Hawkes's earlier novels hold up as his best contribution to our idea of the postmodern. More interested in landscape than in people, refusing to spell out the significance of his visions, Hawkes foreshadowed the antihumanist disruptions of 1960s experimental fiction. While the public largely ignored his works, critics and fellow writers grew to appreciate Hawkes's refusal to cater to conventional interpretations in what Leslie Fiedler once called our "post-Freudian, post-Einsteinian world" (1961: xiii). As Hawkes said, "The problem is that people don't know that life is a kind of fiction that we create and we accept as 'real.' We need to challenge such realities all the time" (Coover 1996b: xi).

29

Jenny Holzer

Paula Geyh

In early 1977 a series of offset posters bearing an alphabetized list of anonymous aphorisms began appearing throughout the streets of lower Manhattan. Pasted to walls and lampposts, parking meters and public phones, garbage cans and manhole covers, they became a part of the visual and verbal cacophony of the city. Amid the city's signs, graffiti, advertising, political campaigns, and cultural announcements, these messages, later revealed to be a "discursive art" project entitled "Truisms" by Jenny Holzer, were curiously difficult to categorize. Their purposes were unclear, and they seemed to originate from contradictory ideological viewpoints:

ABUSE OF POWER COMES AS NO SURPRISE
AN ELITE IS INEVITABLE
ANY SURPLUS IS IMMORAL
MONEY CREATES TASTE
PRIVATE OWNERSHIP IS AN INVITATION TO DISASTER
SELFISHNESS IS THE MOST BASIC MOTIVATION

All printed in the same typeface and so presumably of equal importance, these pronouncements offered their random audiences no clues as to their intended reception. This "universe of opinion," as Holzer termed it, had to be navigated by individual viewers on their own.

From the late 1970s through the early 1990s, Jenny Holzer helped to shape the cultural space of the postmodern era – a space defined by ubiquitous information technologies; juxtapositions of irreconcilable worldviews; wide-ranging investigations into the foundations of Western and particularly modern thought; the dissolution of the ideal of a unified subjectivity; and the near impossibility of mapping one's subject position in the networks of global consumer capitalism. Holzer's art has simultaneously represented and engaged with these postmodern problematics, and has affected our understanding of them.

Putting into practice one of her early aphorisms: USE WHAT IS DOMINANT IN A CULTURE TO CHANGE IT QUICKLY, Holzer has deployed the technologies of broadcast and print media, and advertising (including LED arrays) as the "medium" of her art. Holzer's work is part of the late twentieth-century conceptual art movement, which does not produce conventional "works of art" (drawings, paintings, sculptures), but instead creates art whose value lies in the power of its ideas – art of the mind rather than art of the eye. Much of conceptual art functions primarily as ideological or political critique: race, class, and gender are key foci. Capitalism and commercial culture, and particularly their entanglement with art and cultural institutions (galleries, museums, etc.), are also frequent targets. Inevitably, this art contains a degree of self-reflexivity regarding its own status and valuation as "art," and its embeddedness in the system of reviews, exhibits, sales, and museum "canonization."

One strand of conceptualist art focuses primarily on language and textuality, and so has been linked to various poststructuralist and "deconstructivist" enterprises in the theory and practice of philosophy, literature, and architecture. Tracing a lineage that goes back to the Cubist and Futurist incorporations of fragments of texts in their paintings, in more recent incarnations it has involved the appropriation of and "transformative play" with various types of discourses. Works by Jenny Holzer, Barbara Kruger, Adrian Piper, and Cindy Sherman might all be seen as part of this particular strand of conceptual art.

Holzer's "Truisms" implicitly invoke an array of similar forms: the political or advertising slogan, the one-liner, the homily, the aphorism, the cliché, the Zen koan. Yet while these other forms variously intend to indoctrinate or sell, amuse, instruct, enlighten, connect (lamely), or confound, the intentions of "Truisms" are more obscure. On the surface, they are clearly calculated to surprise, to provoke thought about these conflicting voices. They might require either an identification with a particular "position" among those offered, or an acceptance of one's own – and society's – ability to sustain contradiction. Many viewers responded by adding their own written commentary to the "Truisms," crossing some out, and editing or revising others – in effect, joining in the conversation. In the spirit of participatory art, from Brecht's plays to the "happenings" of Fluxus and other performance artists, the "Truisms" became collaborations.

As aphorisms from "Truisms" and two later series, "Living" and "Survival," such as PROTECT ME FROM WHAT I WANT, PRIVATE PROPERTY CREATED CRIME, and YOU ARE CAUGHT THINKING ABOUT KILLING ANYONE YOU WANT, began appearing in venues customarily reserved for advertising – on the giant electronic signboards of Times Square and Las Vegas, for example – they created increasingly powerful disruptions of the controlled semiotic fields around them. By speaking from the site of commerce, they implicitly raise questions about the nature of other authoritative voices speaking to us, their command of purportedly "public" space, and the nature of the messages they purvey.

Holzer's various series constitute interventions into the public sphere, in the tradition of numerous other "guerrilla art" movements, particularly the Dadaists, the Surrealists, and the more overtly political Situationists, who appropriated objects and language and inserted them into new cultural contexts, in the process subverting their original meanings and ideological import, and, perhaps more important, reshaping the contexts themselves. Yet since the time of those avant-garde modernist movements, it has become clear that capitalism and consumer culture are the most adept practitioners of these strategies of appropriation and can co-opt even the most radical ideas and images. By positioning themselves among – or often in the spaces of – the messages of consumer culture, Holzer's series turn the tables once again, recouping these strategies for new subversive purposes.

Holzer's "Inflammatory Essays" (which followed "Truisms") self-consciously adopt the form of the manifesto and mimic its impassioned rhetoric, yet they defy easy categorization. While political and artistic manifestos have traditionally combined an explicit critique of the flawed present (often formulated as a moment of "crisis") with a utopian prescription for the future, Holzer's "Inflammatory Essays" are strangely devoid of either. As the critic Janet Lyon observes, they are "eviscerated manifestos – free from all explicit or particularized reference" (1991: 113):

REJOICE! OUR TIMES ARE INTOLERABLE.
TAKE COURAGE, FOR THE WORST IS A
HARBINGER OF THE BEST. ONLY
DIRE CIRCUMSTANCES CAN PRECIPITATE
THE OVERTHROW OF OPPRESSORS. THE
OLD AND CORRUPT MUST BE LAID TO
WASTE BEFORE THE JUST CAN TRIUMPH....
CONTRADICTION WILL BE HEIGHTENED.
THE RECKONING WILL BE HASTENED...
THE APOCALYPSE WILL BLOSSOM.

In the "Inflammatory Essays," Holzer creates generic manifestos, whose "no brand," formulaic quality is reinforced by their uniformity: all of them are exactly one hundred words and twenty lines long, and printed in Times Roman Bold. Depending upon the inclinations of their audience, the "Inflammatory Essays" might be read as affirming the potential of public space as a "political" space. Thus, they might function as a form of rhetorical place-holder or zero, keeping open the possibility of an eruption of dissent or rebellion. Or, they might equally be read as an ironic commentary on, or even a send-up of, impassioned political discourse, or even, as Holzer herself suggests, "as a caution about what happens when people are whipped to a frenzy, and don't think about what they are being fed" (Flynn 1993: 33). In any case, they prompt a consideration, beyond their immediate discursive content, of the form and function of the manifesto itself. In this sense, Holzer's work is connected to other postmodern genres such as "metafiction," works of fiction that explore the conditions and conventions of fiction.

The ambiguity of the meaning of "Inflammatory Essays" is compounded (or perhaps complemented) by the ambiguity of its implied "we." The "we" of the political manifesto is always both determinate and open. If the precise identities of those producing the manifesto are unknown, their allegiances are nonetheless quite apparent. By issuing a manifesto, the speakers intend to extend their "we," while simultaneously articulating (and positioning them-selves against) a countervailing "they." The "Inflammatory Essays," however, leave their "we" entirely open by revealing neither their origins (they are, like all of Holzer's work, "unsigned") nor their opposition. The audience is left to ponder its own, and others', unstated allegiances.

Some of the "Inflammatory Essays" issue from a first-person voice, an individual "me" rather than a collective "we."

> DON'T TALK DOWN TO ME. DON'T BE POLITE TO
> ME. DON'T TRY TO MAKE ME FEEL NICE.
> DON'T RELAX. I'LL CUT THE SMILE OFF YOUR
> FACE. YOU THINK I DON'T KNOW WHAT'S
> GOING ON. YOU THINK I'M AFRAID TO REACT.
> THE JOKE'S ON YOU. . . .

Yet this voice is no more certain than the others; it could belong to anyone with any grievance against anyone else, and any of us might imagine ourselves as either its "I" or "you." Holzer's texts implicitly draw attention to the ways in which one's identity is constructed through language – a key focus of the postmodern investigations into the "subject." In conversation, the referents of pronouns are entirely contingent upon who is speaking at any given point: "I" is a position we assume by speaking, but a moment later, another too assumes the position of "I" in response. "I" (as well as "you," "we," and "they") and the identity it marks out are, then, remarkably contingent and bound to context.

The resonance of Holzer's aphorisms is also bound to context. In the New York City of the 1980s, statements from the "Living" and "Survival" series seemed particularly apt and politically charged commentaries on the stark economic inequities of the Reagan era:

WHAT COUNTRY SHOULD YOU ADOPT IF YOU HATE POOR PEOPLE?

IT TAKES A WHILE BEFORE YOU CAN STEP OVER INERT BODIES AND GO AHEAD WITH WHAT YOU WERE WANTING TO DO.

PUT FOOD OUT IN THE SAME PLACE EVERY DAY AND TALK TO THE PEOPLE WHO COME TO EAT AND ORGANIZE THEM.

DON'T WATCH THE UNDERCLASS IT'S MORE LIKELY THAT THE WARLORDS WILL KILL YOU.

Unlike in most of the "Truisms" and the "Inflammatory Essays," the voice of the "Living" and "Survival" series seems more identifiable as Holzer's own, or at least as that of a "leftie-liberal," as she terms herself (Howell 1988: 124). The political tensions inherent in these works are heightened by their incongruous and subversive appearance on discreet bronze wall-plaques "with the look of authority, or the establishment," as Holzer notes, like those that identify the office of a government official or the benefactor of a library, museum, or other institution. In these, as in all of Holzer's work, to paraphrase McLuhan, the medium is (at least half of) the message. Form is also content. Like many other postmodern works of art and literature, Holzer's investigate not just the forms of ideology but also the ideology of forms. The "Living" and "Survival" series' "play" with form results in deadly irony.

Holzer's early works were parasitically attached to building walls, creating a contrast between the fragile, subversive paper messages and the concrete, "established" walls; or they insinuated themselves into the buildings alongside other plaques, playing upon the dissonance between their "establishment" form and their insurrectionary words. In more recent works, including the "Under a Rock" series, the "Laments," and the Venice installation, her signs in effect become architecture. The merging of signs and architecture is itself one of the hallmarks of postmodern architectural design. While architecture has always been a semiotic art, in the late twentieth century there has been a particular convergence of advertising signage and vernacular architecture across the American landscape. Robert Venturi, Denise Scott Brown, and Steven Izenour's *Learning from Las Vegas* celebrated the pervasiveness of the architectural form they dubbed "the decorated shed," inaugurating an "architecture of communication over space" (1972: 8).

Holzer's "Under a Rock" exhibitions consisted of texts carved (in a script used on government monuments) on polished black marble benches. The spotlit benches were surrounded by LED signs, one positioned in the front of the room and the others arrayed along the walls at the head of the benches. The arrangement of the space invoked a combination of church sanctuary, cemetery, and movie theater. Written from the point of view of the perpetrator, bystander, or victim of dark crimes (things that crawl out from under a rock), these texts are narrative vignettes of terrorism, sex, and murder.

CRACK THE PELVIS SO SHE LIES RIGHT. THIS IS
A MISTAKE. WHEN SHE DIES YOU CANNOT REPEAT
THE ACT. THE BONES WILL NOT GROW TOGETHER
AGAIN AND THE PERSONALITY WILL NOT COME
BACK. SHE IS GOING TO SINK DEEP INTO THE
MOSS TO GET WHITE AND LIGHTER. SHE IS
UNRESPONSIVE TO BEGGING AND SELF-ABSORBED.

The "Under a Rock" series is thematically – and architecturally – linked to the subsequent "Laments," a series of thirteen stone sarcophagi (in the exact dimensions of real coffin lids, including ones for children and infants), arranged in spotlit rows with LED signs at their heads. In "Laments," Holzer sought to give voice to the final thoughts of the dead, to give them "a chance to say what they couldn't say" (Flynn 1993: 34). Written in part as a response to the untimely deaths caused by the AIDS epidemic, these inscriptions also have a political edge; there is rage behind these evocations of "those lost for no good reason" (Auping 1992: 93). Holzer's "Laments" are among her most explicitly political – and polemical – works, and in this, they are very much a part of the politicization that has marked American art of the late twentieth century.

Holzer's installation at the 1990 Venice Biennale constituted a virtual retrospective or archaeology of her art. The installation was arranged within the four rooms of the American Pavilion. On either side of its entrance were two darkened antechambers. Their floors were inscribed with "Truisms" (the "ground" of Holzer's work) translated into different European languages, and stone benches encircled their perimeters. In one room, the benches were inscribed with texts from the "Inflammatory Essays", in the other, with a series of meditations on motherhood. Reflecting Holzer's own recent experiences with childbirth and mothering, they are the most personal – and at times the most furious – of her works.

I AM INDIFFERENT TO MYSELF BUT NOT TO MY
CHILD. I ALWAYS JUSTIFIED MY INACTIVITY
AND CARELESSNESS IN THE FACE OF DANGER
BECAUSE I WAS SURE TO BE SOMEONE'S
VICTIM. I GRINNED AND LOITERED IN GUILTY

ANTICIPATION. NOW I MUST BE HERE TO
WATCH HER. I EXPERIMENT TO SEE IF I CAN
STAND HER PAIN. I CANNOT....

I AM AFRAID OF THE ONES IN POWER WHO KILL
PEOPLE AND DO NOT ADMIT GRIEF. THEY
WILL NOT STAY IN A ROOM WITH A DYING
BABY. THEY WILL NOT SPEND THE DAYS IT
CAN TAKE.

These texts appeared in different forms in the two remaining rooms of the installation as well. In what became known as the "Mother and Child" room, the first text in the series ("I AM INDIFFERENT TO MYSELF") was carved in a stone tablet set in the middle of the polished marble floor. On the back wall of the darkened room, slender vertical LED signs reached from floor to ceiling, each a red stream of text mirrored in the floor below, creating an effect of fire flowing into water. Sometimes the texts were inverted, so that they could only be read in their reflection. This inversion echoes Holzer's dualistic representation of woman as both protector and perpetrator, life-giving and death-bringing, which challenges the traditional gender dichoto-mies that allow women only the passive (as opposed to the male, active) half of these traits. The structural elements of the installation – the play of dark and light, solid and "liquid," fire and water – reinforced the dualities that emerge in the texts themselves – mother and child, self and other, life and death, power and vulnerability, love and loathing. As in all of Holzer's works, the form here is finally inseparable from the content.

The progression of the rooms was marked by an ascending intensity of emotion generated by the different presentations of the texts. In the final room the lines of text streamed through the room, flowing over the bodies of the viewers and reflecting up from the shining marble floor, creating a fiery deluge of nearly unbearable visual intensity. The force – and aggression – of this presentation rendered the texts all the more impassioned and inescapable, yet it also caused the eye to look away and the messages to disintegrate into a chaotic storm of piercing, blinking light. This last room shifted the focus of the installation from the content of the texts themselves to the medium in which they – and so much of our own discourse and that of the world surrounding us – are cast. Its strange concatenation of the singular and the commonplace, the emotional and the technological, of personal meditations and mass communications, conjured the postmodern techno-environment of information blitzes and media overload, and became a fitting culmination of Holzer's role in shaping the postmodernist artistic and cultural landscape.

30

Fredric Jameson

Sean Homer

Postmodern theory has consistently been seen to challenge and undermine the central tenets of Marxist thought, especially the centrality it accords to class struggle as the driving force of history, the need for an analysis of the social as a "totality," and the primacy of the economic over political and cultural concerns. According to Jean-François Lyotard's (1984) influential formulation, postmodernity is characterized by an incredulity to all grand, universal, or master narratives: the Enlightenment narrative of a progressive instrumental reason, the psychoanalytic narrative of Oedipal desire, and above all the Marxian narrative of human emancipation. In its stridently nominalist and anti-foundationalist rhetoric postmodernism rejects all universal explanatory systems and the privileging of homogenized groups, such as the working class, in favor of an analysis of discrete micronarratives and particular identities. Postmodernism, in short, represents a fundamental epochal shift in which the older forms of explanation are no longer adequate or credible. Jean Baudrillard has pursued this argument further through his claim that a radical break has taken place within capitalism itself whereby we now exist in a hyperreal world of cyberspace, free-floating images, and mediatized events. Therefore, key Marxian categories, such as the distinction between use-value and exchange-value, are now obsolete as they depend upon an essentially anthropological conception of human need which has been eclipsed by a new economy of signs and simulacra. Marxism, with its nostalgia for the historical referent and latent essentialism, is quite simply redundant in this "unreal" reality of the postmodern world.

Marxism and Postmodernism

Not surprisingly, the response from many Marxists to the concept of postmodernism has been hostile (see Callinicos 1989; Wood and Foster 1997).

Terry Eagleton (1996), for example, acknowledges the value of postmodernism in placing on the political agenda issues of gender, race, ethnicity, and identity but at the same time sees it as a radically impoverished resource. Postmodernism, he argues, tends to undermine its own radicalism by promoting a series of caricatures or "straw figures" – the Enlightenment, Marxism, totality, History (with a capital H), the subject, essentialism, hierarchy, and identity – which it can then extravagantly and ostentatiously knock down. Postmodernism thus undercuts the very foundations of political solidarity and agency, ultimately denying the possibility for any real or meaningful social change. Eagleton does not, unfortunately, give an account of the historical conditions of postmodern ideology and for this we must turn to the North American Marxist theorist, Fredric Jameson.

In 1984 Jameson published what was to become one of the most singularly influential articles to emerge from the debate upon postmodernism; indeed, according to Perry Anderson, "Postmodernism, or, The Cultural Logic of Late Capitalism" served to "redraw the whole map of the postmodern at one stroke – a prodigious inaugural gesture that has commanded the field ever since" (1998: 54). This essay is itself a montage of two earlier interventions by Jameson, that is, "The Politics of Theory: Ideological Positions in the Postmodernism Debate" (1984a), and his 1982 Whitney Museum address, "Postmodernism and Consumer Society" (1985). In the first of these essays Jameson mapped the opposing ideological positions that were emerging around the concept of postmodernism, arguing that whatever stance one adopted with respect to postmodernism, be it positive or negative, it could always be shown to project a particular vision of history.

If – following Lyotard and Baudrillard – a structural break with capitalism can be said to have taken place, then the Marxian critique and its emancipatory narrative are, at a stroke, invalidated and the path seems to lead inexorably to post-Marxism in one form or another. If, on the other hand, postmodernism can be shown to represent a systemic transformation which at the same time retains all the essential characteristics of capital then Marxism retains its explanatory force. For Jameson, therefore, what was required was neither a facile celebration nor entrenched repudiation of postmodern culture but a genuinely historical and dialectical analysis of its emergence and conditions of possibility.

"Postmodernism and Consumer Society" marks Jameson's first attempt to delineate the key features of this culture, albeit with a rather heterogeneous list of names, styles, and forms, ranging from the poetry of John Ashbery to the films of Godard, from the architecture of Robert Venturi to punk rock of The Clash, from the music of Philip Glass to the French new novel. The importance of this essay, however, lies not with who is included or excluded from this taxonomy but in its development of two essential characteristics of Jameson's theorization of postmodernism, that is, his contention that postmodernism ushers in a radically new experience of space and time. There has been a significant decline, according to Jameson, in our sense of history, narrative, and memory and simultaneously an erosion of aesthetic depth and critical distance. This experience finds aesthetic representation through the related concepts of pastiche and schizophrenic temporality.

Pastiche and Schizophrenia

Jameson contrasted postmodern pastiche with modernist conceptions of parody. Parody, he suggests, plays on the uniqueness of a style; it "seizes on [its] idiosyncrasies and eccentricities to produce an imitation which mocks the original" (1985: 119), but in doing so it retains an implicit linguistic norm against which the original is being judged. Above all, parody retains a subversive "other" voice. As an imitation of a particular unique individual or personal style parody also rests on assumptions about the nature of the subject which, since the poststructural dissolution or decentering of the subject, are no longer held to be tenable. Pastiche, on the other hand, whilst sharing many of these features, is a neutral practice. It lacks parody's "ulterior motive," its satirical impulse, and any sense of a norm against which the original is to be compared. Language has now disintegrated into a proliferation of private languages and discourses. Postmodern literature does not simply "quote" popular texts as a modernist such as Joyce may have done, but rather incorporates those texts within itself to the extent that the boundaries between them are effaced. This process of "de-differentiation," as Jameson defines it, between previously distinct cultural realms, specifically between "high art" and "mass" or "popular" culture, is frequently cited as postmodernism's democratizing and popularizing tendency, hence its radical political edge. The full aesthetic realization of postmodern pastiche is to be found in what Jameson designates as "nostalgia films." The classical nostalgia film, writes Jameson, "while evading its present altogether, registered its historicist deficiency by losing itself in mesmerized fascination in lavish images of specific generational pasts" (1991: 296), the privileged generational moments being the 1930s and 1950s. Postmodern pastiche is symptomatic, contends Jameson, of a general loss of historicity and our incapacity to achieve aesthetic "representations of our own current experience" (1991: 21).

It is not just that our sense of history has waned, however, but that our very sense of temporality itself has changed and can now be characterized as essentially schizophrenic. Taking his definition of schizophrenia from Lacan, Jameson deploys this category in a descriptive rather than a clinical sense. Lacan saw schizophrenia as primarily a language disorder, a failure to accede fully into the symbolic order, the realm of language; it, therefore, represents a break in the chain of signification. For Lacan the schizophrenic's failure to fully grasp language articulation will affect his or her experience of temporality, or, more accurately, he or she will experience a lack of temporal continuity. The schizophrenic, therefore, is condemned to a perpetual present, an "experience of isolated, disconnected, discontinuous material signifiers which fail to link up into a coherent sequence" (1985: 119). This lack of temporal continuity has the corresponding effect of making the present more intense and vivid, the signifier in isolation becoming ever more material or "literal." These twin features of pastiche and schizophrenia result in postmodernism's pervasive flattening of space and the displacement of diachronic time with synchronic immanence.

Periodizing Postmodernism

These two essays still lacked, however, an account of the historical preconditions for the emergence of postmodern culture which Jameson himself had called for, and it was this analysis that the "Cultural Logic" essay provided in an extraordinary *tour de force*. Drawing on the work of the Marxist economist Ernest Mandel, Jameson sought to anchor postmodern culture in the objective transformations of the economic order of capital itself. Contrary to many postmodern theorists he argued that postmodernism does not mark the emergence of a new historical epoch but the intensification and restructuration of the social and productive relations of capitalism. In *Late Capitalism* (1975) Mandel identified three distinct moments of capitalist development: market capitalism, imperialism or monopoly capitalism, and our present age, mistakenly defined as postindustrial capitalism by some but more properly defined as multinational or late capitalism. Mandel's periodization is based on a theory of "long waves"; capitalism develops through a cyclical movement of boom and bust every seven to ten years but we can also detect within the history of capital larger cyclical movements that take place approximately every fifty years. These longer cyclical movements are linked to the development of new technologies of production and reproduction and mark a higher stage of capitalism, or to put it another way, an intensification of capitalist relations of production (see Homer 1998 for a fuller explanation of Mandel's work).

For Jameson, the term postmodernism does not designate a particular aesthetic or discrete style but rather a *periodizing* concept which serves to "correlate the emergence of new formal features in culture with the emergence of a new type of social life and a new economic order" (1991: 113). This new economic order emerged post-World War II, around the late 1940s or early

1950s for the United States and in the late 1950s for Europe. The key transitional decade, though, is seen to be the 1960s. Postmodernism clearly retains many of the features of high modernism – for example, its self-consciousness, the disruption of narrative forms, its cultural eclecticism and sense of parody – but to see postmodernism simply as a continuation of modernism is to fail to grasp the transformation that these features have undergone and above all to fail to take account of the social position of the older modernism. Postmodernism and modernism, writes Jameson, "remain utterly distinct in their meaning and social function, owing to the very different positioning of postmodernism in the economic system of late capital and, beyond that, to the transformation of the very sphere of culture in contemporary society" (1991: 5). With modernism the sphere of culture was seen to have retained a degree of semi-autonomy; whether from the left or right, it retained an oppositional stance and critical distance toward capital. Postmodern culture has become fully integrated into commodity production in general, annulling its oppositional and critical stance. Postmodernism, then, is what Jameson calls a cultural dominant, a notion that allows for "a range of very different, yet subordinate, features" (1991: 4), as it presupposes the residual characteristics of modernism as well as emergent characteristics of post-postmodern culture. As a concept it allows for both continuity and difference.

Critique of Jameson's Periodization

Jameson's achievement was breathtaking and for the first time provided a comprehensive account of the historical specificity of postmodernism but it also raised a number of critical issues that it failed to adequately address. As Mike Davis (1985) has pointed out, there appears to be a certain discrepancy between Jameson's periodization and Mandel's. For Mandel, the term "late capitalism" designates that period of economic history which clearly began after World War II. Jameson's periodization of postmodernism is somewhat equivocal; he defines it both as the period post-World War II and the moment emerging from the late 1960s and early 1970s. Jameson seeks to clarify this situation in the introduction to *Postmodernism*:

> the economic preparation of postmodernism or late capitalism began in the 1950s, after the wartime shortages of consumer goods and spare parts had been made up, and new products and new technologies (not least those of the media) could be pioneered. On the other hand, the psychic *habitus* of the new age demands the absolute break, strengthened by a generational rupture, achieved more properly in the 1960s. (1991: xx)

Jameson goes on to argue that the crystallizing moment of crisis for both the economic and the cultural spheres was the oil crisis of 1973. However, this still does not appear to resolve the discrepancies between Mandel's periodization and his own. For instance, while David Harvey (1989) and Edward Soja (1989) share much of Jameson's analysis of postmodernism and acknowledge his influence on their own work, they disagree in this one important respect.

What divides these otherwise mutually sympathetic analysts of postmodernism is essentially which side of the economic crisis of the early to mid-1970s they see as the economic preconditions for postmodernism itself. Jameson argues that it is the pre-1970s boom, while Harvey and Soja locate postmodernism's economic basis in Thatcherite monetarism and Reaganomics. Postmodernism may have emerged in the 1970s but it came of age in the 1980s and is now irredeemably associated with the conspicuous consumption of that decade, in other words, with the rise of that new breed of entrepreneurs and young high-earning financial service workers, the so-called Yuppies. Thus, Frank Pfeil argues that, contrary to Jameson's notion of postmodernism as the cultural expression of the global logic of late capitalism, postmodernism is a much more local phenomenon. Postmodernism, writes Pfeil, is "a cultural-aesthetic set of pleasures and practices created by and for a particular social group at a determinate moment in its collective history" (1990: 98). Christopher Norris (1990) also locates the emergence of postmodernism in a context of more recent political defeats and especially within Europe of the legacy of May '68 and the wholesale retreat from politics of a generation of French intellectuals. In particular Norris identifies the collapse of the Althusserian-structuralist paradigm as at once discrediting Marxism *tout court* and legitimating a pervasive anti-realist and epistemologically relativist stance, as the displacement of questions of politics proper into issues of aesthetics and ethics. Jameson goes some way in endorsing this more limited analysis of postmodernism as "an ethos and a 'life-style' . . . the expression of the 'consciousness' of a whole new class fraction . . . variously . . . labelled [the] professional-managerial-class, or more succinctly as 'the yuppies'" (1991: 407). He also accepts that postmodernism "is essentially a much narrower class-cultural operation serving white and male-dominated elites in the advanced countries" (1991: 318), but always with the rider that it is the first truly "global" North American cultural phenomenon.

The Politics of Space

The central problem with the cultural logic thesis is that it remains at too high a level of abstraction; on the one hand, Jameson presents a persuasive account of an individual subject's experience of the disorientating world of global

capital, and, on the other, a very generalized theory of the structural transformations of the system itself. What this work lacked, and the monumental
Postmodernism, or, The Cultural Logic of Late Capitalism (1991) conspicuously
failed to deliver, was any systematic account of the mediations between the
individual subject and the world system. The key categories of mediation
employed here, as with Jameson's previous work, were commodification and
reification. Postmodernity was seen to mark a further expansion of an essentially Lukácsean conception of reification whereby the commodity form had
now penetrated the last enclaves of resistance to capital, that is, the aesthetic,
the Third World, and the Psyche. Capitalism, in other words, had become the
first truly universal system and postmodernism its cultural expression. One of
the problems with this account was that it appeared to rule out the possibility
for any form of resistance to the new global market and hence the possibility of
historical change. The dilemma posed for our present political imagination
was starkly revealed in Jameson's notion of a new postmodern political
aesthetic of "cognitive mapping," or something we might have termed in
pre-postmodern times as "class consciousness."

   The notion of cognitive mapping derives from the urban studies of Kevin
Lynch in the 1960s where it designated a subject's ability to cognitively locate
him or herself in the new urban landscapes of postwar North American cities.
Jameson expanded the concept to now include a subject's ability to mentally
represent or map his or her experience in relation to the global economy.
Jameson's account of his own experience of postmodern spatiality, in particular his reading of the interior of the Bonaventure Hotel, has been remarkably
influential, but it is questionable to what extent this experience can be
generalized (see Homer 1998: 128–51). Indeed, for Jameson postmodern
spatiality seems to remain "alarming" and "disorienting," and faced with
the "horror of multiplicity" of contemporary space he was unable to perceive
of any form of its transcendence or negation. Above all, what this dialectic
of immediate perception and inconceivable totality lacked was any indication
or analysis of the group, institutional, regional, or national forms of mediation
that might intervene between them, that is to say, forms of mediation that
at once shape individual identities and subjectivity and at the same time
provide the space for political resistance to the otherwise relentless logic of
reification.

Speculation and Finance Capital

In his most recent work on postmodernism (1998), Jameson has sought to
clarify this relation between global capital and discrete cultural artifacts
through the structural role played by finance capital and speculation within

the new global economy. As with his original notion, Jameson finds his ideas at once confirmed and facilitated by Giovanni Arrighi's *The Long Twentieth Century* (1994). Ostensibly a history of capitalism, Arrighi's book, argues Jameson, provides "a new structural understanding of features of capitalism not yet fully elucidated" (1998: 136), that is, the problem of *finance capital*. Arrighi's elaboration of the nature and operation of finance capital serves to crystallize all the problems and questions that have arisen from the early 1980s onwards and especially in the relationship between economics and culture. Finance capital does not represent an entirely novel or complete break with previous modes of capital investment but the dialectical expansion of capital itself:

> Speculation, the withdrawal of profits from the home industries, the increasingly feverish search, not so much for new markets (these are also saturated) as for the new kind of profits available in financial transactions themselves and as such – these are the ways in which capitalism now reacts to and compensates for the closing of its productive moment. Capital itself becomes free-floating. (Jameson 1998: 140–1)

What Jameson is calling "free-floating capital" here is not an entirely fictional realm of finance completely divorced from the material production and consumption of goods and services, but it exists on the floors of the world's stock markets in the form of speculation rather than through the production of goods on the factory floor. The advantage of Arrighi's work over Jameson's previous use of Mandel is that it forestalls the teleological implications of the classical market, monopoly, and late capitalism model whilst retaining a conception of capitalist development as discontinuous and expansive. Furthermore, Arrighi's dialectic of money, capital, and speculative finance is a process that is internal to capital itself, as a process of decline and renewal at every higher stage of capitalism. Therefore, it can be seen to provide one of the keys to understanding the recent transformations in culture, through the intensification of *abstraction* from money through investment capital to finance capital. In other words, a theory of abstraction that closely follows Jameson's earlier notion of the reification of the image or sign, from realism (whereby the image is still tied to its referent), to modernism (when the image becomes severed from its referent), to postmodernism (where reification penetrates the image itself and rends signifier and signified asunder). As this process is internal to capital it can be rendered at either a systemic level – in terms of successive modes of production – or, alternatively, at more specific levels of analysis – as in the operation of particular financial markets. Thus Jameson is also able to deploy this notion of abstraction at a system level – as with the dialectic of realism, modernism, and postmodernism above – or within the context of specific genres or cultural forms – the analysis of film, for example, or specific styles of music.

Conclusion

Jameson's most recent studies on architecture and land speculation as well as the transformation of the image in contemporary culture provide us with some of the most sustained and provocative attempts yet to elucidate the relations between a global economy and postmodern cultural practice. There remain problems with this project, not least the fact that Arrighi's thesis was formulated against Mandel's theory of long waves, and this begs the question of where Mandel's work is to be located in Jameson's conceptualization of postmodernism. Furthermore, Arrighi's work has also been criticized for being theorized at such a high level of abstraction that it can provide us with little understanding of the actual workings of capital markets today. Finally, there remains the question of agency and the possibility for social transformation, and this directs us toward a much closer examination of different forms of mediation and cultural practices in a postmodern world. In conclusion, the unquestionable importance of Jameson's work on postmodernism remains his attempt to ground this most slippery and ephemeral of phenomena in the objective transformations of the global economy. More than any other figure in postmodern debates, he has consistently argued for the necessity of historicizing this vituperatively ahistorical concept and eschewing moralizing judgments for a fully dialectical analysis. Jameson has constantly brought to the fore the material conditions of this apparently immaterial world of postmodernity.

31

Charles Jencks

Hans Bertens

One of the best-known and most influential critics of contemporary architecture, Charles Jencks (b. 1939) has often been credited with bringing the terms "postmodern" and "postmodernism" into circulation. Although this attribution has no basis in historical reality – he himself has acknowledged the literary critic Ihab Hassan as his source – it is still appropriately suggestive because it illustrates the impact of his writings, more in particular his theorizing of postmodern architecture.

Jencks was not the first to do so. In his 1966 book *Complexity and Contradiction in Architecture*, the architect Robert Venturi had already taken a stance against modernist architecture's "easy unity of exclusion" (Venturi 1972: 16) and had made a plea for an architecture whose "elements" would have to be

> hybrid rather than "pure," compromising rather than "clean," distorted rather than "straightforward," ambiguous rather than "articulated," perverse as well as impersonal, boring as well as "interesting," conventional rather than "designed," accommodating rather than excluding, redundant rather than simple, vestigial as well as innovating, inconsistent and equivocal rather than direct and clear.

"I am," Venturi concluded his list of, at the time, highly provocative preferences, "for messy vitality over obvious unity" (16). Architecture should "evoke...many levels of meaning and combinations of focus" (16) instead of the single meaning and single focus elicited by modernist architecture. This does not necessarily mean that all traces of modernism must disappear from the new, messily vital architecture that Venturi has in mind. Although *Complexity and Contradiction* is primarily interested in rehabilitating premodern architectural styles – in particular Mannerism and Baroque – it by no means excludes modern elements from its plea for hybridity and pluralism. Venturi's attack on modernism is not so much aimed at the actual architecture as at the purist and puritanical – "Protestant" in Charles Jencks's term – ideology that governs it. As Jencks, mixing his religious metaphors in attributing an Index to Protestantism, would put it much later, "Ornament, polychromy, metaphor, humour, symbolism, place, cultural identity, urban context and convention were put on the Index and all forms of decoration and historical reference were declared taboo" (1996: 22).

This distinction between ideology and its concretized products – the actual buildings that we see – is of vital importance to theorists like Venturi and Jencks, who both reject the purist and exclusivist ideology that they attribute to the modernist architects, even if they, at least occasionally, can still admire their architecture. In fact, for Jencks, as we shall see, this distinction plays a crucial role in his definition of architectural postmodernism.

Although by 1981 Jencks's name was already so bound up with postmodern architecture – or perhaps even postmodernism in general – that Ada Louise Huxtable could call him "the acknowledged guru of Post-Modernism" (Huxtable 1981: 10), he had not been the first to connect postmodernism and architecture. After Sir Niklaus Pevsner and Philip Johnson had occasionally used the term in the later 1960s, it had entered the vocabulary of architectural criticism in 1974 when it had begun to be adopted by a number of New York-based architects and critics, including Robert Stern, Paul Goldberger, and Douglas Davis. Jencks first used it the following year, in an article called "The Rise of Post-Modern Architecture." (While virtually everybody else has dropped the hyphen, still often used in the mid-1970s, between "post" and "modern," Jencks has retained it in order to distinguish "Post-Modernism" – as a contemporary movement in architecture, literature, and the arts – from "post-modernism" – the sociocultural condition of the late twentieth and early twenty-first century – and "postmodernism" – the deconstructivist movement in architecture and its poststructuralist equivalents in the other arts.) However, even if Jencks was not the first to see the relevance of the new term for contemporary architecture, he is undisputably the one who really put it on the architectural map with his 1977 *The Language of Post-Modern Architecture* (revised and expanded again and again through the 1970s and 1980s) and other highly influential publications.

In 1975, Jencks's postmodernism (*pace* his own Post-Modernism) is first of all a new pluralism that has come to replace modernism's monism. It includes what he calls "ersatz" architecture, consumer-oriented architecture, a new "social realism," and radical traditionalism. Its inclusiveness is illustrated by a passage from an article, "A Genealogy of Post-Modern Architecture," published two years later. A "strong postmodernist," Jencks tells us in 1977,

> would have to design mixed metaphors like Utzon, indulge in historicism and eclecticism like Venturi, be regionalist like Neo-Liberty and the Barcelona

School, adhocist like Goff, Erskine and Kroll, use a different style for each job like Saarinen and Kitutaka, use them semantically like Kurokawa, incorporate the pluralism of various codes like Takeyama, be sensitive to urban context like Jane Jacobs and Leon Krier, indulge in ironic parody like Mozuma Monta or Thomas Gordon Smith, and commit travesty and traditionalesque – like the Madonnas of Madonna Inn. (1977a: 269)

Still, in spite of this catholicity, we see a pattern emerge in this apparently random listing of contemporary developments, even if Jencks himself is at that point not yet fully aware of it. By the time of the second edition of *The Language of Post-Modern Architecture*, published in 1978, the pattern has crystallized. In that second edition, Jencks introduces his landmark definition of postmodern architecture as "double-coded." Postmodern architecture

speaks on at least two levels at once: to other architects and a concerned minority who care about specifically architectural meanings, and to the public at large, or the local inhabitants, who care about other issues concerned with comfort, traditional building and a way of life. Thus, Post-Modern architecture looks hybrid . . . (Jencks 1978: 6)

In its attempt to communicate simultaneously with two – or more – widely different constituencies, postmodern architecture is inevitably double-coded: "Hence the double-coding, the architecture which speaks to the elite and the man on the street" (8).

In the "Postscript" added to *The Language of Post-Modern Architecture*'s third edition of 1981, Jencks further refines his definition of postmodernism. As I have already pointed out, Jencks has much more of a quarrel with the ideology of modernist architecture – its yearning for purity, its exclusivism, and its universalistic pretensions – than with the actual architecture itself. This should not surprise us: even if he felt no genuine admiration for at least some of modernism's architectural achievements, as an advocate of pluralism Jencks would hardly be in a position to excommunicate modernism (if I may stay with his religious metaphors). However, he does much more than merely tolerate modernism. In 1981, Jencks fundamentally revises his earlier double-coding in that he now decides that one of the two codes involved is always that of modernism: postmodern architecture is "double-coded, an eclectic mix of traditional or local codes *with Modern ones*" (Jencks 1981: 133; emphasis added). Postmodern architecture may be double-coded in any number of ways, but one of the two codes always refers back to modernism.

This is an important, and very influential, refinement of Jencks's earlier position. What it means, for instance, is that simple imitations of earlier styles can have no place in his postmodernism. It also excludes much of the suburban

and/or commercial architecture discussed in publications such as Robert
Venturi et al.'s *Learning from Las Vegas* (1972), which had tended to see the
often strikingly pluralist developments in those sectors in postmodern terms.
For Jencks, a situation in which a number of styles merely coexist peacefully
under the umbrella of pluralism no longer qualifies as postmodern. Jencks
wants a palpable tension between the codes that make up a postmodern
building or work of art. His postmodern architects, "like Post-Modernists
generally, send a mixed message of acceptance and critique. In a word their
double-coding confirms and subverts simultaneously" (Jencks 1996: 30). In
this mixed message, this double code, modernism is always represented: "all
the creators who could be called post-modern keep something of a modern
sensibility, some intention which distinguishes their work from that of revi-
valists... Post-Modernism has the essential double meaning: the continuation
of Modernism and its transcendence" (30).

As we have just seen, the hybridity implicit in double-coding had interesting consequences for Jencks's categorization of contemporary architecture.
However, double-coding did not only exclude the most conservative contemporary architecture, it also excluded what to many observers seemed the most
revolutionary architecture of the time: the Centre Pompidou in Paris, Norman
Foster's Hongkong and Shanghai Bank in Hong Kong, the then new Lloyd's
building in London, or even the less striking but still innovative Westin
Bonaventure hotel in Los Angeles that Fredric Jameson would a few years
later see as typically postmodern. For Jencks, this architecture is "an exaggeration of several Modern concerns such as the technological image of a building, its circulation, logic and structure" (Jencks 1981: 133). This "late
Modern" architecture is "pragmatic and technocratic in its social ideology
and from about 1960 takes many of the stylistic ideas and values of Modernism
to an extreme in order to resuscitate a dull (or clichéd) language" (Jencks 1986:
32). Although Jencks is willing to admit that late-Modern architecture sometimes allows itself ironic gestures in the direction of postmodernism (as in the
case of Philip Johnson's AT&T building), with its interest in high-tech
solutions and its exposed technology it is essentially single-coded and self-
referential.

When Jencks branched out, after the mid-1980s, and began to include
painting, literature, and postmodern philosophy in his discussions of postmodernism, his "late-Modern" category immediately proved useful, offering,
for instance, a seemingly natural fit for Derrida's deconstruction and other
radicalizations of arguably modernist concerns with language, representation,
and identity. In fact, after the mid-1980s Jencks increasingly comes to see
"late-Modernism" in terms of an obsessive and ultimately sterile self-pre-
occupation, even if he repeatedly expresses his admiration for, for instance,
Foster's Hong Kong building. We must see this in connection with Jencks's

growing and more general unease with the ever-increasing fragmentation that he finds in contemporary society. It is this unease that in 1987, in a book titled *Post-Modernism: The New Classicism in Art and Architecture*, leads him to suggest that a new architectural consensus may be emerging:

> The argument of my book is to say that Free-Style Classicism underlies both the art and architecture of the third phase of Post-Modernism, starting roughly from the 1970s and continuing until the present. And it is more or less a consensus, a world consensus, though it has many sub-styles, like the International Style had . . . The general reason for all this happening is the need for a universal language, a public language. (Jencks 1987: 45)

In painting Jencks saw a similar desire for consensus. Noticing "a return to a traditional concern with content" (1986: 25) in contemporary painting, he argued that "We can see in this return to the larger Western tradition a slow movement of our culture, now worldwide, back to a 'centre which could not hold' (to misquote Yeats)" (38).

With this general drift toward a consensus postmodernism, Jencks's original definition of postmodernism as two codes, or languages, uneasily and often antagonistically cohabiting within one and the same architectural design or artistic work, loses much of its bite. Jencks keeps on insisting on irony and on double-coding, but there is little irony or tension left in postmodern classicism. Although in the course of the 1990s he would seem to distance himself again from the idea of a "universal" postmodern classicism – partly, no doubt, because the paintings that served to illustrate his arguments had been devastatingly critiqued – Jencks's postmodernism comes to serve ever more broadly representational ends: "There is the intention to confront the present with the past, to question and subvert from within the dominating culture, to *represent the complexity of contemporary life through double coding*" (Jencks 1996: 43; emphasis added). Postmodernism now signals the pluralism of the contemporary world in which once inimical views and attitudes live in relatively peaceful coexistence.

Seen in this light, postmodernism is the surface manifestation of a fundamental sociocultural change: "one of the deep reasons for Post-Modernism is the reassertion of the presence of worldliness, fecundity, variety and embodied spirituality: that is, a cosmic orientation based on contemporary science" (Jencks 1996: 9). In the 1990s, Jencks's postmodernism acquires a strong utopian dimension. It comes to stand for emancipation, freedom, diversity, tolerance – in short, for the forces of life and light. For Jencks postmodernism's drive toward freedom and equality – in which he includes the feminist movement and the emergence of multiculturalism – is not a historical coincidence, but reflects the nature of the universe itself: "At all events the universe story is one of increasing complexity . . . and evolution towards ever-increasing feeling, sensitivity, mental power and organisation" (71). Although there is no guarantee that "a benign state will [ultimately] prevail," our current evolution toward pluralism, toward a far greater tolerance of diversity and complexity than modernity could ever muster, is for Jencks a sign that at least for the time being our postmodern society is in tune with the universe itself.

32

Barbara Kruger

Paula Geyh

The postmodern era has witnessed a fundamental transformation of centuries-old attitudes toward art. Conceptual art, in particular, challenges ideas of art as the "original" product of individual genius, created in elite isolation from the realm of popular, commodity culture. Photography and graphic art – media that implicitly undermine distinctions between the original and the copy, the hand-made and the mass-produced, and finally between "high" aesthetic and "low" popular art – have been the preferred media of many conceptual artists such as Barbara Kruger, Jenny Holzer, Cindy Sherman, and Sherrie Levine.

Barbara Kruger's striking high-contrast black-and-white images overlaid with slashes of red framing slogans in bold-faced type are among the most recognizable of recent conceptualist works. Reminiscent of both Dada photo-montage and the graphic art of the Russian avant-garde of the 1920s (which critiqued bourgeois society from the outside), Kruger's art aims to disrupt conventional modes of seeing and perceiving. Her critiques, however, are launched from inside the art world as well as outside it. This dual positioning in itself generates multiple ironies. Kruger's massive piece featuring a black-and-white reproduction of Michelangelo's Sistine Chapel fresco of Adam receiving the spark of life from the hand of God, overlaid with a text reading, "You invest in the Divinity of the Masterpiece," simultaneously critiques classical aesthetics, from Kant to high modernism, and relies upon them for its impact. The piece's acquisition by the Museum of Modern Art deepens the irony of its criticism of the convergence of art and commerce, though it remains uncertain whether its appearance there undermines the museum or itself, both or neither.

Such ironies are endemic to Kruger's dialogical or contrapuntal fusions of image and text. Rather than using images to illustrate her words or words to define her images (the two customary relations of words and images in combination), Kruger's works juxtapose conflicting words and images to produce powerful semiotic dissonances. The images are appropriated from advertising, photography annuals, how-to handbooks, and news and documentary photographs. The words are her own, but they frequently echo or evoke contemporary clichés, advertising slogans, and the rhetoric of political propaganda. We have been conditioned, "programmed," to perceive the meaning of images as virtually transparent (particularly in the case of advertising and news images), a conditioning that facilitates the unquestioning acceptance of the illusions and ideologies they proffer. Kruger's works attempt to "deprogram" their viewers through texts (the slogan-like phrases overlaying the images) that expose, displace, deflect, or rebut the images' messages. In the process, her works seek to demystify such images, to reveal how power and desire inhere in them.

The locus of power (the power of domination, of control, of definition), the ruling "you" against which Kruger's work is directed, is never explicitly identified: it must be inferred by the viewer. Confronting the image/text, the viewer is forced by Kruger's method of direct address to identify the likely "you" addressed by the work and then adopt a position in relation to it, either assuming the place of that "you" or of the implicit "I" or "we" who is speaking. This process of taking up a "position" within the system produced by the work reminds the viewer of the crucial role discourse plays in constructing subjectivity, one's sense of self – a key preoccupation and target of postmodern critical thought and practice. Another effect of this method is to collapse the viewer's aesthetic distance from the work of art: "I'm interested in making an active spectator who can decline that You or accept it or say, It's not me but I know who it is," Kruger has said (Squiers 1987: 80).

While the "you's" are never named, it is possible to identify some of them, if only provisionally. Surveying the range of Kruger's art, it appears that they are often male and nearly always malevolent – violent, greedy, repressive, racist, sexist, homophobic – a sort of amalgam of the dark side of the American character as it is expressed in both individuals and in its government and economic system. Her "you" thus takes the form of both particular individuals and more broadly conceived "types" or collectivities standing in for "the system." Another way to understand these opposing "you's" and "I's," as art critic Ken Johnson suggests, is as "imagined personifications of the dominant power on the one hand and the insurgent resistance on the other.... [Their confrontation is a] ritualistic evocation of a kind of mythic contest between titanic antagonists – between the revolutionary son (or daughter) and the tyrannical father" (1991: 131).

Some of Kruger's most resonant works are directed against Big Brother-like forces of repression: the image of a shadowy figure wearing a fedora and holding his finger up to his mouth in a "shushing" gesture, overlaid with the statement, "Your comfort is my silence"; the close-cropped image of a man's eyes, looking through a spyglass, with the words, "Surveillance is Your Busywork" superimposed on it; and two shadowed faces without mouths separated by a chasm into which the words "You destroy what you think is difference" tumble. To even mention this "you" is, of course, a transgression of the rules it lays down, but even more than that, it is a reversal of the order of dominance itself: here the silenced talk back, voicing a very public "j'accuse." No other era has been as concerned with giving voice to groups who have been silenced throughout history as the postmodern has. Kruger's art can be seen as a counterpart to postmodern texts that chronicle "history from below," that is, from the vantage point of workers and the poor, women, and marginalized ethnic and racial groups whose experience has traditionally been omitted from the historical record. Who speaks with authority, whose stories are told, whose words count – these questions haunt works by Kruger like the one depicting the shattered face of a Greek statue emblazoned with the words "Your fictions become history." In some works, such as the "flag" installation, the questions (arrayed in the form of the American flag) are asked directly: "Who is beyond the law? Who is bought and sold? Who is free to choose? Who does time? Who follows orders? Who prays loudest? Who dies first? Who laughs last?"

While many of Kruger's critiques are directed against the power of the state, this is only one part of a much broader understanding of power as dispersed through myriad "sites" and institutions (e.g., the family, the church, the school, the media, the market), ideological state apparatuses, as Louis Althusser famously called them, and the discourses through which they operate (e.g., morality, religion, knowledge, news, and advertising). These various sites must be seen as part of an interlocking network of social organization and control, each reinforcing one another and the whole. In postmodern America, the market, with its unparalleled ability to infiltrate and colonize nearly every part of our lives, may be the most powerful of these forces. Kruger's own sense that there is "nothing outside the marketplace," that she "live[s] and speak[s] through a body which is constructed by moments which are formed by the velocity of power and money" is reflected in both the form and content of her work (Mitchell 1991: 435). The red frames that surround her works are meant to signal their status as commodities; they are, in effect, a packaging device. "Kruger's works operate," art critic Amelia Jones suggests, "by mimicking the strategies of the commodity, which 'seduce, dislocate and deter'" (1991: 158).

Kruger's works, it should be noted, are also often found in the space of consumer advertising: on billboards, bus shelters, posters, matchbooks, caps, and T-shirts. Such placement inevitably redounds upon the sites themselves, raising questions such as, what is the meaning of "public" space (and should "public" be synonymous with "commercial")? who decides the allocation of such space? where is the space of political struggle? These questions are crucial not just for an understanding of Kruger's work, but also for our understanding of postmodern spatiality and how it is being transformed by the forces of global commodity capitalism. The extent of its power is suggested by Kruger's image of an exploding house on which appears the comment, "Your money talks," and another of shadowy pants legs and men's dress shoes below the legend, "You make history when you do business."

Kruger's "anti-ads" aim to interrupt our unquestioning reception of the messages of the market by exposing their underlying assumptions and hidden agendas. "Buy me I'll change your life," reads one that features the picture of a particularly repulsive stuffed toy resembling a deformed Donald Duck. Another, the image of a hand presenting a business card that reads "I shop therefore I am," evokes the Cartesian formula of self and suggests the extent to which advertising encourages us to define our identities through the products we consume. The art world, too, is implicated in these systems of pervasive representation; works of art have long served to "advertise" or lend legitimacy to particular ideologies and their ways of seeing. And art, too, is a commodity: "When I hear the word culture," one of Kruger's slogans (emblazoned across the face of a ventriloquist's dummy) reads, "I take out my checkbook." In tiny type in the corner by the dummy's mouth, it says, "We mouth your words."

Among the postmodernist critiques of the power of representations is Jean Baudrillard's argument that the postmodern era has brought a sort of apotheosis of the "simulacrum," an image, that has come to replace – to stand in for or function as – the real. Many of Kruger's works are directed against a particular form of such images: the stereotype. Though their functioning resembles that of other images, the stereotype is an especially potent force in shaping us as social subjects and structuring our thought and responses to ourselves and others. It initiates a process that Louis Althusser, in his analysis of ideological state apparatuses, referred to as "interpellation," the "hailing" of a subject by an agent of the social order, indicating a particular, preestablished subject position which the subject is invited (or compelled) to "recognize" and accept as his or her own. By responding to this "hail" or address, we take up our prescribed roles in the social order: diligent worker, dutiful wife, law-abiding citizen, devout worshipper, loyal follower, and so on.

The messages of many of Kruger's works suggest that such "recognitions" as often as not constitute cases of misrecognition: "You thrive on mistaken identity," one accuses. Another asserts, "We construct the chorus of missing persons." These works endeavor to interrupt the process of interpellation by calling attention to the stereotype and its function as an instrument of power that "presents" what it wishes you to see and obscures what it does not. "Kruger," the critic Craig Owens has noted, "proposes the mobilization of the spectator" (1984b: 104). This mobilized spectator is encouraged to "read against" the intended meaning of stereotypical messages and images. In an early series, Kruger modeled such resistant readings by stamping pictures of a ranch house, of a woman's modestly folded hands, and of a woman cowering on a bed, with the words "Container," "Perfect," and "Tradition" – each a repudiation of our preprogrammed interpretations of these familiar images.

The power of visual representations to determine our images of ourselves and others has been an important focus of postmodern critique. Kruger has described her work on several occasions as "a series of attempts to ruin certain representations and to welcome the female spectator into the audience of men" (Squiers 1987: 79). Gender roles – the ways in which society defines what it is to be "masculine" or "feminine" – have been a constant preoccupation of Kruger's work. Several pieces have critiqued constructions of masculinity: "We don't need another hero," reads the slogan superimposed on the image of a little girl admiring a little boy's display of his bulging biceps. Kruger's critique extends to how masculinity is negotiated among groups of men. The repressed homoerotic desire of fraternal organizations, for example, is revealed by an image of fraternity rough-housing tagged with the observation: "You construct intricate rituals which allow you to touch the skin of other men."

The majority of Kruger's work on gender roles, however, has focused on the construction of women's subjectivity. One of her most well-known works is a close-up of a woman's face, the eyes covered with two perfect leaves, framed by the text: "We won't play nature to your culture." This piece evokes one of the gendered binaries which have structured Western thought and philosophy since Plato: nature associated with the female, culture with the male. This binary opposition has positioned woman as secondary to man, the "other" to his self, and associated her with the lesser, negative side of such paired, hierarchical opposites as presence and absence, thought and emotion, and master and slave. Kruger's image of a woman's face mutating into that of an animal, emblazoned with the statement, "I will not become what I mean to you," suggests the feminist response to the long history of patriarchy.

Within Western systems of visual representation, particularly as they have been manifest in art and, more recently, in film, photography, and advertising, the "gaze" has generally been coded as male. Woman has been the object, not the subject of the gaze; the spectacle, not the spectator (an observation echoed in one of Kruger's works featuring the face of a recumbent woman, eyes closed, being caressed and regarded by a man whom we only glimpse. In parallel lines, like bars across the image, appear the words, "We are being made spectacles of"). The gaze itself is a form of power. In a sense, the gaze immobilizes, freezing its object within the spectator's frame of reference – a point reiterated by Kruger's image of the silhouette of a woman, sitting and bent down, the outline of her body fastened by nails against the background of a wiry grid, across which are stretched the words: "We have received orders not to move." Throughout her career, a primary purpose of Kruger's artistic practice has been to expose this and other mechanisms through which our representations, in all their myriad forms, shape and finally imprison us, and through this exposure, free us from their tyranny.

33

Thomas Kuhn

Arkady Plotnitsky

Thomas Kuhn (1922–96) would be a reluctant postmodernist at best. Thus, he joins a number of major figures whom, or at least whose ideas, we associate with postmodernism (Derrida, Foucault, Irigaray, Deleuze and Guattari, among others) but who would themselves resist this association. Arguably, the main reason for this resistance is that these thinkers appear to associate the term with much that is different and sometimes in conflict with their ideas, including those (according to this view) misappropriated by postmodernism itself. There are good reasons for this view and for their, sometimes sharp, criticism of postmodernism. Accordingly, the application of the term "postmodernist" to their ideas requires considerable caution, caution not always exercised by commentators. I would argue, however, that it is not out of place. I would also argue that some of these thinkers do not always sufficiently grasp certain aspects of postmodernist thought and culture, including the postmodernist deployment or implications of their own ideas, especially when this deployment works against the grain of their thought, as sometimes happens in Kuhn's case. The situation is hardly surprising and is not a matter of misunderstanding or incoherence of thought on the part of these thinkers. Instead it appears to be a decoherence – a structural split from a single or totalizing wholeness – proper to the radical, irreducible heterogeneity of the landscape of postmodernism and postmodernity. (It may be useful, even if provisional, to distinguish these terms and, correspondingly, the adjectives "postmodernist" and "postmodern," referring by the first to philosophical ideas, wherever manifest – say, in philosophy, art, and politics – and by the second to postmodern culture, which, one might argue, amounts to our contemporary culture.) At the same time, this type of heterogeneity allows for other relationships between radical philosophical thinking and postmodernism. An obvious example would be Jean-François Lyotard's work, both expressly postmodernist and, philosophically, close to that of Kuhn and others just mentioned.

Thus, while complex and ambivalent, the connections between Kuhn and postmodernism are more logical or even inevitable than arbitrary. Moreover, some of the key ideas of Kuhn and postmodernism share a common genealogy – namely, that descending from both (post-)Darwinian biology and the radical epistemology of quantum physics. These connections are in Kuhn's case not coincidental, even leaving aside that Kuhn received his Ph.D. in physics before he moved on to his work in the history and philosophy of science. While science played the most decisive role, the ideas of most key figures in the history of modern biology and quantum physics (and some, such as Erwin Schrödinger and Max Delbrück, worked in both fields) may also be traced to proto-postmodernist aspects of nineteenth- and early twentieth-century philosophy, literature, and the arts. Conversely, the relevance of evolutionary biology and genetics, quantum mechanics, and other key developments in modern mathematics and science to the work of Kuhn and other figures here mentioned is hardly in doubt or surprising in view of the significance of new mathematics and science for modern intellectual history. Contemporaneously with the appearance of his most famous work, *The Structure of Scientific Revolutions* (1962), Kuhn interviewed the founders of quantum physics, and specifically Niels Bohr. These interviews appear to have had a major impact on his thought and subsequent works, bringing them closer to the more radical postmodernist epistemology. I shall sketch the key elements of Kuhn's thought and work before elucidating these connections.

Kuhn appears to have been a reluctant revolutionary even in his own field. That is, he appears to have been reluctantly pushed into his views of the history (evolutionary and revolutionary) of science by the rigor of his investigation, rather than by the desire to implement (however rigorously) an independent revolutionary idea. Ironically, the case is similar to that of Max Planck, the discoverer of quantum physics in 1900. Planck was reluctantly forced into his ascription of, in certain circumstances, discontinuity to light, previously believed to be a continuous, wave-like phenomenon in all circumstances. I simplify for the moment the nature of Planck's discovery and related history, and of the quantum phenomenon itself, whose properly quantum-theoretical understanding was never accepted by Planck himself and several other founders of quantum theory – Einstein and Schrödinger among them. These questions are masterfully analyzed by Kuhn in his great *Black-Body Theory and the Quantum Discontinuity, 1894–1912* (1978). The book also contains significant new insights into the relationships between continuity (evolution) and discontinuity (revolution) in the history of science, which bring Kuhn even closer to postmodernist epistemology. That in both cases new relationships between continuity and discontinuity are at stake is not accidental and is part of the common genealogy of Kuhn's ideas and postmodernism.

What, then, defines Kuhn's view of modern science and makes it revolutionary? Kuhn's two arguably most famous concepts are "the paradigm shift" – a radical, discontinuous transformation of the conceptual view governing the preceding ("normal") developments of science – in the course of scientific revolution, and "incommensurability," which defines the (irreconcilable) relationships between different paradigms. Kuhn's usage of the term "paradigm" is unstable, as he acknowledges. It has been suggested that there are over twenty (different) uses of the term in Kuhn, and that he fell in love with it, as, one might add, did our (postmodern) culture. These variations, however, are not incoherent or arbitrary, and to some degree are even necessary. To indicate some of them, in *The Structure of Scientific Revolutions* paradigms are initially defined as "models from which spring particular coherent traditions of scientific research" (1996: 10). Then the concept is expanded to a much broader cultural definition. It is "what the members of scientific community share" while "conversely, a scientific community consists of men [and, one presumes, women] who share a paradigm" (1996: 176). The book, however, also uses the term "paradigm" in more narrow but, for Kuhn, sometimes more significant senses, for example, that of a "constellation of group commitments" or "disciplinary matrix" or a "shared example," through which one's ("paradigmatic") scientific understanding and practice in a given field develops. Indeed, he sees this latter sense of the term as the book's most significant, as well as least understood, contribution (1996: 187–91). Kuhn is also sensitive to the degree in which incommensurability applies to possibilities of persuasion, the (eventual) transition from one paradigm to another, and so forth. Here his thinking sometimes stops short of a more radical but also more comprehensive and, thus, perhaps ultimately more effective view of incommensurability. In a rough outline, the pre-Kuhnian view of the process and/or progress of science was based on the idea of (by and large) continuous development. In the course of this development, scientific facts, theories, and methods are "added, singly or in combination, to the ever growing stockpile that constitutes science technique and knowledge" (1996: 2). In other words, in this view these developments take place within the same, even if diversified, paradigm or commensurable set of paradigms. Theories or parts of theories may of course be corrected or discarded within that process, for example, in accordance with the "Popperian" concept of falsification of theories by experiment. (Karl Popper's own view is a more complex matter.) This type of understanding (there are variations) is correlative and is an outgrowth of the modern, Enlightenment program, specifically as considered by Lyotard (for example, in conjunction with what he calls the "metanarratives" of modernity). By contrast, Kuhn's "paradigm-shift" view introduces a far more complex and dynamical perspective on the history of scientific knowledge, without an Enlightenment-inspired nostalgia for a unified picture or for progress toward a single goal. (There are of course local forms of progress.) We find key "postmodernist" parallels and resonances in Foucault's "episteme" and Lyotard's "differend" (both perhaps influenced by Kuhn).

These are crucial ideas, both in general and specifically in the context of postmodernism. I would argue, however, that Kuhn's insights must be seen as correlative to, even if not the consequences of, the joint workings of two other, perhaps more fundamental, factors which link Kuhn to postmodernist philosophy and epistemology even more essentially and firmly.

The first is the role of chance in scientific discovery and practice, crucial across the postmodernist landscape. Ultimately, Kuhn's understanding of chance brings it to the radical limit of the idea of chance found in quantum theory and, more implicitly, in post-Darwinian evolutionary biology and genetics.

The second, at a certain level more fundamental, is the constitutive, rather than auxiliary, role of culture in the determination and, to use Lyotard's term (crucial for his understanding of science and scientific knowledge), legitimation of science. This view of the importance of culture defines Kuhn's thought as "constructivist" in juxtaposition to the (more traditional) realist view that leaves this constitutive role strictly to nature, while giving culture, at most, an auxiliary position. It may be observed that the constitutive role of culture in Kuhn and other constructivist theories may be seen as parallel to the irreducible and constitutive, rather than, again, auxiliary, role of observational and measuring technology in the constitution of the experimental data of quantum physics. According to Bohr, it is this role that is ultimately responsible for other key ("strange") features of quantum physics and its radical – proto-postmodernist – epistemology. This argument was familiar to Kuhn and, I would argue, had a major impact on all of his thought.

It may be argued that it is this constitutive role of culture that is largely responsible for both Kuhnian chance and other key features of Kuhn's matrix – discontinuity, paradigm shift, incommensurability, and so forth – and necessitated its departure from the preceding theories of scientific knowledge. No paradigm, even if narrowed down (as indicated above), no shift of paradigm, and no incommensurability of paradigms can be rigorously considered outside their constitutive cultural frameworks, even though Kuhn may not have taken this point to its ultimate limits. Ultimately, however, the situation is best seen as defined by the complex reciprocity of all these various elements, including the role of observational technology in quantum physics, or of chance and culture. It is conceivable that (again, analogously to quantum-mechanical epistemology) the efficacity of all these elements and of the relationships among them, now all seen as effects, is inaccessible by means of any of them, and ultimately by any means and in any terms that are, or will ever be, available to us. This is, arguably, epistemologically the most radical view of the situation, even if not quite Kuhn's own, although he comes close to it in his later thought. It may, however, be attributed to other radical thinkers, for example, to Nietzsche, Bataille, Bohr, Derrida, and de Man, if not quite (or not without qualification) to Deleuze, Foucault, and Lyotard.

While (especially toward the end of his life) at most a qualified realist, Kuhn was also a qualified and, again, reluctant (cultural) constructivist. He was compelled to envision more complex (as against the preceding history of science), and more reciprocal and symmetrical relationships between nature (or mind) and culture in the determination and legitimation of science. This complexity in no way diminishes the significance of culture in this process, but instead places it within a more complex economy. In some respects, this view is closer to more recent developments in constructivism than to the more traditional *social* constructivism of, say, David Bloor's school and of related developments in science studies, elaborated in the wake of the work of Kuhn, Paul Feyerabend, Imre Lacatos, and several earlier thinkers, in particular Ludwik Fleck. In truth, these approaches are rarely strictly "constructivist" (that is, to the point of suspending the role of nature absolutely). The difference, however, in the balance of determination and legitimation of science, social and extra-social construction, (social or other) constructivism and realism, or other (more radical) forms of unconstructivism, is crucial. It is this balance that ultimately determines the (epistemologically) radical nature of a given theory, such as Kuhn's.

In closing *The Structure of Scientific Revolutions*, Kuhn appeals to Darwin's theory of evolution as a key model for "the evolution of scientific ideas," indeed a "nearly perfect analogy," even though he (rightly) cautions that the analogy "can be pushed too far" (1996: 172). The analogy and Kuhn's argument reemerge at a crucial point on relativism in an important 1969 "Postscript" (1996: 205–6). Kuhn observes that "the most significant" as well as, to many, "the least palatable" of Darwin's suggestions is "the abolition of [the] theo-logical kind of evolution." For "The *Origin of Species* recognized no goal set either by God or nature" (1996: 172). By analogy, Kuhn and other radical theorists of scientific knowledge (or key postmodernist thinkers) do not deny that there is progress to science. But they do question – and may even deny – that this progress is toward a particular (single) goal, or that it can be seen as proceeding along a single line of development. This view, however, is even more disturbing and unpalatable to the proponents of traditional views of science and knowledge than an outright denial of progress, which would be much easier to argue against and which is indeed problematic from the radical perspective just outlined. (This latter point is often missed by commentators on radical thought, critics and admirers alike.) Evolution (biological or scientific) proceeded through a complex interplay of continuous and discontinuous pro-cesses (evolutions/revolutions), within which the role of chance is irreducible and is primarily responsible for the suspension of teleology. An analogous view defines quantum physics, where there can be no question of attempting a causal or realist analysis along the lines of classical physics, and much of postmodernist epistemology, influenced as it is by both of these scientific theories. This view also irreducibly localizes evolutionary ("historical") chains and hence the narrative structure of our knowledge, very much in accordance with Lyotard's definition of postmodernist (and postmodern) sensibilities: incredulity toward and suspension of totalizing "grand narratives" and "metanarratives."

Ultimately, the understanding of chance implied in this view reaches new limits, at least in the more radical approaches in all these areas – quantum physics, biology, and postmodernist philosophy. Indeed this understanding may be said to define twentieth-century thinking about chance in the work of such figures as Nietzsche, Blanchot, Lacan, Deleuze, de Man, and Derrida. We may call this understanding postclassical or nonclassical. (Not all postmodernist theories subscribe to it, especially those based on or appealing to chaos theory, which is not radically noncausal in the same sense.)

Classically, chance or, more accurately, the appearance of chance is seen as arising from our insufficient (and perhaps, in practice, unavailable) knowledge of a total configuration of forces involved and, hence, of the lawful necessity that is always postulated behind a lawless chance event. If this configuration becomes available, or if it could be made available in principle (for it may, again, not ever be available in practice), the chance character of the event would disappear. Chance would reveal itself to be a product of the play of forces that is, in principle, calculable by man, or at least by God. Most classical mathematical and scientific theories and classical philosophical views of probability are based on this idea: in practice, we have only partially available, incomplete information about chance events, which are nonetheless determined by a complete architecture of necessity behind them. This architecture itself may or may not be seen as ever accessible in full or even partial measure, which may make such a theory indeterministic in so far as it disallows exact or, as in the case of chaos theory, even statistical predictions concerning the behavior of the systems involved. The *presupposition* of necessity is, however, essential for and defines the classical and specifically modern view as causal and as realist. Realist theories may be described most generally by the presupposition that their objects in principle possess independently existing attributes no matter whether we can, in practice or in principle, ever describe or approximate them or not. Subtle and complex as they may be, all scientific theories of chance and probability prior to quantum theory – and many beyond it – and most philosophical theories of chance are of the type just described. They are realist and causal, even if not necessarily deterministic.

The *nonclassical* understanding of chance or reality (which ultimately implies the impossibility of using such a concept) is fundamentally different.

Nonclassical chance is irreducible not only in practice (which, as I explained above, may be the case with classical chance) but also in principle. There is no knowledge, in practice or in principle, that is or will ever be available to us and that would allow us to eliminate chance and replace it with necessity. Nor can one postulate such a (causal/lawful) economy as unknowable (to any being, individual or collective, human or even divine), but existing, in and by itself, outside our engagement with it. This qualification is crucial, for, as I explained above, some forms of the classical understanding of chance allow for this type of (realist) assumption. By contrast, nonclassical chance, such as that which we encounter in quantum physics, is irreducible to any necessity, knowable or unknowable. According to Bohr, "it is most important to realize that the recourse to probability laws under such circumstances is essentially different in aim from the familiar application of statistical considerations as practical means of accounting for the properties of mechanical systems of great structural complexity." Bohr adds an extraordinary sentence, which may be adopted as a definition of postmodernist epistemology at its radical limit, and which was undoubtedly familiar to Kuhn: "In fact, in quantum physics we are presented not with intricacies of this kind, but with the inability of the classical frame of concepts to comprise the peculiar feature(s)... characterizing the elementary [i.e., quantum] processes" (Bohr 1987, 2: 34). Indeed it may remain (forever) unexplainable why statistical predictions are possible under these conditions, but they are and they work excellently. Ultimately, according to Bohr, we here confront "an essential inadequacy of the customary viewpoint of natural philosophy for a rational account of physical phenomena of the type with which we are concerned in quantum mechanics." Indeed, the latter "[entail] the necessity of a final renunciation of the classical ideal of causality and a radical revision of our attitude towards the problem of physical reality," and ultimately perhaps a final renunoiation of the classical ideal and perhaps any available or conceivable concept of reality as well (Bohr 1983: 146). This, I would argue, applies to much of postmodernist epistemology and Kuhn's views of both quantum physics and the way we can understand science and culture. In his Rothschild Lecture at Harvard in 1992, Kuhn stated the same point: "I am not suggesting, let me emphasize, that there is a reality which science fails to get at. My point is rather that no sense can be made of the notion of reality as it has ordinarily functioned in the philosophy of science."

In the case of scientific evolution/revolution as considered by Kuhn, this epistemological situation is, as I argued, correlative to the irreducible role of cultural determination and legitimation in the project of science and to the complexities of the interactions between nature and culture. Now, however, physical or biological "nature itself" (to the degree such a concept is possible under these conditions) offers us, at least, partial models for these complexities. (It is worth noting that one need not reach the level of the quantum constitution of the systems involved in order to encounter them in biology.) Both are crucial references for Lyotard as well. Indeed part of his critical, or deconstructive, argument in *The Postmodern Condition* (1984) is the following. If one wants to understand human culture on the model of nature or mathematics, as has been customary throughout modernity, one might also want to be more attentive to what nature (or science) and mathematics tell us. And they (specifically quantum physics, chaos theory, algebra and topology, and post-Gödelian mathematical logic) appear to convey to us a very different – postmodern and perhaps still more radical – message.

I would now like to comment further on the question of reality and constructivism, which I shall define in terms sufficiently broad to accommodate both Kuhn and other views more customarily associated with constructivism. According to this definition, most postmodernist epistemology would be constructivist, although differences and nuances must be kept in mind. Constructivist ideas have had a considerable impact in recent years in a variety of fields, most prominently in the philosophy and history (or sociology) of science, say, from Bloor to Bruno Latour. These ideas have become a major force in postmodernism and postmodern culture.

In question in constructivist and postmodernist philosophy alike is how real are the various conceptions of reality we form, beginning with the idea of reality itself; that is, how well, if at all, they correspond to what actually exists in the world, rather than only reflect our view of the world. This question still assumes that we can in fact ascertain anything about the world that would be independent of our interaction with and our view of it. This assumption defines what is called *realism*, and it is fundamentally questioned and often denied by constructivism. The latter is often accompanied by *relativism*, that is, the view (found in Kuhn as well) that our understanding of the world is defined by our particular interactions with it, interactions specific to us and not others. Our particular interactions with and views of the world may of course be affected by our interactions and "negotiations" with those who have different views of the world. In this (relativist) view, the world that we (objectively?) share is the outcome of these negotiations. This understanding, however, leaves space for irreducibly incommensurable views as well. Constructivists or postmodernists do not, by and large (one does encounter more radical views), deny that the world exists or is real or even objective in this particular sense. Nor do they deny that there is a certain material world that would continue to exist, were we no longer there to interact with it. They question (and some deny) the (realist) claim that we can endow the world with properties that can be claimed as independent of such interactions and negotiations, since, they argue, any such definition would be inescapably affected by these interactions and negotiations. In other words, the constructivist world or, if you like, constructivist "reality," is reciprocal with respect to our interaction with this world, while the realist world and reality are independent and self-contained. As Niels Bohr once said, in a constructivist vein, of the quantum-mechanical epistemology: "the new situation in physics has so forcibly reminded us of the old truth that we are both spectators and actors in the great drama of existence" (1987, 1: 119). We can never only observe the world but always shape it and, even more so, our view and sense of it merely by virtue of our existence in the world.

The constructivist view, as just outlined, corresponds closely to Bohr's philosophy of quantum physics, to which Kuhn's epistemology is indebted as well. Bohr's epistemology also and perhaps most fundamentally deals with what is ultimately inaccessible to knowledge. On this point, Bohr and, at least by implication, Kuhn depart from most constructivists, in particular Feyerabend, in so far as the quantum world as such is seen as and treated as inaccessible to our knowledge or experience. This understanding is crucial to making the overall framework radically and irreducibly nonrealist. It makes any conceivable notion of reality inapplicable, if not meaningless, at this level – that is, at the level of the ultimate constituents of nature. Ultimately, Kuhn appears to have come, with Bohr's help, to this type of conception, which is as difficult and for some (Einstein among them) impossible to accept as anything that nonclassical, such as postmodernist, epistemology has to offer. For Kuhn, there is thus an irreducible "loss" in representation and knowledge, that is, in relation to the way classical knowledge would function. For one cannot think here in terms of some preexisting or possible, if unavailable, knowledge or representability. This inaccessibility is crucial to quantum theory. But it may also be seen as corresponding to the most radical and most rigorous epistemological frameworks associated with postmodernism, such as those of Nietzsche, Bohr, Bataille, and Derrida, or, at their best, Heidegger, Foucault, and Lyotard.

We are now ready to bring together various trends linking Kuhn and postmodernism, and more firmly position Kuhn in relation to postmodernist theory and the culture of postmodernity. Even the first is (and, in truth, has always been) a complex phenomenon, let alone the second, which amounts to the whole of contemporary culture (in its postmodernist unsummability). Both are inevitably and even irreducibly, if again heterogeneously, conjoined. Lyotard's title and subtitle, "The Postmodern Condition" (relating to the contemporary culture) and "A Report on Knowledge" (a theoretical assessment of the character of knowledge under this condition) indicate this conjunction, which is characteristic of much postmodernist thought. The book itself (along with other works that supplement it) explores it throughout. One finds elements or at least echoes of similar explorations in Kuhn's works, specifically in *The Structure of Scientific Revolutions*. Given the limits of space, I shall, by and large, bypass the relationships between Kuhn's work and postmodern culture. These are not negligible, extending from the rhetoric of paradigm shifts (it is pervasive) to the academic and public debates concerning modern science and its relation to society. However, by way of conclusion, I shall summarize the relationships between Kuhn's thought and postmodernist theory, specifically epistemology, which may be ultimately most germane in assessing these relationships in any event.

From this perspective, postmodernist theory may be seen as the radical critique of the views of knowledge, meaning, truth, interpretation, communication, narrative, and so on, which have traditionally defined the thought and culture of modernity. At its limit, this critique extends to the radical epistemology outlined above. Kuhn and a number of major postmodern figures have reached or come close to this view. Certainly, Lyotard's famous definition of the postmodern as "that which in the modern, puts forward the [irreducibly?] unrepresentable in representation itself" (1984: 81) relates to and depends on this epistemology, even if it is more difficult to be certain how far Lyotard would go here. I also leave aside other aspects of Lyotard's "definition," in particular the distinction between the modern and the postmodern in terms of our attitude toward the "loss" in representation (nostalgia for versus the affirmation of "the unattainable"), rather than only in terms of epistemology itself. Ultimately, I would argue, the epistemology is different, too. Indeed the presence of nostalgia changes the epistemology, and it certainly prevents one from embracing a radical postmodern epistemology. On the other hand, Lyotard's analysis of postmodernity and postmodernism in terms of narrative or (following Wittgenstein) language games can be easily linked to the present considerations. Certainly, Lyotard and others here mentioned are right to relate this radical loss in (re)presentation to a radical and radically decentered ("postmodern") plurality or heterogeneity – conceptual, cognitive, linguistic, narrative, cultural, or other at every level. (Kuhn's "incommensurability" may be best seen from this perspective as well.) Both postmodernism and postmodernity are indissociable from and inconceivable without this. Other key elements of all these theories – discontinuity, chance, incommensurability, or, more accurately, the irreducible interplay of continuity and discontinuity, necessity and chance, the commensurable and the incommensurable, culture and nature, and so forth – are correlative of this epistemology.

The configuration just outlined does not exhaust postmodernism but perhaps relates to what is, at least epistemologically, deepest and most radical in it, or in Kuhn's work. Indeed both may themselves be best seen not in terms of classically causal connections but instead in terms of such correlations – heterogeneously interactive and interactively heterogeneous links, links that are (epistemologically) postmodernist and (culturally) postmodern.

34

Jacques Lacan

James A. Steintrager

One hallmark of Lacan's work is its syncretism. Fields as diverse as phenomenology, linguistics, anthropology, and theoretical mathematics mingle with psychoanalysis, creating a complex and evolving amalgam. Another and related hallmark is Lacan's infamously dense and allusive idiolect, which has frustrated many a reader and is no doubt partially the result of sustained rhetorical self-stylization. If postmodernism has a style that could be characterized as baroque, even Gongoristic, then Lacan stands out as one of its exemplars. Yet, for Lacan, language by its very structure bars human subjects from unity and sets in motion the never fulfilled movement of desire. This, along with his concern that the role of the analyst both in therapy and the classroom be emphasized rather than hidden behind a veil of objective detachment, suggests that the generous reader might consider this difficulty and self-stylization heuristic.

Jacques Lacan was born in 1901. He was trained in psychiatry, and received his doctorate in 1932 for a thesis on paranoia. He produced relatively few written works; the major texts were gathered in a collection published in 1966 and simply entitled *Écrits* ("writings"), a rubric that evokes by way of contrast his principle medium: oral presentation. Most of his teachings were elaborated in the seminar that he held in various venues in Paris from 1953 to 1980 – the seminar twice being expulsed from sponsoring institutions. Lacan's career was in fact marked by controversy. In 1952, he helped lead the secession of a group of analysts from the Société psychanalytique de Paris. The International Association of Psychoanalysts subsequently excluded from its ranks members of the breakaway group, the Société française de psychanalyse. Such was the institutional response to Lacan's innovative and nonconciliatory approach. He died in 1981. These references may serve to position Lacan historically. The explanatory power of such biographical information, however, is itself put into doubt by Lacanian analysis. Such analysis rejects the notion that the proper name – Lacan's name in this case – refers one to a concrete entity whose characteristics can be elaborated and anchored to this support. Rather, the proper name is itself a signifier that carries with it the slipperiness of all signifiers. Who was Lacan? To provide a definitive answer to such a question would run counter not only to the spirit but, more importantly and decisively, to the *letter* of Lacan's teachings.

Mirrors, Speech, and Something Else: Lacan's Three Orders of Human Experience

A key contribution of Lacan's early work is his elaboration of the mirror stage. Unable to control either its environment or its own body, the infant sees reflected in the mirror (or in the image of another) a *Gestalt* that promises a future wholeness. It is at this moment that the psyche finds itself structured in terms of an alienating exteriority: the image of wholeness is situated outside of the subject but precipitates the formation of the ego as its internalized correlate. That is, the "I" is not the name for an essential subjective core; it is a function that is produced by identification with something other. The mirror stage encapsulates what Lacan sees as the paradox of demand: if the subject wants to consider itself whole, then it must ask to be recognized as such by another; but such a demand simply confirms dependence. For this reason, the joy associated with the promise of the mirror stage is tempered by an inevitable aggressivity. If these formulations have a Hegelian ring to them, there is little doubt that they owe much to the master–slave section of the *Phenomenology of Mind*. In contrast to Hegel, however, the dialectic of self and other that Lacan describes admits of no synthesis that would sublate the contradiction on which it is based. Lacan insisted that the mirror stage not be taken as a phase that would be passed through by the infant and left behind. Rather, it remains as a structure that forms the kernel of the order of human experience known as the Imaginary. As etymology implies, the Imaginary is conceived first and foremost in visual terms. As Lacan's thought developed the importance of the Imaginary – with its emphasis on objects and identifications – would cede to an ever greater concern with language.

The Imaginary has its roots in the phase of Lacan's work most inflected by phenomenology. In 1953, Lacan delivered an address entitled "The Function and Field of Speech and Language in Psychoanalysis." It was a manifesto of the linguistic turn that Lacan hoped to bring to psychoanalysis. Although, much like the mirror stage, the Imaginary would never be left behind, its dominance would henceforth indicate a regression in either analytic teaching or the analysand's therapy. Lacan thus labels the analysand's recourse to the Imaginary *parole vide* or empty speech. Using Ferdinand de Saussure's understanding of language as a grouping of coupled signifiers and signifieds, the values of which are constituted by their place in a system of differences rather than seen as positive or essential, Lacan transforms psychoanalysis into an investigation of the subject's relation to such differentially organized structures. In addition to Saussure, the structuralist linguistics of Roman Jakobson and Emile Benveniste as well as the structuralist anthropology of Lévi-Strauss become touchstones in the theorization of what Lacan calls the order of the Symbolic. The objects and identifications associated with the Imaginary are now viewed as dependent on their relation to this other order. In fact, Lacan tends to designate this order as that of the Other, suggesting that language remains extrinsic and alien to the speaking subject. The analysand's recognition of this dependence on the alterity of language is labeled *parole pleine* or full speech.

Indeed, what Lacan often calls his "return to Freud" consists primarily of analyzing those texts of the founding father of psychoanalysis that emphasize language. Lacan then translates these texts into structuralist terms. He thus recasts Freud's central discovery, the unconscious, with reference to Saussurean linguistics – but he does so with a crucial twist. While taking up Saussure's foundational coupling of signifier/signified, Lacan insists that the two sides of this linkage belong to heterogeneous networks and that any such linkage is provisional. This heterogeneity is graphically symbolized by the bar (/) separating the two aspects of the linguistic sign. Rather than stressing the signified or concept, Lacan instead claims that the signifier – or what he often calls "the letter" – conditions by the specificity of its own laws the signified. In so doing, he pushes the signifier to the fore as that which both institutes and characterizes the unconscious. To quote the standard formulations in this regard: "the unconscious is structured like a language" and "the unconscious is the discourse of the Other." These two formulations must be seen as complementary. In the first place, the unconscious is that which speaks in the subject (in spite of the resistances to this truth brought about by the ongoing presence of the ego as an Imaginary function). In the second, this speech of the Other can only be grasped by linguistic or, better, rhetorical analysis. The Other makes itself heard through the tropes of metaphor and metonymy (Lacan's replacement terms for Freud's "condensation" and "displacement," both processes associated with the way in which dreams manifest the unconscious). Metonymy characterizes the underlying insistence of desire in the signifying chain of discourse: the contiguity of signifiers allows for the continual displacement of the expression of desire along this chain. Metaphor provides the structure of the symptom, as one signifier is substituted for another, the latter now in the position of the hidden signified of the manifest signifier. In both cases, it is the relative autonomy of the signifier – the fact that signifiers are not irrevocably linked to signifieds – that makes possible the speech of the Other.

In a related move, Lacan reformulates the Oedipal saga in terms that convert content (the narrative of the male child's negotiation of sexual desire, fear of castration, renunciation of the mother and identification with the father) into structure and form. The supposedly real father becomes the linguistic and cultural network that situates the child – provides the child with a name and thus a position – even in advance of language acquisition. Castration anxiety is no longer the perceived threat to the penis, but rather the renunciation entailed by language and culture: the repression of the Imaginary quest for wholeness and the acceptance of the linguistic structures that will henceforth govern the subject. Lacan designates this double act of naming and denying with a pun: *le nom-du-père* (in French, it is impossible to distinguish aurally the difference between the "name of the father" and the "no of the father"). Lacan's subject thus only comes into being as the subject of language – subjected to language – and then only as a split subject – finding the direction of its desire only in language and yet separated even further by language from the original and now repressed quest for unity.

Clearly, Lacan's emphasis on language has little to do with reference. The subject of language actually gives up on any possible recourse to the world of "real" objects by entering into the play of signification. That said, Lacan designates the third order of psychoanalytic experience as the Real – and what exactly this means is one of the more controversial aspects of his teaching. A provisional answer is simply that the Real is that which lies outside of and yet supports the Imaginary and Symbolic orders. The Real cannot be accessed directly – any imagining of it fails to grasp it just as any discussion of it is simply more speech – and yet its presence is felt as an inevitable resistance. Thus, while eschewing the notion that language simply represents psychic or external reality – surely a sign of the postmodern insistence that "reality" is constructed rather than found – Lacan's contructivism does posit something beyond language and images. This beyond is constitutive of the subject's experience and yet unavailable to analysis except as rendered in paradoxical formulations. As Lacan would remark, the Real is "the impossible."

Psychoanalysis as Discipline and Science

Throughout his career, Lacan scrupulously sought to avoid reducing psychoanalysis to biological determinism or behaviorism. He makes clear that even the mirror stage, which is supported with biological references, produces an aggressivity that we cannot understand as simply the presence of an aggressive instinct. The distinction between the biological and the psychoanalytic becomes starker still with the insistence on language and structure: the Symbolic is an emergent order, the laws of which determine what the human subject is.

The human is thus differentiated from the rest of the biological world as the "subject that speaks." According to Lacan, psychoanalysis can claim the status of a discipline with a delimited object of study because the specificity entailed by language simultaneously engenders the unconscious. But the scientific status of psychoanalysis in general and of Lacanian psychoanalysis in particular has never gone uncontested. For some, the ubiquitous graphs, idiosyncratic logical formulae, and references to topology and probability theory are extraneous at best and fraudulent at worst. Lacan seems to have considered them absolutely essential to his teaching. This is because they underwrite the scientificity of psychoanalysis. This is not scientificity in the sense of the study of claims that can be falsified. Rather, it is the structuralist dream of providing formal descriptions of previously content-oriented disciplines such as linguistics, anthropology, and literary studies. Formalization is indeed the common thread that links the literary morphologies of Vladimir Propp, the synchronic analysis of signifiers and signifieds in Saussure, and the structural description of myths in Lévi-Strauss. Lacan, like so many others, no doubt hoped that psychoanalysis could raise itself to the level of science through the use of what he called "little letters" (referring to the variables used in his various schemata).

But if Lacan was one of the first to adopt the high modernist dream of structuralism, he was also one of the first to render problematic structuralism's claim to be external to the systems that it examines. Lacan illustrates this, for example, in the schema of the four discourses. In this schema a subject's specific relation to signification defines various positions (those of the university, of mastery, the analyst, and the hysteric). Taking up the position of the psychoanalyst implies one just as fully in the structures of signification as does the position of the academic and even the patient. For this reason, Lacan conceives of psychoanalysis as a science that can neither effect closure nor avoid the paradoxes of self-reference. The relationship of psychoanalysis to modernity as a project to rationalize human interaction has been ambiguous from the outset. Does Freud's discovery of the unconscious spell an end to extending the realm of reason, or does it mean that light can be shed even on the darkest realms of the psyche? If, according to Jean-François Lyotard, the defining characteristic of postmodernism is the rejection of grand explanatory narratives, then psychoanalysis, Freudian and Lacanian, has surely been one of these narratives and simultaneously, by decentering the conscious subject, an undermining of the stable point of enunciation of such narratives. Although Jacques Derrida and others have critiqued psychoanalysis on the grounds that it finds itself wherever it looks, it is only fair to say that Lacan in particular sought to explore the inevitable reflexivity of psychoanalysis rather than to foreclose it.

Affinities, Critiques, and Adaptations

Important differences notwithstanding, Derrida's practice of deconstruction shares with Lacan the use of Saussure's linguistics as a tool by which to undermine notions of the subject as autonomous and present to itself. Similarly, Lacan's exploration of the slipperiness of signification in terms of metaphor and metonymy bears comparison to Paul de Man's thesis that the irreducibly rhetorical aspect of language is a barrier to conclusive understanding. Deconstruction can be viewed in a sense as a radicalization of the Lacanian notion that language is structurally incapable of delivering on its promise to convert division into unity, lack into wholeness, absence into presence.

If the path of deconstruction seems to lead us away from questions of practice – a contention worthy of debate – several prominent theorists have sought to foreground the political stakes of Lacan's enterprise. A notable example is Louis Althusser, who attempted to incorporate Lacanian ideas into his structuralist Marxism. Althusser suggests that we only become subjects when "interpellated" into the symbolic networks of various ideological state apparatuses such as the education system. Yet, as influential as Althusser's theory of "interpellation" has been, it does not adequately capture the Lacanian conception of experience: the entry into language only further alienates the subject; it does not provide a comfortable position in the Symbolic order.

Other Marxist-oriented critics have voiced suspicion that psychoanalysis, including certain aspects and interpretations of Lacan's work, only serves to mask and ingrain capitalist ideology. Gilles Deleuze and Félix Guattari thus take aim at the Oedipus complex, which they see as functioning to perpetuate exploitation by normalizing the essential unit of capitalist relations of production: the nuclear family. Here they suggest that Lacan's recasting of the Oedipus complex in structuralist terms only further hides this function behind a scientific facade. And yet, they see in other aspects of Lacan's work the potential for radical and revolutionary critique. For his own part, Lacan rejected the claims of Marxism to provide a convincing account of subjectivity. One the one hand, language cannot be reduced to part of a superstructure. It is not simply the carrier of a historically contingent ideology, but rather must be described in terms of universal and formal laws proper to it. On the other hand, language is not part of a material, economic base – although Lacan does insist that signifiers themselves are material.

Lacan's impact on feminist thought in France and abroad has been sizable, although most feminists have tended to approach his work with ambivalence. Jane Gallop, for example, has suggested that Lacan's very style of presentation

– masculine and masterful – helps perpetuate patriarchal attitudes. Others have appreciated Lacan's insistence that the category of gender must be understood as an effect of signification rather than in terms of essential attributes. Film theory, often in conjunction with feminism and gender studies, has taken up many Lacanian concepts in order to explore how the "gaze" of the camera situates and thus produces the viewer. The notion of "suture," the technical procedures such as shot/countershot by which films insert the spectator into a subject position, has gained wide currency. It should be noted, however, that Jacques-Alain Miller, himself a psychoanalyst and the editor of Lacan's seminars, originally coined the term "suture" to describe how lack is constitutive for the subject. That is, "suture" did not originally describe the way in which the viewer's Imaginary is stitched to the film's Symbolic. That said, there is a certain amount of irony in the frequent accusations of heterodoxy and misconstruction leveled by disciples of Lacan at his interpreters and adapters. After all, Lacan was himself considered heretical by many in the psychoanalytic community – a charge that he appears to have relished. The obscurity of his style, moreover, has done little to discourage misinterpretation. Lacan apparently thought that ambiguity and wordplay would keep his teachings from sliding into doctrine. More importantly, however, Lacan's style forces the reader or listener to rediscover what he promulgated as the fundamental truth of the unconscious: that it operates according to the laws of the letter.

35

Ernesto Laclau and Chantal Mouffe

Philip Goldstein

In *The Postmodern Condition* Jean-François Lyotard claims that the "grand narratives" in which God, the class struggle, or social progress explain historical change can no longer justify Western technocracy (1984: 60). Post-Marxist theory accepts this and critiques traditional Hegelian Marxism, which claims that society evolves in distinct historical stages realizing a predetermined telos – the communist society. In particular, the post-Marxist theory of Laclau and Mouffe describes the "hegemonic" ideological practices constructing modern cultural identities and, by deepening the Enlightenment tradition, seeks to foster an alliance of women's, African-American, postcolonial, gay, working-class, and other "new social movements." Derived from Antonio Gramsci, this notion of ideological hegemony rejects traditional Marxist theory, which considers the economic contexts of social life predetermined and the historical development of society teleological, as well as Althusserian Marxism. The critique of traditional Marxism takes into account the nightmarish experiences of the former USSR and promotes a radical extension of the Enlightenment tradition, but the critique of Althusser dismisses not only his subjectless science but also a discourse's institutional determination, what Michel Foucault calls the nexus of knowledge/power.

In *For Marx*, Louis Althusser, whose work initiates post-Marxist theory, admits that Marx initially adopted Hegelian humanism but maintains that Marx eventually rejected this humanist view and established a scientific Marxism; as Althusser says, the "rupture with . . . all philosophical humanism is not a secondary detail; it is one with the scientific discovery of Marx" (1969: 234). Althusser emphasizes Marx's scientific objectivity and the importance of the working class but faults both Stalinist and Hegelian Marxism.

Laclau and Mouffe also critique the Hegelian belief that predetermined historical stages and contexts explain social development; however, by their time the Soviet Union is close to its demise, the Western working class has turned conservative, and poststructuralist theories and independent movements of women, blacks, homosexuals, and others have developed. Laclau and Mouffe accept, as a result, Althusser's notion of ideology but not his distinction between science and ideology.

Laclau and Mouffe agree that the ideological apparatuses of the state interpellate or construct a subject and, thereby, reproduce themselves, as Althusser claims; however, they defend Gramsci's notion of ideological hegemony because they deny that a Marxist science can resist its ideological practices and grasp the objective truth. They adopt, in addition, the post-structuralist belief that, since objects do not simply or literally mirror their sociohistorical contexts, the distinction between object and context, discursive and nondiscursive practices, or "thought and reality" breaks down; in Laclau and Mouffe's terms, "[s]ynonomy, metonomy, metaphor . . . are part of the primary terrain itself in which the social is constituted" (1985: 110).

Laclau rejects the Hegelian notion that the working class will achieve full humanity once it overthrows the capitalist system; however, more negative than Althusser, he complains that traditional Marxism treats the working class as a privileged agent achieving "full presence" in a "transparent" communist society because the "rationalist naturalism" of traditional Marxism preserves the apocalyptic ideals of the Christian theology which this Marxism opposes. That is, Christian theology maintains that the sacrifice of God overcomes evil and redeems humanity but situates the historical process of salvation beyond human understanding. Traditional Marxism considers the working class the agent of human salvation and the historical process a secular, scientific matter, but Marxism still expects the working class to overcome evil and redeem humanity (see Laclau 1993: 76–8; 1996: 9–15).

Post-Marxism claims, by contrast, that hegemonic ideological discourses construct stable but partial or dislocated subjects whose antagonisms ensure that they fail to achieve the "full presence" or closure sought by both Marxism and Christianity. In traditional terms, the discursive conflicts by which contending political parties seek to impose their hegemony explains values and identities more fully than ruling-class interests or social structures do because, incomplete or dislocated, such structures produce only partial identities. Antagonism or dislocation does not imply a positive new context or Hegelian "aufhebung," as traditional Marxists say. The subject remains fissured because the antagonism of diverse social contexts or the dislocation of social structures matters more than the systematic contradictions and predetermined structures of the traditional view (Laclau and Mouffe 1985: 122–34).

Laclau and Mouffe suggest, moreover, that the antagonisms of the working class, women, minorities, and others expose the fissures within the literal meanings and conservative identities imposed by hegemonic ideological practices. The conflicts and struggles of these social movements undermine these literal meanings and conservative identities and entitle these movements to democratic rights. Laclau maintains, as a consequence, that a successful politics does not seek the revolutionary transformation of capitalist society; a successful politics requires strategic argument whose success predetermined working class or other socioeconomic contexts cannot ensure in advance. The social movements properly defend their separate interests or their political independence; however, since what establishes identity is contextual oppositions, antagonisms, or exclusions, not essences or transcendent selves, each movement must also construct equivalences establishing a hegemonic bloc. To establish these equivalences, movements use terms like "justice" and "equality," but Laclau considers them floating signifiers, not universal or transcendent truths.

Numerous scholars have noted how elegantly this account of the fissured subject and the floating signifier endows Lacanian psychoanalysis, to which the account is indebted, with broad political import; however, some critics object that Laclau's theory echoes the conservative belief that free enterprise has triumphed and that Soviet communism, as well as Marxism, have died; as Terry Eagleton says, the postmodern opposition to traditional Hegelian Marxism disables radical opponents of the capitalist system just when that system has gotten more powerful than ever (Eagleton 1990: 381; see also Miklitsch 1994: 169).

Laclau and Mouffe's belief that hegemonic discourses construct the contingent identities allowed by dislocated socioeconomic structures does destroy the traditional faith in revolutionary social transformation; however, Laclau and Mouffe's explanation of Soviet communism illustrates and justifies their belief. On the one hand, Laclau and Mouffe grant that the Leninist account of the vanguard party explains the Stalinist features of Soviet communism (see, for example, Brzezinski and Freidrich 1956). The Soviet party grew more and more dictatorial because Leninist theory gave the party the exclusive possession of the scientific truth and the exclusive right to define and to represent the working class and its interests (Laclau and Mouffe 1985: 56–7). On the other hand, Laclau and Mouffe accept the liberal historians' belief that, more than Marxist theory, the authoritarian character and the socioeconomic difficulties of late nineteenth-century Russia explain the growth of the Stalinist system (see Cohen 1985; Lewin 1988). They, too, assume that Stalinism brought together a feudal peasantry, an industrial working class, Czarist bureaucrats, and various other groups belonging to very different historical stages; however, rejecting a cultural continuity with feudal Czarism, Laclau and Mouffe argue that what Leon Trotsky called Russia's "uneven development" explains Stalinism. That is, emerging simultaneously, not in chronological succession, Russia's diverse groups created an anomalous situation in which the frail bourgeoisie could not undertake the modernizing tasks assigned it by established historical schema. These tasks, which included educating and industrializing Soviet society and creating large urban centers and even an independent and democratic civil society, fell instead upon the Russian working class (Laclau and Mouffe 1985: 50–4). In other words, since the Soviet communists articulated diverse democratic demands and simultaneous socioeconomic structures, the communists' ideological hegemony, not the fixed, class identity and distinct historical stages of traditional Marxism, explain the Soviet experience.

Contrary to various Marxists, Laclau and Mouffe maintain that the Soviet experience has subversive epistemological import: it shows that the Hegelian belief in purposive historical development reduces contingency, negation, antagonism, or dislocation to ephemeral experiences and, as a result, blindly eliminates the multiple signification of history's "uneven development" or "overdetermined" events.

Critics also complain that, by granting discourse "an absolute autonomy" or "central role in social and political life," Laclau and Mouffe "find no alternative short of total contingency, indeterminacy and randomness" (see Larrain 1994: 104). Laclau and Mouffe do consider "the social" an indeterminate or irreducible discourse, rather than established structures reproduced by institutional practices. Indeed, they reject the Foucauldian notion that institutional practices reproduce established social structures even though Michel Foucault also criticizes humanist and Althusserian views.

That is, like Laclau and Mouffe, Michel Foucault dismisses humanist notions of theoretical self-consciousness and Althusserian ideas of an autonomous science. He discusses the breakdown of the phenomenological tradition, not Marxism's humanist or Stalinist limitations. Indeed, he says that the study of the Gulag exposes the limits of Marxism (Foucault 1980: 134–7). He too rejects, however, the Althusserian opposition of ideology and science because he considers science "one practice among many," not a privileged discourse. He rejects as well the Hegelian theory of historical development. He says that contradiction has many levels and functions within and between discursive formations and does not represent a difference to be resolved or a fundamental principle of explanation (Foucault 1968: 149–56).

Even though he dismisses humanist notions of theoretical self-consciousness and Althusserian ideas of an autonomous science, he maintains that ideology or discourse imposes conformity but resists ruling–class purposes (see Butler 1993: 9–11). Like Althusser, who claims that the ideological apparatuses of the state resist ruling–class intentions but still reproduce the state, he maintains that distinct historical configurations of power and knowledge regulate the body, institutions, and even society.

Laclau and Mouffe reduce such normalizing configurations of knowledge and power to "functional requirements" of the Althusserian "logic of reproduction" and emphasize the subversive potential of theoretical critique. Their account of the subject undermines the liberal consensus legitimating art, ethics, science, and other public spheres – cf. Jürgen Habermas – but not because Laclau rejects the Enlightenment tradition. Laclau considers politics a matter of hegemonic articulation or argument, not an obligatory pursuit of consensus, but he favors the radical extension of the Enlightenment tradition. He does not accept these disciplinary divisions of "modernity" because he dismisses not only the Althusserian distinction of science and ideology but also the Foucauldian notion of knowledge and power. Laclau and Mouffe argue that theoretical critique resists such institutional conformity and exercises subversive force. As Anna Marie Smith says, "Against Althusser, then, they would say that... we never arrive at a situation in which a ruling force can become so authoritative that it can totally impose its worldview onto the rest of the population" (1998: 71). Smith overstates Althusser's "functionalism" but gets Laclau and Mouffe's position right: they assume that poststructuralist theory can transcend the divisions of modern disciplines and their institutional contexts and expose the antagonisms, dislocations, or fissures which, in Smith's terms, incite "concrete struggles towards progressive social change" (1998: 60).

As a result, Laclau's post-Marxism approximates the messianic Marxism of Jacques Derrida more closely than the genealogical histories of Foucault. Derrida does not foster an alliance of new social movements or favor a radical extension of Enlightenment democracy, yet Derrida critiques the "onto-the-ology" of traditional Marxism and rejects the institutional reproduction of the subject.

For example, he argues that, in the name of science, Marx condemns the spiritual or spectral other whose recurring phantoms derail the communist movement; however, he fails to exclude this spectral other, whose presence reasserts itself as the revolution's spirit or in other ways (Derrida 1994 [1993]: 106–9). Derrida maintains that Marx's critique, which includes not only the spirit or specter but also ideology and commodity fetishism, opposes but fails to exclude them because they are already within Marxism, part of Marx's revolutionary spirit or communist movement. Laclau fears that this logic of the specter can include a totalitarian path, but he considers this logic a hegemonic logic; as he says, "I have nothing to object to" (Laclau 1995: 88).

Derrida goes on to claim, however, that true communism requires a messianic concept of justice. As the "indestructible condition of any deconstruction" and the vital "legacy" of Marx (Derrida 1994 [1993]: 28), this messianism affirms a transcendent sense of an other. Laclau complains that Derrida treats openness to the other as an ethical obligation, not a political or hegemonic construct (Laclau 1995: 95), but he accepts what Derrida terms the affirmative messianic and emancipatory promise of Marxism (1995: 75); however, by undermining "sedimented layers of social practice" and revealing the decisions grounding them, the absolute hospitality to a religious or messianic other always already part of us subverts more than a program of transcendent "onto-theological" truth or purposive "teleo-eschatological" action. In addition, this absolute hospitality resists all academic, scientific, or established discourses as well.

Laclau and Mouffe forcefully demonstrate that a postmodern notion of ideological hegemony undermines the Hegelian humanism of traditional and Stalinist Marxists and justifies a broad democratic alliance of trade unionists, feminists, minorities, and other "new social movements" which have emerged since the 1960s; however, Laclau accepts the Derridean notion of a messianic Marxism because he fears that institutional practices deny theoretical critique and impose a functionalist conformity. As a result, his post-Marxism effectively dismisses not only Stalinist communism or bureaucratic working-class organizations but all established progressive groups, including trade unions, left-wing political parties, and the humanities' newly instituted women's, African-American, ethnic, or gay studies and programs. To secure progressive reforms in the 1990s, when the so-called culture wars have so terribly divided and discredited academia, post-Marxist theory adopts Laclau and Mouffe's notion of a radical democratic politics, not Althusser's broad distinction between science and ideology, and a Foucauldian concept of institutional determination, not the theoreticist fear of functionalist conformity, because the Foucauldian concept explains a discourse's methodological conflicts and historical changes and justifies established groups and programs.

36

Robert Lepage

Jennifer Harvie

The main feature of Robert Lepage's work as a theater director which aligns it with postmodernism is its textual openness – its challenge to dominant structures of meaning and its playful, spectacular multiplication of possible meanings. And the postmodern debates which critics of Lepage's work have most strongly engaged it with have to do with the contested political effectiveness of postmodern performance; for instance, the degree to which Lepage's playful – but not explicitly political – postmodern performance compels politicized audience responses. This essay examines how critics see Lepage's work as textually open and what values they attribute to this openness, concluding with some critics' championing of the work for what they see as its politically engaged deconstructive metatheatricality. It then examines in more detail debates around the political effectiveness of postmodern performance to question: the value of the hermeneutic openness, or indeterminacy, attributed to Lepage's work; the description of Lepage's work as deconstructively metatheatrical; and the significance of Lepage's institutional engagement with a variety of structures, including his own multimedia production company, and the international theater festivals that increasingly make up his contexts of production. I argue that Lepage's work can be seen, most positively, to offer a playful and creative postmodern challenge to conventional hierarchies of drama production and dramatic meaning. I conclude, however, that it can be seen more negatively – and, I believe, more persuasively – to succumb to the kind of political passivity, and negligence, that postmodern art is so often accused of practicing.

Textual Openness

Critics regard much of Lepage's work as textually open and, for the most part, they laud this openness for the challenge it presents to representational certainty, and particularly to the dominance of ideologically coercive (because ideologically naturalizing and textually closed) mimetic realism in twentieth-century performance. They see it as ideologically liberating because it encourages audiences to engage creatively with the shows in constructing their meanings, instead of simply submitting passively to a heavily inscribed and prescriptive meaning.

This openness starts with the shows' authorship, which is not accomplished solely by Lepage but is multiple and dispersed amongst the members of his companies. Shows are developed through processes of collective exploration, starting from found material resources, which inspire improvisation work, which leads to the devising of text. The devising of Lepage's largest pieces – including *The Dragons' Trilogy* (Théâtre Repère, 1985), *Tectonic Plates* (Théâtre Repère, 1988), *The Seven Streams of the River Ota* (Ex Machina, 1994), and *The Geometry of Miracles* (Ex Machina, 1998) – is explicitly attributed to Lepage and his companies (Charest 1997: 170–96). Even in his productions which use pre-authored scripts – including *A Midsummer Night's Dream* (Shakespeare, Royal National Theatre, London, 1992) and *A Dream Play* (Strindberg, Kungliga Dramatiska Teatern, Stockholm, 1994) – and in his solo shows – *Vinci* (1986), *Needles and Opium* (1991), and *Elsinore* (1995) – authorship can still be seen as dispersed as Lepage collaborates extensively with other creators, most obviously the performers, but also designers of scenography, costume, and sound.

The gestation of Lepage's works is frequently long and often notoriously public, so that the openness – or instability – of their meaning too is long and public. Lepage does not hesitate to show work-in-progress, even in world premieres of his work at often very prestigious festivals. *The Seven Streams of the River Ota* premiered at the 1994 Edinburgh Festival and was radically different over the eight nights of that run (Wehle 1996: 30). Over the three years it was produced (1994–6), the show took on many different forms, including versions of three, five, and eight hours' duration (Lepage and Ex Machina 1996, n.p.). His shows' scripts are so volatile they are seldom published – *The Seven Streams of the River Ota* and *Polygraph* (Lepage and Brassard 1997) – are the two exceptions. Further, the form of any of Lepage's theater work is not necessarily stable even in its location within that medium. Both *Le Polygraph* (1996) and *No* (1998), Lepage's two films after *The Confessional* (1995), extrapolate material from his stage productions of *Polygraph* and *The Seven Streams of the River Ota* respectively. As much as some critics scorn what they see as Lepage's lack of professionalism in presenting work-in-progress, more critics celebrate Lepage's process of creation for its openness and great creative potential, for both theater makers and audiences.

The textual openness introduced in Lepage's work in its devising is enhanced in its presentation, particularly in its use of narrative, languages, images, media, and performance styles. Critics frequently characterize the narratives of Lepage's productions as fragmented (Bunzli 1999: 91), having "multiple enigmatic storylines and overlapping scenes" (McAlpine 1996: 130) and thereby challenging audiences' expectations that dramatic works should have both a linear and a dominant – or simply a master – narrative. They observe that the discourses of Lepage's productions are, similarly, multiple and challenge the dominance within much drama of spoken and written text over other semiotic systems. The main languages Lepage uses are English and Québécois French, but his productions often use more languages, including Chinese in *The Dragons' Trilogy*, sign and semaphore in *Tectonic Plates*, and German and Czech in *The Seven Streams of the River Ota*. Partly, multiple languages in Lepage's shows act as realistic signifiers for the cultural variety and heterogeneity of the contexts he depicts. However, they also act potentially to destabilize language's apparent coherence and authority by demonstrating the differences and inconsistencies between languages, especially when Lepage's proliferating languages are translated only partially or not at all. Further, in their sheer multiplicity, Lepage's languages emphasize their own status as systems of communication and provide a potentially pleasurable metatheatricality – metatheatrical because the productions foreground their own representational systems, and pleasurable because the audience may recognize its own cultural condition of mediation, and may feel invited to enjoy its own fluency in reading representation.

Alongside verbal discourses, visual signification and visual transformation proliferate in Lepage's productions. Indeed, Lepage's work is perhaps best known for its visual trickery and bravura, for the way alterations in a performer's positioning on a grand piano can transform it into a gondola in *Tectonic Plates*, or the way lighting changes can instantly transform a house's walls in 1980s Japan into corridors in a concentration camp in 1940s Europe in *The Seven Streams of the River Ota* (Lepage and Ex Machina 1996: 45). Through this emphasis on the visual, the conventional dominance of linguistic meaning within the theater is challenged. Further, the visual imagery itself is often unstable or simultaneously multiple in Lepage's productions, so that visual meaning is itself in flux, polyvalent, and requires active interpretation (Girard 1995: 160). In the second scene described briefly above, for instance, visual signs indicate both the past and the present, Japan and Europe, simultaneous, conflicting and coinciding. The shows' use of multimedia – often including film, slides, and live video projection – further destabilizes language's dominance. In a similar vein, the shows are internally eclectic, in style and media – combining naturalism, non-naturalism, puppetry, dance, and so on (Garner 1994: 227). This stylistic proliferation potentially foregrounds the shows' own stylistic construction, and confounds audiences' expectations of homogeneous and consistent style and of how to read and make sense of the performance, producing again, more varied readings.

In many respects – thematically, stylistically, in their use of representational media – Lepage's work can be understood by that familiar postmodern descriptor, pastiche. For some critics, the irreverent selection and assembly characteristic of pastiche produces unexpected new meanings, productively breaks down unnecessary – and unproductive – creative boundaries, and encourages playful audience engagement. What it risks is another question, to which I shall return later.

The openness or indeterminacy that I have described as characteristic of the processes and forms of Lepage's work is picked up too in its themes. First, the work is often self-consciously concerned with the effects of representational practices – who makes what meanings and how those meanings affect others – and thereby problematizes its own representational practices and their effects. *Polygraph*, for instance, is concerned with the making of a semi-fictional film, and *The Geometry of Miracles* is concerned with the effects of different forms of spatial design, including choreographed movement and architecture. Second, the work is overwhelmingly concerned with what critic James Bunzli has described as *décalage*, or displacement (Bunzli 1999: 84ff.). Often, this displacement is geographical, as Lepage's shows are notoriously concerned with travel, but it may also be temporal and is always cultural. By example, this narrative and thematic exploration of displacement may encourage audiences to explore the displacements of meaning and subjectivity which the work's open textuality permits.

Critics attribute the variety of features of Lepage's work which I have gathered under the heading "textual openness" with numerous positive effects. The multiplicity and mobility of meaning this textual openness produces is seen as democratic and culturally productive, permitting varied and multiple readings by active audiences, and responding to different conditions of reading and the different priorities of different readers. Amongst these multiple meanings, some may appear contradictory, and some may be fantastical, so that not only the logical, the singular, and the dominant are favored and conventional hierarchies of meaning are challenged. Particularly, critics see this openness as permitting the productive expression of difference: linguistic difference, most obviously, but also cultural difference and sexual difference, as in *Tectonic Plates* and *The Seven Streams of the River Ota*, both of which play with the ambiguity of characters' genders, and even sexes. They see it as pleasurable, permitting audiences to revel in the creative play of interpretation and to explore "different" meanings and and – by extrapolation – identities. Finally, they see it as politically engaged through a deconstructive metatheatricality, a self-consciousness about the methods of representation which compels audiences to question, first, those methods, second, its own relationships with them, and third, the meanings it makes with them.

The Politics of Postmodern Performance

But these claims in praise of Lepage's work and of its political value raise broader questions about the viability of a politically effective postmodern performance in general. In his influential article, "Toward a Concept of the Political in Post-Modern Theatre," Philip Auslander, after Hal Foster (1985), argues that postmodern performance can no longer be politically transgressive now that "the seemingly limitless horizon of multinational capitalism" provides no limits to transgress (Auslander 1997: 60) and the ability of any representation to challenge dominant culture has been shown by poststructuralism to be compromised by all representation's potential complicity with the dominant. However, postmodern performance can, Auslander argues, be politically resistant, or offer "strategies of counterhegemonic resistance by exposing processes of cultural control and emphasizing the traces of nonhegemonic discourses within the dominant without claiming to transcend its terms" (Auslander 1997: 61). This is not, he argues, a political theater but a theater of politics; political engagement is "a *result*, but not the *object*" (Auslander 1997: 71). And we may see this description of Auslander's as corresponding to what I described above as the work of Lepage's shows, work which highlights and leaves volatile and problematic its representational processes but which does not explicitly engage in political debate. For Baz Kershaw, the value of Auslander's argument is limited because it describes theater makers as politically passive: political action may happen in response to the work of their performance, perhaps, but not through their own volition (Kershaw 1996: 144). To more accurately attribute political will and effect, Kershaw argues, it is important to consider the work's context of performance and reception (Kershaw 1996: 149). For my analysis of the political effectiveness of Lepage's postmodern work, these debates raise productive questions: is Lepage's work actually politically resistant; even if it is, is that resistance politically passive; and how may consideration of the work's contexts of production revise my analysis of its political effect?

Auslander himself admits that some postmodern work itself raises "the question of what constitutes a potentially counterhegemonic appropriation of an image, and what merely restates the image," presumably, in the latter case, without compelling its audience to pursue political critique (Auslander 1997: 64). Certainly Lepage's work has been read in this light, which sees it as not actually, in many respects, politically resistant. From this perspective, the postmodern, open, unfixed qualities of Lepage's work are identified as not politically engaged in a number of ways: they trivialize cultural specificity, both geographical and historical cultural specificity; they indulge the vague and nostalgic instead of documenting and interrogating the historically specific; and they prioritize pleasure at the expense of achieving critique, deconstructive or otherwise. Hodgdon argues that Lepage's 1992 production of *A Midsummer Night's Dream*, for instance, dehistoricized and abstracted the cultural forms of Indonesia to use it as a "culture of sensuality" (after Pavis 1992; Hodgdon 1996: 84). Elsewhere, I have made a similar argument about *The Seven Streams of the River Ota*'s "Far Orientalist" treatment of Japan (after Morley and Robins 1995; Harvie forthcoming). Lepage's postmodernity is not, in this analysis, politically resistant but apolitical. Instead of seeing Lepage's work as self-consciously – and in a deconstructive mode – self-referential and metatheatrical, this critical line of analysis further tends to see Lepage's work as decadently hypertheatrical, overwhelming potential irony and critique with self-satisfied and self-interested play, and producing not political response but a chronic failure of political critique. Reviewing *The Seven Streams of the River Ota*, James Frieze writes, for instance, that it provided "an intense but strangely vacuous experience" (Frieze 1997: 137).

There are further contextual concerns which radically qualify the political effectiveness – or, simply, the political effect – of Lepage's work, particularly its attribution of democratic openness. I will concentrate on some of the institutional contexts of his work here. First, there is his recently formed company, Ex Machina. Although it is certainly possible to see Lepage as insistent on a democratic dispersal of authorial power in his productions, it is nevertheless also possible to see him as monopolizing much of the authority – and certainly much of the credit – for the productions. Hunt compares him to the all-encompassing actor-creator and cites Lepage's own term for his artistic approach: "global" (1989: 104). Harvie and Hurley emphasize that Lepage is, after all, the most likely "deus" of his multidisciplinary production company formed in 1994, Ex Machina (1999: 299). The context of production of Lepage's shows is, increasingly, major international theater festivals. The appearance of Lepage's shows in these geographically varied contexts may appear democratically to foster even more multiple and varied readings. On the other hand, the variety of those readings is potentially compromised both by the homogeneity of the festivals' programming – internally as well as from country to country – and by the festivals' elitism. Indeed, Lepage's participation in this circuit may be seen to indulge and exploit the iniquities of late capitalist global culture – inextricably aligned with the postmodern by Jameson (1991) – as the shows address solely the patrons who can afford to attend these usually very expensive festivals (Harvie and Hurley 1999: 308). Finally, Lepage's work exhibits what might be seen as a particularly postmodern split between local and international affiliations. While his work is increasingly developed in the Caserne, Ex Machina's own dedicated production facilities in Québec City, paid for largely by Québécois and Canadian government grants, that work nevertheless continues to be shown predominantly outside Québec. This, again, demonstrates his work's openness (here, to international markets and audiences). It demonstrates also exploitation of the cultural specificity provided by Québec (namely funding), and potential evacuation of that cultural specificity through the work's neglect of the Québécois audience in pursuit of an international one (Harvie and Hurley 1999: 309).

Lepage's innovative, spectacular theater practices challenge conventional performance's textual dominance, narrative linearity, and generic homogeneity. They continue to provide audiences with pleasure, creative stimulation, and new – and potentially more democratic – ways of making new and more diverse meanings. More damagingly, their openness risks sacrificing cultural and historical specificity, and the fine line they tread between metatheatricality and hypertheatricality risks emphasizing irony's pleasure at the expense of its critique. Finally, their apparent lack of self-reflection – let alone self-critique – on the economically and culturally elite contexts of their own production undermines their apparent dedication to the democratic production of meaning and the destabilization of hierarchy. As much as these are problems of Lepage's productions, they may also – more generally – be problems of postmodern culture, and they may be problems of and for Lepage's audiences. What is at stake, after all, is not simply what shows he makes, but what his audiences make of them.

37

Emmanuel Levinas

Peter Atterton

The Jewish philosopher Emmanuel Levinas (1906–95) is without question the most original and important ethical thinker in postmodernism. His ethics of compassion for the Other, an ethics that begins with the face of the neighbor rather than with freedom, that emphasizes goodness and responsibility rather than the formalism of universal laws, almost single-handedly gives the lie to the claim that postmodernism is little more than an exuberant textual nihilism devoid of any serious moral content. Yet Levinas hardly invokes the image of the quintessentially French *philosophe* of postmodernism. In his work we find none of the wordplays, pastiche, and parody that characterize so much of the movement. It may even be said that Levinas's thinking goes against the grain of contemporary thought in its refusal to abandon ethics. However, the fact that the two leading representatives of postmodernism, namely, Jacques Derrida and Jean-François Lyotard, have found in Levinas's ethics important resources for their own respective critiques of Western reason should make us think twice about consigning Levinas to a tradition that he was among the first to call into question. As someone who provides an intellectual foundation for the best of postmodern theory, as well as providing it with an ethics that so many of its detractors have falsely accused it of lacking, Levinas can rightly be called a key thinker in postmodernism.

Ethics as First Philosophy

The guiding principle of Levinas's philosophy is that ethics is *prima philosophia*. It is a principle that encapsulates the spirit of his thinking and serves as the basis for his first extended critique of the Western philosophical tradition, *Totality and Infinity*, published in 1961. In its search for truth, philosophy, according to Levinas, has mostly been "ontology." It has privileged thematization and knowledge at the expense of neglecting or concealing the absolute priority of ethics. This privilege shows itself in the way philosophy attempts to comprehend the nature of reality by subordinating what exists to an all-encompassing rational structure or "totality." Confined within the totality, particular beings are understood as the bearers of attributes they share with other beings, whereby they are divested of their individuality and become conceptually "the same." For Levinas, the only being capable of resisting such totalization is the human Other. The Other absolutely resists all philosophical attempts at knowing and calls into question the violence and injustice of ontology. This calling into question occurs in the "face-to-face" encounter with the Other which "precedes ontology" (*Levinas* 1969 [1961]: 42). Here ethics and justice consist in recognizing in the face of the neighbor someone who is destitute and proletarian, whose very destitution provokes my shame and calls me back to my responsibilities. Exposed to the defenseless nudity of the face, "I am not innocent spontaneity but usurper and murderer" (1969: 84), and thus have always to make amends. To respond to the face with responsibility requires all the resources at my disposal without my ever being able to say that I have done enough. This is not the alarming "overload" of responsibilities denounced by moral philosophers in the Anglo-American tradition, but the situation of the I divested of its arbitrary freedom, and delivered over to the infinity of responsibility for the Other where duties grow in the measure that they are fulfilled (1969: 244). Between me and the Other there is no common measure in that what I have the right to demand of the Other is incommensurable with what the Other has the right to demand of me (1969: 50). Responsibility thus lies "beyond the justice of universal laws" (1969: 247).

The starting point of these reflections was phenomenology. But it soon became apparent that phenomenology was stretched beyond its limits when it came to describing what does not show itself in terms of any horizon. Hence, immediately following the publication of *Totality and Infinity*, Levinas embarked upon a discussion of the face by "situating it with respect to the phenomenology it interrupts" (1989 [1963]: 356). The result was the introduction of "the trace," a concept that Levinas would place at the center of his second major work, *Otherwise Than Being*, published in 1974. It was a concept that also found its way into major work of other philosophers, most significantly Derrida, for whom it provided a means of deconstructing metaphysics.

The Trace of Levinas in Derrida

In *Of Grammatology* (1967), Derrida incorporated into his own thinking

*the concept of the trace that is at the center of the latest work by Emmanuel
Levinas and his critique of ontology . . . which has determined the meaning of
being as presence and the meaning of language as full continuity of speech.*
(Derrida 1976 [1967]: 70)

The importance of Levinas's trace for Derrida resides primarily in its ability to
free deconstruction from the double bind of using metaphysical language in
order to overcome that language – a problem not only for deconstruction but
also for Levinas's own ethics. In "Violence and Metaphysics: An Essay on the
Thought of Emmanuel Levinas," written in 1964, Derrida called into question
Levinas's claim in *Totality and Infinity* to have broken with ontology in the
name of ethics. While Derrida at the time argued that no such decisive break
was possible given Levinas's dependence on the language and conceptuality of
ontology (Derrida 1978 [1968]: 143), the indications are that later Derrida
came to see the trace as a way of mitigating that dependence. The trace, which
is not a sign in the conventional sense, whose properties of signification belong
to elements of language related to extralinguistic entities, ruptures the signifier–signified relation by making it impossible to say *who* or *what* is present in
it. As the trace of a certain absence that defers the decision as to the referent of
its term, it signals the relation of *différance* within the text of philosophy,
frustrating its logocentric and phonocentric pretensions.

This is, of course, Derridian parlance and naturally gives rise to the question
of whether Levinas would recognize himself in the project of deconstruction.
To this question, one would have to answer both yes and no. In his only essay
devoted to Derrida, "Wholly Otherwise," appearing in 1976, Levinas made a
point of expressing what he called "the pleasure of a contact made in the heart of
a chiasmus." However, while he acknowledged "the primordial importance of
the questions raised by Derrida" (Levinas 1991 [1976]: 10), he remarked upon
the way in which these questions implicitly reestablish the ontology they are
meant to undermine. "To say that this lack [of presence] still belongs to Being is
to revolve in the circle of Being and nothingness" (Levinas 1991: 7). However,
this did not prevent Levinas from finding in deconstruction an ethical meaning
apparently not found by its author:

> What appears to the deconstructive analysis as truly lacking in itself is not the
> *surplus* – which would still be . . . a residue of ontology – but the *better* (*le mieux*)
> of proximity; an excellence, and elevation, ethics before Being or the Good
> beyond Being. (Levinas 1991: 7)

These lines perform the double reading characteristic of deconstruction itself.
In the measure that Derrida's work converts the "surplus" found within the
text of philosophy into something like a *deficit* of presence, it appears still to be

determined by ontology. Hence, it too could be charged with continuing what Levinas calls the "destruction" (1987: 154) (not deconstruction!) of ethical transcendence (Bernasconi 1982: 37). On the other hand, to the extent that it also reveals the proximity of the Other beyond ontology, deconstruction would have to be interpreted as having an underlying ethical significance.

While it may seem ironic to find Levinas "turning the tables," as it were, on the master of deconstruction in this way, especially when we consider that Derrida was one of the first to use the logic of negation against Levinas, it is a clear indication of the trace of Derrida's thinking in Levinas's own. By this, I simply mean that Levinas appears to have learned an important lesson from Derrida, and from Heidegger before him: namely, that to contradict Hegel is to reconfirm Hegel. To dispute the hegemony of presence by pointing to its deficiency is to reinstate the disputed hegemony by defining deficiency in its own terms. Not that Heidegger and Derrida, of course, are prepared to give Hegel the last word in philosophy. Each thinker announces the end of philosophy in a quite different sense from Hegel, for whom it entailed the final reconciliation of thought with the thinker, leaving nothing outside reason to be known. Where does Levinas stand in relation to the discourse of the end of philosophy that has come to dominate the postmodernist debate?

The End of Philosophy and Humanism

That Levinas does not fully accept the idea that philosophy is at an end, whose totalizing and neutral implications he called into question in *Totality and Infinity* (1969: 298), is clear from an interview given in 1981:

> It is true that philosophy, in its traditional forms of ontotheology and logocentrism – to use Heidegger's and Derrida's terms – has come to an end. But it is not true of philosophy in the other sense of critical speculation and interrogation. Reason is never so versatile as when it puts itself into question. In the contemporary end of philosophy, philosophy has found a new lease of life. (1984: 69)

The last claim is reminiscent of the refutation traditionally leveled at skepticism – a *self*-refutation to the extent that the Pyrrhonian skeptics were more than prepared to put their own negative assertions into question. If Levinas, then, is unwilling to embrace the notion of the end of philosophy with the same zeal as many of his contemporaries, his hesitancy betokens anything but a failure of skeptical nerve and an uncritical attachment to traditional ways of thinking. For it is precisely the inability of proponents of the end of philosophy to break old habits – totalization, neutralization, and dogmatism – that provokes Levinas's skepticism.

In *Otherwise Than Being*, speaking of the end of humanism, another shibboleth of postmodernism, Levinas writes, "Modern anti-humanism . . . is true over and beyond the reasons it gives itself. It clears the place for subjectivity positing itself in sacrifice, in a substitution which precedes the will" (1978: 127). Levinas appears unconcerned by the fact that very few antihumanists would couch their thinking in explicitly ethical terms. What does it matter when we now know better than to trust authorial intentions? Levinas's notion of subjectivity cannot be equated with anything found within the tradition, and thus is not answerable to the same critique. Indeed, Levinas even shares that critique, though it has for him a quite different meaning from that found in the work of Heidegger, Foucault et al. "Humanism has to be denounced only because it is not sufficiently human" (Levinas 1978: 128). It is not human enough because true subjectivity, according to Levinas, is not defined by rational autonomy but by responsibility for the Other. Here the presumption of responsibility precedes the assumption of responsibility. "The will is free to assume this responsibility in whatever sense it likes; it is not free to refuse this responsibility itself; it is not free to ignore the meaningful world into which the face of the Other has introduced it" (Levinas 1969: 218–19). Clearly, there remains a residue of will and spontaneity in Levinas's ethics, an element of freedom that no ethics worthy of the name can spirit away. The least that can be said is that for Levinas ethics does not begin with freedom, but with obligation. Unlike traditional morality, in which "ought implies can" (Kant), Levinas's ethics entails "ought" as the indispensable condition for "can." The "can" of practical reason implies the relation with the Other who "invests" (84) the will by liberating it from arbitrariness and delivering it over to the infinite demands of asymmetrical responsibility. Levinas acknowledges the scandalous nature of such asymmetry from the point of view of a traditional ethics of reciprocal obligations. Indeed, he even appears to celebrate it: "There is something more important than my life. And that is the life of the other. That is unreasonable. Man is an unreasonable being" (Levinas 1988 [1976]: 172). *Pace* Aristotle. *Pace* Kant.

Levinas, Lyotard, and Justice

If Levinas offers Derrida resources for a meditation on *la différance*, he provides Lyotard with a basis for thinking *le différend*. In *Just Gaming*, appearing in 1979, Lyotard repeatedly appealed to Levinas in the course of insisting on the singularity of the language game of prescriptions ("justice") and its incommensurability with denotative statements. "This is what, for me, makes the thought of Levinas so important" (Lyotard 1985 [1979]: 22); "What interests me so much in someone like Levinas, is the forceful attention of the original character of requests" (Lyotard 1985: 25); "A game of prescriptions without interest . . . Levinas is categorical on this, and I think he is quite right" (Lyotard 1985: 53).

Nevertheless, Lyotard is not an uncritical admirer of Levinas's work. Despite the lack of any foundational criteria with which to judge it, eliminated by his incredulity toward grand narratives, he gives notice of the manner in which his own thinking consists in "betraying" it. He writes,

> It is obvious that the very way in which I take over [Levinas's] doctrine . . . is alien to his own. In his view . . . truth is not ontological truth, it is ethical. But it is a truth in Levinas's own terms. Whereas for me, it cannot be the truth. (Lyotard 1985: 60)

The critical flaw in Levinas's thinking, according to Lyotard, consists in privileging one language game over all the others. For Lyotard, there exists a multiplicity of language games, each with its own set of rules, pragmatically organized around three distinct "poles" of discourse: the "Western" or epistemological pole, marked by the desire for totalization; the "Jewish" or prescriptive pole; and the "pagan" pole, which includes the retelling of myths and popular narratives in artistic works and traditional cultures. Although Levinas's thinking is explicitly bound to the second pole, to the extent that it ignores the abundance of other ("pagan") language games that make up the third pole, it implicitly reinstates the first pole in the most traditional of gestures. In other words, Levinas settles the differend of obligation in a litigious manner by passing judgment on all discourses, as though there were a universal rule of judgment between heterogeneous genres, which Lyotard denies.

There is no question that Levinas, like Plato, gives preeminence to the Good and judges everything else in its light, including art: "There is something wicked and egoist and cowardly in artistic enjoyment. There are times when one can be ashamed of it, as of feasting during a plague" (Levinas 1987: 12). Levinas's criticism of art, however, pales in comparison with his denunciation of what he calls "paganism," a brand of discourse that Lyotard elevates precisely because it does "not have any truth value in the sense of speculative discourse" (Lyotard 1985: 38). For Levinas, by contrast, it constitutes a throwback to a primitive or nascent stage of humanity in awe of what he derisively calls the "sacred":

> Here we have the eternal seduction of paganism, beyond the infantilism of idolatry, which long ago was surpassed: *The Sacred filtering into the world* – Judaism is perhaps no more than the negation of all that. . . . The mystery of things is the source of all cruelty towards men. (Levinas 1990 [1963]: 232)

If there is an unquestioned bias in Levinas's thinking it is perhaps not so much his privileging of ethics over everything else as the privilege he extends to Judaism in his examples of ethics. It is a bias that nevertheless goes unchallenged by Lyotard, who indeed leans the same way: "the absolute privileging of the pole of the addressee, as the only site in which the social body can hold, is to be found in Jewish thought. By which I mean the thought of Levinas" (Lyotard 1985: 37).

Whether or not Lyotard is correct to assimilate the language game of prescription to Jewish thought, he is surely mistaken to characterize Levinas's thought in terms of the "absolute privileging" of the addressee of obligation. In Levinas, it is never the self who has priority, but the Other who delivers the self over to the demands of infinite responsibility. To be sure, Levinas does not give priority to the Other to the exclusion of all others. For there is in Levinas's thinking the foundation of a socialist politics, the necessity to introduce parity and equality into the one-sidedness of the face to face in danger of becoming an *égoïsme à deux*, neglectful of the rest of humanity. "The third party looks at me in the eyes of the Other – language is justice" (Levinas 1961: 213). It is the need for this third-party justice that justifies the return to philosophy and provides a *raison d'être* for ontology, according to Levinas, henceforth called upon to engage reflective judgment in the absence of criteria. This fundamental insight is missing from Lyotard's reading.

Like Lyotard, Levinas is a thinker of the differend to the extent that he acknowledges the inapplicability of a single rule of judgment that would totalize both the Other (addresser) and the I (addressee). However, he differs from Lyotard precisely in so far as he will not settle for anything less when it comes to the problem of third-party justice, which requires that rules of genre be found in order to attenuate the violence that emanates not just from ontology, but, paradoxically, from ethics itself. To privilege the Other at the expense of ignoring justice produces a wrong no less serious, and perhaps more irreparable, than the damages incurred by the litigious practices of the totality. *It is in the name of justice to all the potential addressers of imperatives that the search for truth is itself justified*, and why Levinas would regard Lyotard's resistance to the scientific language game, and his call for "little narratives," for dissent and not consensus (Lyotard 1984: 66), as ethically unsound and unjust. In "Secularization and Hunger," written shortly after the famine that caused some one and a half million deaths in Ethiopia (1971–3), he writes:

> The condemnation of technology – which moreover is diffused throughout public opinion by means of all the perfections of the technology of broadcasting – has itself become a comfortable rhetoric, forgetful of responsibilities to which a "developing" humanity, more and more numerous, calls and which, *without the*

development of technology could not be fed. (Levinas 1998 [1976]: 9 modified translation)

If Levinas considers the Enlightenment idea of progress to be ethically indispensable, it is not because he considers science and technology to be the final goals of humanity. It is because they are needed for the "development" of the Third World. The sacred must be supplanted by secularization, where the land is no longer something to be worshipped, but something in which to plant food for half of the world's population who currently do not have enough. This requires not less but more scientific consensus, not less but more mass agricultural techniques. To the extent that Western science and technology are needed by the Third World, we should perhaps question ourselves about our right to call them into question in these postmodern times.

38

David Lynch

Joseph Natoli

If you put two films aside, *Eraserhead* (1976), Lynch's bizarro at the very edge of the modernist, avant-garde independent, and *Dune* (1984), his failure to go Hollywood mainstream, what you have in *Blue Velvet* (1986), *Wild at Heart* (1990), and the TV series *Twin Peaks* (1990) is a screening of postmodern views, an expression of a postmodern attitude, a primer of postmodernity.

Postmodernity allows us no still point, no center, and no place to rest. The center is everywhere. The life-world *is* in motion with respect to almost everything, not only in the present but in the past and in that part of the future that is constructed here in the present. The self is not outside the flux or at the still center, nor is consciousness peering into the wellsprings of the flux. Consciousness is not peering into the foundation of things, of the world. We are inside the flux. We are most tellingly – and for modernists, most unfortunately – *inside* the language we use and therefore it is equally valid to see it as using us.

The self is also *outside* itself; it is in the world, disseminated, scattered, consisting of intersecting selves that the world, language, contingencies, culture conjoin within clusters, motifs of identity that are multiple, not continuous, not cohering, not unified. What does this imply? That if you are like Jeff Beaumont in *Blue Velvet* and gazing out of the closet at the Blue Lady, there is no subject–object space – much beloved and much needed by modernity – between you and the Blue Lady, between you in the closet – which is like the frame of your life-world – and the room out there. What you are inside is already what is outside. You can make pronouncements from the inside about what you think is going on outside, what the outside means to you, but another observer observing your observing would be able to see your couplings of self and world, the distinctions of the marked space of the world that are in you, the contingencies that have been marked out by the culture and are equally marked out by your observations. *Blue Velvet* pulls us out of the closet of distanced, private, dominating subjectivity and puts us on our knees within the reality we dreamed we were separate from and dominated. The play of the film is the play of subject/object switches, a playing of the game "Who's in Charge of Reality Here?" Jeff seeks in true Enlightenment style to sew up the mystery of the severed ear; he wants to delve into what was previously hidden from him. He assumes the role of the investigative detective, the data-gathering empiricist. And he winds up flung into the messiness of a world his story of control cannot control. The Blue Lady reverses their roles: she puts a knife to his throat and orders him to do what she wants. "Don't look at me!" she shouts. We don't want to be Jeff at that point; the classic realist spin is unspun. If we're not Jeff, who are we? Who is in control here? And so our own subjectivity is put on the line and the stakes of the film are now as high as they can get: we have lost control of our viewing and are viewing our loss of control. It is unsettling. Frank Booth in turn reverses roles with the Blue Lady. "Don't you look at me!" he yells at her. Dominating subjectivity is his, not hers. She is an object; women are caught in a terrible story that will not die: they are objects, subject to the male gaze. "Show it to me," Frank orders her. She is her sex; she is not a person but a part of anatomy.

We hear the words to the song "Blue Velvet" a number of times in the movie and each time the song changes for us as the context of our listening – where we are in the film – changes. We connect word and world from within our own reality frames, frames contrived from various proportions of the social, the cultural, and the personal. What the mixture is defies empirical analysis or rational exploration. But worlds collide; Jeff's reality frame – his neat Lumberton reality – intersects Frank's dark and violent reality. "Don't go to Lincoln," Jeff's spinster aunt cautions him. But how can he avoid it? How can you keep your rendering of reality from being interrupted by what that rendering leaves out? Do you think because you are chaste and sober there will be no more cakes and ale in the world? The unmarked space of the world cannot be clocked by the sound of the tree-falling timescape of Lumberton. Love should be as pure and purifying as Sandy says it is; but "love" is a signifier that can be and has been connected in other and far different ways. "Hit me!" the Blue Lady orders Jeff. If you love me, hit me. "Love is a bullet from a gun," Frank tells Jeff. What is "love" but what the stories we live in make of it?

Lynch's characters live within recognizable stories and bring the world to meaning from within those stories. We recognize them because they come out of popular culture; they are the same stories that fill our own heads and shape our reality frames. The hyperreal isn't some unknowable Platonic realm: it's *Mister Rogers's Neighborhood*. "Hi, neighbor," Frank jovially greets Jeff for the first time. "Want to go for a ride, neighbor?" Jeff throwing a rock at a can is Huck Finn all over again; Jeff on the trail of a crime the way Frank and Joe Hardy were on the trail of a crime; Sandy speaking of robins coming to fill the world with love is accompanied by choir music from across the street: that old-time resurrecting religion story; Sandy's mom is right out of *Leave It To Beaver*; Jeff's own family right out of the Andy Hardy films; Sandy and Mike the football captain are sweethearts at Archie Andrews's Riverdale High School; Frank's caught up in the Oedipus story retold by Freud; all of Lumberton is Main Street Disneyland. And Lynch's fascination with sex and violence is not simply tied to his own idiosyncratic bent, nor simply because they are "box office." They are obviously fascinations – blue velvet fetishes – of American culture. And the stories we live in about them, the way we hook up with these potent signifiers, does not cover what they may be unmarked by our stories. Lynch does not simply mark that space definitively or evaluatively but rather plays us into the depth and strangeness of our responses to both, a sort of poststructuralist revisiting of our forged chains of signification.

When the highest share of America's TV audience watched Lynch's *Twin Peaks* week after week they were moving across the profound surfaces of postmodern lives, although Lynch contextualized the show within two popu-lar TV genres: the soap opera and the murder mystery. Everything went on as if we were watching a cross between *Days of Our Lives* and *Murder She Wrote*. When it became clear that FBI agent Dale Cooper was more of a mystery than the mystery he was supposed to be solving and the inhabitants of the town of Twin Peaks were taking us way beyond our own sense of realism into unset-tling and disturbing territory, the veneer of both soap opera and murder was cracked. While a soap opera forks off into multiple realities it never takes a viewer into a reality frame the viewer is not already in or comfortable with or able to digest easily because that frame has already been taken for a test drive in the culture. In fact, soaps like to spin plot filaments recently spun in the headlines or elsewhere on TV, or in film or talk shows etc. *Twin Peaks*, on the other hand, takes us down those lost highways toward places we have never been, do not know, have nothing to say about, and are therefore uneasy about. We're not only down strange roads but we're not at the wheel, and Lynch has only been fooling us into thinking we are at the wheel. We get revenge by not tuning in.

Because the premiere launched a murder mystery – who killed Laura Palmer? – *Twin Peaks* also got identified as a TV murder mystery, one that we can follow week after week, gathering clues, following red herrings, and then finally figuring out who done it. But Lynch disappoints here too; the show overspills the murder mystery format. The red herring trails turn out to be a fascination for Lynch. They are not there to mislead; they assume center stage, only to be displaced by something else, also thought originally to be peripheral. For weeks the Laura Palmer murder seems to be replaced by a log, or a slice of cherry pie, or someone's battle with a curtain rod, or crazy dreams, or incest – anything and everything but the murder. Agent Cooper, our ratiocinative agent of discovery, perforates his investigation with inconsequential, mundane fascinations, finally pursuing a line of investigation based on his dreams. Agent Cooper's mind wanders finally down weird, dreamlike corridors, and the effort to connect those surreal passages with the "real world" of the dead body of a young woman finally produces the same frustration in the TV mystery fan as it did in the soap opera fan.

So Lynch was spinning us away from the classic realist spin but toward what? Network executives demanded the murder be solved to placate the expectations of murder mystery fans; plots needed to be tied together; characters needed to be demystified; words needed to make sense; dreams needed to be separated from reality; some point of view had to be projected; some hero had to come forward to save the day, to save the show. It didn't happen. The show plunged in ratings and never saw a third season, perhaps a first for a TV show that just a year before had swept the rating charts. *Twin Peaks*, along with *Blue Velvet* and *Wild at Heart*, went into the "cult" (read "weirdo") section of the video stores. What all this meant was that a depiction of a postmodern world had gotten filtered through naive realist, Enlightenment modernist, and twentieth-century modernist expectations. Lynch was showing us on screen and on TV a shifting of reality-making ways. Lynch was creating the very means by which we could recognize a postmodern world, the world he was introducing in *Twin Peaks*; but we saw it in already entrenched ways and therefore saw it as a personal vision of an eccentric but talented filmmaker. And lest Lynch didn't get the message that TV was bound heart and soul to the realist formula of hero identification–clear-cut categories of right and wrong–fathomable metanarrative–victory over all obstacles–satisfying closure–reconfirmation of the viewer's sense of realism, it would be repeated for him in 1999 when his ready-to-debut new TV series *Mulholland Drive* was at the last minute canceled by ABC. What they previewed was too "disturbing."

Wild at Heart is a road movie: the young heading west, no particular destination in mind, but intent on escaping what constrains their youth, their wildness, their love of freedom. Fit *Wild at Heart* into a powerful American mythos. "The world is wild at heart and something weird on top," Lula says in this film, a variation of "It's a strange world," the comment Sandy makes more than once in *Blue Velvet*. Lula tries to fit herself in the *Wizard of Oz*, translating everything into a trek down a Yellow Brick Road, trouble from the Wicked Witch of the West, a dissolution of all the bad things in her life, an answering of all her questions, and a discovery of the true home where the heart is. Unfortunately, reality doesn't oblige the plots of Hollywood films. Lula begins her journey west already haunted by her father's death and by rape and abortion. And as she surfs the dials on the car radio and hears nothing but sick, sordid, and weird news, she screams out in protest. Do these news reports create the weirdness of the world, or does the weirdness of the world create these reports? She and Sailor dance wildly in the desert and embrace, their love somehow rising above the wildness of the world, their wildness at heart somehow crushing the weirdness of things. But ahead is pure contingency: a car crash that takes the lives of two young lovers, Lula and Sailor surrogates. Chance, neither forestalled by Enlightenment reason which presumed to forestall it nor by postmodern narrative which doesn't presume to grasp reality or chance, can suddenly knock us off the Yellow Brick Road. Ahead is the vile Bobby Peru, who will confound Lula's notion of true love with the cravings of her own sexual appetite, an appetite seemingly disconnected from the "true love" she has for Sailor. "Love" becomes a floating, tormented signifier. "Why are there people like Frank Booth in the world?" Jeff asks in *Blue Velvet*. Or like Bobby Peru in *Wild at Heart*? Why are there disturbing people in the world? Why does our Yellow Brick Road story get disturbed by the stories of David Lynch? Why can't we live in the stories of reality that we project and impose upon reality? Why can't human nature and human behavior be what Dorothy and the Tin Man and the Cowardly Lion and the Scarecrow know they are?

Sailor lives in a world in which the rebel Elvis crosses with Brando the "Wild One," but these stories gradually fall apart and leave him uncertain as to who he really is. An identity in crisis, a self fracturing, splitting up into multiple images as different stories mirror his face differently. The snakeskin jacket that Brando wore in the film version of Tennessee Williams's *Battle of Angels*, the jacket that symbolized his individuality and love of personal freedom, is now Sailor's but the jacket confers no special powers. Individuality and personal freedom, like love, are caught up within stories of the same, and these stories can never hold off clashes with other stories, other configurations of being in the world. At the film's end, Sailor is beaten up by a street gang and while lying semi-conscious on the ground sees and hears the Good Witch who directs him back to the "true love" story. His mad rush over cars stopped in traffic is right out of a Doris Day/Rock Hudson movie. He sings, broken nose turned blue, "Love Me Tender" to Lula as the film credits roll and audience laughter responds to the hokey ending. We're laughing at our extremely weird capacity to laugh at our own tender and loving confabulations of reality. And then we rush out to continue down the Yellow Brick Road of our own concoction. But in *Wild at Heart* Lynch leads the break off the Yellow Brick Road, off Main Street, Disneyland. Plural lives, plural hearts.

39

Jean-François Lyotard

Hans Bertens

In 1983 and 1984 the debate on the postmodern considerably widened its scope as the result of a number of seminal publications: Jean Baudrillard's *In the Shadow of the Silent Majorities* and *Simulations* (both 1983), Fredric Jameson's "Postmodernism and Consumer Society" (1983) and its much revised and expanded version that appeared the following year under the title "Postmodernism, or, The Cultural Logic of Late Capitalism," and Jean-François Lyotard's "Answering the Question: What is Postmodernism?" (1983) and *The Postmodern Condition: A Report on Knowledge* (1984), the translation of his 1979 *La Condition postmoderne: Rapport sur le savoir*. Each of these interventions generated a great deal of excitement, not least because they were relatively untheoretical – at least as compared with Derridean deconstruction – while they still seemed to offer sweeping analyses of contemporary culture. Baudrillard's "hyperreal" and Jameson's "cultural logic of late capitalism" almost directly articulate the deep uneasiness of left liberal intellectuals with Reaganism, while Lyotard's more philosophically inspired view of the postmodern seemed to put a whole range of contemporary events and phenomena in their proper place.

The remarkable influence of Lyotard's brief study must be attributed to this explanatory power, which derived in large measure from its specific angle: Lyotard was the first to analyze developments in the sciences and in Western philosophy along postmodern lines. (Ihab Hassan, from whom Lyotard had borrowed the term "postmodern" – in his 1978 *Au Juste* he had still used the term "pagan" – had made some overtures in this direction, but had never really followed them through.) Perhaps as important is that Lyotard offered a succinct and sweeping definition of the postmodern that since 1984 has been repeated countless times: "Simplifying to the extreme, I define *postmodern* as incredulity towards metanarratives" (Lyotard 1984: xiv).

But let us first look briefly at Lyotard's intellectual career before his sudden international fame in the mid-1980s. A two-year stay in colonial Algeria

(1950–2), during which he became acutely aware of the evils of colonialism, converted Lyotard to Marxism and from 1954 until 1964 he was an active member – with a good many intellectuals of his generation – of the Socialisme ou barbarie group. After leaving the group he was active in a rival group until 1966, when he took his definitive leave of Marxism, a decision he saw vindicated by the events of May 1968 – or at least by the official Marxist response to them.

In 1971 Lyotard published *Discours, figure*, a critique of representation in which we recognize the skeleton structure of his later definition of the postmodern. *Discours, figure* pits libidinal energy – in the Freudian sense – against discursive representation. This energy does not manifest itself discursively but through images, events, and so on, which because of that offer better access to "truth" than discourse. The book, then, is a "defense of the eye" against the dominance of discursive activity (in which Lyotard includes reading) in modern Western society. (The sociologist Scott Lash later developed this argument into a fundamental opposition between a predominantly discursive modernity and a predominantly figurative postmodernity – a postmodern sociocultural formation dominated by communication through images. See his *Sociology of Postmodernism* of 1990.) For Lyotard the debate between structuralists on the one hand and phenomenologists on the other – determining structure versus self-determined subject – ignores that which underlies both structure and subject: desire. This fundamental realm of desire is the realm of difference, of true heterogeneity. This heterogeneity cannot manifest itself in standard discourse, but can be glimpsed in the unexpected, the transgressive, in figurative art that does not strive for coherence, harmony, and completeness.

In *Économie libidinale* of 1974, this interest in desire has become a radical championing of its unbridled manifestations. *Discours, figure* privileges the figurative in so far as it acts as a direct expression of desire, but places it, with the discursive, in a larger framework. *Économie*, however, presents the libidinal as endless and autonomous "transformations of energy" and is prepared to see the subject only in those terms – the discursive is now nothing but a thin and artificial veneer: "The subject is product of the representation machine, it disappears with it." As Albrecht Wellmer has put it: "for Lyotard, subject, representation, meaning, sign, and truth are links in a chain which must be broken as a whole ... Neither art nor philosophy have to do with 'meaning' or 'truth,' but solely with 'transformations of energy,' which cannot be derived from 'a memory, a subject, an identity' " (Wellmer 1985: 340). In his celebration of unconstrained and undirected libidinal energy Lyotard comes very close to admiring the irrational vitalism that Gerald Graff and others saw in the American counterculture of the 1960s.

More interesting for my purposes here is that *Économie libidinale* begins to develop Lyotard's characteristic interest in pluralism and singularity. In a discussion of monotheism and – pagan – polytheism, Lyotard argues that a polytheistic religious system like that of ancient Rome has a number of advantages over monotheistic religions. With its many gods and goddesses – all of which serve distinct roles – polytheism recognizes the fact that human experience is not undivided. There is a god or goddess for every occasion and every act, and because the relations between them are not necessarily fixed the diversity of human experience is not only recognized but is also not subjected to a rigid taxonomy. The heterogeneity of the polytheistic pantheon does justice to the heterogeneity of experience. Monotheism – from this perspective the scourge of the West – subordinates all diversity and difference to one final instance, one final perspective, and in so doing fundamentally denies it. Paganism – the happy-go-lucky organization of experience in relatively autonomous categories, each of them covered, so to speak, by a distinct (and usually fallible) divine being – *privileges* heterogeneity and stands for the incommensurability (*Économie* uses Leibniz's term "incompossibility") that Lyotard will later, from *The Postmodern Condition* onwards, see as the central characteristic of the "postmodern condition."

As we have already seen, in *The Postmodern Condition* – to finally turn to Lyotard's most influential work – this "condition" is defined as "incredulity towards metanarratives." Lyotard sees the project of modernity as driven by so-called metanarratives, that is, the supposedly transcendent and universal truths that serve to justify and legitimate modern Western culture. The universalist ambitions of modernity characteristically find their legitimation through "an explicit appeal to some grand narrative, such as the dialectics of Spirit, the hermeneutics of meaning, the emancipation of the rational or working subject, or the creation of wealth" (Lyotard 1984: xxiii). The modern pursuit of knowledge, for instance – the project of science, broadly speaking – is either justified by a political metanarrative that we have inherited from the Enlightenment or by a philosophical one that derives from German idealism. In the political version the pursuit of knowledge is justified by a view of history that sees history in terms of emancipation. To simplify this, knowledge serves to bring us closer to universal freedom. Philosophically, the pursuit of knowledge finds its legitimation in "a philosophy of history which construes the process of history as a realisation of Reason in the sciences" so that ultimately the principle of universal knowledge functions as the legitimating instance (Honneth 1985: 151). Another metanarrative that is referred to in the quotation I have just given – that of "the creation of wealth" – argues that the free market, in other words, an economic organization along capitalist lines, will ultimately benefit each and all of us and not just the entrepreneurs who usually rake up the first proceeds.

The Postmodern Condition presents two central arguments. The first is implicit in the term metanarrative: for Lyotard even the most fundamental legitimations of the project of modernity have no empirical foundation – they are, literally, stories that we tell ourselves in order to convince ourselves of their truth. In this privileging of language, Lyotard moves away from the exclusive focus on desire that we find in *Économie libidinale* and connects his thinking with Derrida's deconstruction and, especially, Foucault's discourses. Second, for Lyotard, the metanarratives of modernity have lost their power to convince: "Speculative or humanistic philosophy is forced to relinquish its legitimation duties" (1984: 41). The transcendent, universalist legitimations of modernity no longer have the power to hold things together. The best that we can put forward to replace them is legitimation through performativity – "the best input–output equation" – but such utilitarian, instrumental, legitimitations have only limited applicability. Essentially, postmodern legitimation is nonperformative and immanent. Postmodern legitimation, as Nancy Fraser and Linda Nicholson have put it, is "plural, local, and immanent . . . Instead of hovering above, legitimation descends to the level of practice and becomes immanent in it" (Fraser and Nicholson 1988: 87).

With the transition from modernity to postmodernity, meta- or grand narratives have given way to "*petits récits*," to modest narratives that have a limited validity in place and time and that are sometimes identical with what Lyotard, borrowing from the later Wittgenstein, calls "language games." These language games, which are not subservient to one overarching principle or universal language, together constitute the sociocultural formation that we call postmodernity. They range from Wittgenstein's "models of discourse," that is, various forms of utterance – denotative, performative, prescriptive, etc. – that all follow their own specific set of rules, via the discourses that are employed by social institutions and professions, to the narratives that Lyotard also calls *petits récits*. A language game that doubles as such a *petit récit* ("little narrative") may serve to regulate and implicitly to legitimate a whole culture – it may contain "deontic statements prescribing what should be done . . . with respect to kinship, the difference between the sexes, children, neighbors, foreigners, etc." (20) – but that legitimation is always immanent: "Narratives . . . define what has the right to be said and done in the culture in question, and since they themselves are part of that culture, they are legitimated by the simple fact that they do what they do" (23).

It is the coexistence of a whole range of often widely different and always immanently legitimized language games, and the coarticulation of the various voices that make up a specific game, that for Lyotard guarantee a progressive politics. The only moves that are therefore never permitted are those of "terror": "By terror I mean the efficiency gained by eliminating, or threatening to eliminate, a player from the language game one shares with him" (63). Terror, which leads to enforced consensus, intervenes with the free flow of the game and damages its political potential, which for Lyotard finds concrete actualization in diversity, uncertainty, and undecidability. As he put it in a 1988 interview:

> The real political task today today, at least in so far as it is also concerned with the cultural . . . is to carry forward the resistance that writing offers to established thought, to what has already been done, to what everyone thinks, to what is well known, to what is widely recognized, to what is "readable," to everything which can change its form and make itself acceptable to opinion in general. (Van Reijen and Veerman 1988: 302)

It is *dissensus* that enables an emancipatory politics and dissensus can only exist by the grace of heterogeneity: the continuing diversity of language games and of difference within single games.

This radical privileging of dissensus also is the driving force behind Lyotard's second major contribution to the debate on the postmodern: his rewriting of the Kantian sublime as the "postmodern sublime." In an article published originally in 1982 and presented in Ihab and Sally Hassan's *Innovation/Renovation* of 1983, Lyotard argues that the modern sublime is essentially a "nostalgic" sublime because through its form it still "continues to offer to the reader or viewer matter for solace or pleasure" (Lyotard 1983: 340). The postmodern, avant-gardistic, sublime, however,

> puts forward the unpresentable in presentation itself; that which denies itself the solace of good forms, the consensus of taste which would make it possible to share collectively the nostalgia for the unattainable; that which searches for new presentations, not in order to enjoy them but in order to impart a stronger sense of the unpresentable. (Lyotard 1983: 340)

Consensus can never take us beyond the beautiful (to speak of beauty is to invoke preexisting norms); dissensus, however, can lead into the realm of the sublime which evokes "contradictory" feelings that are "deep and unexchangeable" (Lyotard 1986: 11) in the sense that they cannot be shared. The confrontation with the sublime, with the unpresentable, leads to the radical openness that Lyotard prizes above everything else.

Lyotard's great and continuing importance for the debate on the postmodern lies in his insistence on translating the micro-aporias of Derridean deconstruction to a level of far more general undecidabilities – the "differends" of his 1983 book *Le Différend*. In a period of ever-increasing (capitalist) homogenization and (liberalist) consensus, Lyotard has reminded us again and again of the value of difference and of incommensurability, and of the important function served by artistic expressions that in their reaching out for the postmodern sublime once again bring home the message of heterogeneity and of *le différend*.

40

Trinh T. Minh-ha

E. Ann Kaplan

Much of the confusion and passionate, sometimes acrimonious, debates about postmodernism have been due to critics not carefully distinguishing the specific terrain involved in any one scholar's, journalist's, or policy-maker's voice. Postmodern literary and aesthetic theory is one thing; postmodernism as an abstract philosophical category another; postmodernism taken up by, or applied to, international capitalism, or to a postmodern subject of psychoanalysis, yet different again.

From the moment interest in postmodernist theory in the American academy developed in a big way (around 1984), feminists and Marxists in the humanities worried about its potentially dangerous political implications. But others found fascinating and exciting the overthrowing of established academic modalities that postmodernism permitted, and the kinds of texts (horror film, off-beat TV, performance art, subcultural art, etc.) that it brought newly into view. Many thought that, as adapted to America, postmodern theories helped explain and account for what people had already sensed as some kind of new, perhaps disturbing, cultural era. Others, however, loudly denounced postmodernism either as merely the latest intellectual "fad," without serious import, and somehow "dangerous" in propagating undesirable values – decentering, destabilizing, undoing what people had always relied on for order. These issues have not resolved themselves. They remain open, and postmodernism is still contested, problematic, even as postmodern paradigms begin to shift perhaps into something I try to define elsewhere as "millennial" (Kaplan 2000).

I tried to clarify this conjuncture in 1988 by distinguishing within academia two differing strands of humanities postmodern thinking, which I called "complicit" and "utopian" (Kaplan 1988). By complicit, I meant an apocalyptic fascination or celebration of the end of totalizing narratives, and also of the (implicitly white male) humanist subject, that could end up serving corporate capitalism's need (in an era of international finance and companies with multiple global sites) for decentered, even fragmented, fluid subjects. By "utopian" I had in mind contrary efforts of French feminists Luce Irigaray, Hélène Cixous, or the early Julia Kristeva, to see fluid subjectivity and the end of totalizing narratives as freeing women from the constraints of a "feminine" that was always already male-defined and placed in totalizing narratives aimed at serving white male needs.

I think this distinction made sense at the time, but I would now note that both the complicit and utopian kinds of postmodern theorizing responded to the fears and fantasies of largely white intellectuals as subjects: it spoke to their old views of an America and the world that had seemed permanent and stable but that now no longer made sense. Postmodernism opened up liberatory possibilities for white intellectuals without Marxism's specific class constraints, or socialist-feminism's gender constraints – and thereby entered into a problematic confrontation with both Marxism and feminism. Feminists and some minorities, as noted, worried about celebrating the death of the subject when women and the marginalized had barely gained the status of "subject." It seemed that the subject whose death male theorists were celebrating was largely white and male. Meanwhile, many were ambivalent about how postmodern digital technologies (which preoccupied theorists in media and theater arts) would change their (modernist) world. In James Cadello's words, fears included the need to bring technology in line with the ends it was to serve – humanities, personality, sociality, morality.

There is no doubt about the lasting impact of postmodernist theories on intellectual discourse – a sign that its perspectives have some basis in cultural and political realities. But scholars are manifesting the impact in varied ways. Diverse feminists have come to differing conclusions about postmodernism : Australian Meaghan Morris was one of the first to embrace postmodernism and to argue that feminism, in its profound critique of patriarchal culture, was already postmodern, *avant la lettre* (Morris, 1988); Barbara Creed (also Australian) was one of the first feminist film scholars to see the importance of postmodern theories for interpreting Hollywood cinema (Creed 1987). Political philosophers such as Nancy Fraser, Linda Nicholson, and Seyla Benhabib, working from socialist-feminist or Habermasian positions, saw postmodernism as encouraging political cynicism and hedonism, while scholars in Queer Theory engaged the new gendered subjectivities that postmodern theory opened up spaces for. Meanwhile, African-American media and art theorists have also taken up interesting and complex positions: Michele Wallace saw the potential of postmodernism, while worrying about its lack of attention to race, and bell hooks argued that Black life – in its forced fragmentation and dispersal, its inability to ground itself because of slavery – had always been postmodern (see on this Kaplan 2000).

Taking issues regarding race to the global context, perhaps most contested has been how postmodernism intersects with postcolonialism. Postcolonialists confront the new multinational capitalism: who could have predicted in the 1980s the rapid upsurge in the American stock market? Its recurrent shakiness and decline? Or the equally incredible continuing advances in digital technologies, accompanied by a frenzied development of new hard- and software? In 1985, Donna Haraway (with her familiarity with science) studied the new biotechnologies and examined their increasing impact on society that feminists and Marxists seemed to be ignoring. The enormous growth of this technoscience as a huge profit-making industry, along with the major advances in digital technologies, were determining factors behind a need for a new humanities research paradigm in the mid-1980s. These industries are currently producing new subjects – largely young males – whose activities are changing the world, and seemingly confirming the notion that the "market" is replacing "nation" as a global signifier.

But male theorists have hotly debated the application of postmodern theories to nations like India (Ahmad 1992) and continents like Africa (Mudimbe 1988). In the wake of pioneering research by (among others) Edward Said, Gayatri Spivak, Homi Bhabha, and Arif Dirlik on imperialism and postcolonialism, Arjun Appadurai more explicitly links postcolonialism and postmodernism in discussing the complexities of the near millennium – a moment when the old divide between the "local" and the "global" has been dramatically challenged by new kinds of flows of people and technologies (Appadurai 1990).

Following upon all this, women scholars in development have in turn taken complex and again contradictory stances toward postmodern theory. They question whether or not it has any relevance for their research and for practices in developing nations. An excellent overview of how specialists in gender and development view postmodernism may be found in a volume edited by Marianne H. Marchand and Jane L. Parpart, called *Feminism, Postmodernism, Development* (1997). After reviewing postmodernist critiques in the humanities and social sciences, and relationships between postmodernism and feminism, the authors suggest that there is a need to undermine the traditional "equation between development, modernity and the West" (1997: 12). They cite authors who "question the universal pretensions of modernity, and the Eurocentric certainty of both liberal and Marxist development studies." Such authors point out that "much of the discourse and practice of development has exaggerated Western knowledge claims, dismissed and silenced knowledge from the South and perpetuated dependence on Northern 'expertise'" (12). However, Marchand and Parpart are aware of some of the dangers of postmodern thinking: "The celebration of differences and multiple identities has provided welcome plurality and richness to feminist analysis but in its extreme form, it raises questions about the ability of women to speak for each other, to mobilize political action and to call for the defense of women's rights" (18).

However, from the less usual feminist postcolonial perspectives in the arts and humanities, one artist/theorist who deals with postmodernism from a postcolonial standpoint (going back as far as 1983), and refutes many of the objections to postmodernism as an elitist, Western white male phenomenon and set of concerns, is film scholar/practitioner Trinh T. Minh-ha. Trinh's influence on multicultural theorists and artists in terms of integrating a postmodernist and postcolonial perspective can hardly be overstated.

As Trinh has remarked, the idea that "postmodernism" is somehow a Western discovery or theory is mistaken. Postmodernism implicates everyone, and non-Western cultures have contributed to and participated in postmodernist theorizing as much as others. Trinh's first contribution is to work out from the level of subjectivity, not from that of broad abstractions in the manner of the male theorists mentioned. Trinh focuses on how to make oneself a "subject" within struggles against the state and make women's concerns central; how to link the specificity of one's particular context and struggles with those of women in different national, cultural, and geographical locations, etc. (See Kaplan 1997.)

Second, Trinh's very aesthetic and artistic practice performs postmodernism: for she notes that each film demands its own strategies and that these strategies emerge in the process of the filming. Trinh does not go into a project with a preconceived idea of how the film will go, or even, it seems, of what her aims are. She discovers what she needs to do in the process of the doing. Trinh has described herself as working between genres, between different modes of address, between different codes – something that has been defined as a main aspect of postmodernism. Her practices always come to a point where they reach the limit of what is cinema and what is not cinema; what is Art and what is not Art; what is politics and what is not politics. Each work is a throw of the dice. Each film is a boundary event that leads spectators to constantly ask where that limit is. In each film form *is* content (Trinh 1995).

Third, the postmodern concept of multiple, shifting, "I's" – usually stated as an abstract defining characteristic of postmodernism – is actualized in Trinh's texts. This idea has been a major, pioneering concern of Trinh's, developed over many years in her films and writings. The films and writings enact multiple positions, instead of just describing them: in her hybrid texts, language and image work together, whether the text is film, book or article. In developing this postmodern notion within the postcolonial frame, Trinh challenges previous constructions of interracial looking relations, which begin with the subject–object structure, and emphasize people of color as the deplored "object," or the Kristevan abject. While it has been, and remains, crucial to unpack this Western binary – to challenge, reverse, and resist it – Trinh moves toward another concept of interracial looking relations. Her films practice a place beyond the usual subject/object Western binary, manifesting multiple "I's" confronting "multiple I's" in the Other. Her films challenge the notion of something fixed. Subjectivity is not opposed to objectivity but has its own range of activity. In their very hybridity, Trinh's works transgress categories and boundaries mainstream cinema erected for its profit and convenience out of Western habits of classifying, categorizing, differentiating. For example, in her first film, *Reassemblage*, Trinh already practices many of these aspects of her work. In accordance with the understanding of multiple "I's," Trinh attempts in *Reassemblage* to avoid making the narrator of the film one unitary subject (herself as narrator). Her voice speaks within many different discourses.

Postcolonial women artists like Trinh are working to perform an alternate concept of postmodernism – one that takes advantage of the collapse of totalizing colonialist discourses without, however, falling into either the postmodern apocalyptic, suicidal frenzy of what I called the "commercial" postmodernism; or the opposite, utopian liberatory fantasy; or, finally, the despairing stances of many white feminist responses to the present conjuncture. Trinh rather demonstrates the strengths and possibilities of women of color to utilize the undeniable postmodern, postcolonialist moment for their own ends, their own needs, their own futures.

41

Toni Morrison

Thomas B. Hove

Although she regards herself first and foremost as an African-American writer, Toni Morrison's work shares several features with a widespread tendency in postmodern fiction – shared by American writers as diverse as Leslie Marmon Silko, Ishmael Reed, and Thomas Pynchon – to confront, question, and ultimately supplement dominant cultural narratives. Morrison's fictions repeatedly challenge cultural traditions defined by patriarchal, assimilationist, and totalizing standards. Ever since her first novel, *The Bluest Eye*, came out in 1969, she has set herself in opposition to the European American white mainstream by portraying and celebrating unique, powerful voices of marginalized women from American history and contemporary American life.

Formally, Morrison's impulse to supplement totalizing narratives is reflected in her characteristic fictional technique of letting a variety of voices from the African-American present and past offer their own accounts of themselves. This technique serves several important purposes: it resists the imperialistic impulses associated with the effort to formulate one and only one version of our world and the people in it, particularly with regard to America and African-Americans; it invites readers to participate in the construction of truth and meaning by learning a sympathetic tolerance for a variety of voices; and it highlights the fact that the protagonist throughout Morrison's fiction is not a single heroic figure but rather the collective, which in her work refers to all the members, past and present, of the African-American community. Morrison's humanitarian concerns are obviously much wider, but the African-American community remains her central focus because she wants to retrieve, celebrate, and preserve its accomplishments, values, and traditions in the face of global and mainstream American threats to its survival.

Against this racially charged social backdrop, Morrison's work can be read as a series of reactions against a patriarchal, ethnocentric white version of modernism and cultural politics. In her insistence on the centrality of African-American culture to her characters' lives, she challenges not only the values of the high modernist tradition but also its forms, especially its linguistic forms. In her article "Unspeakable Things Unspoken" (1989), for example, she comments on her deliberate attempts to give voice to certain forms of black speech that only African-American audiences would be familiar with. "Quiet as it's kept," the first phrase of *The Bluest Eye*, inaugurates this tendency in her career. Another small but notable example of this tendency is her use of the sound-effect "sth" in both *Beloved* (1987) and *Jazz* (1992). This small example also evokes Morrison's frequent attempts to translate linguistic forms from the oral to the written tradition without allowing the official forms of written convention to eradicate the forms and expressions characteristic of oral traditions.

As is commonplace in postmodern theory and fiction, Morrison emphasizes the centrality of language not only as a repository of culture but as the primary medium of social interaction. In both its form and content, her fiction dramatizes the importance of controlling language and using it as a resource for liberation, self-expression, recognition, and communion. At the same time, however, her fiction documents the various ways language can be misused for purposes of domination, oppression, dehumanization, and extermination. Morrison has commented most directly on these issues in her 1993 Nobel Lecture, in which she narrates the fable of a blind, black woman storyteller whose cultural authority is mockingly challenged by a group of youths from the dominant culture outside of which she lives. Initially, the woman puts the children off with an enigmatic response that challenges them to decide whether they wish to perpetuate humiliating social practices through language or instead use language as a medium for exchanges of love and respect. When she begins to see that the children have come to her not out of a cruel impulse to mock her with linguistic trickery but rather out of a genuine desire to learn from her, she invites them to join her in the communion of language. The fable ends on a note of hope that language, particularly in its narrative form, can bring people from hostile social backgrounds together in an act of shared creation. "Look," the old woman says. "How lovely it is, this thing we have done – together." Examples of such cooperation and reconciliation via language abound throughout Morrison's fiction, usually when her characters realize that their shared language ought to work against the divisions and conflicts set in motion by competitive or oppressive forces in the white mainstream.

But in spite of these moments of cooperation and reconciliation, Morrison's fictional and nonfictional works carefully balance hope with an unflinching acknowledgment of the forces that can imprison language and misuse it as an instrument of predatory domination. The most obvious example of this misuse is the enterprise of classifying humans according to skin color and "race." As with recent social-scientific and historiographic treatments of race, Morrison illustrates how such classificatory schemes have been used not only to justify inhumane practices like slavery but also to help perpetuate them by supplying bogus justifications for their continuance. This enterprise is most vividly portrayed through the figure known as "Schoolteacher" in *Beloved*, whose actions embody the connections between linguistic classification and dehumanizing social practices. The worst of these practices are, for obvious historical reasons, those inflicted by whites on blacks, for example the Biblical and pseudo-scientific classificatory schemes that were used to justify chattel slavery. Morrison also documents the self-destructive legacy of these schemes within the African-American community by showing the variety of ways her black characters mistreat one another on account of differences in shading. For example, the "8-rocks" of *Paradise* (1998), named after a particularly dark grade of coal, found the town of Ruby because whites, Indians, and lighter-skinned blacks have rejected them. But within their self-enclosed community, the dark-skinned 8-rocks come to regard themselves as an aristocracy, and some of them justify their abuses of power by appealing to the bogus criterion of skin color. In this instance and several others, Morrison suggests the need for more fluid views of social identity, an aim she shares with contemporary social scientists who have taken up arms against divisive social practices based on pseudo-biological classificatory schemes.

On the creative rather than essayistic side of her challenges to hegemonic narratives and oppressive misuses of language, Morrison sets out to lend eloquent expression to the people, stories, voices, and forms of life that these narratives have typically disregarded, devalued, and silenced. Some examples of these traditionally neglected forms of life are the following: a rejected and sexually abused young girl (Pecola in *The Bluest Eye*); a radically independent social outcast (Sula from *Sula* [1973]); a folkloric family history initially lost to the vicissitudes of oral transmission and geographic displacement (*Song of Solomon* [1977]); people who do not fit existing racial identities (Jadine from *Tar Baby* [1981], Golden Gray from *Jazz*); two lonely orphans and a deaf-mute woman (Twyla, Roberta, and Maggie from "Recitatif"); a woman who is forced to kill to prevent her child from being seized by her former slaveowner (Sethe from *Beloved*); a teenaged girl murdered by her middle-aged lover (Dorcas from *Jazz*); a commune made up of outcast women (the Convent women from *Paradise*). Within the stories that focus on these marginalized figures, Morrison frequently alludes to actual historical incidents that have until only recently been left out of official historical records. This was one of the purposes of *The Black Book*, a documentary history she edited and which presents an extensive collage of African-American cultural documents. But her fiction, much like that of Ishmael Reed, incorporates a wide variety of scenes from African-American history that challenge triumphalist versions of mainstream American historiography: Margaret Garner's desperate infanticide (*Beloved*); the 1917 race riots in East St. Louis (*Jazz*); the neglect, mistreatment, and irrational hostility toward black veterans of the two world wars (*Sula, Song of Solomon, Jazz, Paradise*); the unpunished 1955 murder of Emmett Till (*Song of Solomon*); the 1963 bombing that killed four girls in a Birmingham church (*Song of Solomon*). Similarly, Morrison's only full-length work of literary criticism, *Playing in the Dark* (1992), calls attention to a hitherto suppressed "Africanist presence" in American literary history.

In keeping with her emphasis on communal concerns, Morrison's fictions work against the elitist high modernist ideal of the individual hero or genius who transcends the limitations of his or her community. Most of the time, Morrison debunks her characters when they pursue quests for solitary fulfillment and disregard collective concerns, as in her treatments of Milkman's quest for gold (*Song of Solomon*), Sethe's and Beloved's sadomasochistic relationship (*Beloved*), Joe Trace's yearning for lost youth (*Jazz*), and the 8-rocks' efforts to preserve their "pure" community from global forces of social change (*Paradise*). By contrast, when Morrison's initially self-centered figures display some form of altruistic or communal concern, it is a sign of their potential redemption, which most often lies in a closer state of communion with their geographic or ancestral African-American roots. If one follows this theme throughout her work, one can see why Morrison continually asserts her difference from the European-American modernist tradition. Instead of allowing herself to be inserted in that tradition, she claims that what she tries to do in fiction has more in common with jazz and with the African-American oral traditions in which she grew up. These inspirations for her fiction should constantly be kept in mind, for they remind those who want to assimilate her into traditional European-American cultural traditions that she considers her African-American cultural identity as the most important basis of her artistic endeavors.

Nevertheless, it is a logical consequence of literature's circulation in global society that Morrison's fictional technique can also be compared usefully with that of non-African-American writers, particularly because her narrative forms share many surface features with them even though their origins differ. For example, she has often been compared to Woolf and Faulkner, both of whom Morrison happened to study in graduate school. In addition, her work is permeated with many of the classic Hellenic and Hebraic themes and motifs from Western art and culture. Usually, however, when Morrison uses Western themes and motifs, she is trying to suggest that her characters are making the wrong moves, as when Milkman and Guitar's quest for gold echoes Jason and the Argonauts' morally dubious quest for the Golden Fleece. By contrast, Morrison's characters most often find authenticity, value, and redemption in African and African-American folk traditions. But Morrison does not simply replace one system of cultural authority with another, for she also subjects these folk traditions to critical scrutiny, especially when they manifest patriarchal values. The most memorable instance of such a use and critique of African and African-American folk traditions appears in *Song of Solomon*, where Solomon's flight to freedom from slavery is questioned by a woman who wonders how many family members he left behind in the thralls of slavery. This example illustrates what might be labeled a moral norm in Morrison's fiction: what's good is what's good for the community as a whole, not for some isolated member of it unaware of his or her ties and obligations to others.

Sometimes, Morrison's style achieves a modernist grandeur that threatens to swallow her fictions' social subject matter into itself. But her constant focus on the communal concerns and political survival of the African-American community, as well as her acknowledgment of the unique identities of individuals within that community, resist the modernist bent toward privileging aesthetic mastery over social engagement. The best illustration of her art acknowledging its limits occurs at the end of *Jazz*, where the narrator acknowledges her inability to fully define the people she is trying to imagine. This narrative move reflects a step back from the modernist tendency to allow the aesthetic to absorb the actual, as in the work of Henry James and Faulkner, whose characters often conspicuously think and speak according to the syntax, cadences, and vocabulary of their author's peculiar style.

A more important line of comparison for Morrison herself, lies in her narrative technique's affinities with the call- and-response pattern of African oral storytelling. According to one current critical consensus, "non-Western" oral traditions invite a collaborative and democratic relation between storyteller, subjects, and audience. Morrison's recurring technique of moving from one narrative voice to another works against the model of narrative authority that allows one primary voice or style to absorb all other voices into its overarching, complex coherence. To a degree, Morrison's use of multiple points of view resembles Faulkner's attempt in *Absalom, Absalom!* to portray the same events from a variety of perspectives and according to a variety of interpretations. But while Faulkner's principal narrators Quentin and Shreve eventually seem to master the material they reconstruct by solving the mystery of the Sutpens' motivations, Morrison's narrators are more willing to acknowledge the limitations of their knowledge and to admit that human motivation poses mysteries that we will never fully be able to penetrate or define. This epistemological impasse is also reflected in Morrison's treatment of ethics. If the motivations of Morrison's characters are ultimately impenetrable, then ethical decisions and judgments must always be tentative, provisional, and based on varying degrees of uncertainty. Morrison brings out this ethical problem most vividly in *Beloved*, which avoids siding with only one of the variety of reactions to Sethe's attempts to kill her children rather than allow the slaveholders to abduct them back into slavery.

Morrison's characters remain mysteries also because their identities do not conform to traditional patriarchal or mainstream expectations. Her most interesting characters have decentered subjectivities, for both positive and negative reasons that lead to sometimes fulfilling, sometimes damaging consequences. Morrison's female protagonists are typically outcasts with no coherent sense of identity, and there are at least two causes for their lack of coherence. On the one hand, her strong females refuse to submit to the traditional roles available to them in their communities, usually because these roles have been imposed by either white or patriarchal interests. On the other hand, without any satisfactory social traditions to fall back on, or without any open-minded communities that will accept their unique identities, Morrison's women must strike out on their own and create new, nontraditional identities for themselves. Some of these women – Pecola from *The Bluest Eye*, Twyla and Roberta from "Recitatif," Violet from *Jazz*, and the women who come to the Convent in *Paradise* – have no stable sense of identity because they are victims who have been rejected, neglected, or abused. Other women – *Sula*, Pilate from *Song of Solomon*, Jadine from *Tar Baby*, Sethe from *Beloved*, Dorcas from *Jazz*, and Connie from *Paradise* – willfully place themselves in opposition to the people and traditions that demand their conformity and threaten their quests for authenticity. Ultimately, both types of women must carry out improvisatory quests for identity, and they complete these quests with varying degrees of success.

Inevitably, these women's quests run parallel to their encounters with and navigations through racial politics. The two most interesting encounters with racial politics are the stories of Sula (*Sula*) and Jadine (*Tar Baby*). Morrison has described Sula as "quintessentially black, metaphysically black... new world black and new world woman extracting choice from choicelessness, responding inventively to found things. Improvisational. Daring, disruptive, imaginative, modern, out-of-the-house, outlawed, unpolicing, uncontained and uncontainable. And dangerously female" (Morrison 1989: 25). Sula must resist the customs and gender roles expected of her in the traditional black community of Medallion. Jadine from *Tar Baby*, on the other hand, embodies Morrison's most extensive treatment of an African-American woman coming to terms not only with gender roles but with the problems and freedoms of racial indeterminacy. Although Jadine is light-skinned enough to be accepted by the white-dominated fashion industries of Paris and New York, she is haunted by ethnic inauthenticity and by a sense of having betrayed the African side of her ethnic heritage. Other characters who illustrate the cultural and personal problems associated with racial ambiguity are Maureen Peal (*The Bluest Eye*), Milkman's mother Ruth and her father

Dr. Foster (*Song of Solomon*), Dorcas (*Jazz*), and Golden Gray (*Jazz*). The sociological significance of these stories lies in the variety of ways they challenge the simple-minded, oppressive American practice of defining "blackness" according to the "one-drop" rule, and of characterizing blackness as something to be reviled, a theme Morrison addresses from a literary-historical standpoint in *Playing in the Dark*.

In conjunction with her resistance to totalizing worldviews, all of Morrison's novels conclude in a semantically open-ended way. In *The Bluest Eye*, Pecola's identity disintegrates, and the consequences of her pregnancy are left shrouded in mystery. At the end of *Song of Solomon*, Guitar lunges murderously at Milkman, but Morrison never reveals whether the two men fall to their deaths or Milkman miraculously "rides the air." *Tar Baby* concludes with Jadine disappearing, for better or worse, to Paris as her ex-lover, Son, embarks on an uncertain quest with supernatural overtones. "Recitatif" leaves its characters' racial identities, their attitudes toward each other, and their memories of cruelties both suffered and committed indeterminate. In the final chapter of *Beloved*, the narrator self-contradictorily claims, "This is not a story to pass on," and Morrison never allows us to pin down who or what, exactly, Beloved is. At the end of *Jazz*, Joe and Violet Trace seem to have learned how to love each other, but the narrator expresses her uncertainty about understanding the true nature of their relationship. Finally, *Paradise* ends with the citizens of Ruby hushing up their slaughter of the Convent women, but there are signs that the community cannot ward off influences from the outside world forever. Such open-ended conclusions confirm that Morrison refuses to settle upon one worldview as definitive, or to leave her readers satisfied that everything coheres in a world riven by slavery and its legacies of oppression and racially based hostility. Nevertheless, Morrison invites her readers to build with her and her characters something out of this world's rubble that might be new and beautiful – as the storyteller of her Nobel Lecture says, "Together."

42

Thomas Pynchon

Dominic Pettman

Someday he will know everything, and still be as impotent as before.
Byron the Bulb *(Pynchon 1975: 654)*

To many literary scholars and critics, Thomas Pynchon is the quintessential postmodern author. More than a mere recluse, "Thomas Pynchon" is the proverbial signifier without a verifiable signified; a writer whose personal mythology is as complex, ironic, and enigmatic as his body of work. In the 1960s and 1970s, when articles by Foucault and Barthes were announcing the death (or at least the demotion) of the author, Pynchon was explicitly deconstructing the established hierarchies between the key coordinates of author, biography, genius, and text.

The scholarly fetish of the author – as opposed to the author-function – was quickly thwarted by any attempt to profile or interview Pynchon. Nobody seemed to know where he lived, or even what he looked like. Only one photograph attested to his actual existence, and this dated back to his college days. Indeed, the mystery surrounding Pynchon was further enhanced by his decision to send a double-talking comedian to accept his National Book Award in 1974. (Such an archetypal "postmodern absence" was later satirized by Malcolm Bradbury in his 1987 novel *Mensonge*.) The interminable attempt to uncover the "truth" about Pynchon uncannily mirrors the fruitless quests of his characters. It is this apparent need for "facts" – for epistemological certainty – which gives the narrative momentum in all of Pynchon's works.

Already in his first novel, *V* (1963), we have the formal and conceptual blueprint which would inform his writing for the subsequent four decades, and would cement his place in the postmodern pantheon. This book rushed into the fleeting cultural vacuum left after the Beats and before Pop-Art, transcending the narcissistic angst of the former, and anticipating the ironic playfulness of the latter. Liberally utilizing postmodernism's three Ps – parody, pastiche, and paranoia – *V* told of the search for a woman known only as "V," jumping from Florence, Paris, Malta, Southwest Africa, and the Suez between 1899 and 1945. This stunning debut led to comparisons with everyone from Bellow, Heller, and Vonnegut, to Swift, Sterne, Jarry, and even Joyce. At least one reviewer coined the phrase "American picaresque" in response to the neo(n)-Byzantine excesses of the novel's style and scope (Plimpton 1963).

Pynchon's second novel, *The Crying of Lot 49* (1965), is more compact and linear in structure, following housewife Oedipa Maas through the intriguing events which occur in the wake of the (alleged?) death of her ex-lover, Pierce Inverarity. Although this novel is much shorter than his other works, it represents a streamlined compendium of the tropes and tribulations which have come to be termed "postmodern": self-reflexivity, undecidability, floating signifiers, the collapse of high into low culture, depthless characters, epiphanic multiplicity, historical confusion, proliferating micro and counter-narratives, and the (failed) attempt to cognitively map the semiotically saturated present.

Oedipa becomes mixed up in an underground group called The Trystero, who seem to be running a clandestine postal service, along with several other secret social systems. Their symbol is the muted horn and peppers the narrative as much as Oedipa's environment, beckoning her to make sense of the mysteries which seem to lie just outside her understanding. Moreover, the name "Oedipa" is itself a red herring, tempting the reader to decode the text through overly familiar hermeneutic models such as psychoanalysis. Is she really searching for her father? Does "father" equal "God" in this context? And if so, are both dead? But before we even apply these questions to the narrative, Pynchon cheekily reminds us of his own dictum: "If you can get people to ask the wrong questions, you don't have to worry about the answers."

Any Archimedean point or stable frame of analysis soon becomes unstuck by Pynchon's radical rendering of doubt. As a consequence, the classically trained reader soon becomes lost in a seemingly meaningless universe, which nevertheless promises a possible revelation. The text manipulates us into becoming an extradiegetic version of Oedipa herself, looking for clues which will explain our immersion-in-flux. "You could waste your life that way," says Oedipa, "and never touch the truth" (Pynchon 1990: 80).

This is a pertinent point in the so-called "post-political era" of nihilistic relativism, for there is little doubt that Pynchon is the godfather of the current generation of paranoiacs and conspiracy theorists who, ironically or not, believe in the *X-Files* slogan that "The Truth is Out There." Often linked with science fiction writers such as Philip K. Dick, Samuel Delany, and – more recently – Neal Stephenson, Pynchon's metafictional approach to writing destabilizes any kind of semiotic certainty. Of course, postmodernists were not the first to question the reality behind appearances – and metafiction was practiced at the dawn of the novel by Laurence Sterne; however, this new generation of writers set the precedent for wallowing in such uncertainty by dismantling formalistic "structures of intelligibility" (Bennett 1985: 32). Gone is the internal angst of a Beckett, Sartre, or Dostoevsky character, replaced by the ironic parody of modernist detachment.

Moreover, Pynchon's spectral presence – along with his frequent references to an overarching *plot* – emphasizes the complicit relationship between fiction, metafiction, and the desire to sculpt this chaotic universe into some kind of order (along with all the ethical and political baggage that such a desire carries with it). His work, therefore, both laments and celebrates the loss of any stable basis for epistemological verification. In doing so, Pynchon ironically pre-empts the genuine contemporary passion for conspiracy theory, a temptation which Jameson has described as "a degraded attempt ... to think the impossible totality of the contemporary world system" (Jameson 1991). Agent Fox Mulder is therefore a child of Pynchonian aesthetics; a pop-culture icon who sincerely seeks the truth, and yet simultaneously winks at an audience hungry for more false revelations. For this reason, there is no aesthetically satisfying closure at the end of *The Crying of Lot 49*, and it provocatively avoids any attempt to explain the riddles of the narrative. It doesn't finish – it simply stops.

I have signaled Pynchon's use of parody to destabilize not only the reader's relationship to the text, but the text's relationship to itself, and to any kind of production of meaning. Let us therefore return to the remaining terms in the three *P*s of postmodernism: pastiche and paranoia, beginning with the former. Postmodern texts, whether they be books, artworks, or architecture, often borrow from both the realist and modernist modes of representation, frequently switching randomly from one register to the other. They do so in order to produce "radically indeterminate texts which foreground the illusory nature of all interpretative constructs" (Bennett 1985: 32). (A "progressive knotting into," in Pynchon's anti-Gordian language.)

Where the modernist relies on "detachment, awareness and observation," the postmodernist exploits "complicity, doubt and participation" (McHale 1986). Likewise, the former unveils "reality" through the technique of multiple perspectives, whereas the latter negates the very notion of a shared reality through multiple ontologies. (In a different context it would be fruitful to further unpack these notions in relation to both Derrida's notion of *différance* and Lacan's greasing of the Real; see Berressem 1993).

In 1973, Pynchon published *Gravity's Rainbow*, which has been read as a pastiche of canonical texts such as *Moby Dick*, *Don Quixote*, *Commedia*, *Gargantua and Pantagruel*, *Ulysses*, and indeed, the hubristic designs of litera-

264 Dominic Pettman

ture (and literary criticism) in general (see Newman 1986). This book took the thematic concerns of his previous novels and inflated them into a gigantic, sprawling, bubblegum-baroque *magnum opus*, which seemed to push "the new Uncertainty" to its limits (Pynchon 1975: 302). Where Joyce created one of literature's most complex and convincing characters in Leopold Bloom, Pynchon invented Tyrone Slothrop – a character whose costumes and qualities change so often that he eventually evaporates altogether. Joyce created a diegetic universe which discredited the various grand narratives which had hitherto given European culture a certain amount of coherence. Pynchon produced a master text which refuses the very notion of mastery.

Continuing where *V* left off, *Gravity's Rainbow* traces the symbolic and apocalyptic trajectory of Germany's V2 rocket into an era obsessed with the technical fusion of sex and death. Between the ominous launch and final descent into "terminal orgasm," Pynchon presents us with a Disney-meets-Bosch panorama of European politics, American entropy, industrial history, and libidinal panic which leaves a chaotic whirl of fractal-patterns in the reader's mind. Such technical excesses prompted one reviewer to state that Pynchon creates "a concatenated jigsaw puzzle" rather than "an esthetically coherent literary structure" (Locke 1973). But as we have seen, this demotion of formal control is a sign of the postmodern text, which joyfully abandons the modernist's desire for God-like control of his or her material. Pynchon is not evoking a new language to express unprecedented perceptions, but ambivalently regurgitating the deafening noise of cultural feedback.

And yet, there is a remarkable subterranean symmetry to *Gravity's Rainbow* – a structural logic which, once again, constantly teases the reader into making some sort of sense of events as they unfold. Sudden jumps in perspective, narrative voice, tone and genre, are all designed to disorient. These "palimpsested" excursions into the archive, however, promise an imminent rescue for the reader, for they provide decoy lifebuoys in the guise of genealogical precedents. But while Swift, Faulkner, Melville, Rilke, and Eliot have all been invoked to provide a conceptual grid for understanding the millennial epic of *Gravity's Rainbow*, the elliptical trajectory of the narrative continually foils convenient symbolic equivalences (for instance, the V2 rocket does and does not perform the same function as the great white whale).

What makes this novel postmodern, in contrast to its literary forebears, is its ventriloquistic approach to intertextuality. Indeed, Pynchon's penchant for pastiche displays a particularly acute form of his generation's compulsion for quoting artistic antecedents. (At one point in the story, Slothrop even begins to hear quotation marks when people are speaking to him [241].) Critics have also pointed out the novel's mimetic debt to the cinema, not only in its continuous reference to the movies, but also its metaphoric utilization of filmic techniques (jump-cuts, splicing, close-ups, freeze-frame, etc.). *Gravity's*

Rainbow itself – that is, the actual book the reader holds in his or her hands – is an exercise in low-tech, high-cerebral multimedia.

Indeed, this blending of different discourses is where Pynchon transcends the modernists who preceded him. In assimilating not only the styles of former literary periods (Jacobean drama, detective fiction, eighteenth-century rhetoric, quasi-Biblical parables, etc.) but the vocabularies of the sciences and industry (Pynchon studied physics and engineering in addition to English at Cornell), *Gravity's Rainbow* dissolves the ideological distinctions between the humanities and technology. Critic Peter Cooper claims that Pynchon's "profound and varied use of science may be his most important contribution to contemporary letters," allowing Pynchon to set the tone for such postmodern offshoots as cyberpunk, and other panicky reflections on the technological penetration of self and society (Cooper 1983: 111).

As a result – and perhaps more than any other writer of fiction – Pynchon has most exhaustively covered the hyperreal terrain mapped by postmodern prophet Jean Baudrillard. His entire oeuvre addresses the conflict which occurs when the opacity of the sign collides head-on with "the transparency of evil." Indeed, Pynchon's early enthusiasm for the work of Marshall McLuhan has influenced his depiction of human interaction with machines, and the exponential alienation which can result from an age where "reality" seems like the industrial waste-product of an omnipresent media. Simulacra are everywhere in Pynchon's novels, prompting the postmodern crisis of knowledge, representation, and agency, and finally leading back to Oedipa's flirtation with solipsism: "Shall I project a world" (Pynchon 1990: 82).

In *V* people hot-wire their brains to televisions, have sex with cars, and eroticize prosthetics, anticipating the techno–organic excesses of Burroughs, Ballard, and Cronenberg. The unifying principle in these proto-cyberpunk passages is paranoia, the third term in our three *P*s, and the word which will forever be associated with Thomas Pynchon. All of his work describes the bureaucratic web in which the subject now finds him- or herself enmeshed, and dramatizes Foucault's insights into surveillance, control, and the panopticon: "that city of the future where every soul is known, and there is no place to hide" (Pynchon 1975: 566). The lesson of *Gravity's Rainbow* is, therefore, that we all inhabit Deleuze's technocapitalistic interface between paranoia and schizophrenia.

Paranoia is rampant in The Zone, a *mise-en-abîme* for *Gravity's Rainbow*'s shell-shocked aesthetics, as well as the nerve-shredding suspense of Cold War deterrence theory, and the cruel inevitability of cultural thermodynamics. It is also a surreal territory mapped onto the contemporary moment: an era which has discovered that (to quote Robert Musil) "pseudo-reality prevails." The Zone therefore represents the not-Kansas of liminality: an in-between state of limbo and inversion which now permeates those areas of life once deemed "normal." It is here that Pynchon most flexibly exercises his mandate to "junk cause-and-effect entirely, and strike off at some other angle" (Pynchon 1975: 89). And it is here that entropy – another key word in Pynchon's universe – holds sway.

The temptation when talking about Pynchon, as the above may illustrate, is to indulge in the buzzwords of postmodern lingo, which have become "as comfortable and familiar as a worn-out couch in a graduate student lounge" (Scott 2000: 42). It is important to note, however, that Pynchon's radical interrogation of contemporary confusion also represents an explicitly political extension of postmodern aesthetics: the rejection of officially sanctioned discourses, the suspicion of ethical imperatives to conform to normative behavioral models, and the revision of History as a master-signifier which dictates concrete facts and corresponding moral lessons. (The cause-and-effect of secular sense-making systems, he tells us, is merely a "diversionary tactic" [Pynchon 1975: 167].) These concerns – which were always present in Pynchon's heretical underground movements – have become more prominent in his two most recent works, *Vineland* and *Mason & Dixon*. The former explores the legacy of the 1960s counterculture in the Reagan – Orwellian 1980s, and the latter traces the geohistorical fault-line carved through the heart of America. Both express a keen awareness of mundane political realities; an awareness which previously lay just beneath the surface of his earlier works.

Thus, to relentlessly emphasize the chaos and confusion of his work is to neglect Pynchon's erudite celebrations of the colloquial, the ironic, and the darkly absurd; all filtered, of course, through the dominant influences of his time – jazz, rock 'n' roll, drugs, and the acceleration of the great American spectacle. Indeed, the passing years have proved that Pynchon is not merely the navel-gazing, technically gifted craftsman that he is often made out to be, but one of the most perceptive practitioners of a certain kind of reenchantment. In his own words, Pynchon creates "arabesques of order competing fugally with...improvised discords" (quoted in Wood 1984).

Like the enigmatic V2 rockets that threaten The Zone, Pynchon's unpublished books buzz both menacingly and enticingly over our heads – sometimes for decades. Even now, somewhere on the globe, there is a cultish-fan or literary critic with a reverse-Pavlovian pup-tent, salivating with the unconscious premonition of impact. Only after Pynchon's next book actually explodes, however, will we hear it approaching.

43

Robert Rauschenberg

John G. Hatch

In 1953 Robert Rauschenberg (b. 1925) acquired a drawing from the American Abstract Expressionist painter Willem De Kooning. He then spent a month diligently erasing the markings and eventually presented to the public the infamous *Erased De Kooning Drawing* (1953: Collection of the Artist). Although commonly seen as an attack on De Kooning's work and that of his fellow Abstract Expressionists, whose dominance of the American art scene by the 1950s may have seemed overbearing for a young artist, the piece was meant to be a point of departure rather than an effacement or eradication of the immediate past. In fact, Rauschenberg admired the work of De Kooning, who, of all of the Abstract Expressionists, was the one closest to sharing some of the objectives Rauschenberg strove for in his own pieces. The gesture of erasing the work marked a reopening of the visual field, a move away from the convention of closed meaning suggested by a "finished" work, ironically a drawing in this case, and introducing an infinite realm of possibilities or action (Zweite 1994: 21–2). In turn, "meaning" is shifted from the controlling hand of the artist to the mind of the viewer; the finished drawing would have inevitably been prescriptive, the viewer would have attempted to "divine" what De Kooning was trying to say with the various markings which would have unmistakably been his own. As for the erased work, can one really say that it is a "Rauschenberg"? Can one actually speak of an author or maker since what "author" there was, has been erased? Rauschenberg has not so much made as unmade a work which carries no traces of his hand as maker of an image in any traditional sense. There is no image and all that remains of any image has to be recreated by the viewer either in the form of attempting to imagine what De Kooning's drawing may have looked like or mentally recreating Rauschenberg's action: an action which we all could have undertaken. To complicate matters further, how does one classify this work in terms of medium? Is it a drawing when, other than the paper, it bears none of the characteristics that would allow it to be classified as a drawing? As with most of Rauschenberg's work, this piece does not concern itself with the notion of the integrity of the medium that would be one of the hallmarks of Clement Greenberg's burgeoning modernist aesthetics.

The *Erased De Kooning Drawing* introduces us to most of the issues Rauschenberg's work addresses. An important aspect of his work is a move away from the realm of prescriptive idealism to a more direct, less interpretative engagement with reality on the part of the artist. Rauschenberg's "White Paintings" of 1951 address the modernist heritage of the monochrome work as an absolute and utopian philosophical statement that dates back to Kazimir Malevich's famous "White on White" series of 1917–18. Where the Russian painter saw the move toward the pure white canvas as a nonobjective presentation of the evolution of human consciousness to a pure spiritual state of existence, Rauschenberg takes the canvas and uses it as a field which records the shadows of the viewer facing the work, essentially reversing key aspects of the Malevich works. The "White Paintings" act as "receptor surfaces," to use Leo Steinberg's term, which embrace what Rauschenberg saw as the ephemeral and chaotic quality of the world around us (Steinberg 1972: 84). Again, the issue of authorship emerges in that Rauschenberg painted the canvases, but the images and or meaning are generated by the viewer, not the artist. Similarly, one could question the authorship of Rauschenberg's *Automobile Tire Print* (1953), which involved the American composer John Cage driving his Ford Model A, with its tires inked with black house paint, along 22 feet of attached sheets of paper; but again, the point for Rauschenberg is one of the artist engaging in a dialogue with the world around him rather than dictating his impression of what the world should be. In other words, he sought to shift the emphasis from the traditional view of the author as the manufacturer of an interpretation of reality to one of the artist generating opportunities to make us more self-aware or self-conscious of the world surrounding us and our role as participants in understanding it.

Reality emerges in a tangible way in Rauschenberg's "combines," a group of works begun in the mid-1950s that can loosely be defined as sculptural and are constructed using common everyday objects. They represent another step toward fulfilling Rauschenberg's desire to have his works "look more like what was going on outside the window" (Taylor 1990: 146). By using common objects such as table legs, beds, and light bulbs, the combines allow a greater level of interpretative accessibility to the viewer and thus, as Rauschenberg put it, "give the spectator a far more active role" (cited in Spector 1997: 233). However, one has to use the term "interpretative" rather loosely since having such familiar, everyday objects present in an art work obviously changes their meaning, although at times Rauschenberg undermines even this by having some of his everyday objects still retain their original function, incorporating, for instance, light bulbs that can be switched on.

Rauschenberg's combines invite viewers to engage with the work on more familiar terms and through the apparent randomness of assemblage of the combines we are prompted to draw out our own interpretation rather than to try to figure out what Rauschenberg himself is attempting to say. This is reinforced, obviously, by Rauschenberg's conscious effacement of himself in these works and subsequent ones. The plainness of the objects eludes a reading tied to the maker of the combine. In turn, the placement of the objects fails to suggest any hierarchical relationship that might imply a specific narrative. Oddly enough, paint is used in the combines and applied with a brush, seemingly conceding to the idea of the gestural mark as an inevitable recorder of the personality of the artist, yet the paint is applied in a simple and matter-of-fact manner that undermines this idea. Also, the colors used tend to be muted, probably as a result of Rauschenberg's dissatisfaction with the fact that his early painted pieces *led* some viewers to associate certain psychological states with the colors, and he wanted to avoid such associations at all costs (Krauss 1997: 209; Brown 1997; 270). So why use paint in the first place? In part, Rauschenberg challenges himself in trying to undermine our conventional understanding of the role of paint in art by playing on our expectations – i.e., of the painted mark as a recorder of an artistic sensibility – and subtly undermining them in a way that serves to strengthen the purpose of his work. In turn, the painted strokes act as a controlling device that levels many of the elements found in the work, thus erasing or neutralizing potential hierarchies or narratives within the work (Feinstein 1990: 45–6). With characteristic succinctness, John Cage summarized what is going on in the combines: "There is no more subject in a combine than there is in a page from a newspaper. Each thing that is there is a subject. It is a situation involving multiplicity." He concludes that "Perhaps after all there is no message" (Cage 1961: 102).

In 1962 Rauschenberg, inspired by the example of Andy Warhol, began a series of silkscreen paintings which moved from the use of real objects in the combines to working with photographs taken from various sources. This change in practice resulted partly from Rauschenberg's growing awareness of how important a role images play in contemporary society, whether they are absorbed via the print media or television. Although it could be argued that moving from physical objects to images as material for his work signals a move away from his works, embodying the life he wished they could somehow capture, Rauschenberg felt that images were just as much a part of the reality we function in as objects are: "I was bombarded with TV sets and magazines by the excess of the world. . . . an honest work should incorporate all of these elements, which were and are a reality" (cited in Kotz 1990: 99). But he stopped making combines also because he felt he was becoming too familiar with the process involved in making them and, thus, controlled or directed meaning was beginning to inadvertently appear (Feinstein 1990: 21).

The silkscreen paintings continue to engage with the banal in that they use predominantly images of everyday objects. This use of image rather than object shifts our attention away from the literalness of reality to our interpretation of it. In other words, more emphasis is placed on how we conceptually make sense of reality rather than on the artist's physical engagement with it, which is what the combines inevitably evoke in their use of objects rather than images. In the choice of images and their arrangement every effort is made on Rauschenberg's part to allow as open an interpretation as possible. In terms of the images themselves, Rauschenberg observes: "I prefer images that are less specific so that there is room for everyone's imagination" (Rauschenberg 1987: 77). Some images might appear to indicate a singular reading, like that of John F. Kennedy, yet this type of image simply reinforces the unique experience of each viewer when faced with a Rauschenberg painting. For example, most of those who remember the Kennedy assassination recall vividly where they were and what they were doing, yet there will be no two people who will share exactly the same memory of how they felt when they received word of the event. In a sense, the event may be shared but the personal situation and reaction to it will be unique.

The openness to interpretation of the images selected by Rauschenberg is complemented by their nonhierarchical, or "non-sequential" as he put it, presentation on the canvas. This is what he admired in the work of Leonardo da Vinci, as he noted in a 1961 interview:

> One of the great paintings that left a mark on me is Leonardo's *Annunciation* in Florence. In that canvas the tree, the rock, the Virgin are all of equal importance. There is no gradation.... It was Leonardo da Vinci's *Annunciation* that provided the shock which made me paint as I do now. (Cited in Feinstein 1990: 3)

One of the most remarkable aspects of Rauschenberg's silkscreen paintings is his efforts and ability at further undermining any fixed reading/relationship between the various components presented. As with the combines, the application of paint plays a key role as a leveler of the imagery and any possible hierarchical reading it may engender. Uncontrollable factors such as the legibility of the screened images and the application of color in the screening process do the same. Even his use of calendars assists in this equalizing process: one might view the calendar as an armature for structuring experience, but Rauschenberg undermines this possibility by affixing calendars on some of his silkscreen paintings for the following rather than the current year. Ultimately, Rauschenberg's images are simply presented with no attempt at suggesting a causal link between them or, as he put it in his 1963 text "Notes on Painting": "The concept I ... struggle to deal with ... is oppoed [*sic*] to the logical continuity ... inherent in language ... and communication. My fascination with images ... is based on the complex interlocking of disparate visual facts ... that have no respect for grammar" (cited in Feinstein 1990: 76).

A Rauschenberg work has no beginning or end, no syntactical rules holding the whole together, no pattern directing its form of expression. In fact, Rauschenberg relished as an advantage of the visual arts that there were substantially fewer rules of composition than for written language. He even attempted in two of his published texts, "Notes on Painting" and "Random Order" (both 1963), to loosen the presentation and understanding of language by generating "text" in the form of a visual collage. In a manner akin to Dada collage, photomontage, and optophonetic poetry, Rauschenberg provides a significant number of potential readings depending on where one chooses to start and where one goes next in terms of the various details presented. Each component's possible reading is constantly modified as it is followed by another and then the whole changes yet again when one moves on to the next detail. As Rauschenberg himself notes in "Random Order," "every step is change" (Krauss 1997: 209–10).

Ultimately no two people will emerge with the same reading of Rauschenberg's silkscreen paintings since they mean to elude any singular interpretation or meaning. Rauschenberg certainly does not want to claim that meaning is impossible to find in his works, since the minute one attempts to make sense of a piece, meaning is inevitably generated or created; but it is of a wholly personal nature based on one's own experiences. As he notes:

> I don't like explaining the whys of what I do because I think that robs the unique experiences and eliminates or makes it difficult for somebody to have an independent reaction. For example, in 1949 I said if somebody knows what something else means then the physicality and the actuality and the responsibility of the viewer dies. (Cited in Stuckley 1997: 32–3)

Rauschenberg does not impose his sense of things, or at least tries not to, he simply provides the viewer with the tools and a forum of interpretative activity. This objective is similar to that of the Merce Cunningham Dance Company, with whom Rauschenberg collaborated and for whom he worked in the 1960s; as Steve Paxton, a dancer with the company, explained:

> A Merce Cunningham Dance Company performance is a well-orchestrated noncollaboration. The thesis is that the music, the dance, and the décor each exists on its own unique terms, and they are shuffled into the experience of the audience, each "hand" being unique. (Paxton 1997: 261)

Shortly after he stopped producing silkscreen paintings in 1964, Rauschenberg himself would, make a number of important pieces that would literally be activated by the viewer.

It is probably not surprising, as Andrew Zweite points out, that Rauschenberg's silkscreen paintings began at the time of the publication of Umberto Eco's *Opera aperta* (Milan, 1962), where the latter's notion of the "open work of art" involving a field of possible interpretations and the viewer as a co-producer of the work echoes closely Rauschenberg's own notions on art making (Zweite 1994: 42). It is an idea which a number of artists at the end of the 1950s were beginning to address, many of which Rauschenberg either knew or knew of. In 1961, Rauschenberg published an article on the work of his friend, the Swedish painter, Öyvind Fahlström, and his description of Fahlström's objectives neatly sums up those Rauschenberg strove for as well:

> The logical or illogical relationship between one thing and another is no longer a gratifying subject to the artist as the awareness grows that even in his most devastating or heroic moment he is part of the density of an uncensored continuum that neither begins nor ends with any decision of his.
>
> I recognize the acceptance of this fact in the work of Fahlström whose characters in a plot of painting can take any shape, responding to the openly established dramatics of the picture map. They are free to operate, cooperate, incorporate, collide or collapse, always responding locally without a tasteful sense of the compositional 4 sides of the canvas, which seems to serve only as a sheet of paper needed to record any information. . . . The use of the familiar is obscure, the use of the exotic is familiar. Neither sacrifices completely its origin, but the mind has to travel to follow just as the eye has to change to focus. In the end a viewed painting has been an invitation not a command. (Cited in Feinstein 1990: 76)

44

Ishmael Reed

David G. Nicholls

Ishmael Reed is an indefatigable writer of letters to the editor. American English has many words to describe people like him: "crackpot," "crank," and "kook" come to mind. These people are often accused of paranoid delusions, grandiose fantasies, and a general inability to deal with reality. Reed has not escaped such criticism. But, given his frequent invocation of the trickster figure in his writings, it is difficult to believe that Reed is not keenly attuned to the critical potential of the crackpot's stance. One might even say that the figuration of the author as a cantankerous reader pervades his oeuvre; certain of his writings, such as "The Atlantic Monthly, 1970" (a poem in the form of a letter to the editors), take up this role directly. In nine novels, five collections of poetry, four collections of essays, and numerous works in other genres, Reed has developed a body of work in which he persistently rereads and rewrites the myths and forms of America. His writings proceed from the assumption that the United States is, and always has been, a multicultural society; he draws broadly on popular, folk, and oral sources in American cultures. Reed often engages popular genres such as the Western or the detective novel, unsettling their formulae through parodic reappropriation: "When the parody is better than the original a mutation occurs which renders the original obsolete. Reed's Law" (1989 [1978]: 248). Although Reed identifies with his Irish, Cherokee, and African-American ancestors, he knows that in the US his blackness carries the greatest symbolic weight; he devotes considerable attention to the problem of black masculinity in his art and in his arguments. But this does not prevent him from parodying the masculinist slave narrative genre, as he does in *Flight to Canada* (1976). He relies less than others on the notion of a black literary tradition, preferring instead to draw on a new range of historical references in order to create a multicultural "mutation" of mainstream American culture. His works can be read as dissenting letters to the media establishment in contemporary America.

As such, Reed's writings exemplify many of the characteristics of postmodernist literature. They are parodic, self-reflexive, and ironic, and frequently mix popular culture with high cultural sources. His works trouble the universalist discourse of modernity by introducing the partial, different voices of otherness. Reed's multiculturalism challenges the rationalist logic of Western culture, particularly through his engagement of the syncretic religion of Vodoun. Yet, as we will see, the inexplicable magic of Vodoun does not fully disrupt the expectations for closure reason demands. In many of Reed's works, the forces of his "Neo-HooDooism," hitherto repressed by Western culture, emerge as explanations for narrative events within the autonomous system of his aesthetic. Reed retains the notion of the author as a prime authority, one who defines a dissenting but nevertheless total vision of the world.

Reed's writing career began on the margins of the publishing world. Born in Chattanooga, Tennessee, in 1938, he moved to Buffalo, New York, with his mother at the age of three. At 14, he wrote a jazz column for a local African-American newspaper, the *Empire State Weekly*. Reed would first attract attention for his fiction while studying at the University of Buffalo night school; his English instructor encouraged him to transfer to the day division, where Reed took courses for two and a half years before dropping out and returning to the newspaper. In 1962, he moved to New York City and became part of a circle of experimental writers and journalists. He published his first poems, founded the underground newspaper called the *East Village Other*, and taught a prose workshop at St. Mark's in the Bowery. Upon publication of his first novel in 1967, he moved to Berkeley, California, where he taught at the university and discovered greater artistic freedom than he had felt in New York; he has remained in the Bay Area ever since. Despite his successes with commercial publishers (Doubleday, Random House, and Atheneum, among others) and his affiliation with a major university, Reed has continued to be active in the alternative and small press communities. He has co-founded several literary magazines and presses and the multiculturalist Before Columbus Foundation. Thus Reed critiques mainstream forms and publishers from within while also creating new institutions and aesthetic possibilities on the margins.

We might read his shuttling between the center and the margins of the institution of literature as a model for understanding his critical engagement with the possibilities of postmodern writing. As David Mikics has argued,

> Reed's work suggests how African-American tradition, which generally – not always, but generally – wants to depict the survival of a people and a culture in its original, authentic strength, can be reconciled with postmodernism. (1991: 1)

Mindful though he is of the black writers who have come before him, Reed is not drawn toward the project of creating a redemptive black tradition to parallel that of American literature more generally. "Being a colored poet," he writes in "Jacket Notes," "Is like going over/Niagara Falls in a/Barrel"; he concludes that "what really hurts is/You're bigger than the/Barrel" (1989: 130). Resisting the problematic containment of becoming a "colored poet," he does not use the model of the central institution to create a supplementary institution from the margins; as he stated in an interview with Reginald Martin, "When I say Afro-American aesthetic, I'm not just talking about us, you know. I'm talking about the Americas... The West's Afro-American aesthetic is multi-cultural – it's not black" (Martin 1984: 180). Instead, Reed looks toward a neglected belief system of the African diaspora – VooDoo – for the source of his aesthetic practice, which he dubs "Neo-HooDooism." In VooDoo, he discerns a set of religious practices deriving from African cultures and continuing as a subversive presence in the Americas. Reed's early prose poem, "Neo-HooDoo Manifesto," explains:

> The reason that HooDoo isn't given the credit it deserves in influencing American Culture is because the students of that culture both "overground" and "underground" are uptight closet Jeho-vah revisionists. They would assert the American and East Indian and Chinese thing before they would the Black thing. Their spiritual leaders Ezra Pound and T.S. Eliot hated Africa and "Darkies." (Reed 1989: 20)

In contrast to the high modernism of Pound and Eliot, Reed projects an aesthetic of syncretism in which forms, figures, and temporalities are transmuted: Mikics observes that "he creatively and successfully exploits a particular African-American subculture in order to invent his own brand of critical postmodernism" (1991: 4). As "Black Power Poem" suggests, conjuring up a Neo-HooDoo aesthetic enables an oppositional practice with an African-American inflection:

> A specter is haunting america – the spectre of neo-hoodooism.
> all the powers of old america have entered into a holy alli
> ance to exorcize this spectre: allen ginsberg timothy leary
> richard nixon edward teller billy graham time magazine the
> new york review of books and the underground press.
>
> may the best church win. shake hands now and come
> out conjuring. (Reed 1989: 19)

Reed's Neo-HooDoo aesthetic is well exemplified in his most-anthologized poem, "I Am a Cowboy in the Boat of Ra." As the title indicates, the speaking subject of the poem adopts multiple personae from a vast historical range. The cowboy, that quintessential figure from the Western frontier in American history, is also (principally) Horus, son of the Egyptian Osiris. Osiris, a black fertility god who introduced agriculture and respect for civil and divine laws in Egypt, was sacrificed by his brother, Set; Horus returns to avenge his father's death and to restore order. Reed figures the avenger as a cowboy, and also as Vodoun figure Loup Garoo, an African priest, and a gangster. These changing personae are the faces of the specter of neo-hoodooism that are being exorcised in "Black Power Poem." The cowboy in particular is the avenger who will bring back all that has been repressed through a "holy alliance" (Reed 1989: 19) best exemplified by Cardinal Spellman, whose words on the exorcism of the devil are featured in the poem's epigraph. Reed's puns and shifts of historical register, as when jazz musician Sonny Rollins is noted for "the ritual beard of his axe" (Reed 1989: 17) because his saxophone resembles a hieroglyph's beard, draw connections between ancient Egypt and contemporary black culture in the Americas. These connections are figured in the terms of New World syncretism rather than as a lineage per se. As Shamoon Zamir observes, "it is in his vertiginous blend of New World religion and an Emersonian mythology of Americana that Reed discovers weapons for his Mental War against cultural exclusionism" (1994: 1223). Reed eschews the confessional lyric voice, which many black writers have used to present testimony on the history of their oppression. Instead, Reed's personae dramatize a "struggle for mastery between satire and prophecy" (Zamir 1994: 1206) through which a more active, self-generating hero may emerge.

The thematics of HooDoo pervade his fiction, beginning with his first novel, *The Free-Lance Pallbearers* (1967). Reed engages the heroic possibilities of the cowboy again in his second novel, *Yellow Back Radio Broke-Down* (1969). Here, the hero is Loop Garoo (literally, a werewolf), a black cowboy who uses VooDoo to battle against the forces of conformity. The latter are represented chiefly by the character of Drag Gibson, a decadent white landowner; they are also represented by Bo Shmo (a black social realist who maintains a prescriptive Black Aesthetic) and the Pope. The novel's title suggests the way in which Reed addresses genre: the yellow back (a term for the Western) is broken down through an oral (radio) performance, here a tall tale that begins its address to "Folks" (Reed 1988 [1969]: 9). Reed breaks down the formula of the Western, which typically features the cowboy hero on the frontier enacting Manifest Destiny, by stretching the limits of logic and temporality expected of realism. Though ostensibly set on the nineteenth-century frontier, Reed has the Indian Chief Showcase rescue Loop from Bo Shmo with a giant helicopter. Beyond anachronism, Reed uses the magical possibilities of VooDoo to further the hero's goals. Loop enters Drag's domain as he is attempting to quash a rebellion by democratically minded children in Yellow Back Radio; in this violent spell, Loop's companion in a visiting carnival troupe, Zozo Labrique, is killed. She is a HooDoo priestess and gives Loop a mad dog's tooth on her deathbed. Loop is expected to use this and his knowledge of spells to avenge her death. This he is able to do, principally by putting a terrible itch on Drag Gibson. Eventually the Pope is called in to diagnose the problem; he recognizes that the power of HooDoo, usually repressed by the church, is in Loop's hands. In this sense, then, VooDoo's disruptive power is brought back into the logical expectations of reason, as the cause of previously unexplained events in the novel. Though Reed's novel breaks down many of the assumptions of the plot of the Western, it also saves the cowboy hero at the end: in a parody of the expected ending of such narratives, he rides (and swims) off into the sunset chasing the Pope's ship.

Reed's interest in breaking down generic expectations continues in his other novels. *Mumbo Jumbo* (1972), for example, features a VooDoo priest as the detective in a mystery novel, and the slave narrative is parodied in his *Flight to Canada*. As Michele Wallace has observed in her essay on "Ishmael Reed's Female Troubles," however,

> these genres have in common their validation of the white male center. Reed attempts to displace only the color of the center (like trying to peel the white off snow!), leaving intact, even confirming, the notion of centers and therefore peripheries. (1991: 149)

In this sense, Reed's work encounters a problem typical of postmodernist writing: the difficulty of finding a way of writing that escapes complicity with the forms of rationality one seeks to critique. As Wallace's title suggests, for Reed this problem arises most prominently around the issue of gender difference. In his nonfiction in particular, Reed opposes the ethnic chauvinism of the white establishment in America along with the ideology of feminism. His complaint that in works by black women "black men are spoiled narcissistic brutes" (Reed 1982: 72) and his frequent characterization of black women as lesbians or insatiable sexpots has drawn fire from feminist critics. Reed returns fire by claiming that he is simply defending a besieged group, a group to which he belongs. In a self-interview, Reed asks himself "why you so mean and hard?" His answer: "Because I am an Afro-American male, the most exploited and feared class in this country" (1989 [1978]: 144). This defensive posture is evidenced in his many essays criticizing the mass media's obsession with portraying the black man as criminal. His resistance to centers is apparent in a prize-winning essay, "American Poetry: Is There a Center?" in which he concludes with a friend that the only center is "in every poet's heart" (1994: 265); as Wallace and others have argued, though, the logic of the center in Reed's heart replicates some of the structural and political aspects of the mainstream masculinist center.

As a cantankerous reader and writer, Reed employs the postmodernist gestures of parody, self-reflexivity, and irony in order to revise the myths and forms of the dominant culture in the US. In so doing, he introduces a voice deriving from his own otherness and from his understanding of the multicultural reality of American culture. Reed persistently shuttles between high and low cultural forms and institutions, attacking the central media establishment through his fiction, poetry, essays, and persistent letters to the editor. Through all of these efforts, Reed's voice emerges as that of the active hero, the cowboy, whom he projects and parodies in some of his works. Reed's reconfiguration of black masculinity around the active hero creates a compelling alternative to the aesthetic possibilities of social realism and confessional writing. But, in his preservation of the author's prime authority around this kind of figure, Reed preserves the logic of a centered voice that provokes, in Wallace's words, his female troubles. Nevertheless, Reed's work presents a powerful, creative response to contemporary American concerns.

45

Richard Rorty

Frans Ruiter

Postmodern thought is characterized by its frontal attack on everything that smacks of "representation." The belief that representation is possible is seen as the last foothold of a metaphysical desire for foundation and for universalism. This anti-metaphysical disposition of postmodern thinking is the result of a self-reflexivity – the self-reflexivity of the philosophy of the subject – carried to its extreme. It seems likely, however, that this uncompromising anti-representationalism, anti-foundationalism, and anti-universalism will turn out to have been only a transitional stage in postmodern theorizing, a stage which felt the need to create a sharp cesura with the modern and with the Enlightenment tradition. In the current phase of postmodern thought the avant-gardist gesture of the clean and complete break (a notion that, incidentally, is also thoroughly modern) would gradually seem to have lost much of its attractiveness. Instead, participants in the debate explore the possibilities of doing justice to both the desire for transcendence and universalism and the penchant for self-reflexivity and permanent critique that are inalienable aspects of the Enlightenment (Bertens 1995: 242–3).

If there is any ground to this idea of a gradual shift of emphasis within postmodern thought, we can see the American philosopher Richard Rorty (b. 1931) as a determined precursor of the later phase. The ambivalences (some would say contradictions) in Rorty's philosophy suggest that exploring new territory is a risky business. This is also suggested by the way his philosophy has been received. His critique of the pretensions of "professional" philosophy has provoked pretty violent reactions (Malachowsky 1990; Farell 1994: 117–46; Saatkamp 1995).

His political position has been attacked by radical postmodern "liberals" as well as by neo-conservatives. Jonathan Culler has accused Rorty of a "complacency [which is] altogether appropriate of the Age of Reagan" (Culler 1988: 55), while Richard Bernstein has described Rorty's philosophy as "little more than an ideological apologia for an old-fashioned version of cold war liberalism dressed in fashionable 'postmodern' discourse" (Bernstein 1991: 249). It is in particular this "fashionable" postmodern discourse that on the righthand side of the political spectrum is regarded with deep suspicion: with his historicism and nominalism Rorty has been seen as contributing to the dissemination of a highly irresponsible relativism that undermined the moral foundation of liberal society.

Rorty's involuntary isolation (the paradoxical fate of many of those who seek the middle) is somewhat ironical since there will not be many philosophers who are as fond of the word "we" as he is. Rorty himself, incidentally, claims to feel more at home in the progressive camp (Rorty 1999: 3–20; 1998a: ch. 4). In some ways, then, he is glad to be attacked by the right: "Fortunately, I have gotten as much flak from the right as from the left . . . Had I not, I would have begun to fear that I had turned into a neoconservative in my sleep, like Gregor Samsa" (1987: 575).

Rorty is a philosopher who again and again tries to bridge the gap between diverse philosophical traditions and schools. But it would be wrong to see this simply as motivated by ecumenical passion. It would seem that Rorty takes a sardonic pleasure in bringing together parties who in no way want to be associated with each other. He appreciates rationalistic and logical philosophers like Quine and Davidson just as much as the obscure *Seins*-philosophy of Heidegger; he appreciates the serious Enlightenment philosopher Habermas just as much as the playful deconstructivist Derrida; and he finds the literary writings of Orwell at least as fascinating as those of Proust. Sometimes Rorty evokes the image of a lonesome alchemist who tirelessly tries to fuse incompatible elements.

In order to clarify the many ambivalences of Rorty's philosophy, I will sketch its historical background. Rorty originally earned his reputation in the analytical tradition. Analytical philosophy had developed out of logical positivism after World War II and had by the 1960s become the dominant philosophical school in the United States. Rorty undeniably made his mark as an analytical philosopher. In 1967 he published *The Linguistic Turn*, which collected analytical texts in a much-used reader. He has ever since remained faithful to this "linguistic turn," that is, the idea that language is the beginning and end of philosophical reflection. However, he would give this turn an extra twist. In his next and controversial book, *Philosophy and the Mirror of Nature* (1979), he offered a radical critique of the metaphysical foundations and the scientific pretensions of the analytical tradition. Still, in spite of its anti-metaphysical message, *Philosophy and the Mirror of Nature* positions Rorty as a worthy heir to logical positivism. However, the anti-representationalism that he now links with that perspective bridges the gap with the hermeneutical tradition of continental philosophy. Just like the logical positivists, Rorty thinks that philosophy has primarily worked at finding illusory solutions to illusory problems. Epistemology in particular – ever since Descartes the heart of philosophy – has been led astray. The problem arose when Descartes identified and distinguished a special realm of the mind, a move that introduced the metaphor of the mind as mirror. Ever since, the mind has supposedly mirrored reality.

Descartes's view of things evokes typically epistemological questions. How can we ever know whether the mind does indeed truthfully represent reality? Does it indeed only mirror or does it distort the real? These problems also troubled the epistemology of analytical philosophy in which "language" substitutes for Descartes's "mind" and "representation" replaces his "mirror." Rorty believes that questions such as the above cannot be answered. There is no Archimedean point of view, no "divine perspective" which allows us to compare the real and its image in the mind's mirror: "there is no way to get outside our beliefs and our language so as to find some test other than coherence" (Rorty 1979: 178).

The solution that Rorty proposes is to simply abandon the metaphor of the mirror so that once and for all the problems of the philosophy of the subject would seem to have been solved. This proposal is provocative because it also abandons truth – the correspondence of knowledge and empirical facts – as our ultimate orientation. We will never touch bedrock and arrive at a position that will allow us to claim that our knowledge truly represents the real: "The notion of accurate representation is simply an automatic and empty compliment which we pay to those beliefs which are successful in helping us to do what we want to do" (Rorty 1979: 10).

After the publication of *Philosophy and the Mirror of Nature* Rorty further explored the consequences of his critique and increasingly moved toward the tradition of American pragmatism, which had been more or less marginalized by the rise of analytical philosophy. From the perspective of a pragmatic, nonrepresentational understanding of knowledge, knowledge is not a means to represent the world but an instrument for coping with it. Rorty's choice for pragmatism is to a certain extent also a daring attempt to avoid the aporias of a frantic postmodern self-reflexivity.

For the pragmatist, to build solidarity (consensus) is more central than to achieve objectivity (truth). All that objectivity could possibly mean is an optimal intersubjective agreement with regard to things: "the desire to extend the reference of the us as far as we can." The difference between (objective) knowledge and (subjective) opinion – a constituent opposition within Western philosophy – thus becomes a difference in degree, not in kind. The pragmatist drops "the traditional distinction between knowledge and opinion, construed as the distinction between truth as correspondence to reality and truth as a commendatory term for well-justified beliefs" (Rorty 1991a: 23–4). According to Rorty the only difference between knowledge and opinion lies in the effort needed to create consent, a view that has provoked the charge that he sets up "mob psychology" as the norm for knowledge. This accusation is not quite justified. After all, "admitting that justification is ultimately a matter of sharing a practice rather than, say, attaining self-evident insights does not make the routine results of ordinary epistemic deliberations a matter of arbitrary choice" (Gutting 1999: 24).

New perspectives are successful if they succeed in attracting sufficient support, if they find social acceptance, and not because they correspond to reality. On this view, a social movement such as feminism did not achieve success because it exposed a masculinist misrepresentation of women, but because it introduced a new discourse with regard to the relationship between men and women and gradually succeeded in finding "increasing semantic authority" for this discourse through the creation of supportive groups – literally, the creation of communities of faith (Rorty 1998b, 202–27).

Usually, logical reasoning and recourse to arguments play a subordinate role in changes of perspective: "Logical arguments are all very well in their way, and useful as expository devices, but in the end not much more than ways of getting people to change their practices without admitting they have done so" (Rorty 1989: 78). The catalysts of moral or intellectual progress are "creative misuses of language," "redescription," the "reweaving" of "web[s] of belief" and the introduction of new metaphors. Poets and prophets are not inferior to scientists in this respect and may even be better equipped for this particular purpose.

This view has provoked a wide range of the most diverse charges. Rorty has been accused of idealism (does he not suggest that reality is a creation of the language within which we happen to live?), of relativism (if there is no reality against which we can check our various conceptions of it, all such conceptions are equally true), of political and moral cynicism (how can he, given his assumptions, refute the worldview of, say, Hitler?), of irrationalism (he rejects the supposedly superior normative power of reason), of radical subjectivism, of immoral aestheticism, of reactionary conservatism. Although he "take[s] refutation to be a mark of unoriginality," Rorty has with a good deal of patience and good humor, and without abandoning his basic views, tried to refute these and other accusations in a long series of articles – collected in *Consequences of Pragmatism* (1982), *Contingency, Irony, and Solidarity* (1989), *Objectivity, Relativism, and Truth* (1991), *Essays on Heidegger and Others* (1991), *Truth and Progress* (1998), and *Philosophy and Social Hope* (1999).

We do find minor tactical adjustments in the line of battle. The tendency toward radical subjectivism of the early work is, for instance, played down (cf. Saatkamp 1995: 191) and in his replies to his critics Rorty distances himself from the notion that the mind projects an image on an in itself indifferent reality. That notion is, after all, not much more than an inversion of the unfortunate metaphor that presents the mind as a mirror of reality. Rorty also rejects the charge of linguistic idealism. He admits that he subscribes to the view that we cannot decide "whether language cuts reality at the joints." But that does not imply that there is no reality apart from the language we use to describe it. The problem, however, is that the "nonlinguistic brutality of facts" does not press one single and correct representation upon us and that we lack the means of tricking nature into giving up its secrets, as Bacon still could believe. The idea that our knowledge corresponds with nature "simply [is] one more variant of the notion that the gods can be placated by chanting the right words" (Rorty 1991a: 80). Because of that, the natural sciences cannot get down to reality's bedrock either. "The notion that some one among the languages mankind has used to deal with the universe is the one the universe prefers, the one which cuts things at the joints, was a pretty conceit" (Rorty 1991a: 80). Rorty even claims that the humanities are more vital to contemporary culture than the sciences.

A curious aspect of Rorty's philosophy is that he would seem to represent a radical variety of postmodernism (anti-representationalism, anti-fundamentalism, anti-universalism, anti-rationalism, historical contextualism, nominalism, and so on), but that, as the net result of this radically disruptive philosophical critique, our conceptions and perspectives do not have to be adjusted, even if they have completely lost their founding. For Rorty the real issue is another (and perhaps final) round of secularization. Just like life simply went on after God had been declared dead (in spite of Dostoevsky's fear that with the death of God everything would be permitted), we will now, too, be perfectly able to live in a world that has been divested of its last remnants of transcendental superstition: of a belief in representation, universalism, foundations.

It goes without saying that the left has seen this position in terms of "complacency" and "quietism." As a matter of fact, Rorty's "therapy" has a double aim, seeking to free us from two "cramps" simultaneously: on the one hand the "cramp" that results from the notion that the values of liberal democracy need founding if it wants to avoid being eroded by relativism; on the other hand the "cramp" caused by the conviction that we need radical social change in order to realize a better, fairer society.

The fact that we cannot found liberalism – as, for instance, the social organization that optimally corresponds to the human condition – does for Rorty not necessarily mean that we are condemned to a social relativism that never touches bottom. No matter how we look at things, relativism is an impossible position. The historicism that becomes inevitable when we give up on foundations and universalism offers a way out of the infinite regression of relativism. We can, after all, adopt modern liberal society as our frame of reference (tolerance, openness, equality, justice, solidarity). Following this line, Rorty again and again refers to "our tradition," "our practices," and so on, presupposing a frame of reference that does not need further legitimation (and would never be able to find it either). Because of this, ethnocentrism is for Rorty not something that we must avoid at all costs, but a natural point of departure. It is, moreover, at least as far as liberalism is concerned, also a final destination. In spite of his thoroughly historicist position, for Rorty history has ended, even if the end he sees is different from Fukuyama's: with Fukuyama the end of history is the more or less reasonable and optimal end of the history of ideas, while with Rorty it is the outcome of pure chance (Rorty 1998b: 228–43). For Rorty the ideals of liberalism are "parochial, recent, eccentric cultural developments," but they also happen to represent "the best hope for the species" and are "worth fighting for" (Rorty 1991a: 208). He is unimpressed by the possibility that this judgment may be based on circular reasoning (in the sense that from the perspective of liberal values, liberal society is inevitably the best of all possible societies). Rorty's ethnocentrism, then, has two central aspects: determination (or, in Heidegger's words, "geworfen sein") and decisionism. We are the product of a specific tradition which determines us and we consciously decide to continue it.

How to combine this self-assured ethnocentrism with the irony that Rorty also thinks is of paramount importance? After all, Rorty's "ironist" – a term he presents within quotation marks – has

> radical and continuing doubts about the final vocabulary she currently uses, because she has been impressed by other vocabularies, vocabularies taken as final by people or books she has encountered; ... she realizes that arguments phrased in her present vocabulary can neither underwrite not dissolve these doubts; [and] insofar as she philosophizes about her situation, she does not think that her vocabulary is closer to reality than others, that it is not in touch with a power not herself. (Rorty 1989: 73)

In order to prevent irony from undermining liberal hope, Rorty radically separates the private from the public. The private realm is the playground of irony and the scene for individual self-realization. It can accommodate the most wayward, sublime, or even anti-liberal views, as long as in the public domain the minimal liberal values – "leaving people's private lives alone and preventing suffering" (Rorty 1989: 63) – are respected. Rorty compares the public domain to a bazaar where all sorts of people are engaged in trading things. Such a bazaar, in which people would "rather die than share the belief of many of those with whom they are haggling" is "obviously not a community in the strong sense of community" – *Gemeinschaft* – as used by communitarians such as MacIntyre and Taylor (Rorty 1991a: 209). After the deals of the day have been concluded, people return to their private domain where they are once again among, for instance, their co-religionists, and feel free to express themselves on others and other perspectives. In other words, Rorty opts for public pragmatism combined with private narcissism and aestheticism. The public is a protective "procedural" layer that must guarantee optimal private freedom. The liberal hope that Rorty so often mentions – "the hope that life will eventually be freer, less cruel, more leisured, richer in goods and experiences, not just for our descendants but for everybody's descendants" (Rorty 1989: 86) – is not so much a way of life itself, but rather an instrument for the creation of optimal conditions with regard to the "good life" as privately defined.

This rigid dichotomy between the public and the private has been rather severely criticized. Serious doubts have been expressed with regard to the supposed neutrality of this liberal public framework *vis-à-vis* the private domain. Does not liberalism privilege certain forms of self-realization at the expense of others (Gutting 1999: 60)? Second, can we assume that the minimal liberal consensus that Rorty seems to find in the public domain is really there? As Bernstein points out, "It is never clear why Rorty, who claims that there is no consensus about competing conceptions of the good life, thinks there is any more consensus of justice or liberal democracy" (Bernstein 1991: 245). Fraser has similar doubts: "Rorty homogenizes social space, assuming, tendentiously, that there are no deep social cleavages capable of generating conflicting solidarities and opposing 'we's.' It follows from this assumed absence of fundamental social antagonisms that politics is a matter of everyone pulling together to solve a common set of problems" (Fraser 1989: 104). Finally, we may well ask if such a rigid separation of the private and the public is at all possible. Private views may very well have public consequences and may easily lead to serious conflicts (as in the case of abortion).

All in all, Rorty presents us with a breathtaking balancing act in which he smashes things in the manner of a Nietzschean philosopher without, however, causing much practical damage. The aim of Rorty's project is not only to show us that so-called philosophical differences do not make much of a real difference, but also to put forward a philosophy of his own that does not make a difference either (illustrating the point that philosophy is simply incapable of making a difference).

Rorty entertains the cheerful belief that all sorts of current oppositions, which we now think of the greatest importance, will gradually simply lose their significance. This does not mean that the arguments that Rorty himself has put forward are free of differences and distinctions, but, unlike the deconstructivists, he has a light-hearted (that is, pragmatic) way of dealing with them. He has little affinity with the grim obsessiveness with which the poststructuralists hunt for binary oppositions which they themselves will never be able to escape and which must be deconstructed for ever and ever in order to avoid the trap of logocentrism. He finds their "knee-jerk suspicion of binary oppositions" (Rorty 1991b: 111) baffling and their critique of logocentrism reminds him too much of another fixation, that upon "Satan and the Forces of Darkness" (1991b: 112).

Rorty's philosophy can be seen as an original and interesting experiment that, moreover, undoubtedly articulates an attitude to life that is widespread in the Western world, and in which a basic political consensus with regard to liberal society is coupled with great tolerance for widely diverse personal projects and genuine sensitivity to the multicultural and postcolonial context. This situation demands a subtle balance between particularity and universality. Rorty does justice to both when he makes a distinction between "agents of love" – the "connoisseurs of diversity" whose contribution it is to make the unfamiliar and strange vocabulary of others intelligible – and the "agents of justice," whom he calls the "guardians of universality." The first category calls our attention to marginalized and repressed groups within society, while the second sees to it "that once [these people] have been shepherded into the light by the connoisseurs of diversity, they are treated just as the rest of us" (Rorty 1991a: 206; see also Hall 1994: 176).

(Translated by Hans Bertens)

46

Salman Rushdie

Eyal Amiran

In postmodern thought, there is no ground, or transcendent foundation, for art or for the voice, the traditional signature of the poet. The modernist artist – say, Stephen Dedalus in Joyce's novels – only dreams of flying the nets of his time and place; as postmoderns, Salman Rushdie says, "we have come unstuck from more than land. We have floated upwards from history, from memory, from Time" (1983: 91). But the past is not lost in postmodernism; rather the relation to it is altered. Paradoxically, Rushdie connects the voice with the ground to articulate this vision of a world without solid ground; he also argues that postmodern art finds a more provisional if functional ground in modern art. Rather than articulating a world without semblance of up or down, order, chronology, Rushdie's postmodern fiction has these qualities – only they are not what they had been in the modern world. Part of that argument is made in Rushdie's work by its apparent echoing of the past. There is no real echo, however, for postmodernism; an echo presupposes an origin which is not itself an echo. To appear as the echo of another voice, however, is to have the only foundation possible, one that is always already spectral. It is only because there is no ground for voice that the voice can exist in the first place.

Other voices help form the groundless ground of the postmodern word. An important such parental voice for Rushdie is James Joyce's. Of particular interest is Joyce's discussion of the ground, which is based on a famous forgery from the New Testament. "Thou art Peter," Jesus says to Peter, "and upon this rock I will build my church" (Matthew 16: 18). The sentence was put into the New Testament in the eighth century to secure the dynasty of the Roman Popes against their competition from the Eastern Church. This shaky ground is doubly the figure for questionable foundations, because it is a pun in Latin ("Peter" means rock); "in the beginning was the gest," as Joyce writes in *Finnegans Wake* (1976: 468): the first thing was already double. In *Ulysses*, forgery is sufficient foundation for art, imagination, belief. From Peter on, a line of fathers, an "apostolic succession, from only begetter to only begotten," leads to the present: "on that mystery," says Stephen Dedalus, "the church is founded and founded irremovably because founded, like the world, macro- and microcosm, upon the void" (Joyce 1961: 207). This foundation cannot be undermined because fatherhood is a "legal fiction" and has no solid facts to stand on.

The rock of modern foundations is a kind of fiction upon which Rushdie builds his work. *Midnight's Children*, his masterstroke (published in 1980), is a kind of "cracked digression" (144), or madness, jokingly full of "stupid cracks" (194). The novel's narrator and purported author, Saleem, is cracking up, literally falling apart as he tells his story (37). Not that modernist fiction thinks of itself as a fiction: it sees itself as a kind of higher truth, whereas for postmodernism the truth is a real kind of fiction. Modernist fiction is a well-built world, where everything is necessary. Joyce, Samuel Beckett has said, mastered all his syllables. For Rushdie the desire for solid ground remains, but its ground is forever lost, as Umeed, the narrator, acknowledges in *The Ground Beneath Her Feet* (1999: 62, 351, 359, 388–9). In that novel, Rushdie's ambitious return to the project of *Midnight's Children*, earthquakes and fault-lines make the ground tremble (130). It is a novel in large part about rock music and musicians. Here "rock" has several meanings, including that of ground. The rock star Ormus Cama finds his work "stolen" by other artists who have never heard of him (96), so that he is accused of forgery. Like Stephen Dedalus in *A Portrait of the Artist as a Young Man*, who "forges" the consciousness of Ireland, Rushdie must forge his own life in *Midnight's Children* (394). Saleem, the mind-reading narrator, confesses to producing "stolen originals" in his class work (204), a phrase stolen, as it were, from *Ulysses*. Ormus Cama's father, too, is found out to have built his professional career on forged documents (Rushdie 1999: 132). The same is true of Umeed, who is a photographer. After a delightful passage that echoes the famous ending of *Ulysses* – "yes because it might as well be me as another so yes I will yes I did yes" (1999: 244) – the narrative confesses its stolen art: "There. Now I've removed my mask, and you can see what I really am. In this quaking, unreliable time, I have built my house – morally speaking – upon shifting Indian sands. *Terra infirma*" (244). For Rushdie's postmodern fiction, to reject the stable rock of foundations is to reject the modern world of control, and control of the world. It is also to be founded on that rejection, and bound to return to it.

If in Rushdie's postmodern view "the world is irreconcilable, it doesn't add up" (1999: 351; see 1983: 267), still our fictions must rely on some distinctions to work. We cannot survive the utter collapse of categories (1999: 388–9), hence the apparent paradox of Ormus's "earthquake songs" which, like Rushdie's fiction, praise chaos in highly sophisticated compositions (1999: 390). Nor is historical fact for Rushdie simply a function of narrative – a position associated with Hayden White (1974) – and has no existence outside telling (Rushdie 1980: 529–30). But it is precisely because there are no ground rules that every place or event is unique (1999: 553–4). The effect of the desire for precision is that abnormality, not the normal, is the rule (500). The problem is not the multiplication of forgeries and fictions, but that there are too many good hard facts (1980: 404). For postmodernism, as Katherine Hayles has argued, facts exist in a field of meaning, as true in relation to other facts valued as true by a given system (Hayles 1984: 15–24). That system is, in effect, what Rushdie's fiction imagines, connecting disparate events by a logic that appears – as it does in Thomas Pynchon's novels – ineluctible (e.g., Rushdie 1980: 334). A series of causes and effects may be deduced, depending on the narrative definition of event, of cause, of effect. The groundless is not incompatible with the evidence of fact, and by that same logic, no fact is just one fact. Every postmodern fact exists in several parallel worlds, as Jorge Luis Borges suggests in "The Garden of Forking Paths."

In *Midnight's Children*, the defining facts of artistic imagination lead such multiple lives. They operate metaphorically, and signify in multiple ways. For example, Saleem, the artist, discovers his power one day as a child hiding in a washing chest (191). He can know things through his nose – both mental and bodily presences – and can converse telepathically with the other children born, like himself, with independent India on the stroke of midnight, August 15, 1947. But that basket image also signifies his vulnerability: later in the novel, his friend Parvati-the-witch hides him by making him invisible and weightless in a basket. The basket is a place of both presence and absence. Another such image in the book is that of the sheet: it appears early in the book as a screen that hides Saleem's grandmother from the doctor, who nevertheless can see her in fragments through a hole in the sheet. It is a cinema screen (197) or peepshow (83–4), both an opaque picture window and a window onto a real world behind the picture. To see representation as opaque, a picture of the world and not a window onto the world, is a discovery of the modern (Ortega 1961); here the screen cannot divide the real from representation, and vice versa. Saleem, too, is double: on the one hand the paradigmatic child (recognized as the child of midnight by the Indian prime minister himself), and on the other the unique father of his own parents (309–10), doomed to invent a line of men as fathers (348). He is the embodiment of the new India, and also "an Anglo" (136), the son of an English man and Indian woman who was switched to new Indian parents at birth. He is and is not himself, as Rushdie puts it. He, like the world around and inside him, is a postmodern fact.

There is another metaphor in Rushdie's work for the connection between postmodernism and its unstable modernist ground: the umbilical cord. Where the rock is a spatial metaphor for foundations, the cable provides a temporal figure for the connection between the present and the past. In *Midnight's*

Children the umbilical cord is said to be buried customarily in the foundations of houses to ensure their success (369–70); but it does not always work, and indeed Saleem's parents' house is demolished (409). This metaphor is itself derived from a metaphor. As Stephen Dedalus thinks in *Ulysses*, the umbilical cord is a physical connection between generations, leading back to human origin: "The cords of all link back, strandentwining cable of all flesh" (38). On this cable, thinks Stephen, one may place a phone call to the first parents. It and not Peter's rock is the best foundation. Rushdie combines the navelcord with the rock – the umbilical in the foundations – but he also makes the telephone–umbilical cable connection. "Yes, it must start with the cable," says Saleem (353). In one of the many rebeginnings of the novel, a telegram arrives from a family servant:

> What the telegram said: PLEASE COME QUICK SINAISAHIB SUFFERED HEARTBOOT GRAVELY ILL SALAAMS ALICE PEREIRA.
> "Of course, go at once, my darling," my aunt Emerald told her sister, "But what, my God, can be this *heartboot*?"
> It is possible, even probable, that I am only the first historian to write the story of my undeniably exceptional life-and-times. Those who follow in my footsteps will, however, inevitably come to this present work, this source-book . . . for guidance and inspiration. I say to those future exegetes: when you come to examine the events which followed on from the "heartboot cable," remember that at the very eye of the hurricane which was unleashed upon me . . . there lay a single unifying force. I refer to telecommunications. (355)

Telegrams and telephones, he goes on, were his undoing (also 362). The reference is to the cable that recalls Stephen back to Dublin in *Ulysses*: "Mother dying come home father" (42). Saleem's "cable," like Stephen's, recalls him home on account of an ancestor, only this time his added ancestor is *Ulysses*, the source-book and inspiration. Rushdie refers to Joyce's telephone cable often in the novel; on one occasion he discusses an umbilical cord, telephone, and the poet's voice on the same page (188). Rushdie's postmodern vision relies on the connection with Joyce to show that history cannot repeat itself: if for Joyce it is tragic, for Rushdie it is farce. Rushdie's postmodernism relies on modernist aesthetics, but the rhetorical effect is to foreground the constructed relation, to acknowledge it, to be undone by it. That undoing is what Rushdie's work does: not, therefore, a real demolition, but the notion that fiction cannot be undone because its doing is in part an undoing. It can never begin but can only rebegin, never have foundations because it is always on the line. Modernist writing approaches its own dissolution when, here and there, it articulates this vision.

For Rushdie, postmodernism speaks with the voice of another. Voice is traditionally a figure for authenticity, for the poet's identity. The ground beneath one's feet is also, for the poet, the voice. Postmodernism finds in the idea (so dear to creative-writing programs) that a poet must find her or his "own" voice a nostalgic desire for an organic ground to art. The narrator in *The Ground Beneath Her Feet*, Umeed, cannot sing except as magpies do, stealing others' words: "I must do the best I can with echoes," he says (1999: 57). His antithesis is Ormus Cama, the rock singer who has the gift of the voice, who is thought to be the greatest singer of all time, an Elvis figure who thinks himself "the secret originator, the prime innovator, of the music that courses in our blood" (89). But he imagines and sings songs that others publish unbeknownst to him, and is mistaken for an echo. He is no magpie, not "just another of that legion of impersonators who first rejoiced in, and afterwards rendered grotesque," the success of others (89). He is the real article, only what is real is redefined, just as the term "rejoice" in this phrase itself echoes Rushdie's connection to Joyce. The voice is the rock, says Umeed (157), but that ground is not *terra firma*: the world of music is the "world of ruined selves," where "damage is the normal condition of life, as is the closeness of the crumbling edge, as is the fissured ground" (148).

Rushdie articulates a vision of postmodernism that does not rely on pastiche (Jameson 1991) or on parody to distance itself from the modern culture, history, literature that precede it. Instead a collection of ground rules, double-edged metaphorical relations importantly taken from his invented parent, Joyce, articulate for Rushdie a systemic condition of groundlessness and authentic inauthenticity. For him every ground rule is at least double. Postmodern art for Rushdie is connected to and based on an older world that has itself invented its own private plot of ground.

47

Cindy Sherman

John G. Hatch

There is not much that is particularly novel about Cindy Sherman's first significant body of work, the *Untitled Films Stills,* that launched her public career as an artist in 1977. They are little more than a series of sixty-nine images portraying female types inspired largely by 1950s and 1960s European films. They are all black and white photographs and the images are, on occasion, poorly constructed so that one can catch a glimpse of some of the technical equipment used in shooting the scene. Yet, these photographs have a disturbing appeal to them and, as one begins to inquire about the various decisions involved in their fashioning, they disclose a manifold complexity which belies their apparent simplicity. A careful examination of the *Untitled Film Stills* (1977–80) reveals a work that engages visually a number of seminal contemporary issues addressed by postmodernist theory.

The *Untitled Film Stills* presents a group of images of women in various scenarios or moments, most of them suggesting a captured instant of unguarded intimacy. Each photograph focuses on a single figure in a claustrophobic setting, intimated either technically through a close-up, cropped photographic shot, or physically by presenting the figure in a constricted space or isolated in a vast open locale. These devices are meant to act as metaphors for a type of psychological entrapment. This is complemented by the powerful voyeuristic appeal of these photographs, generated largely because they offer us private moments of another person's life. This appeal is reinforced by our desire to know more about what is going on. In most of the images the individual is reacting to something which is not given to us. An implied narrative context is suggested by the very nature of the photographs and their intimation that what has been captured is but a fragment or instant in time of some unfolding story; this effect is reinforced by the glances or gazes of the figures. Moreover, the very title of the series suggests that these images have been pulled from a narrative. As such, there is an important temporal element at play here which could not have been managed as successfully were these works presented as a series of paintings. Sherman herself had planned a career as a painter while a student at the State University of New York in Buffalo and her paintings were largely in a realist vein, reproducing images from photographs and magazines (Siegel 1988: 270). However, her contacts with fellow students like Robert Longo, her attraction to film and performance art, and a fascination with dressing up and playing out roles (largely in private for her own pleasure), resulted in her interest in adopting photography as an artistic medium despite her difficulties in learning the technical aspects of it (Siegel 1988: 270–2; Brittain 1991: 34–5). Her initial photographic works were largely laid out as a continuous film strip, but this would be abandoned in favor of the isolated still. The former tends to construct a narrative setting and suggests a particular closed interpretation whereas the latter is far more ambiguous, leaving one to wonder as to the set of circumstances that initiated the response or moment recorded.

Sherman's choice of medium is quite significant. In the 1970s, photography was not overburdened by an aesthetic history as was the case with painting, let alone recent painting in so far as it tended toward the excessive and exclusive modernist formalism that frustrated many artists of Sherman's generation (Crimp 1979: pp. 76–7). More importantly, many of the sources for Sherman's work were largely photographic, whether magazine images or film. Her choice of photography was also predicated on her desire to communicate more directly with non-art-educated viewers; as she noted in a 1983 interview: "I like the idea that people who don't know anything about art can look at and appreciate it without having to know the history of photography and painting" (cited in Danoff 1984: 195). This element of accessibility also explains her decision to draw on European film stars rather than American ones, as the latter tended to be too glamorized, whereas actresses like Jeanne Moreau or Sophia Loren often played working-class women (Siegel 1988: 272). In essence then, for Sherman the appeal of photography rests with the level of identification between the image and the viewer, which opens up these works to a greater level of familiarity than that encountered in "High Art," the more so since Sherman's imagery is derived from a broader cultural spectrum. Eventually, Sherman would tackle "High Art" itself in her famous art history series of 1989–90.

Sherman controls every aspect involved in the making of her images. She is the lighting technician, prop person, photographer, and actor. Although much has been made of this fact, many of the decisions involved in creating Sherman's images are not that different from what a figurative painter would undertake (Guimond 1994: 574–82). The key difference rests with the fact that every character is played by Sherman so that there is an important performative aspect to her work that is quite novel. None of her photographs can be read as a self-portrait in any traditional sense of the term. As Sherman herself points out, one does not get a sense of who she is in these works and she shies away from elements that might imply a particular autobiographical reading; she notes: "What makes it successful is when I suddenly don't sense anything about myself in the image" (Brittain 1991: 37). There may to a certain extent be an autobiographical component, but it is presented under the veil of cultural expectations and role-playing in society, as opposed to the seeking out of an essential self. As we shall see further on, Sherman's later work will begin to tackle the question of where individual identity lies.

Ironically, where Sherman maintains complete control over the staging of her images, she consciously and completely relinquishes the reading of the works to the viewer, assuming the role of a passive author: "I want the photos to tell a story, and want to leave it as ambiguous as possible so that different people will have different stories" (Nilson 1983: 77). In another ironic turn, she takes great care in staging and constructing what are for her essentially social constructs of behavior reflected in the various female stereotypes she presents; she puts herself in the position of artificially representing what is already an artificial construction. Some have argued that this simply serves to reinforce the stereotypes of femininity presented in her works, yet her uses of these stereotypes have no context to feed upon in order to reinforce these types: in other words, the figures may be predictable types but they are not presented in the corresponding predictable situation that is necessary to cliché the type in question (Purand 1996: 54). That operation is left to the viewer, in a sense, and the body of responses to some of Sherman's images has led to the recreation of some rather predictable scenarios which, in the end, reveal more about the viewer than the artist (Williamson 1983: 103). Sherman is sometimes surprised at some of the narrative contexts that have been posited for some of her types which, again, primarily reveal the prejudices we hold; in fact, it is always an interesting exercise to survey the varied responses one gets from individuals of various social classes, generations, and gender to Sherman's work (Kellein 1991: 6). Unfortunately, as flattering as the wealth of literature that has appeared dealing with Sherman's work must be for the artist, too much of it has sought to uncover the ultimate narrative context for the figures as if, in a quasi-modernist fashion, there is one singular reading for each work (Krauss and Bryson 1993: 41; Russo 1994: 9). This runs contrary to Sherman's goal of seeking as open an interpretation of her works as possible, a goal akin to what one finds in postmodernist prose fiction (Guimond 1994: 586).

The absence of context for the figures in Sherman's *Untitled Film Stills* echoes the absence of a singular film reference for any of the "scenes." Although many of the sixty-nine photographs in the series have an air of *déjà vu*, none of them has been drawn from one particular film. Rather, they are composites reconstructed from memory by the artist. There is certainly a subtle element of appropriation at play here but had it been as direct as

Sherman selecting a scene from a particular film and recreating it, then the narrative ambiguity of the images would have been lost. One would have easily filled in the gap with the narrative of the film they were derived from, a gap which is their strength (recalling Ludwig Wittgenstein's note to a potential publisher of the *Tractatus* that the best part of the work was what was not found in it). There is one series of works that Sherman produced that is directly related to a story, namely, the photographs she made to accompany the Brothers Grimm fairy tale, "Fitcher's Bird," but as with many fairy tales the lack of detailed narrative advantages Sherman in generating imagery that can continue the type of riveting and frustrating ambiguity that persists in her other images (Sherman 1992). The point of the *Untitled Film Stills* is that these cultural constructs of female identity exist outside of the film medium, that the medium simply reflects cultural stereotypes that are generally accepted as "natural" (Krauss and Bryson 1993: 25).

The ambiguity of Sherman's *Untitled Film Stills* is closely tied to some of the motivations for their production. Sherman herself points out that these images of women attracted her. She even enjoyed putting on makeup, dressing up, and playing parts – a fascination dating back to her childhood days, something most of us can relate to. I should point out that Sherman's mission is to expose cultural constructs of identity in the broadest terms, including those of men. She even toyed with a few images of men in the film series but confessed that she had to abandon them, largely because she could not get comfortable in the roles she wanted to assume (Danoff 1984: 195). No doubt the construction of female identity is the most evident example of cultural role-production today and is that which Sherman can most easily relate to, although the concerns expressed in her work are meant to go beyond female identity construction. But just as Sherman was attracted to the female roles in film she was equally repulsed by them: "I was really torn between an infatuation with those periods and feeling like I should hate them, because [of] those kinds of role models" (Brittain 1991: 36). She especially notes the frustration of being brought up to observe certain standards of acceptable behavior and then coming into conflict with them as they begin to run counter to one's psychological makeup and urges – the conflict, as Sherman herself put it, between "what we should be and what we really feel in our need to act according to our desires" (Carrillo 1999: 77).

A remarkable twist occurs in Sherman's Rear-Screen Projection series of 1980–1. The works are in color and their source seems to be television rather than film. What is remarkable is the fact that the settings now take on the sense of an artificial construction, reversing what one finds with the *Untitled Film Stills*. In these settings the figures seem more genuine, not stereotypical, and their behavior rebellious. This series was not an extensive one, possibly because the message was too simple and blatant. A more subtle alternative is presented in the so-called Centerfold series commissioned by the magazine *Artforum* (1981). These photographs played on the history of the female centerfold, but rather than presenting a male fantasy image of the feminine, they show moments of troubling vulnerability and psychological unease for both the figures depicted and the viewer. In this series, the figure becomes the focal point even more than in Sherman's previous series, where there is very little in terms of a background setting or context, and the subject is presented close-up. In all, the photographs appear to address the clash between expectation and emotional conflict, between social expectations and one's desires. These are still stereotypes, but they are more generalized, emotional stereotypes (Siegel 1988: 273).

To Sherman's surprise the Centerfold series was turned down by *Artforum*, largely because some felt that they simply reinforced certain stereotypes of feminine behavior rather than undermined them. This may explain the next two series, commonly known as the Pink Robe and Color Test series (1981–2), where Sherman's female characters are shown as much more aggressive and self-assertive individuals, eluding, to an extent, any typecasting (although today the "bad girl" role has become stereotyped just as the "angry young man" role was in the 1950s). This breaking away from the idea of role-playing to one of more "genuine" self-expression and assertiveness is complemented by the dress of the figures and their lack of makeup. As Sherman's visual production progresses there is a growing sense of her attempting to peel away the layers of culturally constructed identity (literally with the removal of the makeup in the Pink Robe series) in order to discover what the "self" is. In the Untitled images that follow the Color Test series, some inspired by fairy tales, one witnesses a growing fragmentation of the self to the point where nothing is left but a heap of broken, disjointed objects, bodily fluids, and traces of apparel used in constructing the self, such as sunglasses. Some of the images almost look like the remains of an exploded body. These images that date from 1985 to around 1989 suggest that the result of peeling the layers of cultural constructions off individual identity is the discovery that there is no such thing as a genuine self. Even the body itself, the focal point of Sherman's work throughout most of her career, becomes objectified in the recent Sex Pictures, where prosthetics take the place of living, breathing human beings. Sexuality comes to stand, as Sherman records in her notebooks, as a symbol for various emotions. In a sense, even the biological component of the self is a cultural construction. It is a frightening conclusion but one which seems inevitable and leaves Sherman wondering where she should take her work next; as she records in a 1994 entry in her notebook: "I'm having a hard time finding a direction to move in" (Cruz and Smith 1997: 184).

48

Graham Swift

Wendy Wheeler

The bourgeoisie cannot exist without constantly revolutionizing the instru-
ments of production, and with them the relations of production, and with them
all the relations of society.... Constant revolutionizing of production, un-
interrupted disturbance of all social relations, everlasting uncertainty and
agitation, distinguish the bourgeois epoch from all earlier ones. (Marx, The
Communist Manifesto)

(Berman 1983: 21)

I think it remains true to say that when people think about postmodernism,
what they will have in mind are ideas of fragmentation, decentering, pastiche,
depthlessness, loss of a sense of history and/or a radical questioning of both
historical narratives (the ways in which histories are told) and also big explanatory stories about humankind's place in the world – as told, for instance, by
Hegel and by Marx. Some of these ideas will be associated with "French
theory," and they will be celebrated by some and deplored by others. Fredric
Jameson's essay, "Postmodernism, or, The Cultural Logic of Late Capitalism" (Jameson 1991), remains a classic of the latter kind, while Linda
Hutcheon's work (Hutcheon 1988), on the other hand, is more positive
about the subversive potential of what she calls "historiographic metafiction"
(knowing or canny writing about history *as* a species of fiction); Patricia
Waugh (Waugh 1995) similarly finds value in the postmodern questioning of
the rationalism and positivism of Enlightenment thinking.

Whether truly subversive or not (and, if so, to what ends – see the epigraph
to this chapter), it seems most helpful to understand postmodernism not so
much as a *critique* of modernity (immanent or otherwise) but, rather, as the
crisis of modernity. For, while the two terms are related, "crisis" suggests
something more random in its products than "critique." In this view, shared
in different ways by, for example, Jean-François Lyotard (Lyotard 1984) and

Zygmunt Bauman (Bauman 1993), the *real* condition of modernity – in which "all fixed fast-frozen relations . . . are swept away . . . [and] all that is solid melts into air" – is actually something like the chaos, relativism, and uncertainty of postmodernity. "Modernity," or at least the contingent modernity of Western culture since the scientific revolution of the seventeenth century, is both the unleashing of uncertainties *and* the attempt to sew up this story – of an increasingly Godless, contingent, and meaningless world – with narratives that will give it some kind of meaning. The strongest of these narratives have been those telling a story of the forward march of human emancipation and scientific progress. We are now in the crisis of modernity which we call postmodernity because we are no longer sure that these stories are true. So the current chaos, relativism, and so on, must be understood as symptoms of an ongoing crisis, not as some kind of progress – which they most certainly are not – to be celebrated.

To live in an unintelligible world is intolerable; people *will* have meaning. In the process of losing one kind of world and meaning, people will seek out others – as the intellectual histories of the West during the eighteenth and nineteenth centuries attest. Symptoms of cultural dis-ease can be understood then as, simultaneously, attempts at self-cure. In Swift's *Waterland* (1983), for example, the allegory of siltation and sedimentation – silt: neither water nor land – is offered both as problem (silt blocks things up; stops canals and stories from flowing) and, when the ceaseless work of reclamation is properly done, as the only ground we can ever have. What we reclaim is not the "real stuff" (Swift 1992) of solid truth; it is the sedimented layers of silt, which are the stories of the Fens and the chapters/lessons of both novel and class.

As science took over from religion as the "truth-language" of the Western world, one of the main stories became that of mastering and penetrating the mysteries of the natural world. The core logic of this language was mathematical rationality; its methods were analytical and empirical. Everything, where possible, was to be reduced to its constituent parts so that its workings could be laid bare – preferably to be understood in terms of physics and chemistry. The overall paradigm was mathematical; thus, when Jeremy Bentham tried to reduce the motivations of men and women to their simplest form, he called the result his *felicific calculus* – a *calculation* of maximum happiness.

But as a strategy of mourning (for this is what people must do when they lose things of vital importance, such as God or Meaning), the focus upon analysis of objects in terms of a narrowly conceived view of rationality was profoundly inadequate. Such a view – and the utilitarian practices which stemmed from it – left out much of what is vital to the richness of human experience. As Raymond Williams's *Culture and Society* (1987) charts, it was largely the Romantics who gave voice to the inadequacies of the "scientific" analytic and reductive view. Nonetheless, and as we know, Romanticism, with its inclination toward the moment of symbolic closure and completion, is not without its own problems. Undoubtedly the most ghastly example of the mix of modern scientific and bureaucratic method and Romantic "closure" is, of course, Nazism and the "Final Solution." After World War II, it became increasingly difficult to remain sanguine about either scientific "progress" or Romantic solutions, and it is in this context which the growing crisis of modernity must be understood.

I have argued elsewhere (Wheeler 1999) that Enlightenment modernity can now be understood as a form of failed mourning: melancholia, to use the Freudian term. The postmodernism of the present consists in the attempt to work through that failure (with its splitting, analyzing, fragmenting character-istics) in order to produce a better mourning and a new, or second, modernity. At the heart of the Romantic critique of utilitarianism, and of instrumental reasoning, lay an argument about the importance of the mysteries of the natural world (including humankind) and a central importance attached to the creative vitality with which a person engages with the task of being a human being. It is, thus, certainly creative to be a poet, but it is equally creative to bake a loaf or fashion a chair; the point is that a human being is a person whose labor – of whatever sort – in the world must be his or her own. The difference between mourning and melancholia is that, in the latter condition, the lost "object" (whether religious or romantic – whatever is seen to "complete," or make sense of, the identity of the mourner) is pre-vented from "leaving" by being introjected or internalized. However, once internalized, it is punished for leaving. Melancholia, thus, takes the form of a splitting akin to the splitting of the ego into ego and superego; the lost object becomes, as it were, a permanently "bad" part of the self. Melancholia is characterized by splitting and self-punishment. Mourning is achieved on the basis that the "completing other" is recognized *as* irreducibly other, and the creative center of the self recognized as living, and thriving without need of "completion" from elsewhere. In personal terms, this means the ending of a kind of narcissism in which the individual needs a mirroring mate (the mirroring mate can be an idea as much as a person) for self-completion, and in cultural terms it means an assent to the importance of creativity (which cannot be rule-bound or calculated) against a calculating reason. The mourner, in other words, recognizes her- or himself as a creative individual who is also part of a whole. Mourning is holistic.

It is in these terms that Graham Swift's work can be understood to be thoroughly postmodern. Swift's work offers an exemplary case of the artist who attempts to come to terms with, and to represent, both the possibility and the difficulty of really mourning modernity's losses such as the loss of traditional forms of knowledge with the advent of the absolutely *new* and the loss of the solaces of a personally revealed God. From the first to the last,

Swift's novels explore the failure of romantic conceptions of meaningfulness –
whether in Hegel's story of history as the gradual unfolding of spiritual
knowledge toward the perfect, mutually recognizing, community, or in romantic art's conception of aesthetic knowledge as offering a moment of healing
transcendence in the mystery of symbolic unity.

The task which, over his entire oeuvre, Swift sets himself is that of
imagining how the self-destructive melancholias of modernity can be turned
into the healthy mournings of something that we might call *post*modernity
understood as a precondition for a *new* modernity. Since what we call the
postmodern seems to consist in the struggle between melancholia and
mourning – between nostalgic turns to the past, and a masochistic sense of
social fragmentations, on the one hand, and the attempt to imagine differently
reconstituted communities and selves on the other – we might say that the
outcome of postmodernity, seen as the attempt to live with loss and uncertainty
as a permanent condition, would be the discovery or invention of ways of
being in the world which move beyond the harsh individualism of utilitarian
modernity, and toward a different way of accounting for and valuing human
needs. It is the problem of inventing an aesthetic form capable of telling us
something about the invention of new cultural, social, and political forms – a
"*new* modernity" or "second Enlightenment" – which drives Swift's work.

In *The Sweet Shop Owner* (1980), Swift addresses the problem of the
romantic ideal of history as telling a particular story which can have a telos
or moment of symbolic fullness and unity. In staging his birthday, intended to
draw his estranged daughter home, as a *tableau mort* deathday, Willy Chapman
believes that a moment of symbolic one-ness will be achieved in which he
"would become history"; we do not find out if it works (the implication is that
it does not), but, by problematizing such romantic closure, Swift sets himself
the task of finding an aesthetic form better capable of matching content to
concern. As in the lessons and siltations of *Waterland*, the form he finds is the
many-layered and more open-ended form of allegory. Thus, with *Ever After*,
and as with other contemporary English novelists such as Peter Ackroyd, A. S.
Byatt, and Marina Warner, different stories and periods interpenetrate and
must be read through each other. At its best, this technique allows the past to
have a particular kind of resonance; in *Ever After*, for example, access to the
past (even the relatively recent past of Bill Unwin's childhood and adult griefs)
is always a question of the stories told. As with the story within the story – of
Matthew Pearce's loss of faith in the 1860s – even that is retrospectively
generated: its truth (and it certainly is true; it is a real crisis of faith) lies in
history only in virtue of two events distant in time and only related by the
fragility of memory. The first had *no* significance (is not a part of a significant
history) until the second. The second is the death of Matthew's beloved infant
son, Felix; the first is the fossil of an ichthyosaur encountered by Matthew

embedded in the Lyme Regis cliffs a number of years earlier. Together they fatally shake Matthew's faith. And if history is as fragile as the words and memories in which it is held, so, equally, is identity (memories and words). The outer narrative of *Ever After* hangs around Bill Unwin's suicide attempt following the separate but recent deaths of his mother, wife, and stepfather. The narrative remains caught in terrible indecision between eros and death. Here again, the novel's ending remains open: does Bill end up successfully killing himself at the end or not? Or, to put it another way, does he remain melancholic, or does he learn to mourn? In *Ever After* the answer to that question hangs on the considerable ambiguities of the novel's one concluding sentence: "He took his life, he took his life." Read positively and erotically – taking as possessing – he lives; read negatively in terms of the punishing death drive – taking as taking away – he dies.

In the Booker prize-winning *Last Orders* (1996), Swift finally comes at the problem of mourning, and making, head on. Drawing on and pastiching both Chaucer's *Canterbury Tales* and Faulkner's *As I Lay Dying*, *Last Orders* tells the story of a pilgrimage – not to Canterbury, but through and beyond Augustine's cathedral city, to the Kentish toe of England at Margate: seedy seaside town and home to the once glorious, now faded, funfair called Dreamland. The pilgrimage, of ordinary London friends from Southwark, is the act of commonplace mourning for the soul (see Wheeler 1999). With this, Swift finds a way of allegorizing both sacred and profane ways of making good.

Along with other contemporary novelists, Graham Swift's work shares many of the features which we recognize as postmodern: self-reflexiveness about history and narrative (historiographic metafiction); the use of pastiche; mutually informing interpenetration of past and present; the fragility of the self and its dependence upon memories which may only retrospectively become significant. Where his work becomes significant in ways not approached by many other postmodern writers, however, is in his pursuit of an alternative to romantic symbolism as closure, and in his perception that modernity (and aesthetic modernism) are entirely tied up in a problem about grief and the need to find healthy forms of mourning. If modern art and literature is about finding a way of symbolizing creative community *after grief* (Wheeler 1995), and postmodernity about finding a way to a new modernity, then Graham Swift is one of the few contemporary novelists to have understood – and, in good part, found a way of giving symbolic breath to – this moment.

49

Gianni Vattimo

Nicoletta Pireddu

In the unmappable and heterogeneous postmodern space that turns theory and practice into blurry and unstable objects of study, the thought of Gianni Vattimo occupies a special place – special for reasons which, from a different perspective, might as well be indicted for not being subversive enough. A leading figure in the Italian intellectual *milieu* and increasingly known in the English-speaking world, Vattimo wants to preserve the identity and operational value of philosophy instead of reducing it to textual "discourse" or to a free play of signifiers, and aims at a coherent conceptualization of the postmodern, adopting analytical tools that the postmodern seems to diagnose as in crisis, or even discard as obsolete.

Vattimo's version of the postmodern does not define an atemporal status, as in the case, for instance, of the figural force of Jean-François Lyotard's incommensurable event. Rather, it refers to a particular moment of Western thought, namely, the end of modernity as "the epoch in which simply being modern became a decisive value in itself" (Vattimo 1992 [1989]: 1) – the epoch in which innovation and originality were the supreme values and in which history was conceived as a unilinear progression toward the realization of the ideal of human perfection. If, on the one hand, the dissolution of history as emancipation gives way to "the liberation of differences" (8), hence to "a multiplicity of 'local' rationalities" (9) which disintegrate our sense of a stable reality, on the other hand, this new condition does not want to forsake the possibility of a rational critique. But how can the postmodern still allow us to propose a theory, a positive philosophy, without giving in to the erosion of thought or falling back into the snares of metaphysical foundations?

Vattimo explores the modalities in which twentieth-century philosophy problematizes its dialectical heritage, as illustrated, for instance, by the impossible reconstruction of a unitary past in Benjamin, the falseness of the whole exposed in Adorno's negativity, or Bloch's utopian ontology of the "not yet," according to which the rationality of history announces itself in human experience instead of having already occurred, as in Hegel. However, according to Vattimo, this tendency toward the dissolution of dialectics "goes no further than substituting 'true' being in place of the one that has been revealed as false" (Vattimo 1984: 156), hence it does not radically question the metaphysical myths of reappropriation and totality. Even more recent positions, however, like the thesis of the collapse of metanarratives in Lyotard's *The Postmodern Condition* (1984), are not exempt from aporias, in Vattimo's view. By simply assuming, as Lyotard does, that we are now in a new condition as a result of the confutation of those systems of historical and rational legitimation upon which modernity founded the explanation of reality, we build precisely another master narrative – Vattimo argues – prolonging metaphysical thinking by imposing a new truth upon an old one now dismissed as inadequate (Vattimo 1980: 20–2).

In order for postmodernity to step out of this conceptual loop and legitimize itself, it needs to rethink the philosophical tradition of modernity without attempting to overcome it in Hegelian terms. Drawing from Nietzsche and Heidegger, Vattimo delineates "weak thought" (*Il pensiero debole*) precisely as the distinctive discourse of a condition of knowledge which does not reinstate the strength of the ontological structures, while not trying radically to break with them.

Post-

Nietzsche's nihilism provides Vattimo with an exemplary approach that unmasks all claims to truth and reason as subjective values rather than essences, dissolving, together with foundations, also any ground of comparison, hence of distinction, between an allegedly "real" world and a world of symbols. Therefore it reduces the logical basis of rational metaphysical thought to mere rhetoric, to a delusion of neutrality and objectivity which is in fact an expression of an ideological desire for persuasion and domination. Yet, much of Vattimo's discussion of nihilism in view of "a theoretical proposal for today's philosophy" (Vattimo 1989: 15) starts, more specifically, from Nietzsche's investigation into the possible conversion of passive nihilism (the creation of ideological disguises as a refusal to accept the unmasking and annihilation of supreme values and meaning) into active nihilism (a trust in the power of the will to live after the "death of God," without attempting to construct compensatory fictions). The danger of turning active nihilism into a new metaphysics can be avoided, in Vattimo's view, by taking nihilism as "a theory of the 'disappearance' of Being" (21): where passive nihilism is the process of the vanishing of Being, active nihilism accepts this event as an " 'objective' fact" (21) and responds to it with "a disposition to take risks" (20) that can be defined as "moderate" for it transcends "the interest in self-preservation and, with it, the violence of the struggle for life" (21).

By referring to the dissolution of Being in terms of "ontology of weakness" (21), Vattimo explicitly connects Nietzschean nihilism to the enfeebled, declining nature of Heidegger's Being, which questions the self-evidence, sameness, and stable presence of the metaphysical subject exposing its constitutive temporality and deferment. The key notion that substantiates the weakness of the Nietzschean–Heideggerian attitude *vis-à-vis* its supposedly "strong" models – and that can hence qualify the status of postmodern philosophy *vis-à-vis* modernity – is the term *Verwindung*. Nietzsche's *Human, All Too Human* (1878), with its philosophy of mourning, already synthesizes those implications by positing the need for a movement out of metaphysics without recurring to the category of critical overcoming. Yet it is Heidegger who, from *Being and Time* (1927) on, repeatedly adopts the term *Verwindung* to suggest a "declination" and "distortion" of the category of dialectical overcoming (or *Uberwindung*), but also a "convalescence" from, and "resignation" to, metaphysics. It thus delineates the end of modernity as a deviant alteration of a legacy which cannot simply be abandoned, nor accepted or prolonged, and as a recovery from an illness which leaves, however indelible, traces in us. Along this errant path away from any stable foundation and not culminating in any ultimate truth, indeed, tradition is not repeated but rather rethought, recollected, according to the sense given by Heidegger to *An-denken*. *An-denken* does not connote a process of remembrance, hence of representation, that reconstructs and appropriates an origin or presence or stable structure: metaphysics still speaks to us, yet not in a cogent and authoritarian way, but rather through a sort of transmission that reveals its " 'epochal' openness" (Vattimo 1980: 26). Being is an event that happens and can only be recollected as "always already gone" (26).

When we approach Vattimo's capillary and genealogical analysis of Nietzsche's and Heidegger's philosophy we should keep in mind that his rereading does not want to be a cannibalization of topoi, nor a parodic repetition or a neutral and irreverent pastiche. Rather, it should be seen as a methodological move, a practice of postmodern thought itself: as Vattimo remarks, far from arbitrary, his interpretation of Heidegger is, in its turn, a critical exercise of *Verwindung*, "a distorted acceptance of Heidegger's doctrine" (Vattimo 1992: 38). This observation offers a synthesis of the attitude that postmodern, weak thought can adopt toward its strong past, in Vattimo's view: ʾhe postmodern condition is "without objectification and hence without alienation" (41) in so far as it does not discard inherited categories and values *tout court* but rather approaches them with *pietas*, that is, with the respect and veneration reserved to the monuments and figures of the past precisely in so far as they are passed away. The recognition of the mortality of metaphysical categories – hence of their status as mere remains, ruins, traces – empties *pietas* of nostalgia. Postmodernity is, indeed, an epigonic condition, in that a surplus of historical consciousness hinders the production of the new. Yet, epigonism does not express itself in terms of filial mourning for the loss of a father-like source of authority and legitimation, nor does it engage the postmodern weak "son" in a struggle with a strong precursor, as in Harold Bloom's anxiety of influence. Weak thought lucidly accepts the dissolution of any cogent truth, which is to be exposed and lived fully as a destiny with no alternative, within a finite and circumscribed horizon.

Beyond

Through the key notions of *Verwindung*, *An-denken*, and *pietas* Vattimo shows us how the postmodern way out of foundational thought differs from a dialectical overcoming. To move beyond metaphysics also implies to move beyond its way of conceiving the "beyond" in terms of development and fulfillment, inseparable from a violent attempt to master reality. For the postmodern ontology of weakness this entails acknowledging the rhetorical nature of truth: truth needs to be rethought as a hermeneutical process, hence as formulation and interpretation, instead of an act of disclosure or of reconstruction, when not demonstration, of an already given structure.

Hermeneutics as a cognitive and ethical model is indeed another face of a weak philosophy of postmodernity, and is pervasive in Vattimo's works stretching across two decades, from, for instance, *Al di là del soggetto* (1991) and *The End of Modernity* (1985) through *The Adventure of Difference* (1980), *Etica dell'interpretazione* (1989) and *Beyond Interpretation* (1994). While partaking of a widespread debate on hermeneutics as a form of immanent criticism, the specificity of Vattimo's approach lies in the attempt to recuperate and elaborate on the philosophical meaning of hermeneutics, which in his view has been neutralized precisely by heterogeneous positions and too broad definitions.

A text like *Beyond Interpretation*, for instance, refines previous observations by underlining that hermeneutics is not only simply an anti-foundational theory that unleashes conflicting interpretations. Rather, and this is what mainly matters to Vattimo, it also enacts a "nihilistic vocation" (Vattimo 1997: 2), the impulse of which can be located, once again, in the philosophy of the later Heidegger (hermeneutics as interpretation of the meaning of Being) and in the development carried out by Gadamer (hermeneutics as "linguisticality," constituting human experience in terms of openness to language and through language) (3–4). Vattimo notes that the Gadamerian generalization of hermeneutics has produced a proliferation of commonplaces on the question of truth as interpretation, paradoxically leading hermeneutics back to the metaphysical status of "a finally true description of the (permanent) 'interpretative structure' of human existence" (6). For his part, Vattimo wants to underscore the radically historical nature of hermeneutics itself: as theory, hermeneutics cannot validate itself on the basis of an a priori principle, nor can it ground its truth in objective evidence; rather, it can only uphold its own interpretation in the guise of history (as event and act of narration). Conceived in those terms, the interpretative nature of truth is nihilistic, because as it dissolves into procedure, discourse, language, it reproduces the story of what in Heidegger is the oblivion of being, which endlessly consumes itself in its feeble transmission of tradition. Therefore, the nihilistic formulation of hermeneutics also becomes the postmodern answer to the violence of the metaphysical foundation as much as to the violence which imposes silence and puts an end to the interpretative process.

This answer, Vattimo clarifies, should not be mistaken for an irrational and anti-intellectualist attitude. On the contrary, it asks to be taken as a positive, constructive position aiming at building a new notion of rationality – one that does not fall back into the authenticity provided by a foundational framework, without refusing, by the same token, argumentation *tout court*, as would rather be the case of an aestheticizing, creative-poetic form of philosophy (Vattimo 1997: 97). If hermeneutics is not a polemical rejection but rather a consequence of modernity and, in Heideggerian terms, "can only conceive of itself as . . . the interpretive articulation of its own belonging to a tradition" (108), Vattimo sees rationality as the mere "guiding thread" (109) that helps us orient and reconstruct, from within, the process of our destiny, a destiny which coincides with our weak inheritance of the past. In the impossibility of hermeneutics to go beyond differences, discontinuity, and individual horizons, there also lies its ethical sense. Ethics and responsibility become central in the very moment when, as in the case of postmodern weak thought, we are no longer sustained by foundations, nor guided by imperatives, but rather left with a multiplicity of conflicting argumentations, and locally shared opinions.

Back?

It is not possible to do justice in a few lines to all the pivotal consequences that the hermeneutic-nihilistic turn of Vattimo's philosophy of postmodernity has for the conception of art and the aesthetic experience, the status of science, or politics. However, the most recent developments of Vattimo's thought deserve particular notice, since they open up rather intriguing venues for postmodernity. Such works as *Credere di credere* (1996) or the co-edited volume *Religion* (1998) highlight a shift from the disenchantment associated with the crisis of

the myths and objective truths of modernity to the disenchantment of disenchantment itself, that is, the radical recognition that the very dismissal of the
belief in myths (or of belief *tout court*) is itself a myth (Vattimo 1996: 18).
Vattimo develops this point by exploring the manifest rebirth of a religious
interest and the resumption of the question of faith in contemporary society,
and sees in them the ultimate philosophical response to the consumption of
metaphysical objectification and mythification. Yet, instead of interpreting the
recovery of religion as evidence of a renewed search for foundations, or as an
instance of fundamentalism, he rather takes it as the outcome of hermeneutics'
nihilistic impulse and, simultaneously, as its originary inspiration (suggesting
that it is the Christian inspiration that orients thought in the direction of
nihilism).

The return of the religious in the postmodern world can be explained as the
most faithful accomplishment of nihilism because, by re-presenting a kernel of
sacred contents which were abandoned and are now recalled in a distorted and
reduced version, it exemplifies a weak approach to tradition. In Vattimo's
argument, the term "return" does not so much evoke a recuperation of a
supernatural plenitude or of an ideal of authenticity (Vattimo 1998: 86; 89);
rather, it indicates precisely the *Verwindung* of the Judeo-Christian legacy,
which empties out religion of its transcendental and mysterious characters,
through a process of secularization. In secularization – that is, desacralization,
the reduction of the Lord of the Bible to an effect, a transmission, of the
Biblical text itself, rather than the origin of it – Vattimo hence proposes to see
the meeting point of the postmodern ontology of weakness and of the Christian doctrine of the incarnation of the son of God on the basis of two main
points he had raised earlier. First of all, interpreted as an enfeeblement – a
"reduction" or "*kenosis*" – of God to the level of man (Vattimo 1996: 30–1;
58), incarnation generates the event-like, contingent character of the post-
metaphysical Being (Vattimo 1998: 89; 92), turning the ontology of weakness
into a transcription of the Christian message. Second, the link between a
nihilistic postmodern philosophy and the return of religion as secularization
brings to the foreground the movement away from the violence of metaphysics
in so far as the Christian legacy that Vattimo now identifies in weak thought
implies a dissolution of the violence of the sacred, the end of the metaphysical,
absolute, authoritarian God, disavowed precisely by the figure of the incarnated Christ.

Vattimo's argument about the theology of secularization and the ontology of
weakness seems to come full circle when he invites us to see in the occurrence
of *kenosis*, of secularization, the equivalent of that endless and indefinite
process of consumption of the strong structures of Being which, as noted
above, dismantles the myth of truth as eternal and objective evidence, and
opens the way to the truth of hermeneutics. In so doing, Vattimo's reflections

posit a continuity between hermeneutic ontology and theological hermeneutics on the basis of the inexhaustibility of interpretation. The occurrence, the taking place, of a historical, discursive, and plurivocal post-metaphysical truth coincides, from the point of view of religion, with the event of a God whose transcendence lies in the infinite interpretative process of the Biblical message (Vattimo 1996: 58–61; D'Isanto 1994: 370–1). Just as the nihilistic erosion of the strong structures of being does not lead to the full accomplishment of nothingness (which, as Vattimo underscores, would still constitute an objective presence) (Vattimo 1996: 61), the secularization of the concept of God should not be equated to a negative theology, but, rather, to the experience of positivity and factuality. As Vattimo explains, the return of religion implies simultaneously "createdness as a concrete and highly determined historicity, but also, on the contrary, historicity as provenance from an origin that, as not metaphysically structural and essential, also has all the features of contingency [*eventualità*] and freedom" (Vattimo 1998: 85).

From the Nietzschean announcement of the death of God, in which metaphysics culminates and dissolves, bringing along the crisis of humanism, the nihilism of Vattimo's postmodern thought has led us to the birth of an incarnated divine figure revealing to post-metaphysical philosophy its own provenance from the Hebraic-Christian tradition, and embodying the distortion of such a legacy. Within the horizon of the Incarnation, as Vattimo claims, there takes place that "indefinite process of reduction, diminution, weakening" (93) that translates precisely the significance of nihilism and condenses its constitutive fallenness. Yet in this return to and of religion – where philosophical speculation, the author's personal sensibility, and a popular social phenomenon intertwine – we also perceive a somewhat different formulation of those emancipatory concerns that previously seemed to lie in the "relative 'chaos'" (Vattimo 1992 [1989]: 4) of the postmodern world of differences and local truths. This change of attitude emerges, for instance, when Vattimo presents secularization and the interpretation of the message of the New Testament as essential traits of our salvation (Vattimo 1996: 56–7), or when he locates in the event of the Incarnation the power of conferring on history a redemptive sense (Vattimo 1998: 92). This weak reading of Christian revelation – which, against a tragic and apocalyptic conception of religion, expresses the desire, the hope, to believe, and to find and accept a degree of myth in life without dissecting or unmasking it with the tools of reason and disenchantment (Vattimo 1996: 97) – makes us wonder whether the point of arrival of Vattimo's postmodern discourse is not in fact suggesting a *Verwindung* of *Verwindung*, a way out of postmodernism to be achieved with the very theoretical apparatus of postmodernism itself.

Whether it is the evolution of Vattimo's philosophy that has modified the conception of the postmodern all along, or, rather, the experience of the postmodern that has acted upon his thought producing this ultimate twist, we cannot but be intrigued by the timing that accompanies Vattimo's significant change of focus. Although all these issues were already present in a nutshell in earlier works, their centrality at the outset of a new millennium seems to express a new *Weltanschauung*. After locating the opportunity "of being (finally, perhaps) human" (Vattimo 1992 [1989]: 11) in the emancipatory experience of oscillation and disorientation, it is perhaps with the return of the emotional, spiritual subject that we can leave behind the postmodern "waning of affect" (Jameson 1991: 10).

50

Robert Venturi and Denise Scott Brown

Jim Collins

Despite their resistance to being labeled "postmodernist," the work of Robert Venturi and Denise Scott Brown has been hugely influential in shaping postmodern theory for the past three decades. Venturi's designs, built and unbuilt, are fixtures in any work on postmodern architecture and one in particular – his addition to the National Gallery in London – was one of the most visible battlegrounds between Modernists and postmodernists. While the impact of those projects has been felt most profoundly in the world of architecture and urban planning, the theoretical writings of Venturi and Scott Brown have enjoyed an even broader application. The breadth of that impact is not surprising, given their determination to pursue questions that cross-cut the realms of literary criticism, art history, semiotics, and social theory. Venturi's *Complexity and Contradiction* (1966) and their collaborative study *Learning from Las Vegas* (1972) are benchmark works in postmodern studies because they were among the first rigorous critiques of the Modernist hegemony in the arts and the academy. They articulated a provocative agenda for what many seemed to think was virtually unthinkable, namely, something *after* Modernism – a project that had to be undertaken because the aesthetic of the future had become a hide-bound orthodoxy from the past. It is beyond the scope of this essay to examine even a handful of their most important buildings, so I will focus primarily on this theoretical work. My primary concern will be to demonstrate the ways in which the writings of Venturi and Denise Scott Brown represent one of the most far-reaching attempts to redefine what *culture* means in a postmodern context.

In his preface to *Complexity and Contradiction*, architectural historian Vincent Scully argues that this book is, "probably the most important writing on the making of architecture since Le Corbusier's *Vers une Architecture*, of 1923." Just as Le Corbusier's book became a reference point for Modern architecture, *Complexity and Contradiction* represented the same kind of paradigm shift in terms of architectural discourse. In his preface, Venturi's declaration of principles reveals just how fundamental, and how confrontational, this shift actually was,

> Architects can no longer be intimidated by the puritanically moral language of orthodox Modern architecture. I like elements which are hybrid rather than "pure," compromising rather than "clean," distorted rather than "straight-forward," ambiguous rather than "articulated," perverse as well as impersonal, boring as well as "interesting," conventional rather than "designed," accommodating rather than excluding, redundant rather than simple, vestigial as well as innovating, inconsistent and equivocal rather than direct and clear. I am for messy vitality over obvious unity.... I prefer "both-and," to "either-or," black and white, and sometimes gray, to black or white. (Venturi 1966: 22)

While Venturi called this a "gentle manifesto," it is, in many ways, an anti-manifesto, or perhaps most accurately, a *post*-manifesto because his rejection of the absolutist discourse of the Modernist manifesto in favor of contingency and eclecticism distinguishes it as distinctly postmodern discourse. Equally important is Venturi's advocacy of the use of historical tradition. His manifesto is illustrated by hundreds of marginal photographs, which taken together, present another sort of historical continuum, one which rejects any sort of teleological history of art that would posit Modernism as a final apotheosis. Instead of the valorization of the "shock of the new" that was so fundamental to Modernist orthodoxy, Venturi argues that true contemporaneity can be achieved only through a rigorous awareness of antecedent forms of architecture. He invokes T. S. Eliot's notion of tradition as a model for his project: "it cannot be inherited, and if you want it you must obtain it by hard labor.... This historical sense, which is a sense of the timeless as well as the temporal and of the timeless and the temporal together, is what makes a writer traditional, and it is at the same time what makes a writer most acutely conscious of his place in time, of his own contemporaneity" (19).

It is this critical use of historical tradition which has made Venturi skeptical about certain tendencies within postmodern architecture, perhaps the principal reason why he and Scott Brown have never proclaimed themselves postmodernists as such. Their advocacy of historical appropriation is tied directly to the need for a symbolic architectural language which will make buildings understandable to more than a coterie of architects and patrons. But what complicates Venturi's notion of symbolic language is the diversity of contemporary cultures. The subtlety of this position is perhaps best expressed in his assessment of the strengths and limitations of postmodernism. While he insists that he is "in general agreement with the theoretical bases of Postmodernism," he is critical of its use of history.

Venturi's critique of the "Postmodernists" epitomizes one conception of the postmodern, namely, what Charles Jencks has referred to as free-style classicism (Jencks 1981) or what Charles Moore derided as "party hat" postmodernism. This tendency (perhaps most vividly represented by Philip Johnson's AT&T building in New York City which resembled a Chippendale-style highboy) has been characterized in terms of either a reactionary nostalgia or an irresponsible cannibalization of history. Yet there is another way of defining the postmodern in terms of a much more sophisticated appropriation of historical tradition, one exemplified, to offer only a very brief list, by the buildings of James Stirling and Charles Moore, the novels of Graham Swift and Salman Rushdie, the performance art of Laurie Anderson, and the films of Peter Greenaway. In each case, one encounters not a nostalgic appeal to some lost universal language of good taste but a rigorous meditation on the ways that history shapes the various forms of cultural memory, a variety which forms the very plurality that Venturi sees as the basis for contemporary design. From this perspective, Venturi and Scott Brown are not just in general agreement with postmodernism – they are among its most influential proponents as theoreticians and among its most successful practitioners in terms of their buildings and urban design projects.

Perhaps the best way to appreciate the postmodern dimensions of their work (and to understand why it has had such an impact outside the world of architecture) is to examine the way in which they articulate the interconnectedness of the formal and ideological dimensions of contemporary design in *Learning from Las Vegas*. While *Complexity and Contradiction* delineated the possibilities of a new aesthetic based on eclecticism, hybridity, and historical appropriation, their study of Las Vegas with Steven Izenour explored both the semiotic and ideological aspects of urban design, paying particular attention to the status of the architect *vis-à-vis* the public that was being designed *for*. Just as the earlier work began with an opening salvo aimed at orthodox Modernists, *Learning* challenges the architectural establishment at an even more fundamental level:

> Learning from the existing landscape is a way of being revolutionary for an architect. Not the obvious way, which is to tear down Paris and begin again, as Le Corbusier suggested in the 1920s, but another, more tolerant way; that is, to question how we look at things. The commercial strip, the Las Vegas Strip in particular – the example par excellence – challenges the architect to take a positive, non-chip-on-the-shoulder view. Architects are out of the habit of looking non-judgmentally at the environment, because orthodox Modern architecture is progressive, if not revolutionary, utopian, and puristic; it is dissatisfied with existing conditions. (Venturi, Scott Brown, and Izenour 1972: 3)

It is difficult to say what was most controversial about this opening declaration – that the Strip, normally thought of as the essence of bad taste and the very antithesis of good design, should be studied as an example of successful architecture, or that *progressive* should no longer be considered an unquestioned virtue, or that the role of the architect-as-creative-artist needed to be thoroughly reexamined as well, or that making architecture required, at the most fundamental level, learning *how to look* differently. Looking differently meant asking two interdependent questions – how does architecture become meaningful in contemporary urban environments and how do we evaluate that signifying potential?

What was most radical about this project, then, was that it insisted that architectural quality should be measured not in terms of the self-expression of the architect but as communication between architect and public. Venturi et al. insist that "Las Vegas is analyzed here as a phenomenon of architectural communication. Just as an analysis of the structure of a Gothic cathedral need not include a debate on the morality of medieval religion, so Las Vegas's values are not questioned here. . . . In addition, there is no reason why the methods of commercial persuasion and the skyline of signs analyzed here should not serve the purpose of civic and cultural enhancement" (1972: 4). This desire to investigate how the production of meaning in architecture is not the result of a singular creative act but a complex *interaction* involving a host of participants, both trained and untrained in the niceties of architectural aesthetics, depended on a far more ethnographic definition of culture. The demonization of Las Vegas by the architectural establishment rested on a notion of culture defined in exclusivist terms, i.e., Culture as supreme artistic achievement. But in their appreciation of the architecture of the Strip Venturi, Scott Brown, and Izenour rejected this narrow, endlessly self-confirming definition of culture in pursuit of a far broader understanding of architecture as a form of signifying practice, as one of an endless variety of ways in which a given population represents itself in ways that are locally meaningful.

To consider architecture as a form of popular culture, to even advocate appropriating the iconography of popular culture within their buildings, was perhaps the most controversial aspect of all their study because it challenged the vision of culture which served as the foundation of the entire edifice of architectural criticism. The authors were determined to render explicit the cultural politics lurking within such exclusivist notions of culture. In response to claims that Venturi and company were legitimating "hard-hat politics" in their attempts to understand the nature of suburban architecture, they zeroed in on the elitist nature of these attacks: "One does not have to agree with hard-hat politics to support the rights of the middle-class to their own architectural aesthetics . . . in this Nixon-silent-majority diatribe . . . there is a fine line between liberalism and old fashioned class snobbery" (155). Scott Brown made the crucial point that their incorporation of popular culture did not signal its wholesale acceptance: "After a decent interval, suitable criteria must grow out of the new source. Judgment is merely deferred to make subsequent judgment more sensitive" (Scott Brown 1984).

In their attempt to redefine the operative notions of culture within architectural theory, Venturi and Scott Brown form an integral bridge within postmodernism between Pop Art and British cultural studies. They have written appreciatively of Jasper Johns, Rauschenburg, and Andy Warhol and critics such as Stanislaus von Moos have argued convincingly about the points of contact between Venturi's buildings and the work of Roy Lichtenstein, Richard Hamilton, and Claus Oldenburg. While this connection may be explicit, the comparability of the cultural agendas outlined by *Learning from Las Vegas* and the Centre for Contemporary Cultural Studies at the University of Birmingham needs to be further explored in order to better appreciate the mutuality of concerns, a mutuality that remains underappreciated if postmodern architecture is conceived of merely as buildings in neoclassical costume dress. Despite the lack of common critical terminology, one finds striking similarities in the projects outlined in *Learning from Las Vegas* and in many of the studies devoted to British popular culture, particularly in their attempts to democratize the production of meaning by focusing on how audiences take very active roles in determining what is significant within their environments.

A number of different genealogies have been advanced to explain the evolution of postmodernism but no single critical narrative can really encompass the uneven development it has enjoyed since its history has been so discipline specific (as well as so nationally specific, media specific, etc.). Compelling arguments have been made for the primacy of a number of different explanatory trajectories – that postmodernism is best understood as a broadly defined artistic movement that emerged out of the exhaustion of Modernist aesthetics; or that postmodernism is best understood within the context of philosophy, in which case it may be considered the inevitable extension of poststructuralist theory; or that what we used to call postmodernism was really a nascent form of multiculturalism, in which case the rejection of master narratives in favor of difference, heterogeneity, and contingency is animated by a very different set of historical exigencies. The work of Venturi and Denise Scott Brown represents a vital component in another postmodern genealogy in which affiliations may be drawn in terms of a shared dissatisfaction with cultural hierarchies, a shared determination to challenge the confines of the museum, the archive, and the academy. What animates this tradition is not simply a matter of mixing high art and popular culture, but a fundamental reconsideration of who might be considered a player in the game called culture.

51

Kurt Vonnegut

Todd F. Davis

Kurt Vonnegut's career might best be considered in terms of a porousness of borders or, perhaps more accurately, a complete disregard for borders or boundaries of any kind altogether. Born in Indianapolis, Indiana, in 1922, Vonnegut seems the least likely candidate to ascend to fame as an author of postmodern fiction and an icon of countercultural thought. The son and grandson of architects and the brother of the noted research scientist Bernard Vonnegut, Vonnegut himself remarks that "everything I believe I was taught in junior civics during the Great Depression – at School 43 in Indianapolis, with full approval of the school board. School 43 wasn't a radical school. America was an idealistic, pacifistic nation at the time" (Allen 1988: 103). Characterized by a loyalty to pacifism and a vision for the improvement of the human condition, Vonnegut's fiction and nonfiction demonstrate an undeniable commitment to the celebration of metafictional forms and to the deconstruction of America's most sacred grand narratives. Moving beyond the generic boundaries established by formalist critics, Vonnegut's body of work resists labels, demonstrating the fluidity of form and the futility of dogmatic literary convention. Like the curriculum he learned as a boy at School 43, Vonnegut's work is radical not because of its pronouncements but because its author takes those pronouncements seriously, attempting to translate them into innovative fictional forms while never allowing the rhetoric of such grand narratives as nationalism or Christianity to obscure the horror of humanity's actions toward itself or the planet.

Working against the caricature of postmodernity as a monolithic movement of complete relativism – too often described by its opponents as at best amoral and more likely immoral – Vonnegut poses interesting questions about postmodernism's relationship to issues of peace and justice and, more specifically, social change. Like a latter-day Mark Twain, Vonnegut over the course of his career has used his fame and penchant for joke-telling not only to promote his writing but also his own passionate views on how aid might better be distributed to other countries, how Article II of the Bill of Rights, which concerns the freedom to bear arms, ought to be interpreted, and how women may be far better equipped to lead us into healthier human communities than men, among a host of other diverse and controversial ethical issues. For Vonnegut, following the postmodern tenet that we can know our world only through language, through the fictions we create, does not absolve him of some obligation to the spiritual and physical condition of the planet and those who live upon it.

As a postmodern pragmatist, Vonnegut proclaims in an interview that all we have access to are "comforting lies," not some essential truth placed in the hands of a few cultural elites by God Almighty. Yet even with this kind of dazzlingly irreverent assertion, Vonnegut contends that the comforting lies we tell should in some way redeem our existence, that such *petites histoires* should lead toward the construction of better realities for all who live and the places in which they live. In his own lifetime, he has witnessed the heinous abuses created by the narratives of such "storytellers" as Hitler and Mussolini, Charles Manson and Jim Jones, whose "comforting lies" exploited the very worst traits in humankind. Therefore, the central question for Vonnegut remains: What does one do in a decentered world? The very idealism promulgated by America during Vonnegut's youth drives him toward what can only be described as a form of postmodern humanism. His use of metafictional forms is activist in nature, distinguishing him from such other postmodern authors as Thomas Pynchon and John Barth and aligning him with such contemporary writers as Toni Morrison and Ishmael Reed.

Vonnegut's particular moral vision – wed to the postmodern techniques of what James M. Mellard refers to as the exploded form – finds its roots in his experiences as a soldier and prisoner of war in Dresden, Germany, and his later training after the war as a student of anthropology at the University of Chicago. The bombing of Dresden – the subject of his most celebrated novel, *Slaughterhouse-Five* (1969) – left an indelible mark upon Vonnegut's psyche. After witnessing the awesome power of science in the service of humanity's hatred, he essentially lost faith, explaining that

> for me it was terrible, after having believed so much in technology and having drawn so many pictures of dream automobiles and dream airplanes and dream human dwellings, to see the actual use of this technology in destroying a city and killing 135,000 people and then to see the even more sophisticated technology in the use of nuclear weapons on Japan. I was sickened by this use of the technology that I had such great hopes for. And so I came to fear it. You know, it's like being a devout Christian and then seeing some horrible massacres conducted by Christians after a victory. It was a spiritual horror of that sort which I still carry today. (Allen 1988: 232)

Out of this lost faith, Vonnegut shifts from what might be characterized as his more conventionally modernist narratives – represented by such works as *Player Piano* (1952) and *Mother Night* (1966) – to *Slaughterhouse-Five*, a book that flaunts the boundaries of convention and stands as Vonnegut's most formally postmodern novel to that point in his career. The radical shift in form from any modernist conception of the genre results from Vonnegut's own struggle to find a new paradigm for his experience in Dresden, a cataclysmic moment in time whose truth he discovers cannot be written about in a linear, essentialist fashion. Less a book about his actual experience in Dresden and more a testament to its haunting effects, the novel portrays Vonnegut's struggle and ultimately his defeat to write about such an atrocity. For Vonnegut, World War II and the eventual bombing of Dresden, Germany, may be seen as the results of the kind of absolutism that he crusades against in *Cat's Cradle* (1963), an earlier novel that ends with the complete destruction of the world by the creation of the scientific property Ice-Nine. In *Slaughterhouse-Five*, Vonnegut makes use of a variety of metafictional techniques in order to expose his own struggle with Dresden, and by doing so he establishes an open relationship with the reader that allows for more communication than the traditional modernist paradigm. In the first chapter of *Slaughterhouse-Five*, the author visits his old war buddy, Bernard V. O'Hare, in hopes that their reunion will help him recall the bombing of Dresden. Inserting himself into his created world without comment, Vonnegut makes no attempt to distinguish between "reality" and "fiction." During his visit he meets O'Hare's wife, Mary, to whom the novel is dedicated, and Mary, obviously angered by Vonnegut's presence, accuses Vonnegut of attempting to write a book that will reify the other grand narratives of war:

> "Well, I know," she said. "You'll pretend you were men instead of babies, and you'll be played in the movies by Frank Sinatra and John Wayne or some of those other glamorous, war-loving, dirty old men. And war will look just wonderful, so we'll have a lot more of them. And they'll be fought by babies like the babies upstairs." (1969: 14)

Refusing to accept the metanarratives that her country has offered in defense and even adulation of the war, Mary O'Hare makes Vonnegut promise that "there won't be a part for Frank Sinatra or John Wayne" in his book about Dresden. Not only are there no parts for the likes of Sinatra and Wayne, the actual bombing of Dresden remains on the periphery of the book.

Although Vonnegut's first six novels demonstrate a deep commitment to humanity, that commitment, driven by faith, remains tenuous throughout his career. At no time does Vonnegut become comfortable with the notion that humanity represents the highest achievement of some mythical creator, that our actions are uniquely predestined in some providential plan. Instead, he strives to make sense of our existence, to understand better how he should live in a world absurdly committed to its own destruction. Against the canvas of the devastation he has witnessed, Vonnegut writes novels, as he explains, "to make myself like life better than I do. . . . People will believe anything, which means I will believe anything. I learned that in anthropology. I want to start believing in things that have shapeliness and harmony" (Allen 1988: 109). Before he can make such a radical transition, however, he engages with the very forces that he sees destroying the planet and its inhabitants. In the preface to *Breakfast of Champions* (1973), Vonnegut explains that he must make his head as empty as it was when he "was born onto this damaged planet fifty years ago" (5). And Vonnegut advocates such a plan for us all: "I suspect that this is something most white Americans, and nonwhite Americans who imitate white Americans, should do. The things other people have put into my head, at any rate, do not fit together nicely, are often useless and ugly, are out of proportion with one another . . . I have no culture, no humane harmony in my brains" (5). The key to Vonnegut's attack, his postmodern crusade against all kinds of spiritual and physical abuses, rests in his devotion to a "humane harmony."

The dramatic tension on which Vonnegut builds *Breakfast of Champions* consists of its author's struggle to embrace once again a narrative that attempts to describe the value of the human spirit. As in *Slaughterhouse-Five*, Vonnegut inserts himself as a character into his own artistic creation. In *Breakfast of Champions*, Vonnegut pushes the limits of metafictional art. Rather than appearing simply in the introductory and concluding chapters in order to explain to the reader what the book attempts to do, Vonnegut makes his own fictional epiphany central to the story in *Breakfast of Champions*. While this might not prove problematic in examining the work of some artists, it becomes difficult to discern where the flesh-and-blood author ends and his fictional doppelgänger begins because of Vonnegut's assertion that life itself is a fiction, that all we have are comforting lies. By using such a fictional technique, Vonnegut seems to be mocking our efforts to delineate the boundaries between the world of fiction and the world of fact; in the narrative scheme of *Breakfast of Champions*, he once again asserts, as he did in the preface to *Mother Night*, that we are what we pretend to be. Consequently, when Vonnegut speaks as the fictional narrator of the novel, he in fact speaks for himself. For this reason, it is not unusual to find Vonnegut giving the same speeches in interviews that he gives as a character in his own novels. Unlike other artists, he does indeed conflate the two realities, an indulgence that seems logical to a postmodern harlequin like Vonnegut. Not surprisingly, then, Vonnegut finds the narrative of hope he longs for in the very work of art he has created himself, and, in *Breakfast of Champions*, all roads lead to the Midland City Arts Festival.

Along the way to Midland City, however, Vonnegut takes on the history and practices of American culture in an attempt to destroy those narratives that dehumanize and damage life on this planet. After outlining the history of America in a voice that is childlike in its directness and honesty, Vonnegut dismantles the notion that any of these grand cultural narratives has led to democracy:

> millions of human beings were already living full and imaginative lives on the continent in 1492. That was simply the year in which sea pirates began to cheat and rob and kill them. (10)

Vonnegut claims that what was actually created was a nation where the sea pirates owned human slaves: "They used human beings for machinery, and, even after slavery was eliminated, because it was so embarrassing, they and their descendants continued to think of ordinary human beings as machines" (11). And, once again, Vonnegut the postmodern preacher of humanism decries the mechanization of humanity. In fact, *Breakfast of Champions* may be seen as a righteous lament over our abuse of the land and its people, over the sacrifices we have made to build an economic machine that, in the end, can only consume the earth and all it sustains. Facing such a grim reality, Vonnegut searches for some reason to see people as anything but machines that perpetuate the folly of this destructive American narrative.

In Vonnegut's later novels, an apocalyptic tone of potential doom casts a pall over the hope that resides at the center of each work. In *Galápagos* (1985), he experiments with the idea that the earth and its inhabitants might be better off without the human race as we know it. By having a ghost tell the story of humanity's devolution into seal-like creatures, he illustrates the (self-)destructiveness of our species. Yet he cannot bring himself to dismiss the potential good that also resides within us. As Leon Trotsky Trout, the novel's ghostly narrator and Vonnegut's alter ego, often exclaims about humans in their devolved state, "Nobody, surely, is going to write Beethoven's Ninth Symphony" (259). In this tale of humanity's demise, the planet becomes a safer place; however, the capacity to create and think and feel as fully realized humans is lost, and with this loss life is tragically compromised.

Similar to *Galápagos*, Vonnegut offers potential visions of a sometimes terrifying, sometimes pitiful future in *Slapstick* (1976), *Hocus Pocus* (1990), and *Timequake* (1997). Yet within these visions we also find Vonnegut's postmodern humanism. *Slapstick* suggests that familial community will heal and fulfill us, redeeming our purposelessness by making our existence vital and necessary to others. *Hocus Pocus* demands that we see our "lethal hocus pocus" for what it is. There can be no rhetoric to justify our actions in Vietnam, the novel's narrator Eugene Debs Hartke explains. Instead, Hartke

– just as Vonnegut's grandfather, the German freethinker – suggests that "the greatest use a person could make of his or her lifetime [is] to improve the quality of life for all in his or her community" (176). Finally, in *Timequake*, Vonnegut uses a mixed form – part memoir, part failed novel – to encourage an examination of our past. By plotting a "timequake," he illustrates how what we have done impacts the future, while at the same time he suggests numerous revisions for our present actions. "And even in 1996, I in speeches propose the following amendments to the Constitution," Vonnegut states toward the end of *Timequake*. "*Article XXVIII*: Every newborn shall be sincerely welcomed and cared for until maturity. *Article XXIX*: Every adult who needs it shall be given meaningful work to do, at a living wage" (152). Vonnegut postulates amendments to the Constitution that hardly seem radical; in fact, such amendments, as with much in his social agenda, seem commonsensical, humane, and of utmost importance. The failure to follow such important advice, Vonnegut warns, will lead toward the darkness of apocalypse.

What makes Vonnegut different from many other postmodernists is his refusal to accept complete relativism. He emphatically asserts a single rule for the comforting lies we must tell: "Ye shall respect one another" (1991: 159). This rule already appears in a slightly different form in Vonnegut's early fiction, when Eliot Rosewater, rehearsing what he will say at the baptism of Mary Moody's twins, exclaims, "God damn it, you've got to be kind" (1965: 110). Vonnegut confesses that his single rule for postmodern living is based entirely on a leap of faith. The postmodern morality that characterizes his fictional world presupposes that human life is valuable, and it does so with no possible way to substantiate its claim. Nonetheless, Vonnegut does stand by this claim, continuing to believe in the very fiction he has himself created. At the center of Vonnegut's postmodern humanism is the assertion that life is precious. He is a social prophet who tells his stories with the hope that words can in some way change the dark reality of the present.

52

Hayden White

Ewa Domańska

Although Hayden White (b. 1928) – American theorist and historian of historiography, intellectual historian and cultural critic – often points to his roots in the heritage of European (artistic) modernism, he may be linked with the postmodernist culturalization of the humanities, through the promotion of linguisticality (the best way to understand culture is to approach it as a language), textuality (reality is best construed on the analogy of a text, which means that it may be understood through strategies used to interpret speech, writing, and visual imagery), constructivism (reality – natural, social, or cultural – is not given in an act of immediate perception, but can be grasped by way of imaginative constructs more fundamental for the organization of perceptions than the Kantian categories), and discursivity (knowledge is a product of human consciousness which is not so much mimetic as discursive in nature, therefore what we apprehend as "reality" is actually a discursively produced "reality effect").

White is associated with postmodernist deconstructive thinking in so far as he questions the dichotomies typically used to organize traditional modes of thought – such dichotomous pairs as events and contexts, the literal and the figurative, referentiality and signification. If the characteristics of postmodern scholarship are "hybridity," eclecticism, and a tendency to "blur the boundaries," then White is a perfect example, since his interests in intellectual and cultural history are interwoven with theoretical reflection on the theory and history of historiography. His major achievement was to fuse historiography and literary theory into a more comprehensive field of reflection on the narrative perception of social and cultural reality. White prides himself on his eclecticism and always stresses that whatever originality he has is a result of an application of ideas and concepts borrowed from a wide range of thinkers, older (such as Vico and Hegel) and younger (such as Foucault and Derrida).

White's view of historical discourse combines ideas drawn from modernist writers (such as Stein, Joyce, and Woolf), existentialists (Camus, Sartre), founders of the speculative philosophy of history (Vico, Kant, Herder, Hegel, Toynbee, Marx, Spengler, Weber), anti-positivist theorists of historical studies (Dilthey, Collingwood, Croce), literary theorists, critics, and linguists (Auerbach, Barthes, Burke, Frye, Jakobson), psychoanalysts (Freud, Klein, Lacan), and cultural theorists (Foucault, Jameson). His view stems from a revolt against the positivist approach to history, whose naively realistic understanding of historiography, thinking in terms of binary oppositions (fact versus fiction), advocacy of a correspondence theory of truth and objectivism, and separation of axiology from epistemology, still make history an exceptionally well-protected enclave among the human and social sciences.

White's view is often defined as a rhetorical constructivism based on the conviction that historical facts are not "given to" but "made by" the historian. Following Danto and Barthes, White stresses that "a fact is an event under description" and as such is a purely linguistic phenomenon. Events and facts belong to two different orders of being: the former to reality, the latter to discourse. Historians tend to forget this distinction: while they claim to examine those events whose reality has been established as facts, actually they explain and interpret events which they have described as "facts" and in so doing have already interpreted. While pretending to speak about "the past," they actually speak about textualizations of the past. Thus, argues White, the past does not exist independently of its representations – history is historio-graphy and the historical text is a "literary artifact." In historical studies one cannot verify representations and interpretations of the past by comparing them with an "original." What is possible is to compare various descriptions of the past and to accept the most persuasive one. Consequently, the most important goal of the theory of history is to study historical narration and the rules, conventions, and institutions of historical writing in different times and places in order to uncover their rhetorical modes of production.

White often defines history as a kind of "performative speech," as belonging to the domain of discourse, a domain of cultural production in which speech and writing are conceived to "do" something publicly. Historically, historical discourse has functioned to provide legitimation for the dominant groups of the society in which it is produced: history serves power and the status quo. And this is why it tends to feature description rather than argument as its principal instrument of explanation. For the modern, realistic historian, the best description of a historical phenomenon is the best explanation of it. Whatever explanations historians offer are explanations of the phenomena as they have described them, not of the phenomena themselves. It is because historiography features description (*ekphrasis*) as its principal genre that White insists on historiography's "fictionality." It is the effort to suppress, repress, or mask the fictional elements in historical discourse that marks it as ideological.

Locating in discourse the key points at which fictive elements come to its surface allows us to observe how knowledge and power clash and overlap. Like Foucault, White believes that no human science is free from political implications. Being particularly sensitive to the ideological aspects of historical discourse he points out that it is discourse which determines the differences between the normal and the abnormal, fact and fiction, the relevant and the irrelevant, truth and lie. Thus, it is essential to continuously question the criteria for valorization, which is a task of theory as an aid to critical thought. "No theory, no active thinking," claims White, but there is good and bad theory: "that which is conducive to morally responsible thought, and that which leads away from it." The usefulness of a theory is related to its aim, which is always either political or ethical in character. For White, the objective is to promote "good theory," that is, theory which will ultimately serve humankind.

White is an existentialist in the mode of Sartre and has expressed his own commitment to leftist (socialist) views. As a result, he highlights the issues of free will, individual responsibility, and social problems. He often describes himself as a responsible relativist. For him relativism is "a necessary consequence of skepticism . . . and the most effective instrument in the cultivation of tolerance." Such a strategic relativism implies an appeal for tolerance with regard to the ideas and interpretations of others. Relativism implies the provisional and transient nature of all knowledge, the necessity of contextualizing or historicizing and the plea for a continuous critical testing of theories. At the same time, however, White does not believe that "anything goes"; rather, there is no one and ultimate interpretation of social and cultural phenomena. He believes that historians should strive for a pluralistic (not a universal or transcendental) knowledge, by studying as many different cultural moments and traditions as possible. In so doing, they can escape the kind of provincialism and ideologism that scholarly specialization typically produces. In his debates with his critics over the years, White's main goal has been to make historians realize that each representation of the past is tainted with ideology and that those who accuse others of ideologization do so not to present the past in a way that is more "objective," but because they endorse a different worldview.

In the evolution of White's theories one may distinguish four phases: (1) from the mid-1950s to the mid-1960s: a speculative, idealist phase dominated by an interest in intellectual history and the speculative philosophy of history; (2) from the mid-1960s to the 1970s ("The Burden of History" [1966]; *Metahistory* [1973]; and *Tropics of Discourse* [1978]): a narrativist and tropical phase in which the focus is on the structure of historical narration and the tropological elements of different types of discourse; (3) the 1980s (*The Content of the Form* [1987]): a phase marked by studies of representation in the human sciences and of the relation between narrative discourse and historical representation; and (4) the 1990s ("Historical Emplotment and the Problem of Truth" [1992]; *Figural Realism* [1999]): an ethical and figural phase which is a synthesis of all the previous ones. White is now returning to his interests in the concept of figure (discussed by Auerbach) and its role in historical narration; the question of figural causation, which is discussed in the context of reflections on the use and abuse of history in the culture of the West; the burden of history and the role of memory and oblivion in historical recollection; and the question of the public uses of history.

In the first phase the basic premises of White's theories were formulated. It was marked by his interest in neo-idealists who attacked the positivist approach to history (Dilthey, Droysen, Croce, Collingwood). At that time, White adopted Collingwood's definition of history as a moral discipline providing self-knowledge.

In "The Burden of History," which opens the second phase, we find motifs that appeared in earlier texts, for example, the Nietzschean question concerning the use of history and its role in the modern world. Like Nietzsche, White argued that the historian's task was not to reanimate the past, but to liberate us from whatever constraints it imposed upon us. As he would write later, "The problem may be not how to get into history but how to get out of it." In "The Burden of History" he followed the way of his intellectual predecessors, departing from the analytical and early narrativist debates going on in the influential journal, *History and Theory*, towards literary interpretation. Seeking the common ground of history and literature, he questioned the status of a historiography based on the opposition of the two; he sought to historicize historiography and stressed the role of the imagination in creating images of the past.

Metahistory, which appeared at the climax of high structuralism, on the one hand derived from White's early interests in intellectual history, while on the other it was a product of his later interests in the application of structuralism to the study of various discourses. Today it is considered as the most important work in the theory and history of historiography after World War II – a turning point in a shift toward textualism and constructivism.

Metahistory articulated a research program for the narrativist philosophy of history, becoming the central text in the dispute on the essence of historical writing. It seemed to dissolve the difference between fact and fiction and between real and imaginary events, violating the principles established by Aristotle and confirmed in the nineteenth century by Ranke's constitution of history as a "scientific" discipline. Although White's book exemplified a revolt against the positivist approach to history, in many respects it tried to mediate between the nomological (scientific) and narratological (literary) approach to historical explanation.

In general, *Metahistory* presents history as more constructivist than empirical; an interpretative art rather than a science whose task is to explain. Here tropes replace models, the principles of discourse those of nomological explanation, and rhetorical play the rules of logic. Its formal theory of the historical work also offered useful analytical devices to study the products of historical writing. Treating historiography as a multilevel discourse, White showed that in many ways it is still bound by a way of thinking characteristic of an era when no distinction between science and art was recognized.

The best-known element of White's poetics of historical writing is his theory of tropes (tropology). Following Burke, Jakobson, and Vico, and drawing inspiration from post-Renaissance rhetoric, White proposed a model based on four "master" tropes: metaphor, metonymy, synecdoche, and irony. The "speculative" element in White's tropology was derived from Vico. Like Vico, White approaches the trope (Gr. *trópos*) as a turn, change, a transition from one image in a discourse to another. A characteristic feature of White's tropology is its hierarchy of tropes, with irony featured as a predominant metatrope. Metaphor, metonymy, and synecdoche are conceived as "naive" tropes, since their use presupposes that language is capable of grasping the essence of things in figures. In contrast, irony is related to self-consciousness and to detachment from one's own claims (hence, aporia is the best instrument of ironic language). It represents that particular stage of the development of consciousness in which the problematic nature of language itself is recognized.

In his later articles and books (phase 3), White developed and modified his theory while maintaining its basic premises: narrative is a metacode and a human universal, and thinking about the world has a narrativist character. Reality is a stream of events devoid of meaning. Events occurring in our lives are as amorphous as the historical records studied by historians, and the past as such cannot be understood, since it is composed of meaningless facts, states of affairs, and events. The historian's task is to transpose the "prose" of the historical past into the "poetry" of historiography – to translate the past into history – and the four tropes of anagnorisis serve as a convenient tool for that translation.

The main interests of White's fourth phase reflect the key topics of the current debates in the humanities, and include subjectivity, ethics, and the relation between knowledge and power. The widely discussed article "Historical Emplotment and the Problem of Truth" continues the preceding phase in its concern with the question of limits in representing traumatic historical events, a concern that is closely related to the ethics of analysis and interpretation.

Since the mid-1990s, certain concepts – such as figure, fulfillment, *kairos*, change defined as metamorphosis or transubstantiation, and identity – have been appearing in White's vocabulary more often than before. His interest in the concept of figure (adopted from Auerbach) was already apparent in *The Content of the Form*, but recently this interest has taken a different turn. Using the figure as the fundamental element of discourse, White defines it as "an image" from which and toward which the discourse emanates and turns. This distinguishes figure from trope, which is now defined by White as "a mode of turning from one point in the discourse to another." Thus, one might say that in White's conception of discourse, "figural creationism" has become an alternative for "tropal evolutionism."

For White, the concept of figure paved the way for a new paradigm. Approached in the psychoanalytic terms of Freud and Lacan, it opened up new possibilities of interpretation. A figure is an opening marking the passage from consciousness to the unconscious of discourse, which is ordered figurally as well. Following Freud, White seems to be using the notion of figuration to recover discourse's foundation in consciousness. Whereas Freud used the idea of figuration to explicate the different modes of mediating between the manifest and the latent dimensions of the dreamwork, White stresses that figuration is fundamental to the understanding of poetic creativity and invention. In this context, one may suggest that since historical knowledge always operates *post factum*, there is a kind of historical causality that is inevitably projected backwards. This suggests an alternative to the traditional notion of historical causation, which always presumes that cause precedes effect: a kind of retrospective and retroactive causation, in which the future can be seen as producing the many pasts that precede every present. From this perspective the study of the figure points to new fields of research and interpretation which so far have remained in the discursive unconscious.

53

The Wooster Group

Greg Giesekam

Discussion of the Wooster Group has become a recurrent motif of recent accounts of theater and postmodernism. The playful collaging of found materials and daily life activities with high and popular cultural forms and texts, the use of pastiche and quotation along with a high degree of intertextuality, the ironic, self-aware performances, the fragmentary, processual structuring which resists attempts to impose a unifying meaning, are just some aspects of the company's work which have contributed to its being portrayed as the postmodern theater group par excellence, a status which may initially seem out of proportion with the relatively few productions mounted over twenty-five years and the numbers of audiences who have seen their sporadic performances in New York and on the international touring circuit. Somewhat paradoxically, these productions have become canonized as postmodern classics, despite insistence by company members that they have no great interest in theory. In particular, the work has become the site of struggle over postmodern theater's potential for enacting a resistant politics, notably in debates between Auslander (1987), Schechner (1987), and Birringer (1988).

Appropriately enough, the Group emerged out of another company (Richard Schechner's Performance Group), with some debate over when one can mark the shift from one to the other and what characteristics of the earlier group remain in the practices of the later. Although it was in 1975 that, independently of Schechner, Elizabeth LeCompte, Spalding Gray, and a few others produced *Sakonnet Point*, the first of four productions (the *Rhode Island Trilogy* and *Point Judith*) which came to be seen as Wooster Group shows, it was not until 1980 that the Performance Group was formally disbanded and the lease of its premises in Wooster St., New York, was transferred to the Wooster Group. In common with much experimental work in New York in the 1960s and 1970s, the Performance Group's work had been influenced greatly, and contradictorily, by the writings of Brecht and Artaud, both of whom also figure largely in the intellectual genealogy of certain strands of postmodern thought. Brecht's dismantling of the apparatus of illusionistic naturalism, his emphasis on historicizing action and on disturbing conventional relationships of identification between actor and text and audience and actor, and Artaud's vision of a more visceral, irrational, and anti-representational theater which rejects the dominance of a literary text, appear also in the Wooster Group's developing approach to production.

The initial impetus for *Sakonnet Point* came from Spalding Gray's desire to develop a piece from improvisation – with little idea of what the performance might concern. *Sakonnet Point*, "more dance than theatre" and an attempt "to find a form analagous to Cezanne's painting" (LeCompte, in Savran 1986: 59), explored images and memories of childhood. The title refers to a place on Rhode Island Gray visited as a child and some of the material was suggested by Gray's memories; but it was shaped as much by other performers' responses to ideas and found objects brought to rehearsal. Using a collagist soundtrack of Tchaikovsky, children's songs and birdcalls, and task-based acting which abstained from a psychological approach, this "mood piece" was clearly influenced by Robert Wilson, in whose workshops Gray had participated and whose *Deafman Glance* LeCompte admired for "its musical rather than logical form" (Savran 1986: 4). The second production, *Rumstick Road*, derived more clearly from autobiographical material, with a soundtrack composed largely (and controversially) of taped discussions which Gray had with various relatives and his mother's psychiatrist about events surrounding his mother's suicide. Again, however, the three performers (Libby Howes, Ron Vawter, and Gray) did not literally represent the figures on tape but, rather, created a parallel series of physical actions which emerged from their responses to it. During the development of these productions LeCompte's role as a director orchestrating the collaborative devising process became established.

A key development in the next two productions was the incorporation of critical renderings of extracts from major twentieth-century theatrical texts. A dismembered version of T. S. Eliot's *The Cocktail Party* was threaded through *Nayatt School*, and *Point Judith* included Gray performing a thirteen-minute version of Eugene O'Neill's *Long Day's Journey into Night*. Most subsequent Wooster Group productions have incorporated a classic text as part of the "found" materials used in their creation, usually collaged with texts and performances lifted from popular culture, as well as action sequences devised by the company.

Other characteristic approaches developed during these performances included: the use of a series of scenic elements which recur from show to show in different ways (e.g., a red tent, a skeletal house structure, a long table); the adoption of a predominantly demonstrational, frontal style of performance, in which roles are enacted rather than characters impersonated; the use of the performers' own names on stage – although they are not usually "playing themselves" as such; the practice of reading from scripts of texts used, thus highlighting the pre-scripted (and prescribing) nature of the text; high-speed delivery of text which disregards the sort of inflections associated with more naturalistic acting; the presence of a raisonneur/emcee figure who introduces, orchestrates, and comments on the onstage action; the frequent use of music, both classical and popular, usually played on gramophones in view of the audience and often providing an ironic contrast with concurrent text and action or an ironically excessive accompaniment to them; the use of obscene or pornographic actions and texts as a disruptive device; the use of dance which seems to irrupt upon the action in a nondiegetic fashion; the use of video alongside the live performances.

Despite seeming liberties LeCompte takes with the texts used, she claims they are generally texts which she regards highly, although this may be tempered by particular reservations about them: her work then attempts to stage the event of the Group's confrontation with the text in question. Thus *Route 1 & 9* (1981) developed out of LeCompte's fascination with Thornton Wilder's *Our Town*. She was attracted to its humanism and its nostalgic image of America but also disturbed by its enshrined place within the American imagination. The performance began with a twenty-minute video of Ron Vawter reproducing a lecture by Clifton Fadiman exploring the play's themes and placing it within a liberal humanist perception of art's consolatory and universalizing role. Vawter's deadpan performance and the way in which the "lecture" was staged and filmed created an ironic frame for viewing the excerpts of *Our Town* which followed. These were played in soap-opera "close-up" on video monitors which hovered above live performers in blackface who carried out a comic house-building routine, held a wild party, and performed a series of Pigmeat Markham vaudeville sketches.

Dramatic texts used in subsequent productions include: Miller's *The Crucible* in *LSD* (...Just The High Points...) (1984), Flaubert's *La Tentation de St. Antoine* (*Frank Dell's The Temptation of Saint Antony*, 1987), Chekhov's *Three Sisters* (*Brace Up!*, 1990 and *Fish Story*, 1993), O'Neill's *The Emperor Jones* (1993) and *The Hairy Ape* (1997), and Stein's *Dr. Faustus Lights the Lights* (*House/Lights*, 1997).

In each case various layers of activity and other texts are accrued around the initiating text, often in ways which may seem quite random to a spectator, but which usually derive from various associative leaps made during the devising process. (The shows are usually devised over a long period, with different versions being shown publicly en route; with productions staying – and evolving – in the repertoire for up to five years, there is considerable development between early and later performances.) So, in the case of *LSD*, one of the group had brought in a recording of Timothy Leary speeches. Fascinated by

the tone of his voice and a sense of paranoia in it, LeCompte decided (in the
first version of the production) to precede *The Crucible* with twenty minutes of
the recording, producing an association between the McCarthyite witch-hunts
which lay behind *The Crucible* and more recent witch-hunts around drugs.
After Arthur Miller took out an injunction against what he saw as the Group's
parodic playing of *The Crucible*, Michael Kirby wrote a script modeled on the
play. Meanwhile, Leary's babysitter provided the Group with her recollec-
tions of life at Leary's Millbrook commune. These were included, alongside
memories of Leary's son, Jackie. As the *Crucible* text was increasingly surrounded by other material to do with the 1960s counterculture, the group
decided to film themselves rehearsing the play after taking acid; a detailed
recreation of their behavior formed the basis of Part 3 of the show. To this was
added a film of Ron Vawter in Miami – soon after he had appeared in *Miami
Vice*, along with recreations of debates between Leary and the Watergate
burglar Gordon Liddy (who had worked for the CIA in Miami). This became
the occasion to include some spoof Latin American dancing. The production
refused to manipulate these various strands of text and action toward some
tidy, unifying interpretation of the events presented. Instead, its "messiness"
embodied the conflicting viewpoints within the group and in wider society
about the issues and figures dealt with.

If this collection of materials sounds potentially confusing, *LSD* seems like
an old-fashioned "well-made play" in comparison with the subsequent *Frank
Dell's The Temptation of Saint Antony*. Here the Group's working materials
included: Ingmar Bergman's *The Magician*; Gustave Flaubert's *La Tentation
de St. Antoine*; dances devised in conjunction with Peter Sellars; Geraldine
Cummins's *The Road to Immortality*; a biography and recordings of Lenny
Bruce; a video in which the performers mimicked nude chat shows found on
the cable television Channel J; a film made with Ken Kobland – *Flaubert
Dreams of Travel But the Illness of His Mother Prevents It*; the Spanish dance
troupe from *LSD* – Donna Sierra and the Del Fuegos; various other found
visual and filmic images – including a picture of Willem Dafoe as Christ in
Scorsese's *The Last Temptation of Christ*; along with various incidents and
interruptions which occurred during the rehearsal process.

While champions of the Group have highlighted the potentially deconstructive effects of the complex juxtapositions of imagery and texts in their
work, hostile critics have attacked the supposed mangling of the classic texts
found therein and described the collagist approach as willfully confusing.
Claims to the production of open texts have been turned on their head by
accusations that the profusion of materials and performance styles, along with
their allusive nature, leads to work which closes out all but a few "super-
competent" spectators capable of the games of cultural cross-referencing and
intertextuality which they evoke. In contrast with attempts to see them

pursuing a Brechtian project of estrangement and historicization, Framji Minwalla claims that,

> Brecht's dialectic forces a re-examination of assumptions more effectively than the jagged disruptions present in the Wooster Group's work. Brecht demands that we judge but from an informed perspective; the Wooster Group suggests that we accept and absorb, and this from a condition of emotional saturation that leads to emotional paralysis. (Minwalla 1992: 9)

Even David Savran, whose 1986 study contributed much to an understanding of their working processes, found that *Saint Antony* left him "increasingly skeptical of those artists (and critics) who produce a cultural critique so subtle and so endlessly skeptical that it finally does little else than deconstruct itself" (Savran 1991: 53).

The Group has exposed itself to such charges not just through the work but in discussions of it. LeCompte and others have insisted that the work does not seek to propose particular messages or meanings, political or otherwise. Like Lyotard's postmodern artist who "works without rules in order to formulate the rules of *what will have been done*" (Lyotard 1984: 81), LeCompte argues that it is only "after the fact certain things become obvious, but they're never obvious to begin with." She asserts that she is primarily interested in allowing the elements in her work "to be in the space together, without this demand for meaning. That's not what I'm about" (Kaye 1996: 254, 256). Furthermore, Wooster Group members have consistently rejected the idea of a polemical art, resisting the temptation of producing closure in such work. Such an attitude has sometimes exploded in their own faces. The portrayal of racist stereotypes in the blackface Pigmeat Markham routines of *Route 1 & 9* led to charges of racism which resulted in their losing their funding from New York's Council for the Arts; the sustained use of pornographically sexist dialogue in the first part of *Point Judith* prompted walkouts by female spectators and charges of sexism, while the pornographic film sequence at the end of *Route 1 & 9* was attacked for its supposed exploitation of the actress involved. Undeterred, later works such as *House/Lights* and *The Emperor Jones* have continued to use blackface and pornographic imagery. While the Group has acknowledged that it may have been "safer" to include some framing commentary which distanced itself from the attitudes portrayed, it has argued that to do so would be both dishonest, since they would not claim to be entirely free of racist and sexist attitudes themselves, and less disturbing to the spectators, who could be left complacent in their belief that they are free of such attitudes.

In the face of such refusal to occupy a moral highground, defenders of the work have tended to take one of two routes. One is effectively to attempt to incorporate the work into a more discursive or thematizing mode of analysis which, while recognizing a lack of intentionality and noting disturbances provoked by certain elements in the work, privileges aspects of the performances which are more open to progressive political interpretation. So, for example, we are invited to read the blackface performance in *Route 1 & 9* as overtly critiquing the all-white world of Wilder's play or to interpret the fact that the men in part two of *LSD* speak into microphones, while the women do not, as an image of patriarchal oppression. While such attempts may sometimes be locally persuasive, they underestimate the extent to which, in performance, the shows work more through the pulsing of varying "intensities," bearing in mind Jameson's claim that such intensities in postmodern work generally have no clear cognitive value. On the other hand, commentators such as Kaye and Auslander have acknowledged the work "risks pursuing a confusion of the politically radical and the reactionary" and is "open to charges of unthinking complicity with the material it incorporates" (Kaye 1994: 128). They would suggest, however, that the politics of the work lies in the very disturbance it creates, in its refusal to work toward closure and in the way in which the style of performance itself tends to undermine the actor's presence and authority, thus demanding that spectators make their own judgments on the material. Needless to say, critics of the anti-representational elements in much postmodern work have been skeptical of such attempts to delineate a resistant postmodernism in the Group's work.

In the face of such pressure to defend the work politically, it is perhaps inevitable that few are willing to validate the Wooster Group's work on the basis of its libidinal pleasures. And yet when I remember shows I have seen or discuss them with others who have seen them, what usually springs to mind, beyond some of the darker, more grotesque elements, is the sheer playful exuberance of the *performances*: the virtuosity of the way the performers shift style, tone, and personae at the drop of a hat, or the comic and sensual excess of the dances in productions such as *Route 1 & 9, LSD*, and *Brace Up!* (where the sight of the whole company doing a beautifully orchestrated Polynesian dance brought the house down in Glasgow).

Anyone familiar with Scott Lash's tracing of postmodernism as a "figural" formation – from Nietzsche, through the Surrealists, Artaud, Sontag, and early Lyotard (in *The Libidinal Economy* [1974]) – will recognize in this listing a focus on sensation and the libidinal in contrast with the discursive thrust of modernism. While the Group's work does at times approximate to a more discursive Brechtian tradition, and while LeCompte refers to her formalist tendencies in composition, and these aspects are evident in the work, it is generally more shaped by such figural concerns and evokes responses which are more libidinal than cognitive. As such, what claims it may make for some degree of political engagement rest or fall on the sort of arguments associated with such a tradition, with it always being open to the charges of naivety and irresponsibility that will be brought against such an approach by those who desire an art which more clearly displays its moral or political commitment and which searches out more "popular" audiences than those found at the Performing Garage or on the avant-garde touring circuit.

Bibliography

Ackroyd, Peter. (1982). *The Great Fire of London*. London: Hamish Hamilton.
——. (1983). *The Last Testament of Oscar Wilde*. London: Hamish Hamilton.
——. (1985). *Hawksmoor*. London: Hamish Hamilton.
——. (1987). *Chatterton*. London: Hamish Hamilton.
——. (1989). *First Light*. London: Hamish Hamilton.
——. (1992). *English Music*. London: Hamish Hamilton.
——. (1993 [1976]). *Notes for a New Culture*. London: Alkin Books.
——. (1993a). *The House of Doctor Dee*. London: Hamish Hamilton.
——. (1993b). London Luminaries and Cockney Visionaries. The LWT London Lecture. Victoria and Albert Museum, December 7.
——. (1995). *The Englishness of English Literature*. In Javier Pérez Guerra (ed.), *Proceedings of the XIXth International Conference of AEDEAN*. Vigo: Universidade de Vigo, pp. 11–19.
——. (1996). *Milton in America*. London: Sinclair Stevenson.
——. (1998a). *An Interview with Peter Ackroyd*. http://boldtype.com/1998/ackroyd/interview.html.
——. (1998b). *The Life of Thomas More*. London: Chatto and Windus.
——. (1999). *The Plato Papers*. London: Chatto and Windus.
Ahmad, Aijaz. (1992). *In Theory: Classes, Nations, Literatures*. London: Verso.
Allen, William Rodney. (ed.). (1988). *Conversations with Kurt Vonnegut*. Jackson: University Press of Mississippi.
Althusser, Louis. (1969). *For Marx*. Trans. Ben Brewster. London: Verso.
——. (1971a). *Lenin and Philosophy*. Trans. Ben Brewster. New York: Monthly Review Press.
——. (1971b). "Ideology and Ideological State Apparatuses." In *Lenin and Philosophy, and Other Essays*. Trans. Ben Brewster. London: New Left Books.
——. (1976). *Essays in Self-criticism*. Trans. G. Lock. London: New Left Books.
——. (1993). *The Future Lasts Forever*. Trans. R. Veasey. New York: The New Press.
——. (1996). *Writings on Psychoanalysis: Freud and Lacan*. Ed. Olivier Corpet and François Matheron. Trans. Jeffrey Mehlman. New York: Columbia University Press.

———. (1997). *The Spectre of Hegel: Early Writings*. Ed. François Matheron. Trans. G. M. Goshgarian. London: Verso.

———and Balibar, Etienne. (1970). *Reading Capital*. Trans. Ben Brewster. London: New Left Books.

Anderson, Perry. (1998). *The Origins of Postmodernity*. London: Verso.

Appadurai, Arjun. (1990). Disjuncture and Difference in the Global Cultural Economy. *Public Culture* 2.2 (Spring), 1–17.

Arnell, Peter, Pickford, Ted, and Bergart, Catherine (eds.). (1984). *A View from Campodoglio: Selected Essays, 1953–1982*. New York: Harper and Row.

Arrighi, Giovanni. (1994). *The Long Twentieth Century*. London: Verso.

Ashbery, John. (1966). *Rivers and Mountains*. New York: Ecco.

———. (1970). *The Double Dream of Spring*. New York: Ecco.

———. (1972). *Three Poems*. New York: Viking.

———. (1974). The Craft of John Ashbery. Interview with Louis A. Osti. *Confrontations* 9.3, 84–96.

———. (1983a). The Art of Poetry XXXIII. Interview with Peter Stitt. *Paris Review* 25.90, 30–76.

———. (1983b). The Imminence of a Revelation. Interview with Richard Jackson. In Richard Jackson, *Acts of Mind: Conversations with Contemporary Poets*. University, Alabama: University of Alabama Press, pp. 69–76.

———. (1984). John Ashbery. Interview with Ross Labrie. *American Poetry Review* 13.3, 29–33.

———. (1985). John Ashbery: Interview with John Murphy. *Poetry Review* 75.2, 20–5.

———. (1993). Entretien avec John Ashbery. Interview with André Bleikasten. *La Quinzaine Littéraire* 16.28, 7–8.

Ashmore, M. (1989). *The Reflexive Thesis: Wrighting Sociology of Scientific Knowledge*. Chicago: University of Chicago Press.

Auping, Michael. (1992). *Jenny Holzer*. New York: Universe Publishing.

Auslander, Philip. (1982). *Presence and Resistance*. Ann Arbor: University of Michigan Press.

———. (1987). Toward a Concept of the Political in Post-Modern Theatre. *Theater Journal* 39.1, 20–34.

———. (1992). *Presence and Resistance: Postmodernism and Cultural Politics in Contemporary American Performance*. Ann Arbor: University of Michigan Press.

———. (1997). *From Acting to Performance: Essays in Modernism and Postmodernism*. London: Routledge.

Auster, Paul. (1982). *The Invention of Solitude*. New York: Penguin.

———. (1985). *City of Glass*. New York: Penguin.

———. (1986a). *Ghosts*. New York: Penguin.

———. (1986b). *The Locked Room*. New York: Penguin.

———. (1987). *In the Country of Last Things*. New York: Viking Press.

———. (1989). *Moon Palace*. New York: Penguin.

———. (1990). *The Music of Chance*. New York: Viking Press.

———. (1992a). *The Art of Hunger*. Los Angeles: Sun and Moon Press.

———. (1992b). *Leviathan*. New York: Penguin.

———. (1999). *Timbuktu*. New York: Henry Holt.

Bachman, I. (1998). Material and the Promise of the Immaterial. In I. Bachman and R. Scheuing (eds.), *Material Matters: The Art and Culture of Contemporary Textiles*. Canada: YYZ Books, pp. 23–34.

Bailey, J. (1996). *After Thought: The Computer Challenge to Human Intelligence*. New York: Basic Books/HarperCollins.

Bakhtin, Mikhail. (1981 [1934–5]). Discourse in the Novel. In M. Holquist (ed.), *The Dialogic Imagination*. Trans. C. Emerson and M. Holquist. Austin: University of Texas Press, pp. 259–422.

———. (1965). *Rabelais and His World*. Trans. Helene Iswolsky. Bloomington: Indiana University Press.

———. (1986). Towards a Methodology for the Human Sciences. In C. Emerson and M. Holquist (eds.), *Speech: Genres and Other Late Essays*. Trans. V. McGee. Austin: University of Texas Press.

Balderston, D. (1993). *Out of Context: Historical Reference and the Representation of Reality in Borges*. Durham, NC and London: Duke University Press.

Banes, Sally. (1998). *Subversive Expectations: Performance Art and Paratheater in New York 1976–85*. Ann Arbor: University of Michigan Press.

Barker, James R. (1989). An Interview with John Fowles. *Michigan Quarterly Review* 25.4 (Autumn), 661–83.

Barth, John. (1956). *The Floating Opera*. New York: Appleton Century Crofts.

———. (1958). *The End of the Road*. New York: Doubleday.

———. (1960). *The Sot-Weed Factor*. New York: Doubleday.

———. (1966). *Giles Goat-Boy*. New York: Doubleday.

———. (1967). The Literature of Exhaustion. *Atlantic Monthly* 220.2, 9–34.

———. (1968). *Lost in the Funhouse*. New York: Doubleday.

———. (1972). *Chimera*. New York: Doubleday.

———. (1979a). *LETTERS: A Novel*. New York: G. P. Putnam's Sons.

———. (1979b). The Literature of Replenishment: Postmodernist Fiction. *Atlantic Monthly* 245.1, 65–71.

———. (1982). *Sabbatical: A Romance*. New York: G. P. Putnam's Sons.

———. (1984). *The Friday Book: Essays and Other Nonfiction*. New York: Perigee Books.

———. (1987). *The Tidewater Tales*. New York: G. P. Putnam's Sons.

———. (1991). *The Last Voyage of Somebody the Sailor*. Boston: Little, Brown.

———. (1994). *Once Upon a Time: A Floating Opera*. Boston: Little, Brown.

———. (1995). *Further Fridays: Essays, Lectures, and Other Nonfiction, 1984–1994*. Boston: Little, Brown.

———. (1996). *On with the Story*. Boston: Little, Brown.

Barthes, Roland. (1967 [1953]). *Writing Degree Zero*. Trans. A. Lavers and C. Smith. New York: Noonday Press.

———. (1967 [1964]). *Elements of Semiology*. Trans. A. Lavers and C. Smith. New York: Hill and Wang.

———. (1972 [1957]). *Mythologies*. Trans. A. Lavers. New York: Hill and Wang.

———. (1974 [1970]). *S/Z*. Trans. R. Howard. New York: Hill and Wang.

——. (1975 [1973]). *The Pleasure of the Text*. Trans. R. Miller. New York: Hill and Wang.

——. (1976 [1971]). *Sade, Fourier, Loyola*. Trans. R. Miller. Baltimore: Johns Hopkins University Press.

——. (1977 [1966]). Introduction to the Structural Analysis of Narratives. In *Image/ Music/ Text*. Trans. Stephen Heath. New York: Hill and Wang, pp. 79–124.

——. (1977 [1968]). The Death of the Author. In *Image/ Music/ Text*. Trans. Stephen Heath. New York: Hill and Wang, pp. 142–8.

——. (1977 [1971]). From Work to Text. In *Image/ Music/ Text*. Trans. Stephen Heath. New York: Hill and Wang, pp. 155–64.

——. (1977 [1975]). *Roland Barthes by Roland Barthes*. Trans. R. Howard. New York: Hill and Wang.

——. (1977). *Image/ Music/ Text*. Trans. Stephen Heath. New York: Hill and Wang.

——. (1978 [1977]). *A Lover's Discourse: Fragments*. Trans. R. Howard. New York: Hill and Wang.

——. (1984 [1979]). *Sollers Writer*. Trans. P. Thody. London: Athlone Press.

——. (1985). *The Responsibility of Forms: Essays on Music, Art, and Representation*. Trans. Richard Howard. New York: Hill and Wang.

——. (1990 [1967]). *The Fashion System*. Trans. M. Ward and R. Howard. Berkeley: University of California Press.

——. (1992 [1964]). The Structuralist Activity. In H. Adams (ed.), *Critical Theory Since Plato*. Rev. ed. San Diego: Harcourt Brace Jovanovich, pp. 128–30.

Bataille, Georges. (1953). *Méthode de méditation*. Paris: Gallimard.

——. (1962 [1957]). *Eroticism*. Trans. M. Dalwood. London: Calder and Boyars.

——. (1973). *La Somme athéologique*. Paris: Galllimard.

——. (1986 [1936]). *Blue of Noon*. Trans. H. Mathews. New York: M. Boyars.

——. (1988 [1967]). *The Accursed Share*. Trans. R. Hurley. New York: Zone Books.

——. (1989 [1961]). *The Tears of Eros*. Trans. P. Connor. San Francisco: City Lights.

——. (1992 [1976]). *Theory of Religion*. Trans. R. Hurley. New York: Zone Books.

Baudrillard, Jean. (1975 [1973]). *The Mirror of Production*. St. Louis: Telos Press.

——. (1981 [1973]). *For a Critique of the Political Economy of the Sign*. St. Louis: Telos Press.

——. (1983a). The Ecstasy of Communication. In Hal Foster (ed.), *The Anti-Aesthetic*. Washington: Bay Press.

——. (1983b). *In the Shadow of the Silent Majorities*. New York: Semiotext(e).

——. (1983c). *Simulations*. New York: Semiotext(e).

——. (1988). *America*. London: Verso.

——. (1990a). *Cool Memories*. London: Verso.

——. (1990b). *Fatal Strategies*. New York: Semiotext(e).

——. (1993 [1976]). *Symbolic Exchange and Death*. London: Sage.

——. (1993a). The Precession of Simulacra. Trans. P. Foss, P. Patton, and P. Beitchman. In Joseph Natoli and Linda Hutcheon (eds.), *A Postmodern Reader*. Albany, NY: SUNY Press, pp. 342–75.

——. (1993b). *The Transparency of Evil*. London: Verso.

——. (1994 [1981]). *Simulacra and Simulation*. Ann Arbor: University of Michigan Press.

——. (1994). *The Illusion of the End*. Oxford: Polity.

——. (1995). *The Gulf War Never Happened*. Oxford: Polity.

——. (1996 [1968]). *The System of Objects*. London: Verso.

——. (1996a). *Cool Memories II*. Oxford: Polity.

——. (1996b). *The Perfect Crime*. London and New York: Verso Books.

——. (1998 [1970]). *The Consumer Society*. Paris: Gallimard.

Bauman, Zygmunt. (1993). *Postmodern Ethics*. Oxford: Blackwell.

Bawer, Bruce. (1991). Reading Don DeLillo. In Frank Lentricchia (ed.), *Introducing Don DeLillo*. Durham, NC: Duke University Press, pp. 7–42.

Baxter, Charles. (1994). The Bureau of Missing Persons: Notes on Paul Auster's Fiction. *Review of Contemporary Fiction* 14, 40–4.

Beauvoir, Simone de. (1952). *The Second Sex*. New York: Modern Library.

Belpoliti, Marco. (1996). *L'occhio di Calvino*. Turin: Einaudi.

——. (1991). *Italo Calvino. Enciclopedia: arte, scienza e letteratura*. Milan: Marcos y Marcos.

Benhabib, Seyla et al. (eds.). (1995). *Feminist Contentions: A Philosophical Exchange*. New York: Routledge.

Bennett, David. (1985). Parody, Postmodernism, and the Politics of Reading. *Critical Quarterly* 27.4 (Winter).

Berman, M. (1983). *All That is Solid Melts into Air: The Experience of Modernity*. London and New York: Verso.

Bernardini, Francesca Napoletano. (1977). *I segni nuovi di Italo Calvino*. Rome: Bulzoni.

Bernasconi, Robert. (1982). The Trace of Levinas in Derrida. In R. Bernasconi and D. Wood (eds.), *Derrida and Difference*. Coventry: Parousia Press, pp. 17–44.

Bernstein, R. J. (1991). *The New Constellation: The Ethical-Political Horizons of Modernity/Postmodernity*. Cambridge: Polity.

Berressem, Hanjo. (1993). *Pynchon's Poetics: Interfacing Theory and Text*. Urbana and Chicago: University of Illinois Press.

Bertens, Hans. (1993 [1986]). The Postmodern Weltanschauung and its Relation to Modernism: An Introductory Survey. In Joseph Natoli and Linda Hutcheon (eds.), *A Postmodern Reader*. Albany NY: SUNY Press, pp. 25–70.

——. (1995). *The Idea of the Postmodern: A History*. London and New York: Routledge.

Best, Steven and Kellner, Douglas. (1991). *Postmodern Theory: Critical Interrogations*. London and New York: Macmillan and Guilford Press.

——and——. (1997). *The Postmodern Turn*. New York: Guilford Press.

Birringer, J. (1988). Debating "Ways of Speaking, Loci of Cognition." *Drama Review* 32.1, 4–13.

——. (1991). *Theatre, Theory, Post-Modernism*. Bloomington: University of Indiana Press.

Bloom, Harold (ed.). (1985). *John Ashbery*. New York: Chelsea House.

Bogue, Ronald. (1989). *Deleuze and Guattari*. London and New York: Routledge.

Bohr, Niels. (1983). Can Quantum-Mechanical Description of Physical Reality be Considered Complete? In John Archibald Wheeler and Wojciech Hubert Zurek (eds.), *Quantum Theory and Measurement*. Princeton, NJ: Princeton University Press.

——. (1987). *The Philosophical Writings of Niels Bohr*. 3 vols. Woodbridge, CT: Ox Box Press.

Bondanella, Peter. (1997). *Umberto Eco and the Open Text: Semiotics, Fiction, Popular Culture*. Cambridge: Cambridge University Press.

Borges, Jorge Luis. (1970). *Labyrinths*. Harmondsworth: Penguin.

——. (1989). La Biblioteca de Babel. In María Kodama y Emecé (ed.), *Obras Completas*. Vol. 1. Barcelona.

——. (1999). *Collected Fiction*. London: Penguin.

Bouchard, Norma and Pravadelli, Veronica. (eds). (1998). *Umberto Eco's Alternative: The Politics of Culture and the Ambiguities of Interpretation*. New York: Peter Lang.

Bradbury, Malcolm. (1984). Postmoderns and Others: The 1960s and 1970s. *The Modern American Novel*. Oxford: Oxford University Press.

Brandist, Craig. (1996). The Official and the Popular in Gramsci and Bakhtin. *Theory, Culture and Society* 13.2, 59–74.

Brittain, D. (1991). True Confessions: Interview with Cindy Sherman. *Creative Camera* 308, 34–8.

Brown, T. (1997). Collaboration: Life and Death in the Aesthetic Zone. In W. Hopps and S. Davidson (eds.), *Robert Rauschenberg: A Retrospective*. New York: Guggenheim Museum, pp. 268–74.

Bruckner, Pascal. (1995). Paul Auster, Or the Heir Intestate. In D. Barone (ed.), *Beyond the Red Notebook: Essays on Paul Auster*. Philadelphia: University of Pennsylvania Press, pp. 27–33.

Bryant, Sylvia. (1998). Re-constructing Oedipus through Beauty and the Beast. In Lindsay Tucker (ed.), *Critical Essays on Angela Carter*. New York: G. K. Hall, pp. 83–95.

Brzezinski, Zbigniew and Friedrich, Carl J. (1956). *Totalitarian Dictatorship and Autocracy*. Cambridge, MA: Harvard University Press.

Bunzli, James. (1999). The Geography of Creation: *Décalage* as Impulse, Process, and Outcome in the Theatre of Robert Lepage. *Drama Review* 43.1 (T161), 79–103.

Butler, Judith. (1993). Poststructuralism and Postmarxism. *Diacritics: A Review of Contemporary Criticism* 23.4 (Winter), 3–11.

Caesar, Michael. (1999). *Umberto Eco: Philosophy, Semiotics, and the Work of Fiction*. Cambridge: Polity.

Cage, John. (1961). *Silence: Lectures and Writings by John Cage*. Middletown, CT: Wesleyan University Press.

—— and Helms, Hans G. (1997). Reflections of a Progressive Composer on a Damaged Society. *October* 82, 77–93.

Calabrese, Omar. (1992 [1987]). *Neo-Baroque: A Sign of the Times*. Trans. C. Lambert. Princeton, NJ: Princeton University Press.

Callari, Antonio and Ruccio, David. (eds.). (1996). *Postmodern Materialism and the Future of Marxist Theory*. Hanover: Wesleyan University Press.

——. (eds.). (1998). "Rereading Althusser." Special Issue of *Rethinking Marxism*, 10.3.

Calligaris, Contardo. (1973). *Italo Calvino*. Milan: Mursia.

Callinicos, A. (1989). *Against Postmodernism: A Marxist Critique*. Cambridge: Polity.

Calvino, Italo. (1952). *Il visconte dimezzato*. Turin: Einaudi.

——. (1959 [1956]). *The Baron in the Trees*. Trans. A. Colquhoun. New York: Random House.

——. (1959). *Il cavaliere inesistente*. Turin: Einaudi.

——. (1963 [1957]). *La speculazione edilizia*. Turin: Einaudi.

——. (1963). *La giornata di uno scrutatore*. Turin: Einaudi.

——. (1970). *Difficult Loves*. Trans. W. Weaver. London: Picador.

——. (1973). *The Castle of Crossed Destinies*. Trans. W. Weaver. San Diego, New York, and London: Harcourt Brace Jovanovich.

——. (1974 [1972]). *Invisible Cities*. Trans. W. Weaver. New York and London: Harcourt Brace Jovanovich.

——. (1976 [1965]). *Cosmicomics*. Trans. W. Weaver. New York: Harcourt Brace Jovanovich.

——. (1976 [1967]). *Tzero*. Trans. W. Weaver. New York and London: Harcourt Brace Jovanovich.

——. (1977). *The Nonexistent Knight and The Cloven Viscount*. Trans. A. Colquhoun. New York and London: Harcourt Brace Jovanovich.

——. (1979). *If on a Winter's Night a Traveler*. Trans. W. Weaver. New York and London. Harcourt Brace Jovanovich.

——. (1980). *Una pietra sopra*. Turin: Einaudi.

——. (1983). *Mr. Palomar*. Trans. W. Weaver. San Diego, New York, and London: Harcourt Brace Jovanovich.

——. (1984). *Collezione di sabbia*. Milan: Garzanti.

——. (1985 [1970]). *Difficult Loves. Smog. A Plunge into Real Estate*. Trans. W. Weaver. London: Picador.

——. (1987). *The Uses of Literature*. Trans. Patrick Creagh. San Diego, New York, and London: Harcourt Brace Jovanovich.

——. (1988a). *Lezioni Americane*. Milan: Garzanti.

——. (1988b). *Six Memos for the Next Millennium*. Cambridge, MA: Harvard University Press.

——. (1991). *Perché leggere i classici*. Milan: Mondadori.

——. (1998 [1947]). *The Path to the Spiders' Nest*. Trans. A. Colquhoun (1957). Revised by M. McLaughlin. London: Jonathan Cape.

Cannon, Joann. (1981). *Italo Calvino: Writer and Critic*. Ravenna: Longo.

——. (1989). *Postmodern Italian Fiction: The Crisis of Reason in Calvino, Eco, Sciascia, Malerba*. Rutherford: Fairleigh Dickinson University Press.

Cantor, Paul. (1991). "Adolf, We Hardly Knew You." In Frank Lentricchia (ed.), *New Essays on White Noise*. Cambridge: Cambridge University Press, pp. 39–62.

Capozzi, Rocco. (1989). Keeping in Tune with the Times. In Franco Ricci (ed.), *Calvino Revisited*. Ottawa: Dove House Press, pp. 65–84.

——. (ed.). (1997). *Reading Eco: An Anthology*. Bloomington: Indiana University Press.

Carrillo, C. (1999). Cindy Sherman: la femme aux mille visages. *Oeil-Revue d'Art* 504, 74–9.

Carroll, David. (1987). Narrative, Heterogeneity, and the Question of the Political: Bakhtin and Lyotard. In Murray Krieger (ed.), *The Aims of Representation*. New York: Columbia University Press, pp. 69–106.

Carter, Angela. (1966). *Shadow Dance*. London: Virago.

——. (1967). *The Magic Toyshop*. London: Virago.

——. (1969). *Heroes and Villains*. London: Penguin.

——. (1971). *Love*. New York: Penguin.

——. (1972). *The Infernal Desire Machines of Doctor Hoffman*. Harmondsworth: Penguin.

——. (1974). *Fireworks: Nine Profane Pieces*. New York: Penguin.

——. (1977). *The Passion of New Eve*. London: Virago.

——. (1979a). *The Bloody Chamber*. New York: Harper and Row.

——. (1979b). *The Sadeian Woman: An Exercise in Cultural History*. London: Virago.

——. (1982). *Nothing Sacred*. London: Virago.

——. (1984). *Nights at the Circus*. New York: Viking.

——. (1985). *Saints and Strangers*. New York: Viking.

——. (ed.). (1986). *Wayward Girls and Wicked Women*. New York: Penguin.

——. (ed.). (1990). *The Old Wives' Fairy Tale Book*. New York: Pantheon.

——. (1991). *Wise Children*. New York: Farrar, Straus, Giroux.

——. (1992). *Expletives Deleted*. New York: Vintage.

——. (1993a). *American Ghosts and Old World Wonders*. London: Chatto and Windus.

——. (ed.). (1993b). *Strange Things Sometimes Still Happen*. Boston: Faber and Faber.

——. (1995a). *Black Venus*. London: Chatto and Windus.

——. (1995b). *Burning Your Boats*. New York: Henry Holt.

——. (1997). *Shaking a Leg*. New York: Penguin.

Carter, Howard J. (1987). *I. Calvino: Metamorphoses of Fantasy*. Ann Arbor, MI: UMI Research Press.

Césaire, Aimé. (1972). *Discourse on Colonialism*. Trans. Joan Pinkham. New York: Monthly Review Press.

Champagne, L. (1981). Always Starting New: Elizabeth Lecompte. *Drama Review* 25.3, 19–28.

Charest, Rémy. (1997). *Robert Lepage: Connecting Flights*. Trans. Wanda Romer Taylor. London: Methuen.

Chong, Ping. (1988). *Kind Ness*. In J. Leverett and G. Richards (eds.), *New Plays USA 4*. New York: Theatre Communications Group, pp. 53–94.

——. (1989a). Notes for Mumblings and Digressions: Some Thoughts on Being an Artist, Being an American, Being a Witness.... *Melus* 16, 62–7.

——. (1989b). *Snow*. *Plays in Process*. Vol. 10. New York: Theatre Communications Group.

——. (1990). *Nuit Blanche: A Select View of Earthlings*. In M. Berson (ed.), *Between Worlds: Contemporary Asian-American Plays*. New York: Theatre Communications Group, pp. 1–28.

——. (1991). Untitled Statement. *American Theatre* 8, 40–2.

Civello, Paul. (1994). *American Literary Naturalism and its Twentieth-century Transformations: Frank Norris, Ernest Hemingway, Don DeLillo*. Athens: University of Georgia Press.

Cohen, Stephen F. (1985). *Rethinking the Soviet Experience: Politics and History Since 1917*. New York: Oxford University Press.

Colás, S. (1994). *Postmodernity in Latin America: The Argentine Paradigm*. Durham, NC and London: Duke University Press.

Cole, S. L. (1992). *Directors in Rehearsal*. New York and London: Routledge.

Coletti, Teresa. (1988). *Naming the Rose: Eco, Medieval Signs, and Modern Theory*. Ithaca, NY: Cornell University Press.

Connor, Steven. (1989). *Postmodernist Culture: An Introduction to Theories of the Contemporary*. London: Blackwell.

Conradi, Peter. (1982). *John Fowles*. London: Methuen.

Cooper, Peter L. (1983). *Signs and Symptoms: Thomas Pynchon and the Contemporary World*. Berkeley: University of California Press.

Coover, Robert. (1966). *The Origin of the Brunists*. New York: Putnam.

——. (1977). *The Public Burning*. New York: Viking.

——. (1980). *A Political Fable*. New York: Viking.

——. (1986). *Gerald's Party*. New York: Linden Press/Simon and Schuster.

——. (1987a). *Whatever Happened to Gloomy Gus of the Chicago Bears?* New York: Linden Press/Simon and Schuster.

——. (1987b). *"You Must Remember This." A Night at the Movies, Or You Must Remember This*. New York: Linden Press/Simon and Schuster.

——. (1991). *Pinocchio in Venice*. New York: Linden Press/Simon and Schuster.

——. (1996a). *Briar Rose*. New York: Grove.

——. (1996b). Preface. In John Hawkes, *The Lime Twig: Second Skin: Travesty*. New York: Viking Penguin.

——. (1998). *Ghost Town*. New York: Holt.

Creed, Barbara. (1987). From Here to Modernity: Feminism and Postmodernism. *Screen* 28.2, 47–68.

Creeley, Robert. (1994). Austerities. *Review of Contemporary Fiction* 14, 35–40.

Crimp, D. (1979). Pictures. *October* 8, 75–88.

Crowther, Hal. (1991). Clinging to the Rock: A Novelist's Choices in the New Mediocracy. In Frank Lentricchia (ed.), *Introducing Don DeLillo*. Durham, NC: Duke University Press, pp. 83–98.

Cruz, A. and Smith, E. A. T. (eds.). (1997). *Cindy Sherman: Retrospective*. Chicago and New York: Museum of Contemporary Art and Thames and Hudson.

Culler, J. (1998). *Framing the Sign: Criticism and its Institutions*. Oklahoma City: University of Oklahoma Press.

Danoff, I. M. (1984). Cindy Sherman: Guises and Revelations. In *Cindy Sherman*. New York: Pantheon Books, pp. 193–7.

Davis, M. (1985). Urban Renaissance and the Spirit of Postmodernism. *New Left Review* 151, 67–72.

De Lauretis, Teresa. (1978). Semiotic Models: Invisible Cities. *Yale Italian Studies* (January), 13–37.

———. (1989). Reading the (Post)Modern Text: *If On A Winter's Night A Traveler*, in Franco Ricci (ed.), *Calvino Revisited*. Ottawa: Dove House Press, pp. 131–45.

De Man, Paul. (1989 [1983]). Dialogue and Dialogism. In Gary Morson and Caryl Emerson (eds.), *Rethinking Bakhtin*. Evanston, IL: Northwestern University Press, pp. 105–14.

De Toro, A. (1994). The Epistemological Foundations of the Contemporary Condition. In R. A. Young (ed.), *Latin American Postmodernisms*. Amsterdam and Atlanta, GA: Editions Rodopi, pp. 29–51.

Debord, Guy. (1970). *The Society of the Spectacle*. Detroit: Black and Red.

DeCurtis, Anthony. (1991). An Outsider in this Society: An Interview with Don DeLillo. In Frank Lentricchia (ed.), *Introducing Don DeLillo*. Durham, NC: Duke University Press, pp. 131–41.

Deleuze, Gilles. (1990). Gilles Deleuze: Postmodern Philosopher? *Criticism* 32.4 (Fall), 401–18.

———. (1994a). *Difference and Repetition*. Trans. Paul Patton. New York: Columbia University Press.

———. (1994b). *What Is Philosophy?* Trans. Hugh Tomlinson and Graham Burchell. New York: Columbia University Press.

———. (1995). *Negotiations, 1972–1990*. Trans. Martin Joughin. New York: Columbia University Press.

———. (1996). *Gilles Deleuze and the Question of Philosophy*. Madison, NJ: Fairleigh Dickinson University Press.

———. (1997). *Wising Up the Marks: The Amodern William Burroughs*. Berkeley: University of California Press.

——— and Guattari, Félix. (1983 [1972]). *Anti- Oedipus: Capitalism and Schizophrenia I*. Trans. Robert Hurley, Mark Seem, and Helen R. Lane. Minneapolis: University of Minnesota Press.

——— and ———. (1986 [1975]). *Kafka: Towards A Minor Literature*. Trans. Dana Polan. Minneapolis: University of Minnesota Press.

——— and ———. (1987 [1980]). *A Thousand Plateaus: Capitalism and Schizophrenia II*. Trans. B. Massumi. Minneapolis: University of Minnesota Press.

Derrida, Jacques. (1962). *Edmund Husserl's Origin of Geometry: An Introduction*. Trans. John Leavey. Lincoln: University of Nebraska Press.

———. (1973 [1967]). *Speech and Phenomena, and Other Essays On Husserl's Theory of Signs*. Trans. David B. Allison. Evanston, IL: Northwestern University Press.

———. (1975). The Purveyor of Truth. Trans. Willis Domingo et al. *Yale French Studies* 51, 31–113.

———. (1976 [1967]). *Of Grammatology*. Trans. G. C. Spivak. Baltimore: Johns Hopkins University Press.

———. (1978 [1968]). *Writing and Difference*. Trans. A. Bass. Chicago: University of Chicago Press.

———. (1978 [1964]). *VIOLENCE and Metaphysics*. Trans. A. Bass. In *Writing and Difference*. Chicago: Chicago University Press, pp. 79–153.

———. (1979 [1967]). Living On: Border-Lines. Trans. J. Hulbert. In Harold Bloom et al. (eds.), *Deconstruction and Criticism*. New York: Seabury Press.

———. (1979 [1976]). *Spurs: Nietzsche's Styles*. Trans. Barbara Harlow. Chicago: University of Chicago Press.

———. (1980 [1973]). *The Archeology of the Frivolous: Reading Condillac*. Trans. John P. Leavey. Pittsburgh: Duquesne University Press.

———. (1981a [1972]). *Dissemination*. Trans. Barbara Johnson. Chicago: University of Chicago Press.

———. (1981b [1972]). *Positions*. Trans. A. Bass. Chicago: University of Chicago Press.

———. (1982 [1972]). *Margins of Philosophy*. Trans. Alan Bass. Chicago: University of Chicago Press.

———. (1982a). Of an Apocalyptic Tone Recently Adopted in Philosophy. Trans. John P. Leavey. *Semeia* 23 (1982) and *Oxford Literary Review* 6.2 (1984), 3–37.

———. (1982b). The Time of a Thesis: Punctuations. In Alan Montefiore (ed.), *Philosophy in France Today*. Cambridge: Cambridge University Press.

———. (1984a). Deconstruction and the Other. Interview with Richard Kearney. In Richard Kearney (ed)., *Dialogues with Contemporary Continental Thinkers*. Manchester: Manchester University Press.

———. (1984b). *Signéponge/Signsponge*. Trans. Richard Rand. New York: Columbia University Press. (Parallel French and English translation.)

———. (1985 [1982]). *The Ear of the Other: Otobiography, Transference, Translation: Texts and Discussions with Jacques Derrida*. Trans. Peggy Kamuf. New York: Schocken Books.

———. (1985). *Droits de Regards*. Photographs by M. F. Plissart, with an essay by Jacques Derrida. Paris: Minuit.

———. (1986 [1966]). Structure, Sign and Play in the Discourse of the Human Sciences. In H. Adams and L. Searle (eds.), *Critical Theory since 1965*. Tallahassee: University Presses of Florida, pp. 83–94.

———. (1986 [1974]). *Glas*. Trans. John Leavey and Richard Rand. Lincoln: University of Nebraska Press.

———. (1986). *Memoires: For Paul de Man*. Trans. Cecile Lindsay et al. New York: Columbia University Press.

———. (1987 [1978]). *The Truth in Painting*. Trans. G. Bennington and I. McLeod. Chicago: University of Chicago Press.

———. (1987 [1980]). *The Postcard: From Socrates to Freud and Beyond*. Trans. Alan Bass. Chicago: University of Chicago Press.

———. (1988 [1981]). The Deaths of Roland Barthes. Trans. Pascale-Anne Brault and Michael B. Naas. In Hugh J. Silverman (ed.), *Philosophy and Non-philosophy since Merleau-Ponty. Continental Philosophy-I*. London and New York: Northwestern University Press.

———. (1992 [1991]). *The Other Heading*. Bloomington: Indiana University Press.

———. (1993 [1990]). *Memoirs of the Blind*. Chicago: University of Chicago Press.

———. (1994 [1993]). *Specters of Marx*. New York: Routledge.

——. (1995). *Points... Interviews, 1974–1994*. Stanford: Stanford University Press.

——. (1997 [1994]). *The Politics of Friendship*. London: Verso.

—— and Vattimo, Gianni (eds.). (1998). *Religion*. Stanford, CA: Stanford University Press.

D'Isanto, L. (1994). Gianni Vattimo's Hermeneutics and the Trace of Divinity. *Modern Theology* 10.4, 361–81.

Donato, Eugenio and Macksey, Richard (eds.). (1972). *The Structuralist Controversy*. Baltimore: Johns Hopkins University Press.

Dosse, F. (1997). *History of Structuralism*. Vols. 1 and 2. Trans. D. Glassman. Minneapolis: University of Minnesota Press.

Douglas, Alfred. (1972). *The Tarot: The Origins, Meaning and Uses of the Cards*. Penguin: Harmondsworth.

Dow, William. (1998). Paul Auster's *The Invention of Solitude*: Glimmers in a Reach to Authenticity. *Critique: Studies in Contemporary Fiction* 39, 272–82.

Duras, Marguerite. (1966 [1952]). *The Sailor from Gibraltar*. Trans. Barbara Bray. London: Calder and Boyars.

——. (1966 [1958]). *Moderato Cantabile*. Trans. Richard Seaver. London: John Calder.

——. (1966 [1960]). *Hiroshima, mon amour*. Trans. Richard Seaver and Barbara Wright. London: Calder and Boyars.

——. (1966 [1964]). *The Ravishing of Lol Stein*. Trans. Richard Seaver. New York: Grove Press.

——. (1967 [1950]). *The Sea-Wall*. Trans. Herma Briffault. New York: Farrar, Straus and Giroux.

——. (1968 [1967]). *L'Amante Anglaise*. Trans. Barbara Bray. London: Hamish Hamilton.

——. (1968). *Yes, peut-être* and *Le Shaga*. In *Theatre II*. Paris: Éditions de Minuit.

——. (1973). *La Femme du Gange*. Paris: Benoît-Jacob.

——. (1976 [1973]). *India Song*. Trans. Barbara Bray. New York: Grove Press.

——. (1981). *Agatha*. Paris: Éditions de Minuit.

——. (1985 [1984]). *The Lover*. Trans. Barbara Bray. New York: Pantheon.

——. (1986 [1984]). *La Douleur* (also published as *The War: A Memoir*). Trans. Barbara Bray. London: Collins.

——. (1986). *La Pute de la côte normande*. Paris: Éditions de Minuit.

——. (1988 [1986]). *Blue Eyes, Black Hair*. Trans. Barbara Bray. London: Collins.

——. (1990 [1987]). *Practicalities*. Trans. Barbara Bray. London: Collins.

——. (1992 [1990]). *Summer Rain*. Trans. Barbara Bray. New York: Scribner's.

Eagleton, Terry. (1990). *The Ideology of the Aesthetic*. Cambridge, MA: Blackwell.

——. (1996). *The Illusions of Postmodernism*. Oxford: Blackwell.

Eco, Umberto. (1976 [1975]). *A Theory of Semiotics*. Bloomington: Indiana University Press.

——. (1979). *The Role of the Reader: Explorations in the Semiotics of Texts*. Bloomington: Indiana University Press.

——. (1988 [1956]). *The Aesthetics of Thomas Aquinas*. Trans. H. Bredin. Cambridge, MA: Harvard University Press.

——. (1988). *Foucault's Pendulum*. Trans. W. Weaver. New York: Harcourt Brace Jovanovich.

——. (1989 [1962]). *The Open Work*. Trans. A. Cancogni. Cambridge, MA: Harvard University Press.

——. (1989). *The Aesthetics of Chaosmos: The Middle Ages of James Joyce*. Cambridge, MA: Harvard University Press.

——. (1993 [1963]). *Misreadings*. Trans. W. Weaver. New York: Harcourt Brace.

——. (1994 [1964]). *Apocalypse Postponed*. Ed. R. Lumley. Bloomington: Indiana University Press.

——. (1994a). *The Name of the Rose including the Author's Postscript*. Trans. W. Weaver. New York: Harvest Books.

——. (1994b). *The Island of the Day Before*. Trans. W. Weaver. New York: Harcourt Brace Jovanovich.

——. (1994c). *Six Walks in the Fictional Woods*. Cambridge, MA: Harvard University Press.

——. (2000 [1997]). *Kant and the Platypus: Essays on Language and Cognition*. Trans. A. McEwen. New York: Harcourt Brace.

Ellis, John M. (1997). *Literature Lost*. New Haven, CT: Yale University Press.

Emmet, Paul. (1991). *The Cannibal* to *The Passion Artist*: Hawkes' Journey toward the Depths of the Unconscious. In Stanley Trachtenberg (ed.), *Critical Essays on John Hawkes*. Boston: G. K. Hall, pp. 186–200.

Enck, John. (1991). John Hawkes: An Interview, 20 March 1964. In Stanley Trachtenberg (ed.), *Critical Essays on John Hawkes*. Boston: G. K. Hall, pp. 59–70.

Fanon, Frantz. (1965 [1959]). *Studies in a Dying Colonialism*. Trans. Haakon Chevalier. New York: Monthly Review Press.

——. (1986 [1952]). *Black Skin, White Masks*. Trans. Charles Lam Markmann. London: Pluto Press.

——. (1988 [1964]). *Toward the African Revolution*. Trans. Haakon Chevalier. New York: Grove Press.

——. (1991 [1961]). *The Wretched of the Earth*. Trans. Constance Farrington. New York: Grove Weidenfeld.

Farell, F. B. (1994). *Subjectivity, Realism, and Postmodernism: The Recovery of the World*. Cambridge: Cambridge University Press.

Federman, Raymond. (1993). *Critifiction. Postmodern Essays*. Albany, NY: SUNY Press.

Feingold, M. (1998). Review of *The Emperor Jones*. *Village Voice*, March 24.

Feinstein, R. (1990). *Robert Rauschenberg: The Silkscreen Paintings, 1962–1964*. New York: Whitney Museum of American Art.

Ferman, Claudia. (1997). Carlos Fuentes y *Cristóbal Nonato*: Entre la modernidad y la posmodernidad. *Antipodas: Journal of Hispanic Studies of Australia and New Zealand* (special number), *Specular Narratives: Critical Persectives on Carlos Fuentes, Juan Goytisolo, Mario Vargas Llosa*, 8–9, 97–107.

Fiedler, Leslie A. (1961). The Pleasures of John Hawkes. Introduction to *The Lime Twig*. New York: New Directions.

——. (1971). Cross the Border-Close the Gap. In *The Collected Essays of L. Fiedler*. Vol. 2. New York: Simon and Schuster.

Fimiani, Mariapaola. (1998). Critique, clinique, esthétique de l'existence. In Lucio d'Alessandro and Adolfo Marino (eds.), *Michel Foucault: Trajectoires au coeur du présent*. Paris: L'Harmattan.

Fish, Stanley. (1980). *Is There a Text in This Class? The Authority of Interpretive Communities*. Cambridge, MA: Harvard University Press.

Fishburn, E. (1998). Hidden Pleasures in Borges's Allusions. In E. Fishburn (ed.), *Borges and Europe Revisited*. London: Institute of Latin American Studies, pp. 49–59.

Flynn, Patrick. (1993). Jenny Holzer. *Progressive* 57.4, 30–5.

Fokkema, Douwe. (1984). *Literary History, Modernism, and Postmodernism*. Amsterdam and Philadelphia: John Benjamins.

——and Bertens, H. (eds.). (1986). *Approaching Postmodernism*. Amsterdam and Philadelphia: John Benjamins.

Foster, Hal. (ed.). (1983). *The Anti-Aesthetic: Essays on Postmodern Culture*. Seattle: Bay Press.

——. (1984). (Post)Modern Polemics. *New German Critique* 33, 67–79.

——. (1985). *Recodings: Art, Spectacle, Cultural Politics*. Port Townsend, WA: Bay Press.

Foucault, Michel. (1968). *The Archaeology of Knowledge*. Trans. Alan Sheridan. New York: Pantheon.

——. (1973 [1961]). *Madness and Civilization*. Trans. R. Howard. New York: Vintage Books

——. (1973 [1966]). *The Order of Things*. London: Tavistock Publications.

——. (1977 [1975]). *Discipline and Punish: The Birth of the Prison*. Trans. Alan Sheridan. New York: Pantheon.

——. (1979 [1966]). Pour une morale de l'inconfort. *Nouvel Observateur* 754 (April 23–9, 1979), 82–3. In *Dits et écrits*, ed. Daniel Defert and François Ewald. Vol. 3. Paris: Gallimard (1994), pp. 783–87.

——. (1980). *Power/Knowledge: Selected Interviews and Other Writings, 1972–1977*. New York: Pantheon.

——. (1984 [1969]). What Is An Author? In *The Foucault Reader*, ed. P. Rabinow. New York: Pantheon Books, pp. 101–20.

——. (1984a). Un cours inédit. *Magazine Littéraire* 207 (May 1984), 35–9. Qu'est-ce que les lumières. In *Dits et écrits*, ed. Daniel Defert and François Ewald. Vol. 4. Paris: Gallimard (1994), pp. 679–88.

——. (1984b). What is Enlightenment? In *The Foucault Reader*, ed. P. Rabinow. New York: Pantheon Books, pp. 32–50. Qu'est-ce que les lumières. In *Dits et écrits*, ed. Daniel Defert and François Ewald. Vol. 4. Paris: Gallimard (1994), pp. 562–78.

——. (1985). La vie: L'expérience et la science. *Revue de Métaphysique et de Morale* 90.1 (January–March), 3–14. In *Dits et écrits*, ed. Daniel Defert and François Ewald. Vol. 4. Paris: Gallimard (1994), pp. 763–76.

Foulke, Robert. (1985–86). A Conversation With John Fowles, *Salmagundi*, 367–84.

Fowles, John. (1963). *The Collector*. London: Jonathan Cape.

——. (1965; rev. ed. 1977). *The Magus*. London: Jonathan Cape; Boston: Little, Brown (1966).

——. (1968). Notes on Writing a Novel. *Harper Magazine*, 88–97.

——. (1969). *The French Lieutenant's Woman*. London: Jonathan Cape.

——. (1974). *The Ebony Tower*. London: Jonathan Cape.

——. (1977). *Daniel Martin*. London: Jonathan Cape.

——. (1979). *The Tree*. New York: Ecco Press.

——. (1980 [1964]). *The Aristos*. Tiptree, Essex: Anchor Press.

——. (1982). *Mantissa*. London: Jonathan Cape.

——. (1986). *A Maggot*. London: Jonathan Cape.

——. (1995). *The Nature of Nature*. Covelo, CA: Yolla Bolly Press.

Fraad, Harriet, Resnick, Stephen, and Wolff, Richard. (1994). *Bringing It All Back Home: Class, Gender, and Power in the Modern Household*. London: Pluto.

Frankovits, Alan. (ed.). (1984). *Seduced and Abandoned: The Baudrillard Scene*. Glebe, NSW: Stonemoss.

Fraser, Nancy. (1989). *Unruly Practices: Power, Discourse and Gender in Contemporary Social Theory*. Cambridge: Cambridge University Press.

——, and Nicholson, Linda. (1988). Social Criticism without Philosophy: An Encounter between Feminism and Postmodernism. In Andrew Ross (ed.), *Universal Abandon? The Politics of Postmodernism*. Minneapolis: University of Minnesota Press, pp. 83–105.

Fredman, Stephen. (1990). *Poet's Prose: The Crisis in American Verse*. Cambridge: Cambridge University Press.

Fried, Michael. (1982). How Modernism Works: A Response To T. J. Clark. *Critical Inquiry* 9, 217–34.

Frieze, James. (1997). Channelling Rubble: *Seven Streams of the River Ota* and *After Sorrow*. *Journal of Dramatic Theory and Criticism* 12, 133–42.

Frow, John. (1991). The Last Things Before the Last: Notes on *White Noise*. In Frank Lentricchia (ed.), *Introducing Don DeLillo*. Durham, NC: Duke University Press, pp. 175–91.

Fuentes, Carlos. (1969). *La nueva novela hispanoamericana*. México, DF: Joaquín Mortiz.

——. (1976). *Terra Nostra*. Trans. Margaret Sayers Peden. London: Penguin.

——. (1981). The Art of Fiction (Interview). *Paris Review* 82, 140–75.

——. (1986 [1985]). *The Old Gringo*. Trans. Margaret Sayers Peden and Carlos Fuentes. London: André Deutsch.

——. (1989 [1987]). *Christopher Unborn*. Trans. Alfred MacAdam and Carlos Fuentes. London: André Deutsch.

——. (1993a). *La geografía de la novela*. México, DF: Alfaguara.

——. (1993b). *Tres discursos para dos aldeas*. Buenos Aires: Fondo de Cultura Económica.

——. (1997). *The Crystal Frontier: A Novel in Nine Stories*. New York: Farrar Straus Giroux.

Gaggi. Silvio. (1989). *Modern/Postmodern: A Study in Twentieth-century Arts and Ideas*. Philadelphia: University of Pennsylvania Press.

Gallop, Jane. (1984). *The Daughter's Seduction: Feminism and Psychoanalysis*. Ithaca, NY: Cornell University Press.

Gane, Mike. (1991). *Baudrillard. Critical and Fatal Theory.* London: Routledge.

——. (ed.). (1993). *Baudrillard Live. Selected Interviews.* London: Routledge.

García Canclini, Néstor. (1995 [1990]). *Hybrid Cultures: Strategies for Entering and Leaving Modernity.* Minneapolis: University of Minnesota Press.

Garner, Stanton B., Jr. (1994). *Bodied Spaces: Phenomenology and Performance in Contemporary Drama.* Ithaca, NY: Cornell University Press.

Gasché, Rodolphe (1979). Deconstruction as Criticism. *Glyph* 6, 177–215.

——. (1986). *The Tain of the Mirror: Deconstruction and the Philosophy of Reflection.* Cambridge, MA: Harvard University Press.

Gass, Joanne. (1995). Written on the Body: The Materiality of Myth in Angela Carter's *Heroes and Villains. Arkansas Review* 1, 12–30.

Gass, William. (1968). *In the Heart of the Heart of the Country.* New York: Harper and Row.

——. (1970). *Fiction and the Figures of Life.* New York: Knopf.

——. (1976). *On Being Blue: A Philosophical Inquiry.* Boston: Godine.

——. (1978). *The World Within the Word.* New York: Knopf.

——. (1995). *The Tunnel.* New York: Knopf.

——. (1996). *Finding a Form.* New York: Knopf.

——. (1997 [1966]).*Omensetter's Luck.* New York: Penguin.

——. (1997 [1985]). *Habitations of the Word.* Ithaca: Cornell University Press.

——. (1998). *Cartesian Sonata and Other Novellas.* New York: Knopf.

——. (1999 [1968]). *Willie Masters' Lonesome Wife.* Normal, OK: Dalkey Archive Press.

Gates, Henry Louis, Jr. (1991). Critical Fanonism. *Critical Inquiry* 17, 457–70.

Genette, G. (1982). *Palimpsestes: La littérature au second degré.* Paris: Éditions du Seuil.

Genosko, Gary. (1994). *Baudrillard and Signs.* London: Routledge.

——. (ed.). (1996). *The Guattari Reader.* Oxford: Blackwell.

Gibson, Nigel. (ed.). (1999). *Rethinking Fanon.* Amherst, NY: Humanity Books.

Gibson-Graham, J. K. (1996). *The End of Capitalism (As We Knew It).* Oxford and Cambridge, MA: Blackwell.

Girard, Gilles. (1995). Experimental Theater in Quebec: Some Descriptive Terms. In Joseph I. Donohoe, Jr. and Jonathan M. Weiss (eds.), *Essays on Modern Quebec Theater.* East Lansing: Michigan State University Press, pp. 151–63.

Goehr, Lydia. (1992). *The Imaginary Museum of Musical Works: An Essay in the Philosophy of Music.* Oxford: Clarendon Press.

Goodchild, Philip. (1996). *Deleuze and Guattari: An Introduction to the Politics of Desire.* London: Sage Publications.

Gordon, Lewis R. (1995). *Fanon and the Crisis of European Man.* New York: Routledge.

——, Sharpley-Whiting, T. Denean, & White, Renée T. (eds.). (1996). *Fanon: A Critical Reader.* Oxford: Blackwell.

Grabar, O. (1992). *The Mediation of Ornament.* Princeton, NJ: Princeton University Press.

Grace, Sherrill E. (1984). Courting Bluebeard with Bartók, Atwood, and Fowles: Modern Treatment of the Bluebeard Theme. *Journal of Modern Literature* 21.2, 245–62.

Graham, John. (1966). John Hawkes on his Novels: An Interview with John Graham. *Massachusetts Review* 7, 449–61.

Gramsci, Antonio. (1978). *Selections from the Prison Notebooks*. Ed. Quintin Hoare and Geoffrey Nowell -Smith. New York: International Publishers.

——. (1985). *Selections from the Cultural Writings*. Ed. David Forgacs. Cambridge, MA: Harvard University Press.

Gray, S. (1978). Playwright's Notes. *Performing Arts Journal* 3.2, 87–91.

——. (1979). About Three Places in Rhode Island. *Drama Review* 23.1, 31–42.

Greenblatt, S. (1995). Culture. In F. Lentricchia and T. McLaughlin (eds.), *Critical Terms for Literary Study*. Chicago: University of Chicago Press, pp. 225–32.

Greiner, Donald. (1991). The Photographer's Sight and the Painter's Sign in *Whistlejacket*. In Stanley Trachtenberg (ed.), *Critical Essays on John Hawkes*. Boston: G. K. Hall, pp. 211–19.

Guattari, Pierre-Félix (1996 [1986]). The Postmodern Impasse. Trans. Todd Dufresne. In Gary Genosk (ed.), *The Guattari Reader*. Oxford: Blackwell, pp. 109–13.

Guerard, Albert. J. (1950). Introduction. *The Cannibal*. New York: New Directions.

Guerlac, Suzanne. (1997). *Literary Polemics: Bataille, Sartre, Valéry, Breton*. Stanford: Stanford University Press.

Guimond, J. (1994). Auteurs as Autobiographers: Images by Jo Spence and Cindy Sherman. *Modern Fiction Studies* 40.3, 573–92.

Gutting, G. (1999). *Pragmatic Liberalism and the Critique of Modernity*. Cambridge: Cambridge University Press.

Habermas, Jürgen. (1987 [1983]). *The Philosophical Discourse of Modernity*. Trans. F. Lawrence. Cambridge, MA: MIT Press.

——. (1999). *Wahrheit Und Rechtfertigung. Philosophische Aufsätze*. Frankfurt am Main: Suhrkamp.

Haft, Adele J., White, Jane G., and White, Robert J. (eds.) (1987). *The Key to The Name of the Rose*. Harrington Park: Ampersand Associates.

Halimi, Serge. (1997). *Les Nouveaux Chiens de Garde*. Paris: Liber-Raisons d'Agir.

Hall, D. L. (1994). *Richard Rorty: Prophet and Poet of the New Pragmatism*. Albany, NY: SUNY Press.

Hall, Stuart. (1988). *The Hard Road to Renewal: Thatcherism and the Crisis of the Left*. London: Verso.

Hardt, Michael. (1993). *Gilles Deleuze: An Apprenticeship in Philosophy*. Minneapolis: University of Minnesota Press.

Harlan, D. (1997). The Return of the Moral Imagination. In *The Degradation of American History*. Chicago: University of Chicago Press, pp. 105–26.

Harris, Mary Emma. (1987). *The Arts at Black Mountain College*. Cambridge, MA: MIT Press.

Harvey, David. (1989). *The Condition of Postmodernity*. Oxford: Blackwell.

Harvie, Jennifer. (forthcoming). Transnationalism, Orientalism, and Cultural Tourism: *La Trilogie des dragons* and *The Seven Streams of the River Ota*. In Joseph I. Donohoe and Jane Koustas (eds.), *Robert Lepage: Theater sans frontières*. East Lansing: Michigan State University Press.

—— and Hurley, Erin. (1999). States of Play: Locating Québec in the Performances of Robert Lepage, Ex Machina, and the Cirque du Soleil. *Theatre Journal* 51.3, 299–315.

Hawkes, John. (1950 [1949]). *The Cannibal*. Norfolk, CT: New Directions.

——. (1951). *The Beetle Leg*. New York: New Directions.

——. (1961). *The Lime Twig*. Introduction by Leslie A. Fiedler. New York: New Directions.

——. (1964). *Second Skin*. New York: New Directions.

——. (1971). *The Blood Oranges*. New York: New Directions.

——. (1974). *Death, Sleep, and the Traveler*. New York: New Directions.

——. (1976). *Travesty*. New York: New Directions.

——. (1979). *The Passion Artist*. New York: Harper and Row.

——. (1981). *Virginie: Her Two Lives*. New York: Harper and Row.

——. (1985). *Adventures in the Alaskan Skin Trade*. New York: Simon and Schuster.

——. (1993). *Sweet William: A Memoir of Old Horse*. New York: Simon and Schuster.

——. (1996). *The Frog*. New York: Viking Penguin.

——. (1998). *Whistlejacket*. New York: Weidenfeld and Nicolson.

Hayles, N. Katherine. (1984). *The Cosmic Web: Scientific Field Models and Literary Strategies in the 20th Century*. Ithaca, NY: Cornell University Press.

Hebel, U. J. (ed.). (1989). *Intertextuality, Allusion, and Quotation: An International Bibliography of Critical Studies*. New York: Greenwood Press.

Heidegger, Martin. (1962 [1927]). *Being and Time*. Trans. J. Macquarrie and E. Robinson. New York: Harper and Row.

——. (1996). The Age of the World Picture. In T. Drucker (ed.), *Electronic Culture and Visual Representation: Technology and Visual Representation*. New York: Aperture, pp. 47–61.

Herman, David. (1997). "Structuralism's Fortunate Fall." *Postmodern Culture* 8.1. <http://jefferson.village.Virginia.edu/pmc/text-only/issue.997/review-1.997>.

——. (under review). Sciences of the Text.

Hodgdon, Barbara. (1996). Looking for Mr. Shakespeare after "the Revolution": Robert Lepage's Intercultural *Dream* Machine. In James C. Bulman (ed.), *Shakespeare, Theory, and Performance*. London: Routledge, pp. 68–91.

Holland, Eugene W., (1999). *Deleuze and Guattari's Anti- Oedipus: Introduction To Schizoanalysis*. London and New York: Routledge.

Holland, Norman. (1975). *5 Readers Reading*. New Haven, CT: Yale University Press.

Homer, Sean. (1998). *Fredric Jameson: Marxism, Hermeneutics, Postmodernism*. Cambridge: Polity.

Hong, T. (1995). Ping Chong. In H. Zia and S. B. Gall (eds.), *Notable Asian-Americans*. Detroit: Gale Research, pp. 54–6.

Honneth, Axel. (1985). An Aversion against the Universal: A Commentary on Lyotard's *Postmodern Condition*. *Theory, Culture and Society* 2.3, 147–57.

hooks, bell. (1991). *Yearning: Race, Class and Gender*. Boston: South End Press.

Howell, John. (1988). Jenny Holzer: The Message is the Medium. *ARTNews* (September), 122–7.

Hoyningen-Huene, Paul. (1994). *Reconstructing Scientific Revolutions: Thomas S. Kuhn's Philosophy of Science*. Trans. Alexander J. Levine. Chicago: University of Chicago Press.

Huffaker, Robert. (1980). *John Fowles*. Boston: Twayne.

Hume, Kathryn. (1992). *Calvino's Fictions: Cogito and Cosmos*. New York: Oxford University Press.

Humphrey, Chris. (2000). Bakhtin and the Study of Popular Culture: Re-Thinking Carnival as a Historical and Analytical Concept. In Craig Brandist and Galin Tihanov (eds.), *Materializing Bakhtin*. London: Macmillan, pp. 164–72.

Hunt, Nigel. (1989). The Global Voyage of Robert Lepage. *Drama Review* 33, 104–18.

Husserl, Edmund. (1970). The Origin of Geometry. In *The Crisis of the European Sciences and Transcendental Phenomenology*. Trans. David Carr. Evanston, IL: Northwestern University Press.

Hutcheon, Linda. (1988). *A Poetics of Postmodernism: History, Theory, Fiction*. New York and London: Routledge.

——. (1989). *The Politics of Postmodernism*. London and New York: Routledge.

——. (1993). Beginning to Theorize Postmodernism. In Joseph Natoli and Linda Hutcheon (eds.), *A Postmodern Reader*. Albany, NY: SUNY Press, pp. 243–72.

Huxtable, Ada Louise. (1981). The Troubled State of Modern Architecture. *Architectural Design* 51, 1–2, 8–17.

Huyssen, Andreas. (1986). *After the Great Divide: Modernism, Mass Culture, Postmodernism*. Bloomington: Indiana University Press.

——. (1993). Mapping the Postmodern. In Joseph Natoli and Linda Hutcheon (eds.), *A Postmodern Reader*. Albany, NY: SUNY Press, pp. 105–56.

Inglehart, Ronald. (1997). *Modernization and Postmodernization: Cultural, Economic, and Political Change in 43 Societies*. Princeton, NJ: Princeton University Press.

Iser, W. (1978). *The Act of Reading: A Theory of Aesthetic Response*. Baltimore: Johns Hopkins University Press.

Jameson, Fredric. (1984a). The Politics of Theory: Ideological Positions in the Postmodernism Debate. *New German Critique* 33, 53–65.

——. (1984b). Reviews. *Minnesota Review* 22, 116–22.

——. (1985 [1983]). Postmodernism and Consumer Society. In H. Foster (ed.), *Postmodern Culture*. London: Pluto Press, pp. 111–25.

——. (1991 [1984]). *Postmodernism, or, The Cultural Logic of Late Capitalism*. London: Verso.

——. (1998). *The Cultural Turn: Selected Writings on Postmodernism, 1983–1998*. London: Verso.

Jarry, Alfred. (1963 [1911]). What is Pataphysics? *Evergreen Review* 13, 131–51.

Jencks, Charles. (1975). The Rise of Post-Modern Architecture. *Architecture Association Quarterly* 7.4, 3–14.

——. (1977a). A Genealogy of Post-Modern Architecture. *Architectural Design* 47.4, 269–71.

——. (1977b). *The Language of Post-Modern Architecture*. London: Academy.

——. (1978). *The Language of Post-Modern Architecture*. 2nd ed. London: Academy.

——. (1981). *The Language of Post-Modern Architecture*. 3rd ed. London: Academy.

——. (1986). *What Is Post-Modernism?* London: Academy.

——. (1987). *Post-Modernism: The New Classicism in Art and Architecture.* London: Academy.

——. (1996). *What Is Post-Modernism?* 4th, rev. ed. London: Academy.

Jenkins, K. (1999). On Hayden White. In *Why History?: Ethics and Postmodernity.* London and New York: Routledge, pp. 89–158.

——. (1995). *On "What is History" from Carr and Elton to Rorty and White.* London and New York: Routledge.

Johnson, Barbara. (1980). The Frame of Reference: Poe, Lacan, Derrida. In *The Critical Difference: Essays in the Contemporary Rhetoric of Reading.* Baltimore: Johns Hopkins University Press.

Johnson, Ken. (1991). Theater of Dissent. *Art in America* 79.3, 128–31.

Jones, Amelia. (1991). Modernist Logic in Feminist Histories of Art. *Camera Obscura* 27, 149–64.

Joseph, Branden W. (1997). John Cage and the Architecture of Silence. *October* 81, 85–104.

Joyce, James. (1961 [1922]). *Ulysses.* New York: Random House.

——. (1976 [1939]). *Finnegans Wake.* Harmondsworth: Penguin.

Kagan, Matvei. (1922). Kak Vozmozhna Istoriia? *Zapiski Orlovskogo Gosudarstvennogo Universiteta* 1, 137–92.

——. (1997 [1922–3]). Two Aspirations in Art. Trans. F. Goodwin. *Experiment* 3, 254–64.

Kansteiner, W. (1993). Hayden White's Critique of the Writing of History. *History and Theory*, 32, 273–95.

Kaplan, E. Ann. (1988). Introduction. In E. Ann Kaplan (ed.), *Postmodernism and its Discontents: Theories and Practices.* London: Verso, pp. 1–9.

——. (1997). *Looking for the Other: Feminism, Film and the Imperial Gaze.* London: Routledge.

——. (2000). Postmodernism and Women's Studies. In Victor Taylor and Charles Edsvik (eds.), *The Routledge Encyclopedia on Postmodernism.* London: Routledge.

——, and Sprinker, M. (eds.). (1993). *The Althusserian Legacy.* London: Verso.

Kaye, N. (1994). *Postmodernism and Performance.* Basingstoke: Macmillan.

——. (1996). *Art into Theatre: Performance Interviews and Documents.* London: Harwood Academic Press.

Kellein, T. (1991). Wie schwierig sind Porträts/Wie schwierig sind die Menschen! In *Cindy Sherman.* Basel and Stuttgart: Kunsthalle and Editions Cantz, pp. 5–10.

Kellner, Douglas. (ed.). (1994). *Jean Baudrillard: A Critical Reader.* Oxford: Blackwell.

——. (1989). *Jean Baudrillard: From Marxism to Postmodernism and Beyond.* Cambridge and Palo Alto, CA: Polity and Stanford University Press.

Kershaw, Baz. (1996). The Politics of Performance in a Postmodern Age. In Patrick Campbell (ed.), *Analysing Performance.* Manchester: Manchester University Press, pp. 133–52.

Kotz, M. L. (1990). *Rauschenberg: Art and Life.* New York: Harry N. Abrams.

Krauss, R. (1997). Perpetual Inventory. In W. Hopps and S. Davidson (eds.), *Robert Rauschenberg: A Retrospective.* New York: Guggenheim Museum, pp. 206–23.

——, and Bryson, N. (1993). *Cindy Sherman, 1979–1993.* New York : Rizzoli International Publications.

Kristeva, Julia. (1973). The Ruin of a Poetics. In Stephan Bann and John E. Bowlt (eds.), *Russian Formalism: A Collection of Articles and Texts in Translation.* Edinburgh: Scottish Academic Press, pp. 102–19.

——. (1980 [1967]). Word, Dialogue, and Novel. In *Desire in Language: A Semiotic Approach to Literature and Art.* Ed. L. S. Roudiez. New York: Columbia University Press, pp. 64–91.

——. (1980). *Desire in Language: A Semiotic Approach to Literature and Art.* Ed. L. S. Roudiez. Trans. T. Gora, A. Jardine, and L. Roudiez. New York: Columbia University Press.

——. (1995). Beseda S Iuliei Kristevoi. *Dialog. Karnaval. Khronotop* 2, 5–17.

Kuehl, John. (1975). Interview. In *John Hawkes and the Craft of Conflict.* New Brunswick, NJ: Rutgers University Press, pp. 155–183.

Kuhn, Thomas S. (1985). *The Essential Tension: Selected Studies in Scientific Tradition and Change.* Chicago: University of Chicago Press.

——. (1987 [1978]). *Black-Body Theory and the Quantum Discontinuity, 1894–1912.* Chicago: University of Chicago Press.

——. (1990 [1957]). *The Copernican Revolution: Planetary Astronomy and the Development of Western Thought.* Cambridge, MA: Harvard University Press.

——. (1996 [1962]). *The Structure of Scientific Revolutions.* Chicago: University of Chicago Press.

——et al. (2000). *The Road since Structure: Philosophical Essays and an Autobiographical Interview, 1970–1997.*

Lacan, Jacques (1977 [1966]). *Écrits.* Trans. Alan Sheridan. New York: W. W. Norton.

——. (1977 [1949]). The Mirror Stage as Formative of the Function of the I as Revealed in Psychoanalytic Experience. In *Écrits: A Selection.* Trans. A. Sheridan. New York: W. W. Norton.

——. (1982). *Feminine Sexuality: Jacques Lacan and the École freudienne.* Trans. Jacqueline Rose. New York: W. W. Norton.

Laclau, Ernesto. (1988). Politics and the Limits of Modernity. In Andrew Ross (ed.), *Universal Abandon? The Politics of Postmodernism.* Minneapolis: University of Minnesota Press, pp. 63–82.

——. (1993). *New Reflections on the Revolution of Our Time.* London: Verso.

——. (1995). "The Time is out of Joint." *Diacritics* 25.2 (Summer), 86–97.

——. (1996). *Emancipation(s).* London: Verso.

——and Mouffe, Chantal. (1985). *Hegemony and Socialist Strategy.* London: Verso.

Landry, Donna, and MacLean, Gerald. (1991). Rereading Laclau and Mouffe. *Rethinking Marxism* 4.4 (Winter), 40–60.

Landy, Marcia. (1994). *Film, Politics, and Gramsci* Minneapolis: University of Minnesota Press.

Larrain, Jorge. (1994). *Ideology and Cultural Identity: Modernity and the Third World Presence.* Cambridge: Polity.

LeClair, Tom. (1987). *In the Loop: Don DeLillo and the Systems Novel.* Urbana: University of Illinois Press.

Lecompte, E. (1978). The Making of A Trilogy. *Performing Arts Journal* 3.2, 81–91.

Lefebvre, Henri. (1971 [1968]). *Everyday Life in the Modern World*. New Brunswick, NJ: Transaction Books.

——. (1991 [1947]). *Critique of Everyday Life*. London: Verso.

Lentricchia, Frank. (ed.). (1991). *New Essays on White Noise*. Cambridge: Cambridge University Press.

Lepage, Robert, and Ex Machina (1996). *The Seven Streams of the River Ota*. London: Methuen.

——and Brassard, Marie (1997). *Polygraph*. Trans. Gyllian Raby. London: Methuen.

Levinas, Emmanuel. (1969 [1961]). *Totality and Infinity*. Trans. A. Lingis. Pittsburgh: Duquesne University Press.

——. (1978 [1974]). *Otherwise Than Being or Beyond Essence*. Trans. A. Lingis. The Hague: Martinus Nijhoff.

——. (1984). Ethics of the Infinite Interview. In R. Kearney (ed.), *Dialogues with Contemporary Continental Thinkers*. Manchester: Manchester University Press, pp. 47–70.

——. (1987). *Collected Philosophical Papers*. Trans. A. Lingis. The Hague: Martinus Nijhoff.

——. (1988 [1976]). *The Paradox of Morality*. Trans. A. Benjamin and T. Wright. In R. Bernasconi and D. Wood (eds.), *The Provocation of Levinas*. London: Routledge.

——. (1989 [1963]). The Trace of the Other. Trans. A. Lingis. In M. Taylor (ed.), *Deconstruction in Context*. Chicago: Chicago University Press.

——. (1990 [1963]). *Difficult Freedom*. Trans. S. Hand. Baltimore: Johns Hopkins University Press.

——. (1991 [1976]). *Wholly Otherwise*. Trans. S. Critchley. In R. Bernasconi and S. Critchley (eds.), *Re- Reading Levinas*. Bloomington: Indiana University Press.

——. (1998 [1976]). Secularization and Hunger. Trans. B. Bergo. *Graduate Faculty Philosophy Journal* 20, 3–12.

Lévi-Strauss, Claude. (1963). *Structural Anthropology*. Trans. Claire Jacobson and Brooke Grundfest Schoepf. New York: Basic Books.

Lewin, Moshe. (1988). *The Gorbachev Phenomenon: A Historical Phenomenon*. Berkeley: University of California Press.

Linker, Kate. (1990). *Love For Sale: The Words and Pictures of Barbara Kruger*. New York: Harry N. Abrams.

Locke, Richard. (1973). One of the Longest, Most Difficult, Most Ambitious Novels in Years. *New York Times*, March 11.

Lucy, Niall. (1997). *Postmodern Literary Theory: An Introduction*. Oxford: Blackwell.

Lyon, Janet. (1991). Transforming Manifestos: A Second-wave Problematic. *Yale Journal of Criticism* 5.1, 101–27.

Lyotard, Jean-François. (1971). *Discours, figure*. Paris: Klinksieck.

——. (1974). *Économie libidinale*. Paris: Minuit.

——. (1983). Answering the Question: What is Postmodernism? In Ihab and Sally Hassan (eds.), *Innovation/ Renovation*. Madison: University of Wisconsin Press, pp. 329–41.

——. (1984 [1979]). *The Postmodern Condition: A Report on Knowledge*. Trans. Geoffrey Bennington and Brian Massumi. Minneapolis: University of Minnesota Press.

——. (1985 [1979]). *Just Gaming*. Trans. W. Godzich. Minneapolis: Minnesota University Press.

——. (1986). Complexity and the Sublime. In Lisa Appignani (ed.), *Postmodernism: ICA Documents 5*. London: ICA, pp. 10–12.

——. (1988 [1983]). *The Differend: Phrases in Dispute*. Minneapolis: University of Minnesota Press.

McAlpine, Alison. (1996). Interview with Robert Lepage. In Maria M. Delgado and Paul Heritage (eds.), *In Contact with the Gods: Directors Talk Theatre*. Manchester: Manchester University Press, pp. 130–57.

McCarthy, T. (1991). *Ideals and Illusions: On Reconstruction and Deconstruction in Contemporary Critical Theory*. Cambridge and London: MIT Press.

McDaniel, Ellen. (1981–82). *The Magus*: Fowles's Tarot Quest, *Journal of Modern Literature*. 8.2, 247–60.

McHale, Brian. (1986). Change of Dominant from Modernist to Postmodernist Writing. In D. Fokkema and H. Bertens (eds.), *Approaching Postmodernism*. Amsterdam and Philadelphia: John Benjamins, pp. 57–79.

——. (1987). *Postmodernist Fiction*. New York: Methuen.

——. (1992). *Constructing Postmodernism*. London: Routledge.

McLaughlin, Martin. (1998). *Italo Calvino*. Edinburgh: Edinburgh University Press.

Malachowsky, A. R. (ed.). (1990). *Reading Rorty: Critical Responses to Philosophy and the Mirror of Nature (and Beyond)*. Oxford: Blackwell.

Mandel, Ernest. (1975). *Late Capitalism*. London: Verso.

Mannoni, Octave. (1956 [1950]). *Prospero and Caliban: The Psychology of Colonization*. Trans. Pamela Powesland. London: Methuen.

Marchand, Marianne H. and Parpart, Jane L. (1997). *Feminism, Postmodernism, Development*. London: Routledge.

Marcus, G. (1989). *Lipstick Traces: A Secret History of the Twentieth Century*. Cambridge, MA: Harvard University Press.

Markey, Constance. (1999). *Italo Calvino. A Journey Toward Postmodernism*. Gainsville: University Press of Florida.

Martin, R. (1984). An Interview with Ishmael Reed. *Review of Contemporary Fiction* 4, 176–87.

——. (1998). Addressing the Dress. In M. Berger (ed.), *The Crisis of Criticism*. New York: The New Press, pp. 51–70.

Massumi, Brian. (1992). *A User's Guide to Capitalism and Schizophrenia: Deviations from Deleuze and Guattari*. Cambridge, MA: MIT Press.

Mellard, James M. (1980). *The Exploded Form: The Modernist Novel in America*. Urbana: University of Illinois Press.

Mellors, John. (1975). Collectors and Creators: The Novels of John Fowles. *London Magazine* (February/March), 65–72.

Mikics, D. (1991). Postmodernism, Ethnicity, and Underground Revisionism in Ishmael Reed. *Postmodern Culture* 1, 40 paragraphs.

Miklitsch, Robert. (1994). The Rhetoric of Post-Marxism: Discourse and Institutionality in Laclau and Mouffe, Resnick and Wolff. *Social Text* 45, 167–96.

Minwalla, Framji. (1992). Postmodernism, or The Revenge of the Onanists. *Theater* 23.1, 6–14.

Mitchell, W. J. T. (1991). An Interview with Barbara Kruger. *Critical Inquiry* 17.2, 434–8.

Montag, Warren and Stolze, Ted. (eds.). (1997). *The New Spinoza*. Minneapolis: University of Minnesota Press.

Mooney, William. (1991). Those Pears His Eyes: Paul West's Blind Monologuists and Deaf Auditors. *Review of Contemporary Fiction* 11.1, 267–79.

Morley, David and Robins, Kevin. (1995). *Spaces of Identity: Global Media, Electronic Landscapes, and Cultural Boundaries*. London: Routledge.

Morris, Meaghan. (1988). *The Pirate's Fiancée: Feminism, Reading, Postmodernism*. London: Verso.

Morrison, Blake. (1980). *The Movement: Poetry and Fiction of the 1950s*. Oxford and New York: Oxford University Press.

Morrison, Toni. (1972). *The Bluest Eye*. New York: Pocket Books.

——. (1973). *Sula*. New York: Plume.

——. (1977). *Song of Solomon*. New York: Knopf.

——. (1981). *Tar Baby*. New York: Knopf.

——. (1987). *Beloved*. New York: Knopf.

——. (1989). Unspeakable Things Unspoken: The Afro-American Presence in American Literature. *Michigan Quarterly Review* 28.1, 1–34.

——. (1992a). *Jazz*. New York: Knopf.

——. (1992b). *Playing in the Dark: Whiteness and the Literary Imagination*. Cambridge, MA: Harvard University Press.

——. (1994). *Lecture and Speech of Acceptance Upon the Award of the Nobel Prize For Literature*. New York: Knopf.

——. (1997). *The Dancing Mind*. New York: Random House.

——. (1998). *Paradise*. New York: Knopf.

Moses, Michael Valdez. (1991). Lust Removed From Nature. In Frank Lentricchia (ed.), *New Essays on White Noise*. Cambridge: Cambridge University Press, pp. 63–86.

Mouffe, Chantal. (1988). Radical Democracy: Modern or Postmodern? In Andrew Ross (ed.), *Universal Abandon? The Politics of Postmodernism*. Minneapolis: University of Minnesota Press, pp. 31–45.

Mudimbe, V. Y. (1988). *The Invention of Africa: Gnosis, Philosophy and the Order of Knowledge*. Bloomington: Indiana University Press.

Munslow, A. (1997). *Deconstructing History*. London and New York: Routledge.

Murphy, Margueritte. (1992). *A Tradition of Subversion: The Prose Poem in English from Wilde to Ashbery*. Amherst: University of Massachusetts Press.

Murphy, Timothy S. (1997). Bibliography of the Works of Gilles Deleuze. In Paul Patton (ed.), *Deleuze: A Critical Reader*. Oxford: Blackwell.

Musarra, Ulla. (1986). Duplication and Multiplication: Postmodern Devices in the Novels of I. Calvino. In In D. Fokkema and H. Bertens (eds.), *Approaching Postmodernism*. Amsterdam and Philadelphia: John Benjamins, pp. 135–55.

Natoli, Joseph. (1997). *A Primer To Postmodernity*. Cambridge, MA: Blackwell.

—— and Hutcheon, Linda (eds.). (1993). *A Postmodern Reader*. Albany, NY: SUNY Press.

Nattiez, Jean-Jacques. (1993). *The Boulez–Cage Correspondence*. Cambridge: Cambridge University Press.

Newman, Robert D. (1986). *Understanding Thomas Pynchon*. Columbia: University of South Carolina Press.

Newquist, Roy. (ed.). (1964). John Fowles. In *Counterpoint*. Chicago, IL: Rand McNally, pp. 218–25.

Nietzsche, F. (1986 [1878]). *Human, All Too Human*. Lincoln: University of Nebraska Press.

Nilson, L. (1983). Q & A: Cindy Sherman. *American Photographer* (September), 70–7.

Norris, Christopher. (1982). *Deconstruction: Theory and Practice*. London: Methuen.

——. (1983). *The Deconstructive Turn: Essays in the Rhetoric of Philosophy*. London: Methuen.

——. (1987). *Derrida*. London: Fontana Modern Masters.

——. (1990). *What's Wrong with Postmodernism: Critical Theory and the Ends of Philosophy*. Hemel Hempstead: Harvester Wheatsheaf.

O'Brien, Flann. (1986 [1939]). *At Swim-Two-Birds*. Harmondsworth: Penguin.

Onega, Susana. (1989). *Form and Meaning in the Novels of John Fowles*. Ann Arbor and London: UMI Research Press.

——. (1993a). British Historiographic Metafiction in the 1980s. In Theo D'haen and Hans Bertens (eds.), *British Postmodern Fiction*. Amsterdam and Atlanta, GA: Rodopi, pp. 47–61.

——. (1993b). The Passion: Jeanette Winterson's Uncanny Mirror of Ink. *Miscelánea* 14, 112–29.

——. (1994). "Self" and "Other" in Jeanette Winterson's *The Passion*. *Revista Canaria de Estudios Ingleses* 28 (April), 177–93.

——. (1995). Self, Text and World in British Historiographic Metafiction. *ANGLISTIK. Mitteilungen des Verbandes Deutscher Anglisten* 6.2 (September), 93–105.

——. (1996a). An Interview with Peter Ackroyd. *Twentieth-century Literature* 43.1 (Summer), 208–20.

——. (1996b). Self, World, and Art in the Fiction of John Fowles. *Twentieth-century Literature*, special John Fowles issue, 1.42 (Spring), 29–56.

——. (1997). The Mythical Impulse in British Historiographic Metafiction. *European Journal of English Studies* 1.2 (August), 184–204.

——. (1998). *Peter Ackroyd: The Writer and His Work*. Plymouth: Northcote House and the British Council.

——. (1999). *Metafiction and Myth in the Novels of Peter Ackroyd*. Columbia: Camden House.

——. (2000). Mirror Games and Hidden Narratives in Charles Palliser's *The Quincunx*. In Richard Todd and Luisa Flora (eds.), *Theme Parks, Rainforests and Sprouting Wastelands*. Rodopi: Amsterdam and Atlanta, GA, pp. 151–63.

Ortega y Gassett, José. (1961 [1914]). *Worlds Beyond: Meditations on Quixote*. Trans. E. Rugg and D. Marín. New York: W. W. Norton.

Owens, Craig. (1984a). The Allegorical Impulse: Toward a Theory of Postmodernism. In B. Wallis (ed.), *Art After Modernism: Rethinking Representation*. Boston: Godine, pp. 203–35.

——. (1984b). The Medusa-Effect, or, the Specular-Ruse. *Art in America* 72.1, 97–105.

Parry, Benita. (1987). Problems in Current Theories of Colonial Discourse. *Oxford Literary Review* 9, 27–58.

Pasler, Jann. (1994). Inventing a Tradition: Cage's "Composition in Retrospect." In Marjorie Perloff and Charles Junkerman (eds.), *John Cage: Composed in America*. Chicago: University of Chicago Press, pp. 125–43.

Pavis, Patrice. (1992). *Theatre at the Crossroads of Culture*. Trans. Loren Kruger. London: Routledge.

Paxton, S. (1997). Rauschenberg for Cunningham and Three of his Own. In W. Hopps and S. Davidson (eds.), *Robert Rauschenberg: A Retrospective*. New York: Guggenheim Museum, pp. 260–7.

Pepper, Ian. (1997). From the "Aesthetics of Indifference" to "Negative Aesthetics": John Cage and Germany 1958–1972. *October* 82, 30–48.

Perloff, Marjorie. (1981). *The Poetics of Indeterminacy: Rimbaud to Cage*. Princeton, NJ: Princeton University Press.

——. (1990). *Poetic License: Essays on Modernist and Postmodernist Lyric*. Evanston, IL: Northwestern University Press.

Pfeil, Frank. (1990). *Another Tale to Tell*. London: Verso.

Pifer, Ellen. (ed.). (1986). *Critical Essays on John Fowles*. Boston, MA: G. K. Hall.

Plimpton, George. (1963). The Whole Sick Crew. *New York Times*, April 21.

Plotnitsky, A. (1997). Un-*Scriptible*. In J.-M. Rabaté (ed.), *Writing the Image after Roland Barthes*. Philadelphia: University of Pennsylvania Press, pp. 243–58.

Pritchett, James. (1993). *The Music of John Cage*. Cambridge: Cambridge University Press.

Pynchon, Thomas. (1975 [1973]). *Gravity's Rainbow*. London: Picador.

——. (1984). *Slow Learner: Early Stories*. Boston: Little, Brown.

——. (1990 [1965]). *The Crying of Lot 49*. New York: Perennial Library.

Purand, R. (1996). Cindy Sherman: le caméléonisme mélancolique des Film Stills. *Art Press* 210, 50–5.

Rankin, Elizabeth D. (1973). Cryptic Coloration in *The French Lieutenant's Woman*. *Journal of Narrative Technique* 3 (September), 193–207.

Rauschenberg, R. (1987). *An Interview with Robert Rauschenberg by Barbara Rose*. New York: Vintage Books.

Re, Lucia. (1990). *Calvino and the Age of Neorealism: Fables of Estrangement*. Stanford: Stanford University Press.

Reed, Ishmael. (1967). *The Free-Lance Pallbearers*. Garden City, NY: Doubleday.

——. (1982). *God Made Alaska for the Indians: Selected Essays*. New York and London: Garland.

——. (1988 [1969]). *Yellow Back Radio Broke-Down*. New York: Atheneum.

——. (1989 [1976]). *Flight to Canada*. New York: Atheneum.

——. (1989 [1978]). *Shrovetide in Old New Orleans*. New York: Atheneum.

——. (1989). *New and Collected Poems*. New York: Atheneum.

——. (1994 [1993]). *Airing Dirty Laundry*. Reading, MA: Addison-Wesley.

Resch, Robert Paul. (1992). *Althusser and the Renewal of Marxist Social Theory*. Berkeley: University of California Press.

Resnick, Stephen A. and Wolff, Richard D. (1987). *Knowledge and Class: A Marxian Critique of Political Economy*. Chicago: University of Chicago Press.

Ricci, Franco (ed.). (1989). *Calvino Revisited*. Ottawa: Dove House Press.

——. (1990). *Difficult Games: A Reading of "I racconti."* Waterloo: Wilfred Laurier University Press.

Rincon, C. (1995). The Peripheral Center of Postmodernism: On Borges, García Márquez, and Alterity. In J. Beverley, M. Aronna, and J. Oviedo (eds.), *The Postmodern Debate in Latin America*. Durham, NC and London: Duke University Press, pp. 223–40.

Roberts, Mathew. (1989). Poetics, Hermeneutics, Dialogics: Bakhtin and Paul de Man. In Gary Morson and Caryl Emerson (eds.), *Rethinking Bakhtin*. Evanston, IL: Northwestern University Press, pp. 115–34.

Robinson, Cedric. (1993). The Appropriation of Frantz Fanon. *Race and Class* 35, 79–91.

Rokek, Chris and Turner, Bryan. (eds.). (1993). *Forget Baudrillard*. London: Routledge.

Rorty, Richard. (1979). *Philosophy and the Mirror of Nature*. Princeton, NJ: Princeton University Press.

——. (1982). *Consequences of Pragmatism (Essays: 1972–1980)*. Minneapolis: University of Minnesota Press.

——. (1987). Thugs and Theorists: A Reply to Bernstein. *Political Theory* 15, 564–80.

——. (1989). *Contingency, Irony and Solidarity*. Cambridge: Cambridge University Press.

——. (1991a). *Objectivity, Relativism, and Truth: Philosophical Papers*. Vol. 1. Cambridge: Cambridge University Press.

——. (1991b). *Essays on Heidegger and Others: Philosophical Papers*. Vol. 2. Cambridge: Cambridge University Press.

——. (1996). Response to Ernesto Laclau. In Chantal Mouffe (ed.), *Deconstruction and Pragmatism*. New York: Routledge, pp. 69–77.

——. (1998a). *Achieving Our Country*. Cambridge, MA: Harvard University Press.

——. (1998b). *Truth and Progress: Philosophical Papers*. Vol. 3. Cambridge: Cambridge University Press.

——. (1999). *Philosophy and Social Hope*. London: Penguin.

Ross, Andrew. (1988). *The Failure of Modernism: Symptoms of American Poetry*. New York: Columbia University Press.

Rushdie, Salman. (1980). *Midnight's Children*. New York: Avon Books.

——. (1983). *Shame*. New York: Alfred A. Knopf.

——. (1999). *The Ground Beneath Her Feet*. New York: Henry Holt.

Russo, A. (1994). Picture This: Pleasure and Terror in the Work of Cindy Sherman. *Art Monthly* 181, 8–11.

Rylance, R. (1994). *Roland Barthes*. Hemel Hempstead: Harvester Wheatsheaf.

Saatkamp, H. J. (ed.). (1995). *Rorty and Pragmatism: The Philosopher Responds to His Critics*. Nashville: Vanderbilt University Press.

Sage, Lorna. (1974). John Fowles, Profile 7. *New Review* 1.7, 31–7.

———. (1992). *Women in the House of Fiction*. New York: Routledge.

———. (ed.). (1994). *Flesh and the Mirror*. London: Virago.

Sartre, Jean-Paul. (1965 [1948]). Black Orpheus. Trans. John Maccombie. *Massachusetts Review* 6, 13–52.

Sassoon, Anne Showstack. (1987). *Gramsci's Politics*. Minneapolis: University of Minnesota Press.

Saussure, Ferdinand de. (1959 [1916]). *Course in General Linguistics*. Trans. Wade Baskin. New York: McGraw-Hill.

Savran, D. (1986). *Breaking the Rules*. New York: Theatre Communications Group.

———. (1991). Revolution . . . History . . . Theater: The Politics of the Wooster Group's Second Trilogy. In S.-E. Case and J. Reinelt (eds.), *The Performance of Power*. Iowa City: University of Iowa Press, pp. 41–55.

Sayre, Henry M. (1989). *The Object of Performance: The American Avant-garde since 1970*. Chicago: University of Chicago Press.

Schacht, Richard. (1996). Alienation Redux: From Here to Postmodernity. In F. Geyer (ed.), *Alienation, Ethnicity, and Postmodernism*. Westport, CT: Greenwood Press, pp. 1–16.

Schechner, R. (1987). Ways of Speaking, Loci of Cognition. *Drama Review* 31.3, 4–6.

Schütze, Anke. (1995). "I think after More I will do Turner and then I will probably do Shakespeare." An Interview with Peter Ackroyd. *EESE* 8, 163–79.

Scott, A. O. (2000). The Panic of Influence. *New York Review of Books*, February 10.

Scott Brown, Denise. (1984). Learning from Pop. In Peter Arnell, Ted Pickford, and Catherine Bergart (eds.), *A View from Campodoglio: Selected Essays, 1953–1982*. New York: Harper and Row.

Sharpley-Whiting, T. Denean. (1998). *Frantz Fanon: Conflicts and Feminisms*. Lanham, MD: Rowman and Littlefield.

Sherman, C. (1992). *Fitcher's Bird: Based on a Tale by the Brothers Grimm*. New York: Rizzoli International Publications.

Shoptaw, John. (1994). *On the Outside Looking Out: John Ashbery's Poetry*. Cambridge, MA: Harvard University Press.

Siegel, J. (1988). Cindy Sherman. In J. Siegel (ed.), *Art Talk: The Early 80s*. New York: Da Capo Press, pp. 268–82.

Silverman, Hugh J. (ed.). (1989). *Derrida and Deconstruction*. London and New York: Routledge.

———. (ed.). (1990). *Postmodernism – Philosophy and the Arts*. New York and London: Routledge.

———. (1994). *Textualities: Between Hermeneutics and Deconstruction*. New York and London: Routledge.

———. (1997). *Inscriptions: After Phenomenology and Structuralism*. Evanston, IL: Northwestern University Press.

———. (ed.). (1997). *Philosophy and Non-Philosophy since Merleau-Ponty*. Evanston, IL: Northwestern University Press.

——. (ed.). (2000). *Philosophy and Desire*. New York and London: Routledge.

—— and Aylesworth, Gary E. (eds.). (1989). *The Textual Sublime: Deconstruction and its Differences*. Albany, NY SUNY Press.

Smith, Anna Marie. (1998). *Laclau and Mouffe: The Radical Democratic Imaginary*. London: Routledge.

Smith, Evans Lansing. (1990). *Rape and Revelation: the Descent To the Underworld in Modernism*. Lanham, New York and London: University Presses of America.

Soja, Edward. W. (1989). *Postmodern Geographies: The Reassertion of Space in Critical Social Theory*. London: Verso.

Spector, N. (1997). Rauschenberg and Performance, 1963–67. In W. Hopps and S. Davidson (eds.), *Robert Rauschenberg: A Retrospective*. New York: Guggenheim Museum, pp. 226–45.

Squiers, Carol. (1987). Diversionary (Syn)tactics – Barbara Kruger Has Her Way With Words. *ARTNews* 86.2 (February), 77–85.

Stafford, B. M. (1997) *Good Looking: Essays On the Virtues of Images*. Cambridge: MIT Press.

Stearns, William and Chaloupka, William. (eds.). (1992). *The Disappearence of Art and Politics*. New York and London: St. Martin's and Macmillan Press.

Steinberg, L. (1972). *Other Criteria: Confrontations with Twentieth-century Art*. New York: Oxford University Press.

Stivale, Charles J. (1998) *The Two-Fold Thought of Deleuze and Guattari: Intersections and Animations*. New York: Guilford Press.

Stuckley, C. F. (1997). Rauschenberg's Everything, Everywhere Era. In W. Hopps and S. Davidson (eds.), *Robert Rauschenberg: A Retrospective*. New York: Guggenheim Museum, pp. 30–41.

Stückrath, J. and Zbinden, J. (eds.). (1997). *Metageschichte. Hayden White Und Paul Ricoeur. Dargestellte Wirklichkeit in Der Europäischen Kultur Im Kontext Von Husserl, Weber, Auerbach Und Gombrich*. Baden-Baden: Nomos Verlagsgesellsachft.

Suleiman, Susan Rubin. (1990). *Subversive Intent: Gender Politics and the Avant-Garde*. Boston: Harvard.

Swift, Graham. (1980). *The Sweet Shop Owner*. London: Allen Lane.

——. (1983). *Waterland*. London: Heinemann.

——. (1992). *Ever After*. London: Pan Books.

——. (1996). *Last Orders*. London: Picador.

Tanner, Tony. (1971). *City of Words: American Fiction, 1950–1970*. New York: Harper and Row.

Taylor, John Russell. (1962). *Anger and After: A Guide to the New British Drama*. London: Methuen.

Taylor, P. (1990). Robert Rauschenberg. *Interview* 20.12, 142–7.

Tihanov, Galin. (2000). The *Master and the Slave: Lukacs, Bakhtin, and the Ideas of their Time*. Oxford and New York: Oxford University Press.

Trachtenberg, Stanley (ed.). (1991). *Critical Essays on John Hawkes*. Boston: G. K. Hall.

Trinh T. Minh-ha. (1990). If Upon Leaving: A Conversation Piece. In R. Ferguson et al. (eds.), *Discourses: Conversations in Postmodern Art and Culture*. Cambridge, MA: MIT Press, pp. 44–64.

——. (1991). Interview with Linda Tadi'c. *Release Print* 14.10 (January), 92–9.

——. (1992). Interview in *Film News* (June).

——. (1995). Script of Reassemblage. In Scott Macdonald (ed.), *Screen Writings*. Berkeley: University of California Press.

Tucker, Lindsay. (ed.). (1998). *Critical Essays on Angela Carter*. New York: G. K. Hall.

Unsworth, John M. (1991). Practicing Post-modernism: The Example of John Hawkes. *Contemporary Literature* 32.1, 38–57.

Van Reijen, Willem and Veerman, Dick. (1988). An Interview with Jean-François Lyotard. *Theory, Culture and Society* 5.2–3, 277–309.

Vanden Heuvel, M. (1992). *Performing Drama, Dramatizing Performance*. Ann Arbor: University of Michigan Press.

——. (1995). Waking the Text: Disorderly Order in the Wooster Group's *Route 1 & 9* (the Last Act). *Journal of Dramatic Theory and Criticism* (Fall), 59–76.

Vattimo, Gianni. (1980). The End of History. *Chicago Review* 34.4, 20–30.

——. (1984). Dialectics, Difference, Weak Thought. *Graduate Faculty Philosophy Journal* 10.1, 151–63.

——. (1988 [1985]). *The End of Modernity*. Trans. J. Snyder. Johns Hopkins University Press.

——. (1989). Nihilism: Reactive and Active. In T. Darby et al. (eds.), *Nietzsche and the Rhetoric of Nihilism*. Ottawa: Carleton University Press, pp. 15–21.

——. (1991). *Al di là del soggetto: Nietzsche, Heidegger e l'ermeneutica*. Milan: Feltrinelli.

——. (1992 [1989]). *The Transparent Society*. Trans. D. Webb. Johns Hopkins University Press.

——. (1992). Optimistic Nihilism. *Common Knowledge* 1.3, 37–44.

——. (1993 [1980]). *The Adventure of Difference*. Trans. C. Blamires. Johns Hopkins University Press.

——. (1994 [1989]). *Etica dell'interpretazione*. Bari: Laterza.

——. (1996). *Credere di credere*. Milan: Garzanti.

——. (1997 [1994]). *Beyond Interpretation*. Trans. D. Webb. Stanford, CA: Stanford University Press.

——. (1998). The Trace of the Trace. In J. Derrida and G. Vattimo (eds.), *Religion*. Stanford, CA: Stanford University Press, pp. 79–94.

——and Rovatti, P. A. (eds.). (1983). *Il pensiero debole*. Milan: Feltrinelli.

Venturi, Robert. (1972 [1966]). *Complexity and Contradiction in Architecture*. New York: Museum of Modern Art (1966); London: Architectural Press (1972).

——, Scott Brown, Denise, and Izenour, Steven. (1972). *Learning from Las Vegas: The Forgotten Symbolism of Architectural Form*. Cambridge, MA: MIT Press.

Vipond, Dianne L. (ed.). (1999). *Conversations with John Fowles*. Jackson: University of Mississippi Press, pp. 119–33.

Voloshinov, V. N. (1973 [1929]). *Marxism and the Philosophy of Language*. Trans. L. Matejka and I. R. Titunik. New York: Seminar Press.

Vonnegut, Kurt. (1952). *Player Piano*. New York: Dell.

——. (1963). *Cat's Cradle*. New York: Dell.

——. (1965). *God Bless You, Mr. Rosewater*. New York: Dell.

——. (1966). *Mother Night*. New York: Dell.

——. (1969). *Slaughterhouse-Five*. New York: Dell.

——. (1973). *Breakfast of Champions*. New York: Dell.

——. (1976). *Slapstick*. New York: Delacorte/Seymour Lawrence.

——. (1985). *Galápagos*. New York: Delacorte/Seymour Lawrence.

——. (1990). *Hocus Pocus*. New York: Putnam.

——. (1991). *Fates Worse Than Death*. New York: Putnam.

——. (1997). *Timequake*. New York: Putnam.

Wallace, Michele. (1991). *Invisibility Blues: From Pop to Theory*. New York: Verso.

Waugh, Patricia. (1984). *Metafiction: The Theory and Practice of Self-conscious Fiction*. London and New York: Methuen.

——. (1992). *Practicing Postmodernism/Reading Modernism*. New York: Edward Arnold.

——. (1995). *Harvest of the Sixties: English Literature and its Background, 1960 to 1990*. Oxford: Oxford University Press.

Webb, Kate. (1994). Seriously Funny. In Lorna Sage (ed.), *Flesh and the Mirror*. London: Virago, pp. 279–307.

Wehle, Philippa. (1996). Robert Lepage's *Seven Streams of the River Ota*: Process and Progress. *Theatre Forum* 8, 29–36.

Weiss, Beno. (1993). *Understanding Italo Calvino*. University of South Carolina Press.

Wellmer, Albrecht. (1985). On the Dialectic of Modernism and Postmodernism. *Praxis Inter National* 4, 337–62.

Westfall, Suzanne R. (1992). Ping Chong's Terra in/Cognita: Monsters on Stage. In S. G. Lim and A. Ling (eds.), *Reading the Literatures of Asian-America*. Philadelphia: Temple University Press, pp. 359–73.

Wheeler, Wendy. (1995). After Grief What Kinds of Inhuman Selves. *New Formations* 25 (Summer).

——. (1999). *A New Modernity Change in Science, Literature and Politics*. London: Lawrence and Wishart.

White, Hayden. (1973). *Metahistory. The Historical Imagination in Nineteenth-century Europe*. Baltimore and London: Johns Hopkins University Press.

——. (1974). The Historical Text as Literary Artifact. *Clio* 3.3.

——. (1978). *Tropics of Discourse: Essays in Cultural Criticism*. Baltimore and London: Johns Hopkins University Press.

——. (1987). *The Content of the Form: Narrative Discourse and Historical Representation*. Baltimore and London: Johns Hopkins University Press.

——. (1993, 1994). Metahistory Twenty Years After, Part I: Interpreting Tropology. *Storia della Storiografia*, 24; Part II: Metahistory and the Practice of History. *Storia della Storiografia*, 25.

——. (1998). Twenty-five Years On. *History and Theory*, 37.

——. (1999). *Figural Realism: Studies in the Mimesis Effect*. Baltimore and London: Johns Hopkins University Press.

Whiting, Steven Moore. (1999). *Satie the Bohemian: From Cabaret to Concert Hall*. Oxford: Oxford University Press.

Williamson, J. (1983). Images of "Woman": Judith Williamson Introduces the Photography of Cindy Sherman. *Screen* (November/December), 102–6.

Wolfe, Peter. (1979). *John Fowles, Magus and Moralist*. London: Associated University Press.

Wood, E. Meiksins and Foster, J. Bellamy (eds.). (1997). *In Defense of History: Marxism and the Postmodern Agenda*. New York: Monthly Review Press.

Wood, Michael. (1984). The Apprenticeship of Thomas Pynchon. *New York Times*, April 15.

Woodhouse, J.R. (1968) *Italo Calvino. A Reappraisal and An Appreciation of the Trilogy*. Hull: Hull University Press.

Woolgar, S. (1988). Reflexivity is the Ethnographer of the Text. In S. Woolgar (ed.), *Knowledge and Reflexivity: New Frontiers in the Sociology of Science*. London: Sage, pp. 14–34.

Wooster Group. (1978). Rumstick Road. *Performing Arts Journal* 3.2, 92–115.

——. (1996). *Frank Dell's The Temptation of Saint Antony*. In B. Marranca (ed.), *Plays for the End of the Century*. Baltimore and London: Johns Hopkins University Press, pp. 261–314.

Worton, Michael and Still, Juliet. (eds.). (1990). Introduction. *Intertextuality: Theories and Practices*. Manchester: Manchester University Press.

Zamir, S. (1994). The Artist as Prophet, Priest, and Gunslinger: Ishmael Reed's *Cowboy in the Boat of Ra*. *Callaloo* 17, 1205–35.

Zweite, Andrew. (1994). "Kunst sollte kein Konzept haben." Anmerkungen zu Rauschenbergs Werk in den 50er und 60er Jahren. In *Robert Rauschenberg*. Cologne: Dumont Buchverlag, pp. 17–60.

Index

Lightning Source UK Ltd.
Milton Keynes UK
UKOW03f1206060214

226001UK00002B/118/P

9 780631 217978